F

הכל

*שוחטין ושחיטתן כשרה חוץ מחרש שוטה
וקטן שמא יקלקלו את שחיטתן וכולן *ששחטו
ואחרים רואין אותן שחיטתן כשרה: גמ' הכל
שוחטין *(לכתחלה) ושחיטתן כשרה דיעבד
אמר ליה רב אחא בריה דרבא לרב אשי וכל
הכל לכתחלה הוא אלא מעתה *הכל ממירין
אחד האנשים ואחד הנשים ה"נ דלכתחלה הוא
ויקרא
כז
והא כתיב לא יחליפנו ולא ימיר אותו טוב
ברע או רע בטוב התם כדקתני טעמא לא
שהאדם רשאי להמיר אלא שאם המיר מומר
יוסופג את הארבע ם אלא *הכל מעריכין ונערכין
נודרין ונידרין הכי נמי דלכתחלה והא כתיב
דברים
כג
וכי תחדל לנדור לא יהיה בך חטא וכתיב
קהלת
ה
*טוב אשר לא תדור משתדור ולא תשלם
ס *ותניא *טוב מזה ומזה *שאינו נודר כל עיקר
דברי רבי מאיר ר' יהודה אומר טוב מזה ומזה
נודר ומשלם ואפילו רבי יהודה לא קאמר אלא
באומר *הרי זו   אבל

Opening of the tractate Hullin ("profane") in the Babylonian Talmud. The tractate primarily
deals with the laws of animals slaughtered for food and with other regulations from which the laws
of Kashrut are derived.

THE WORLD OF JEWISH COOKING

GIL MARKS

A FIRESIDE BOOK
PUBLISHED BY SIMON & SCHUSTER

F

FIRESIDE
Rockefeller Center
1230 Avenue of the Americas
New York, NY 10020

First Fireside Edition 1999

Fireside and colophon are registered trademarks
of Simon & Schuster Inc.

Photo credits appear on page 405.

Designed by Barbara Balch

Manufactured in the United States of America

1 3 5 7 9 10 8 6 4 2

The Library of Congress has cataloged the hardcover edition as follows:
Marks, Gil.
The world of Jewish cooking : more than
500 traditional recipes from Alsace to Yemen / Gil Marks.
p.   cm.
1. Cookery, Jewish. 2. Cooking, International. I. Title.
TX714.M3195 1996
641.5'656—dc20   96-2848
                                                              CIP
ISBN 0-684-82491-4
0-684-83559-2 (Pbk)

Acknowledgments

This book owes an enormous debt to many people, both in America and abroad. Among those who shared their recipes, ideas, and time with me are Yusuf Abramov, Stephen Anchin, Adam and Annie Anik, Karen Chera, Talut Keypoor Cohanim, Michelle Comet, Lillian Cooper, Sam Daniel, Esther Davidashvili, Rae Dayan, Louise Defez, Poopa Dweck, Alan and Ellen Federman, Diane Feldman, Sharon Efroymson First, Israel Fridman, Barbara Gilden, Liselotte Gorlin, Dalia Cochavi Kahane, Joan Kekst, Levana Levy Kirschenbaum, Phyllis Koegel, Rose Lawrence, Lily Weiss Levinson, Emile de Vidas Levy, Adina Mishkoff, Nava Levy Mozeson, Barbara Ribakove, Jackie Rivkin Rubin, Aaron and Laya Scholar, Elissa Shay, Stanley Sherman, Miriam Shurabi, David Solomon, Mathilde Turiel, Nach Waxman, Eva Weiss, Stan Zimmerman, and various relatives and friends.

I want to express my gratitude to all the people involved in the production of this book. Most especially I want to thank my editor, Penny Kaganoff, whose encouragement and belief in this book has been indispensable; her assistant, Diana Newman; and my agent, Sharon Friedman.

Very special thanks go to my parents, sisters, brothers, nieces, nephews, and friends, who bore the brunt of many of my culinary experiments and unhesitatingly shared their comments and encouragement.

To my parents,

Beverly and Harold Marks,
for their love and support

Contents

Introduction

The destiny of nations depends upon what and how they eat.

—Jean-Anthelme Brillat-Savarin,
The Physiology of Taste

Jewish cooking reminds me of an old joke that my father tells (as his father did before him) about a Jew on a business trip to Shanghai who was pleasantly surprised to find, of all things, a synagogue in that foreign city. On the Sabbath, the businessman went to the synagogue and much to his amazement discovered it was filled with people with Chinese features chanting the familiar Hebrew prayers. After services, the members of the congregation crowded around the stranger.

"I'm a Jew from New York," the visitor explained.

"You're a Jew?" one of the congregants replied. "Funny, you don't look Jewish!"

American Jews, who are primarily descended from eastern European immigrants, generally associate only their ancestors' customs and foods with being authentically Jewish. (Funny, you don't cook Jewish!) In a similar egocentric vein, Americans tend to divide the Jewish world into two groups—Ashkenazim, who originated in France and Germany, and Sephardim, who originated in Iberia—who were forced from their respective homelands and subsequently became the two largest and most widespread Jewish cultural communities. As a result, Teimanim (Yemenites), the third-largest Jewish ethnic group, are frequently subsumed under the label Sephardim, while Italkim (Italians) are often tagged Ashkenazim. Yet, the Jewish communities of both Yemen and Italy predate those of Sepharad and Ashkenaz, and both produced distinct cultures of their own. In actuality, a mosaic of Jewish cultural communities of varying sizes and antiquity grew up across the globe—including in Iran (Persia), Georgia, Uzbekistan/Bukhara, Azerbaijan, Kurdistan, India (Bombay, Cochin, and Calcutta), and Ethiopia (there were even small communities of Chinese Jews in Kaifeng and Canton, but none of their descendants still identify as Jewish)—based on neither the Ashkenazic nor the Sephardic model, but each possessing its own unique history, customs, and cuisine.

The central feature of Jewish cooking in the Diaspora is adaptation. The history, economics, geography, and climate of each area in which the Jews settled determined what

1

produce was available and what resources were at their disposal. Local fare was incorporated into the Jewish culinary repertoire, while many traditional recipes were either refashioned or forgotten. In every location in which they settled, Jews adopted and modified local dishes, often improving upon them in the process, while symbiotically sharing some of their traditional dishes and culinary touches. (Following the Reconquista in Spain, fifteenth-century Christian writers disparagingly noted the distinctive marks of Jewish cooking—long-simmering stews, the use of olive oil for frying, and the prevalence of onions and garlic in meat dishes. Although religious authorities in Spain, and some other countries as well, concentrated much effort on preventing members of their flock from copying Jewish food, such endeavors were generally ineffective.) At those times when Jews fled an area because of persecution or poverty, they carried these foods to their new homes, thereby spreading this culinary wealth to many diverse locales.

To further complicate matters, even the two primary forms of Jewish cuisine are not monolithic, for Ashkenazic and Sephardic food developed differently in the refugees' new homelands, most of the Franco-German Jews having settled in Austria, Hungary, Romania, the Ukraine, Poland, and the Baltic states; and the Iberian Jews in Turkey, the Maghreb, Egypt, Syria, Iraq, Greece, and western Europe. Indeed, Jews from the Maghreb (northwest Africa) have trouble recognizing many of the dishes of Sephardim from the Levant (the countries bordering on the eastern Mediterranean) and vice versa. Since it was primarily in the Ottoman Empire that the Spanish-Portuguese refugees found haven, the synthesis of Iberian and Ottoman cuisines emerged as the most conspicuous form of Sephardic cooking.

Since the ancestors of the majority of Ashkenazim came from the Slavic regions of eastern Europe (Poland and the Ukraine), it is this form of Ashkenazic cooking that is most widespread and that most Americans associate with Jewish food. Yet even here differences exist. Jewish cooking from western Poland manifests a pronounced Germanic bent, while that from the eastern part of the country is more strongly influenced by Russia and the Ukraine. As a result, western Poles eat more cabbage and much less borscht, herring, and kasha than their eastern counterparts. Jews from southwestern Poland, a sugar-beet-growing region, have developed a preference for sweeter dishes and add copious amounts of sugar to their gefilte fish, kugels, and challah, while those from Galicia (southeastern Poland), where sugar remains an expensive item, generally use much less or no sugar in their cooking. Still, most of the areas in which the Ashkenazim settled had similar produce, and there was constant interaction between these communities through expulsions, trade, and marriages. As a result, enough of a commonality exists between the different styles of Jewish cooking throughout eastern and central Europe that Jews from Bucharest would still recognize as Ashkenazic the food of Jews from Vilnius (Vilna) or Kraków, although they would most assuredly find it much too bland.

Thus, defining Jewish cuisine is no easy task. For while buckwheat, borscht, and beef brisket constitute a prominent part of the Jewish diet in the Ukraine, couscous, *tagines* (stews), and lamb dominate the menu in Morocco, and bulgur, *shorabit khodar* (vegetable and legume soups), and *kibbe* (ground meat and bulgur) are basic in the Levant. Eastern European Jews make sparing use of seasonings—primarily salt, onions, garlic, cinnamon, and ground ginger—while Sephardim liberally indulge in a wide variety of herbs and spices. The cooking fat of choice in northern Europe is schmaltz (poultry fat); olive oil is preferred by those in the Mediterranean region; and lamb fat and sesame oil predominate in the Near East. Jews may literally eat almost anything, from the petite madeleines so cherished by Marcel Proust—his mother was a member of a prominent Alsatian Jewish family—to the grilled organs so beloved by James Joyce's classic character Leopold Bloom.

Jewish food may be as sparing as the meager fare of the impoverished masses who struggled to survive in the shtetlach of the Pale of Settlement (the only portion of czarist Russia in which Jews were permitted to live, stretching from the Baltic Sea to the Black Sea). Or it may be as sumptuous as a feast prepared by Marie-Antoine Carême, one of history's most important chefs and regarded as the founder of France's Grand Cuisine, whose last position was with Baron Edmond de Rothschild in Paris. (That instance was not unique; a number of wealthy Jewish families educated their chefs in the intricacies of kosher cooking.) A few of the dishes eaten by Jews at the end of the twentieth century, such as *cholent* and *hamin* (Sabbath stews), *pastels* (Sabbath pies), and *charoseth* (Passover fruit pastes), originated in Judea more than two thousand years ago. Yet much of what Jews eat today bears little or no relation to the food prepared in ancient Israel, for it was in the Diaspora that modern Jewish cooking developed.

After two thousand years of evolution in almost every country and culture, Jewish cuisine is the cuisine of the world. But if Jewish cooking is universal, what makes a dish peculiarly Jewish? Following Halakah (Jewish law) meant that Jews could not simply adopt all of the dishes of their new homelands. Since the dietary laws exclude such foods as pork, lard, and shellfish, and the mixing of milk and meat, Jews found substitutes for these items. In addition, the Jewish lifestyle—shaped by Sabbath prohibitions, holiday traditions, Torah precepts, and life-cycle events—produced uniquely Jewish dishes that, although based on local foods, often manifested similarities to Jewish dishes from other locales. For example, all Jewish communities incorporate foods mentioned in the Bible—such as almonds, apples, dates, raisins, and honey—as symbolic ingredients in assorted festival dishes. Since many dishes were prepared ahead to be served cold on the Sabbath, vinegar was commonly added as a preservative and often sweeteners or raisins to counter the acidity of the vinegar. As a result, sweet-and-sour dishes proliferate in the Jewish culinary repertoire. And Jews commonly affixed their own special touches to local dishes, such as adding garlic (an item despised by many cultures) and onions, thereby creating extra layers of flavor.

After all is said and done, what is Jewish food? It is food that evokes the spirit of a Jewish community as it celebrates its festivals and life-cycle events. It is a dish that conjures up the joy of millions of Sabbath dinners or resounds with the memory of the *mellahs* (Jewish quarters in Muslim countries), ghettos, and *shtetlach*, in which for millennia Jews struggled to eke out a living. It is the context of Ashkenazim serving honey cake on Rosh Hashanah, strudel on Sukkoth, hamantaschen on Purim, a flourless nut torte on Passover, and cheesecake on Shavuot. It is Sephardim serving leek patties on Rosh Hashanah, eggplant and meat casserole on Sukkoth, doughnuts on Hanukkah, Haman's ear pastries on Purim, sponge cake on Passover, and rice pudding on Shavuot. It is tradition.

Unfortunately, the twentieth century proved unkind to the various ancient Jewish communities, many dating back 2,000 to 2,500 years, almost all of which experienced decimation or outright destruction. The Nazi onslaught laid waste to the great Ashkenazic and Sephardic centers of Europe, and the subsequent Communist control of eastern Europe, for all practical purposes, finished off the remnants. Most of the Jewish communities of the Muslim world were swept away in the face of the nationalism and hatred that emerged in response to the rise of Zionism. Assimilation and emigration spelled the end of many other Jewish communities. Thus, the Jewish community of Poland, which less than fifty years ago surpassed 3,350,000 members, now numbers about 3,000 souls averaging about seventy years of age. Today, barely 1,000 Jews live in Thessaloníki (Salonika), Greece, a city which for several centuries boasted the world's largest Jewish community. The Iranian revolution of 1979 forced tens of thousands of Jews to flee that country and sounded the death knell of a Jewish community that stretched back to the time of Cyrus the Great (ca. 600–529 B.C.E.). In 1992 the last of a fleet of Israeli airplanes packed with a cargo of men, women, and children took off from the airport outside Addis Ababa, effectively drawing to an end the black Jewish community of Ethiopia. In December 1993 the death of an octogenarian in Cochin, in southwestern India, reduced the 2,000-year-old Jewish community of that region to twenty-two elderly people. Today, these once-vibrant Jewish communities exist only in the customs of their descendants living primarily in the two largest Jewish centers extant—Israel and America.

If these Jewish communities no longer exist, why are their foods important? Since food is the part of life that most closely touches people's day-to-day existence as well as their periods of celebration, we can get a taste of a once-vital Jewish community—its nature, history, and customs—through its traditional dishes. By discovering the past, we can learn much about our collective selves. *The World of Jewish Cooking* explores these traditional Jewish foods, their history, and their continuing usage in modern Jewish life.

A Note on Ashkenazim and Sephardim

We remember the fish that we did eat in Egypt for free; the cucumbers and the melons and the leeks and the onions and the garlic.

—NUMBERS 11:5

As the authority and importance of the ancient Judean and then Babylonian communities waned (Judea following the extinction of the patriarchate in 425 C.E.; Babylonia following the Shiite Persian conquest of the country in 945), two important Jewish centers emerged in western Europe—Iberia (called Sepharad, after a city in Asia Minor mentioned in Obadiah 20) and the Rhine River Valley (called Ashkenaz, after a kingdom in the upper Euphrates region noted in Jeremiah 51:27). Although these two medieval Jewish communities were geographically close to each other, their experiences were light-years apart: The Muslims of Iberia generated a relatively liberal, inclusive society, while the Christians of France and Germany developed a restrictive, frequently hostile feudal world. As a result, Ashkenazim and Sephardim, although both of their cultures were based on the Babylonian Talmud, gradually developed differences in areas such as customs, law, liturgy, the pronunciation of Hebrew, and foods.

The Jews of medieval France and Germany found themselves in an alien culinary environment. Their non-Jewish neighbors ate conspicuous quantities of pork and shellfish, used lard for frying, and freely mixed meat with dairy products. They also possessed a completely different attitude toward food and hospitality. As a result, Ashkenazim required a great deal of ingenuity to adapt the local fare. Not that the Jews were missing much, since medieval Franco-German food—at that time, little difference existed between the two countries—tended to be basic and unvaried.

Medieval Jews and Muslims, on the other hand, possessed a similar Middle Eastern attitude toward food and hospitality. Both cultures, for example, attached a special importance to the spiritual cleanliness of food, using only the right hand to touch food and eating from a common serving platter (without using silverware or tablecloths), and gave a religious dimension to entertaining strangers as well as friends. In addition, Muslims eschewed pork and blood, rarely ate shellfish, and only occasionally used dairy products in cooking. As a result, Sephardim easily adopted the dishes of their Muslim neighbors and vice versa. During the course of more than a millennium, Spanish-Portuguese Jews developed a highly sophisticated and distinctive cuisine—a synthesis of Iberian, Arabic, and Jewish influences—one that was much more refined and diverse than that of medieval Franco-German Jews. The high regard for Sephardic cooking was reflected in the Arabic maxim: "Sleep in a Christian bed and enjoy Jewish food."

Still, Ashkenazic and Sephardic cooking were not totally different, since interaction between the two communities sometimes led to a sharing of foods. Therefore, in this collection, if a recipe is common to both Sephardic and Ashkenazic cuisine, two names are given in the recipe title—the first in Ladino (a dialect of Castilian Spanish written in Hebrew) and the second in Yiddish (a form of Middle High German written in Hebrew). In these instances, no geographic identification is given in the accompanying translation. If a dish is exclusive to a specific cultural community or area, however, then a singular ethnic or regional term is employed in the title and the geographic identification follows in the translation.

Kosher-style deli in Los Angeles, 1985. *After a New Haven bakery owned by the Lender family acquired one of the first bagel-shaping machines in 1962, it began to sell frozen bagels, eventually going nationwide. By 1984, when Lender's was sold to Kraft, bagels had become a ubiquitous part of the American diet.*

The Recipes

APPETIZERS

Every man should eat and drink, and enjoy the good of all his labors, it is a gift of God.

—ECCLESIASTES 3:13

Most ancient cultures served all the dishes of a meal at one time, a practice continued today throughout much of Asia. It was the Romans who first introduced the idea of a set order to meals as well as serving small portions of foods at the beginning of the meal to stimulate the appetite and aid in digestion. Ashkenazim follow the Roman-German practice of serving a first course, called a *forespice* (Yiddish for "before food"), to start the meal. The *forespice* may consist of a savory pastry such as a knish or piroshki, a variety meat such as sweetbread or tongue, a smaller portion of a main dish such as stuffed cabbage or stuffed peppers, or a bread spread such as chopped liver or chopped herring.

In the synagogue following morning services on the Sabbath and holidays, Ashkenazim traditionally enjoy a buffet called a kiddush, named after the Hebrew word for the blessing over wine. A kiddush may be a simple affair, consisting of wine or schnapps, a plate of pickled herring, and some *kichlach* (egg cookies) and crackers, or it may be an elaborate sit-down spread. Occasionally, bread rolls accompany the kiddush and it serves as the Sabbath morning *seudah* (meal).

Opposite: **Lighting the Sabbath candles.** Engraving, Venice, 1593. *"On Sabbath eve two angels accompany a man home from the synagogue. If the lamp is burning, the table set, and the couch covered, the good angel declares, 'May it be thus on the next Sabbath, too,' and the evil angel is obliged to answer 'Amen.' But if not, the evil angel declares, 'May it be thus on the next Sabbath, too,' and the good angel is obliged to answer 'Amen.'* (TALMUD SHABBAT 119b).

Middle Eastern dining is very different from European. In ancient Persia, for example, parties centered on wine (see Esther 5:6), and to counter any sour taste in the wine, hosts offered a variety of tidbits to eat. This practice endures as an appetizer assortment known as a meze. A modest meze table—a medley of tastes, textures, aromas, and colors—may feature a half-dozen dishes: both cooked and uncooked, simple and elaborate, hot and cold, and almost always served in small portions. A typical meze includes a variety of spreads, salads, olives, pickles, and bite-sized pastries. A more elaborate affair may contain meat dishes such as fried *kibbe* (meat patties) and *mortadel* (filled meatballs). The meze is generally accompanied with pita bread and fiery condiments such as *z'chug* and *harissa*.

Spreads and Dips

Bread constituted the bulk of the ancient world's diet. Those coarse, hard loaves were very different from the refined breads of the modern world, however, and were generally consumed with a relish or salad to make them more palatable. The Talmud, which contains at least five different terms for relishes used with breads, states, "One who is about to recite the *hamotzi* [blessing over bread] is not permitted to do so before salt and relish is placed before him" (Berachot 40a).

Salata de Berenjena/Putlejela

EGGPLANT SALAD
ABOUT 2 CUPS; 4 TO 5 SERVINGS

By the fourth century C.E., the eggplant had arrived in the Near East from India and quickly became a meze favorite served in numerous ways (the Turks claim to have more than 150 ways of preparing eggplant), including fried in olive oil, then bathed in spices and herbs or smothered in yogurt; stewed with other vegetables; stuffed with meat or rice; wrapped in phyllo or flaky pastry; and, the most popular of all, roasted, then mashed into a creamy paste. The Ottoman Turks spread the concept of mashed eggplant salad to the far reaches of their empire, which at one time stretched from North Africa to the Ukraine.

Thus, eggplant salad became a weekday as well as a holiday favorite in Jewish communities from Marrakech to Odessa.

The seasonings, reflecting regional tastes, vary from place to place: Romanians increase the amount of garlic and add chopped onions to their *putlejela*; Persians add dried mint and a little ground cinnamon to *nazkhatun*; Russians use vinegar instead of lemon juice and add finely chopped raw onion and chopped tomatoes to *baklazhannaya ikra* (*ikra* is a Slavic word for "caviar"); in Calcutta they zest up *brinjal bharta* (*bharta* is the Hindi word for "mashed") with minced green chilies; and Yemenites add tomato puree and *z'chug* (chili paste; see page 379) to their *salada batinjan*. The following is a typical Sephardic version.

1 large eggplant (about 1½ pounds)

2 to 3 tablespoons lemon juice

1 to 2 tablespoons olive or vegetable oil

1 to 2 cloves garlic, crushed

About 1 teaspoon salt

Ground black pepper to taste

2 tablespoons chopped fresh parsley

Black olives for garnish

1. Preheat the oven to 375 degrees.
2. Cut several slits in the eggplant. (If the steam is not vented, the eggplant will burst.) Place on a baking sheet and bake, turning once, until very tender, about 45 minutes. Or roast the eggplant over a gas flame until the outside is charred and the inside is tender, 10 to 15 minutes. (Roasting the eggplant imparts a pleasing smoky flavor.) Let stand until cool enough to handle.
3. Peel the eggplant, removing all the skin. (The skin becomes bitter when burnt.) Pour off any juice. Finely mash the pulp with a fork or, for a smoother consistency, puree in a blender or food processor.
4. Stir in the lemon juice, oil, garlic, salt, and pepper. Cover and let stand at room temperature for at least 30 minutes or in the refrigerator for at least 2 hours to allow the flavors to meld. Store the eggplant salad in the refrigerator.
5. Spread the eggplant mixture on a serving plate, sprinkle with the parsley, and garnish with olives. Serve with bread, crackers, matza, or vegetable crudités.

VARIATIONS

Baba Ghanouj (Middle Eastern Eggplant Salad): Add 3 to 5 tablespoons tahini (sesame seed paste) and ½ teaspoon ground cumin. (Note: *Baba* is the Arabic word for "father," as well as a term of endearment; *ghanouj* means "indulged.")

Israeli-Style Baba Ghanouj: Substitute ¼ to ½ cup mayonnaise for the oil and add 3 to 5 tablespoons tahini, 3 mashed hard-boiled eggs, and 4 minced scallions.

Caponata

ITALIAN BRAISED EGGPLANT
10 TO 12 SERVINGS AS AN APPETIZER, 6 TO 8 AS A SIDE DISH

The Arabs controlled Sicily from 965 to 1060, during which time they introduced many of their favorite foods to the island. Vegetables like eggplant were embraced by the Jews, while at first virtually ignored by most non-Jews. This dish (the name is derived from *cappone*, a Latin term for sweet-and-sour dishes) developed as an eggplant salad for Sabbath lunch: vinegar was added as a preservative, the sugar to counteract the taste of the acid.

Sicily fell under Spanish rule in 1377. Thus, in 1492, the Spanish edict of expulsion was applied to the nearly forty thousand Jews of Sicily. Although this ancient Jewish community disappeared from the island of Sicily (Sicilian Jews organized congregations in Rome, Salonika, Aleppo, and Turkey, preserving their customs until World War II), it left behind one of the area's most famous dishes, caponata. Today, many variations of this dish are found throughout Italy.

2 medium eggplants (about 3 pounds), peeled and cut into 1-inch cubes

About 2 tablespoons kosher salt

¾ cup olive oil

3 medium red or yellow onions, chopped (about 1½ cups)

4 stalks celery, cut into ¼-inch pieces

1 to 2 medium carrots, coarsely chopped

2 cloves garlic, minced

4 cups (2 pounds) peeled, seeded, and chopped tomatoes

1 cup pitted green olives, coarsely chopped

2 to 6 tablespoons red wine vinegar

1. Place the eggplant in a colander, sprinkle with the kosher salt, and let stand for 1 hour. Rinse the eggplant with water and press between several layers of paper towels until it feels firm. (The eggplant can be prepared ahead and stored in the refrigerator for up to 4 hours.)

2. Heat ½ cup of the oil in a large saucepan over medium heat. Add the eggplant cubes and sauté until golden brown and tender but still firm, about 10 minutes. Remove the eggplant and drain off any oil.

3. Heat the remaining ¼ cup oil in the pan. Add the onions, celery, carrots, and garlic and sauté until softened, about 10 minutes.

4. Return the eggplant to the pan and add the tomatoes, olives, vinegar, parsley, basil, and sugar or honey. Cover and simmer over low heat until the vegetables are tender, about 15 minutes. Or bake in a 350-degree oven for about 30 minutes.

5. Stir in the capers and, if needed, salt. Serve warm or at room temperature (the flavors meld as it stands) as an appetizer

1 tablespoon chopped fresh
   parsley
1 tablespoon chopped fresh basil
   or 1 teaspoon dried
1 tablespoon sugar or honey
¼ cup capers, drained
Salt to taste

with crusty bread or crackers or as a side dish with cold meats or poultry. Caponata keeps well in the refrigerator.

VARIATION

Substitute 2 cups tomato juice and ¼ cup tomato paste for the fresh tomatoes.

Hummus bi Tahini

MIDDLE EASTERN CHICKPEA AND SESAME DIP
ABOUT 2 CUPS; 4 TO 5 SERVINGS

Middle Easterners enjoy a variety of spreads and dips prepared by mashing beans (*salatet ful abiad*) and lentils (*salata ades*), long a staple of the region, into a smooth consistency. Unquestionably, the most popular of these legume dishes is a thick chickpea-and-sesame puree called *hummus bi tahini* or, more informally, hummus.

2 cups cooked chickpeas, about
   ¼ cup cooking liquid, or
   water, reserved
3 to 6 tablespoons tahini
   (sesame seed paste), stirred
2 to 3 cloves garlic, minced
3 to 4 tablespoons lemon juice
About 1 teaspoon salt
¼ to ½ teaspoon ground cumin
2 tablespoons chopped fresh
   parsley or coriander
About 1 tablespoon olive oil

1. In a blender or food processor, puree the chickpeas, tahini, chickpea cooking liquid or water, garlic, lemon juice, salt, and cumin. If too dry, blend in enough additional cooking liquid or water to make a smooth paste with the consistency of mayonnaise.

2. Spread the hummus on a plate and sprinkle with the parsley or coriander and drizzle with the olive oil. Serve at room temperature with pita bread or crackers.

Chilbeh

Yemenite Fenugreek Relish
 About ¾ cup

In Yemen, *chilbeh* is used as an all-purpose spread and condiment, much in the manner that Americans use ketchup and salsa. Chilies and tomatoes are relatively modern additions to this spread: chilies for their bite and tomatoes to mellow the flavor. Indian Jews make a version adding their own spice combinations.

2 tablespoons finely ground fenugreek seeds
2 cups cold water
½ cup tomato sauce (or 2 tablespoons tomato puree and ¼ cup cold water)
About 2 teaspoons z'chug (Yemenite chili paste; see page 379) or 1 teaspoon seeded and minced green chili
About 1 teaspoon salt
Ground black pepper to taste

1. Place the fenugreek in a bowl, pour the water over the top, and stir to mix. Let the fenugreek soak in the water for at least 2 hours or preferably overnight (this removes the bitterness).
2. Carefully pour off the water. Stir to form a paste. Add the tomato sauce, *z'chug* or chilies, salt, and pepper. If the paste is too thick to spread—fenugreek expands and firms when exposed to liquid—stir in a little cold water. Store the *chilbeh* in the refrigerator. Serve with pita bread or hard-boiled eggs and as a condiment for any savory dish.

FENUGREEK

Z'*chug* is dominated by the flavor of fenugreek, a squarish, yellow-brown member of the pea family native to the eastern Mediterranean region. The word *fenugreek* is derived from the Latin term *foenum-graecum* (Greek hay), a reference to the use of its leaves as animal fodder. Unheated fenugreek is very astringent, with a celery-like flavor. The legume's attributes emerge when lightly heated, producing a mellow flavor similar to caramelized sugar. (Its principal use in America is in imitation maple syrup.) However, overtoasting results in a disagreeable bitterness. Fenugreek is particularly popular in Yemenite, Ethiopian, Moroccan, Georgian, and Indian cuisine. It is available in Middle Eastern and specialty stores both whole and ground.

Taramasalata

Greek Fish Roe Dip

 About 2 cups; 4 to 5 servings

The foreign influence on Greek cuisine, most notably Ottoman, Persian, and Italian, is clearly demonstrated in the foreign titles of so many of the country's dishes. Versions of fish roe dip can be found throughout the eastern Mediterranean region, but nowhere is it more popular than in Greece.

Taramasalata, a salty, pale-pink-colored dip, is made with the roe of various fish, such as shad and gray mullet, but ever since Jewish merchants introduced carp to the Balkans in the sixteenth century, it has primarily been made from carp roe (*tarama* in Greek).

Unprocessed *tarama* can be found in Greek and many Middle Eastern food stores. Red salmon caviar makes a tasty substitute.

3 slices white bread, trimmed of crusts
About 2 cups water
4 ounces (about ¼ cup) carp roe, shad roe, or red caviar
1 cup olive or vegetable oil
2 large eggs or ¼ cup seltzer
2 to 4 tablespoons lemon juice

1. Soak the bread in the water until soft. Squeeze out the excess liquid and crumble the bread.
2. In a blender or food processor or using an electric mixer, puree the bread and caviar.
3. With the machine on, gradually add the oil, processing until the mixture is smooth and has a mayonnaise-like consistency.
4. Gradually blend in the eggs or seltzer, then the lemon juice. Cover and refrigerate until ready to use. Serve with pita bread, French bread, crackers, or vegetable crudités. *Taramasalata* is traditionally accompanied with an anise-flavored liqueur such as ouzo or *araq.*

VARIATION
Reduce the amount of bread to 1 slice and add 1 large boiled, peeled, and mashed potato.

Gehakte Eier

ASHKENAZIC EGG SALAD
ABOUT 2 CUPS; 4 TO 5 SERVINGS

By the eleventh century, Franco-German Jews had developed the Sabbath custom of eating hard-boiled eggs and salted raw onions, separately. At some point, the two items came together in the form of an egg salad. This dish, also called *eier un schmaltz* (eggs with poultry fat), remains popular among Ashkenazim for such light meals as a *kiddush* (Sabbath morning buffet) or *shalosh seudot* (Sabbath afternoon meal) and at many life-cycle events. The duo of hard-boiled eggs and raw onions was also mixed with other common items to form such favorite Ashkenazic appetizers as *gehakte leber* (chopped liver) and *gehakte hirring* (chopped herring).

Egg salad makes a tasty appetizer or filling for a sandwich. Some people prefer a chunkier texture, while others favor a smoother dish. For a less pungent flavor, sauté the onion in a little schmaltz or oil until golden. You can further vary the flavor and texture by stirring in such additions as chopped celery, sautéed mushrooms, *gribenes* (poultry cracklings), coarsely chopped walnuts, minced green or red bell peppers, and even a little unorthodox caviar and a dash of lemon juice. Yemenites prepare a zesty version, without the schmaltz, adding chopped sour pickles and minced red chilies.

¼ *cup schmaltz (see page 109)*
    or vegetable oil
1 medium yellow onion or
    6 scallions, chopped
    (about ½ cup)
1 to 2 tablespoons chopped
    fresh parsley or dill
About 1 teaspoon salt
Ground black pepper to taste
6 hard-boiled eggs, coarsely
    chopped or mashed
Lettuce leaves for garnish
Paprika for garnish (optional)
Cucumber slices, tomato slices,
    and/or black olives
    for garnish

1. In a medium bowl, combine the schmaltz or oil, onion or scallions, parsley or dill, salt, and pepper. Stir in the eggs: For a chunkier texture, stir until the mixture just holds together; for a smoother texture, blend well. Cover and refrigerate until ready to serve.

2. For individual portions, arrange scoops of the egg salad on a bed of lettuce and, if desired, sprinkle with the paprika. Garnish with cucumber slices, tomato slices, and/or black olives. Serve with crackers, matza, or slices of dark bread or challah.

Hint: Cooking eggs over high heat produces rubbery whites and green rings around the yolks. To prevent this, place the eggs in a single layer in a saucepan and add water to cover by 1 inch. Bring to a boil over high heat. Remove from the heat, cover, and let stand for 15 minutes. Place the eggs in cold water until cool.

Gehakte Leber

ASHKENAZIC CHOPPED LIVER

 ABOUT 3 CUPS; 6 TO 8 SERVINGS

Chopped liver, probably the best known of all Jewish dishes because of repeated references by Jewish comics, is a favorite Ashkenazic appetizer served on the Sabbath, on festivals, and on other special occasions. This dish dates back to the medieval Alsatian communities, renowned for the soft livers of their force-fed geese. (In the seventeenth century, chef Jean-Pierre Close used goose liver raised by Alsatian Jews to invent *pâté de foie gras*.) In eastern Europe, chicken or beef liver, both less creamy than goose liver, were commonly used, but otherwise the dish remained the same. The chopped, broiled liver is supplemented with the Ashkenazic favorites, hard-boiled eggs and onions. Unlike pâté, the texture of chopped liver should be slightly coarse. For a more pungent flavor, do not sauté the onions but add them raw to the *gehakte leber*. Some cooks like to grind several tablespoons of *gribenes* (poultry cracklings) with the liver.

1 pound chicken livers (about 12) or beef liver
Kosher salt
About 6 tablespoons schmaltz (see page 109) or vegetable oil
3 medium yellow onions, chopped (about 1½ cups)
4 hard-boiled eggs, coarsely chopped
About 1 teaspoon salt
Ground black pepper to taste
Lettuce leaves for garnish
Cucumber slices, tomato slices, and/or black olives for garnish

1. Wash the liver and pat dry. Sprinkle lightly with the kosher salt. Place on a rack on a broiler pan and broil on both sides 4 inches from the heat source until light brown and the blood has dripped off, about 5 minutes per side for the beef liver, about 3 minutes per side for the chicken livers. Rinse with cold water. (Because of the large quantity of blood contained in liver, it cannot be made kosher in the same manner as other meats but must be broiled over or under a flame.)
2. Heat 4 tablespoons of the schmaltz or oil in a large skillet over medium heat. Add the onions and sauté until lightly golden, about 15 minutes. Let cool.
3. Process the liver, onions, and eggs through a food grinder or in a food processor until coarsely chopped.
4. Stir in enough of the remaining 2 tablespoons schmaltz or oil to moisten. Season with the salt and pepper. Cover tightly and store in the refrigerator or freezer.
5. For individual portions, arrange scoops of chopped liver on a bed of lettuce and garnish with cucumber slices, tomato slices, and/or black olives. Serve with crackers, matza, or slices of dark bread or challah.

Gehakte Hirring

EASTERN EUROPEAN CHOPPED HERRING
ABOUT 2¼ CUPS; 4 TO 5 SERVINGS

Herring, one of the few fish capable of surviving in the brackish waters of the Baltic Sea, became the primary form of protein for many of the people living in the adjoining lands of Sweden, the Baltic states, western Russia, and eastern Poland; people from western Poland, reflecting a pronounced German influence, ate much less of this fish. Typical of the northern European pantry, herring was generally salted, pickled, dried, or smoked, methods necessary to preserve limited resources during the long, harsh winters.

Chopped herring is a popular eastern European appetizer made from the predominant fish of the area, hard-boiled eggs, and raw onions. Vinegar and sugar or sweet wine are added to create a sweet-and-sour flavor to contrast with the flavor of the fish. In order to make this dish, European cooks soaked, skinned, boned, and pickled their own herring. Today such labor is no longer necessary, since jars of pickled herring are available in most grocery stores.

2 slices challah or white bread, trimmed of crusts, or 2 cups crumbled matza
¼ cup cider or white vinegar
1 (16-ounce) jar pickled herring fillets, drained
2 to 3 hard-boiled eggs, coarsely chopped
1 small yellow onion, chopped (about ¼ cup)
About 1 tablespoon sugar or sweet red wine
Chopped scallions, fresh parsley, or hard-boiled eggs for garnish

1. Soak the bread or matza in the vinegar until moist, about 5 minutes. Squeeze out the liquid.
2. Discard any onions from the herring jar. Rinse the herring well under cold running water and pat dry.
3. In a chopping bowl or a food grinder, chop the herring and bread or matza with the eggs and onion. Or process in a food processor until almost pureed. Check the seasonings, adding sugar or wine to taste. Refrigerate for at least 4 hours to allow the flavors to meld.
4. Mound the herring mixture on a serving plate and garnish with chopped scallions, parsley, or eggs. Serve with rye bread, black bread, crackers, matza, or *kichlach* (egg cookies; see page 321).

VARIATIONS
Herring and Apple Spread: Add ½ cup unsweetened applesauce or 1 to 2 peeled, cored, and minced tart apples.
Lithuanian Herring Salad: Add 1 cup sour cream, 1 teaspoon prepared horseradish, and, if desired, 3 tablespoons chopped dill pickle.

Charkhalis Pkhali

GEORGIAN BEET SALAD
ABOUT 4 CUPS; 6 TO 8 SERVINGS

The agricultural conditions in Georgia lend themselves to high-quality fresh produce. A favorite way of preparing vegetables is *pkhali*—similar to the Turkish *piyaz*—a salad made from a single chopped cooked vegetable. Although many different vegetables are used to make this dish, all *pkhali* have a common denominator—a walnut sauce called *bazha.* The flavor of the finished product varies as the sauce interacts with a particular vegetable. The secret to *pkhali* is allowing it to stand long enough for the flavors to meld. Hosts usually offer several kinds of *pkhali,* as each has a distinct taste. Serve *pkhali* with a bread such as pita or *lavash* (see page 268).

5 medium beets (about 1½ pounds)

About 1 cup bazha *(walnut sauce; see page 375)*

Chopped fresh parsley or coriander for garnish

1. Trim the beets, leaving about 1 inch of the stem intact. Wash the beets, but do not scrub or pierce the skin or the color will bleed.

2. Place the beets in a large saucepan and add water to cover. Bring to a boil, reduce the heat to low, cover, and simmer until tender, 30 to 45 minutes. Drain.

3. When cool enough to handle, slip off and discard the skins. Finely chop the pulp. Stir the *bazha* into the beets. Cover and refrigerate for at least 6 hours.

4. To serve, spread the *pkhali* on a plate, smoothing the top. Score a diamond pattern in the surface and garnish with chopped parsley or coriander.

VARIATIONS

Lobio Pkhali (Georgian Bean Salad): Substitute 3 cups cooked red beans or 1½ pounds shelled, cooked, and drained fresh fava beans for the beets. Garnish with a sliced red onion.

Isanakhi Pkhali (Georgian Spinach Salad): Substitute 2 pounds cooked, squeezed, and chopped fresh spinach or beet greens for the beets. Garnish with coarsely chopped walnuts or pomegranate seeds.

GEORGIAN GOURMET

"Ask anyone from the former Soviet Union," declares Esther Davidashvili, a native of Tbilisi, Georgia, and currently a resident of Jerusalem, "and they'll agree that the food of Georgia is the best of the entire region. People came from all over the former Soviet Union just to experience our cuisine, and the best restaurants in Moscow used to be Georgian."

Situated between the Black Sea to the west, the southern edge of the Great Caucasus Mountains and Russia to the north, and Turkey to the south lies the ancient country of Georgia. This location propitiously placed the region at the crossroads of the spice and silk trades between East and West, accounting for the land's once-legendary wealth.

"The rich Georgian soil yields an abundance of fresh fruits, vegetables, and herbs," Davidashvili notes. "The presence of herbs—coriander is the most popular—is rather pronounced in Georgian cooking, while spices are always used with subtlety. Georgians aren't rice eaters like the Persians and central Asians or noodle eaters like the eastern Europeans. We prefer bread and corn. Georgia is justly renowned for its grapes, wines [which is rather appropriate, since the area may actually be the original home of the vine], and wine vinegars [the predominant souring agent].

"Georgians prefer their food tart—never sweet-and-sour," declares Davidashvili. Georgian cooks found numerous ways to dress up their dishes with an array of pungent sauces. The pride and joy of every Georgian cook is *tkemali*, a sour plum sauce used to flavor a large variety of dishes. A pomegranate sauce called *narsharab* adds a refreshing tartness to dishes. Unquestionably, the most conspicuous element of Georgian cooking is a delicate walnut sauce called *bazha*. "We had several walnut trees in our yard, a common practice in Georgia, and used the nuts in sauces, salads, soups, stews, and confections.

"Since ancient times, Georgians have been masterful shepherds and herdsmen, and meat—primarily lamb—constitutes a major component of the diet," she continues. "Georgians love grilled meats such as shashlik [a form of shish kebab], stews, and dolmas [stuffed vegetables]. Dairy products are found primarily in the form of *matsoni* [Georgian yogurt] and an array of *khveli* [cheeses]." For such a dairy-rich country, it is rather surprising that butter plays such a negligible role in cooking, used primarily to add flavor to baked goods and occasionally for frying. "The preferred fat is *zeti* [oil], usually made from sunflowers and occasionally from walnuts.

"Georgian desserts usually consist of fresh fruit," Davidashvili says. Pastries reflect the Middle Eastern influence of honey-soaked phyllo pastries. "Hospitality is of such importance to Georgians that the dinner table is always kept set in order to promptly serve unexpected guests. We love sitting around the table not only eating but talking and singing—indeed, it is the favorite Georgian pastime."

Georgian Jewish women. *The Russian writer Nemirowitz-Danchansky described his trip to a Georgian Jewish village in the later 1800s: "The noisy streets are crowded with people in colorful attire. The tower of the synagogue resembles a Moslem minaret; it is colorful and is faced with yellow and blue slabs of stone, and it towers above all the houses."*

Pastry Appetizers

Pastel

SEPHARDIC SAVORY PIE
 8 TO 10 SERVINGS AS AN APPETIZER

Two thousand years ago, a favorite Sabbath treat among Babylonian Jews was a fish- or meat-filled double crust pie. The pastry layers represented the double portion of manna, the heavenly bread that the Jews ate during their forty years of wandering in the wilderness of Sinai, collected for the Sabbath and the lower and upper layers of dew that protected the manna. Both the medieval Iberian Jews and the Franco-German Jews adopted this custom. Each Friday morning, Iberian housewives made an oil pastry, while Franco-German Jews prepared *pashtet*, a forerunner of *pâte à choux* (cream puff dough) made from flour, water, schmaltz, and eggs. They first spread a layer of dough into a greased clay pot. Then they spooned in a mixture of ground meat, onions, garlic, and spices and topped the filling with another layer of dough. After the lid was secured, the *pastel/pashtida* was placed in the family oven or, more probably, taken to the communal bakery. Before the onset of the Sabbath the pie was retrieved and placed on a metal rack hanging over the family's hearth. The dying embers of the fire would keep the pie warm until it was eaten for the Sabbath dinner. A medieval story is told of a German Jewish child who was kidnapped by thugs and on the Sabbath cried so incessantly for his *pashtida* that his location was soon discovered.

Partially because of the shortage of meat in Europe beginning in the fifteenth century, this dish disappeared from the Ashkenazic cooking repertoire, although the name survived: in Yiddish, as a term for a type of grain pudding; in Russian, for potato pancakes; and in Hebrew, for both a casserole and a pâté—an appropriate designation, as the original pâtés were wrapped in pastry. Sephardim, on the other hand, continue to prepare a variety of Sabbath pies. Two-crust pastries—variously known as *pastel* ("pastry" in Ladino), *tapada* (from the Spanish *tapar*, "to cover"), *mina* ("mine" in Spanish), *megina*, and, in the Balkans, *inchusa*—are popular Sephardic Sabbath appetizers. During the fall and winter, the filling customarily consists of meat. Vegetables, commonly mixed with cheese, are popular during the spring and summer.

1 recipe oil pastry (see page 42)
  or short pastry (see page 40)
Double recipe Sephardic pastry
  filling (see pages 45–47)
1 tablespoon vegetable oil or
  1 large egg beaten with
  1 tablespoon water
About 1 tablespoon sesame
  seeds for garnish (optional)

1. Position a rack in the lower third of the oven. Preheat the oven to 375 degrees. Grease a deep 11- to 12-inch pie plate or a shallow 2-quart baking dish.

2. On a lightly floured surface, using a lightly floured rolling pin, roll out two-thirds of the dough into a ⅛-inch-thick round about 2 inches larger than the prepared pie plate.

3. Fold the dough in half, then fold again into quarters. Place the tip of the dough in the center of the pie plate, unfold, and gently press into the dish. Trim the dough, leaving a ½-inch overhang. Spoon in the filling.

4. Roll out the remaining dough into a ⅛-inch-thick round slightly larger than the pie plate. Place the dough round over the filling, fold the bottom dough over the top crust, and crimp the edges to seal. Brush with the oil or egg wash and cut several slits in the top to vent the steam. If desired, sprinkle with the sesame seeds.

5. Bake until golden brown, about 40 minutes. Serve warm or at room temperature.

KOSHER

The Hebrew word "kosher" means fit. The laws of *kashrut*, therefore, involve the fitness of food for the Jewish table.

The Bible permits the consumption only of beasts that have split hoofs and chew their cud. Therefore, cattle, sheep, goats, and deer are permissible, while pigs, horses, and camels are *treif* (not permitted, literally meaning "torn"). Leviticus (11:13–20) contains a list of twenty-four varieties of unkosher fowl, including all birds of prey. The identification of kosher fowl is handed down from generation to generation.

In order for even an acceptable beast or fowl to be kosher, it must be ritually slaugh-

tered. Furthermore, since the consumption of blood is strictly forbidden, the blood must be removed by salting and soaking or broiling. In addition, the sciatic nerve and certain fats located in the hindquarter of an animal are forbidden and must be removed.

From the Biblical injunction, one that is repeated three times, "You shall not boil a kid in its mother's milk" derives a restriction on cooking or mixing together meat and dairy products. Foods that are neither meat (*fleishig* in Yiddish and *dela carne* in Ladino) nor dairy (*milchig* in Yiddish and *dela mantika* in Ladino) are known as *pareve* (from a Czech word meaning "pair").

Mina de Maza

SEPHARDIC MATZA PIE

6 SERVINGS AS A SIDE DISH, 4 AS A MAIN COURSE

Mina (Ladino for "mine," as in "an excavation for minerals") is a favorite Sephardic Passover dish consisting of layers of matza and vegetables or meat ingeniously derived from Sephardic pastry pies—also known by such names *pastel, tapada, megina*, and, in Greece, as *pita*. Spring vegetables, most notably spinach, zucchini, and leeks, are the most popular fillings. Meat pies are served at the Passover Seder and as a side dish for dinner during the festival; vegetable *minas*, usually containing cheese, are a part of the *desayuno* (breakfast) served Passover morning with *huevos haminados* (brown eggs; see page 382) and lemon wedges. Double the recipe and bake in a 13-by-9-inch baking pan.

1 tablespoon olive or vegetable oil

4 whole matzot

1 recipe Sephardic meat filling (see page 45) or vegetable pastry filling (see pages 46 and 47)

1 large egg, lightly beaten

1. Preheat the oven to 350 degrees. Spread the oil on an 8- or 9-inch-square baking pan or ovenproof skillet and place the pan in the oven to heat.

2. Soak the unbroken matzot in warm water until semisoft but not mushy, 1 to 2 minutes. Remove the matzot and place on paper towels to drain.

3. Carefully cover the bottom and sides of the prepared pan with 2 matzot, breaking one of them apart to fill in the spaces. Spread with the filling, then cover with the remaining 2 matzot. Spread the egg on the top.

4. Bake until golden brown, about 45 minutes. Let stand about 5 minutes before serving. *Mina* can be prepared several days ahead, stored in the refrigerator, then reheated before serving. Serve warm.

VARIATIONS

Combine the beaten egg with 1 cup mashed potatoes and spread on top of the *mina*.

Layered Mina: Cover the bottom of the prepared pan with 2 matzot, spread with half of the filling, top with 1 additional matza, spread with the remaining filling, and cover with the remaining 2 matzot.

Opposite: **Utensils are immersed in boiling water to make them kosher for Passover.** (Engraving, Venice, 1593.) *Although today most people can afford to purchase a separate set of utensils for Passover, throughout most of history it was necessary to kasher these items though immersion in boiling water.*

Pastilla

MOROCCAN "PIGEON" PIE

8 TO 10 SERVINGS

After arriving in the Ottoman Empire and discovering phyllo, Sephardim sometimes substituted it for the pastry in their pies variously called *mina, pastel,* and *pita.* The most well known version of phyllo pie is the Moroccan *pastilla,* also called *basteya,* made with poultry filling and served on special occasions. It is traditionally assembled in a tin-lined copper pan called a *t'bseel,* but a large baking dish or paella dish can be substituted. Although squab—a young pigeon—is the traditional meat, chicken makes a tasty and more available substitute. *Pastilla* takes a little work to create, but the end result—a delicious filling sandwiched between delicate layers of crisp, flaky pastry—is well worth the effort. For information on handling phyllo, see page 345.

ALMOND FILLING

1 cup toasted blanched almonds, cooled

¼ cup sugar

1 teaspoon ground cinnamon

CHICKEN FILLING

3 tablespoons margarine or vegetable oil

2 medium yellow onions, chopped (about 1 cup)

3 cloves garlic, minced

1 teaspoon ground ginger

1 teaspoon ground black pepper or 12 peppercorns

¾ teaspoon ground turmeric

½ teaspoon saffron threads, crumbled

¼ teaspoon ground allspice

1 (2-inch) cinnamon stick or ½ teaspoon ground cinnamon

1. To make the almond filling: In a food processor, finely grind the almonds, sugar, and cinnamon. Set aside. (The almond filling may be prepared a day ahead and stored in a cool place.)

2. To make the chicken filling: Heat the margarine or oil in a large, heavy saucepan over medium heat. Add the onions and garlic and sauté until soft and translucent, 5 to 10 minutes. Stir in the ginger, pepper or peppercorns, turmeric, saffron, allspice, and cinnamon and sauté for 1 minute.

3. Add the chicken, broth or water, and parsley. Bring to a boil, cover, reduce the heat to low, and simmer until the chicken is tender, about 45 minutes.

4. Remove the chicken. Strain the cooking liquid. (You can reserve the solids and later add to the reduced liquid or discard the solids.) Boil the cooking liquid over high heat for about 20 minutes and reduce to about 1 cup. Meanwhile, remove the meat from the bones and shred.

5. Whisk the reduced liquid into the eggs. If desired, add the strained cooking solids. Cook, stirring constantly, over low heat until the mixture thickens. Pour into a bowl and let cool. (The chicken filling may be prepared a day ahead and stored in the refrigerator.)

4½ to 5 pounds chicken parts
(breasts, thighs, and legs)
4 cups chicken broth or water
½ cup chopped fresh parsley
6 large eggs, well beaten

ASSEMBLY
16 sheets phyllo dough
About ¾ cup (1½ sticks)
    margarine, melted, or
    vegetable oil for brushing
    (see Note)
Confectioners' sugar for dusting
Ground cinnamon for dusting

6. Preheat the oven to 425 degrees. Lightly brush a 10- or 11-inch round baking dish with margarine or oil.

7. To assemble: Line the prepared dish with a sheet of phyllo, draping the excess over the edge. Brush with the margarine or oil. Repeat layering and brushing with 5 more sheets, draping each in a different direction.

8. Spread one-third of the egg mixture on the pastry in the pan. Mix another one-third of the egg mixture with the shredded chicken and pack into the pie shell. Top with 6 additional sheets of phyllo dough, brushing with the margarine or oil and draping the excess as with the other sheets.

9. Spread the remaining egg mixture on the phyllo in the pan, then sprinkle with the almond filling.

10. Fold the pastry edges toward the center of the pie, brushing with the margarine or oil. Top with the remaining 4 sheets of phyllo, brushing with the margarine or oil and tucking in the edges.

11. Bake until golden brown, about 20 minutes. Lightly sprinkle with confectioners' sugar, then sprinkle lines of cinnamon to form a diamond pattern. Let stand at least 10 minutes and up to 30 minutes before cutting into wedges.

SAFFRON

Spikenard and saffron, calamus and cinnamon,
myrrh and aloes, with all the chief spices.
—SONG OF SONGS 4:14

Saffron is made from the red-orange or yellowish stigmas of the purple crocus *(Crocus sativus)*. Since it requires more than eighty thousand blossoms and much manual labor to produce a single pound of saffron, it is far and away the world's most expensive spice. The Arabs introduced these flowers as well as the techniques of preparing them to Spain one thousand years ago.

The more intense the color of the stigma, the better its quality. Saffron gives foods a brilliant yellow color and a slightly bitter flavor. The threads are usually soaked in hot liquid or slightly roasted and ground before being added to a dish. Saffron is a key flavoring in such classical dishes as Moroccan *couscous*, Persian rice *polo*, and Indian *pilau*.

TURKISH DELIGHTS

"The food of Turkish Jews is a lot like our languages: a mixture. We spoke Ladino at home, Turkish in the street, Hebrew in the synagogue, and French in school," says Mathilde Turiel (née Nahum). Her sister, Louise Defez, agrees. "Variety is the hallmark of the Turkish kitchen."

Following the split of the Roman Empire, the eastern part, the Byzantine Empire, spent most of its millennium of existence attempting to spread the Greek Orthodox religion while fending off incursions by Persians, Arabs, Huns, and Slavs. More successful were the Ottoman Turks, originally from the area south of Siberia currently called Turkmeni-stan and Khirghizistan, who gradually gained control over Western Asia. In 1453, the Turks captured Constantinople (renamed Istanbul), bringing an end to the Byzantine Empire. The Ottoman Empire reached its height under Süleyman the Magnificent (1494–1566), whose domain stretched northwest to Hungary, northeast to Georgia, westward to Algeria, and southeast to the Euphrates River.

Sultan Bayezid II (1447–1512) eagerly welcomed tens of thousands of Sephardim, thanking the Spanish monarchs for enriching his kingdom while impoverishing their own. The Sephardim quickly overwhelmed the Roman-iots (Greek-speaking Jews), becoming the dominant form of Jewish culture in Turkey.

"Turkish cooking doesn't use a lot of spices," notes Mathilde. "We rely more on herbs, especially parsley, dill, and mint. Both herbs and spices are used subtly."

"In Turkey, eggplant is the king of vegetables. Sephardim almost never serve plain vegetables, but enhance them with tomatoes, a splash of fresh lemon juice, or herbs. And we use them in dishes such as *fritadas* [omelets], *minas* [pies], and dolmas [stuffed vegetables]. Fresh fava beans with their pods are a customary Passover food. But we don't eat rice or sesame seeds on Passover [unlike many Sephardic communities that permit eating these items]."

Louise adds, "*Tishpishti* [honey-nut cake] was served on Rosh Hashanah night. *Crocon* [honey-nut brittle] is a Turkish specialty traditional on Rosh Hashanah. *Lokmas* [doughnuts] are the favorite Hanukkah treat, but we also make a variety of pastries and always have plenty to serve guests. *Pan d'Espagna* [sponge cake] was served on Shavuot because it was white, a symbol of purity. Purim was a great day for baking, with baklava, *kadayif* [shredded wheat pastry], *travados* [pastry horns], *trigona* [nut-filled phyllo triangles], ladder-shaped cookies symbolizing the gallows on which Haman was hung, and, the most prominent Purim pastry, *shamlias* [fried pastry twists dusted with sugar]. On Purim, everyone used to bake extra to give to the poor."

"Turkish coffee accompanies sweets," Mathilde notes. "After finishing the coffee, a guest returns the empty cup to the serving tray and says, '*Caves d'alegria*' [coffee for joyful occasions]."

DESAYUNO

Following Sabbath and festival morning synagogue services, Sephardim return home to a *desayuno* (Ladino for "breakfast"). This meal is a casual affair primarily consisting of finger foods, most notably a trio of filled pastries: *boyos* (several types of cheese pastry), *bulemas* (phyllo coils), and *borekas* (small flaky turnovers). In texture, *boyos* fall between the very thin, very crisp pastry of *bulemas* and the thicker, less crisp pastry of *borekas*. A typical *desayuno* also features *fritadas* (omelets), *huevos haminados* (brown eggs; see page 382), cheeses, olives, rice pudding, fresh fruit, jams, yogurt, and an anise-flavored liqueur called *ouzo* in Greek, *raki* in Turkish, and *araq* in Arabic. The following three cheese pastries are also served at other dairy meals, including those on Shavuot (see page 315), on Hanukkah (see page 220), and during the week preceding the fast of Tisha b'Av (see page 209).

Boyos de Queso

SEPHARDIC CHEESE PINWHEELS

ABOUT 20 PASTRIES

1 recipe cheese pastry
    (see page 42)
1 cup grated kashkaval
    (see page 30), Cheddar,
    Muenster, or Swiss cheese
1 large egg beaten with
    1 tablespoon water

1. Preheat the oven to 375 degrees.
2. On a lightly floured surface, roll out the dough into a ¼-inch-thick rectangle. Sprinkle with ⅔ cup of the cheese and roll up jelly roll style. Cut into ½-inch-thick slices.
3. Place the slices on a baking sheet, cut side up, and flatten slightly. Brush the tops with the egg wash and sprinkle with the remaining ⅓ cup cheese.
4. Bake until golden brown, about 20 minutes. Serve warm or at room temperature.

Boyos de Pan

SEPHARDIC CHEESE PUFFS
ABOUT 48 SMALL PUFFS

Sephardim generally made bread, for much of history an arduous process, only twice a week, on Mondays and Fridays. After a few days, the bread would become stale. *Boyos de pan* (from *bollo*, Spanish for a bun or small cake) originated as a way to use dry bread by soaking it in water or milk, seasoning the mixture with cheese and spices, then frying dollops of the batter in hot oil. Over the centuries, more sophisticated variations of *boyos* developed, but the common denominator among them has always been cheese.

1 pound lean bread such as French or Italian, torn into small pieces

4 cups grated kashkaval *(see below), Swiss, Gouda, or Cheddar cheese (or 1½ cups grated Parmesan cheese and 1 cup cottage cheese)*

4 large eggs, lightly beaten

2 tablespoons chopped fresh parsley

1 clove garlic, minced

About 1 teaspoon salt

Ground black pepper to taste

1. Preheat the oven to 375 degrees. Grease 2 large baking sheets.

2. Soak the bread in water to cover until soft, about 5 minutes. Drain and squeeze out the water—there will be about 3 cups of bread. Stir in the cheese, eggs, parsley, garlic, salt, and pepper.

3. Drop the batter by heaping tablespoonfuls onto the prepared baking sheets and bake until golden brown, about 25 minutes. Or deep-fry the batter in 1 inch of hot vegetable oil until golden brown on all sides. Serve warm or at room temperature.

VARIATION

Lighter Boyos de Pan: Add 2 cups all-purpose flour, ¼ cup vegetable oil, and 1 teaspoon baking powder.

KASHKAVAL

*K*ashkaval, a popular spun-curd Balkan cheese with a texture similar to *provolone dolce*, is based on the Italian *caciocavallo* (literally "on horseback"), but is made from ewe's milk or a combination of ewe's and cow's milk. It is similar to the Greek *kaseri*. When aged for two to three months, it is mild and used as a table cheese; more mature cheeses are stronger and used for grating.

Bulemas

SEPHARDIC CHEESE COILS

ABOUT 30 PASTRIES

Traditional *bulemas* are made from a thinly stretched yeast dough, but there is also an easier version made from store-bought phyllo dough. Coating the yeast dough with oil produces flaky layers similar to phyllo.

¾ teaspoon active dry yeast

1 cup warm water

About 2 cups all-purpose flour

½ cup vegetable oil

½ teaspoon salt

1 cup grated Parmesan or
*   Romano cheese*

2 cups Sephardic cheese,
*   eggplant, or spinach filling*
*   (see pages 45 and 46)*

1. In a large bowl, dissolve the yeast in ¼ cup of the water. Add the remaining ¾ cup water, ½ cup of the flour, 1 tablespoon of the oil, and the salt. Stir in enough of the remaining 1½ cups flour, ½ cup at a time, to make a soft dough. Place on a lightly floured surface and knead until smooth and elastic.

2. Pour the remaining oil into a 13-by-9-inch baking pan. Form the dough into 1-inch balls and place in the baking pan, turning to coat in the oil. Cover with plastic wrap and let stand for 15 minutes.

3. Preheat the oven to 375 degrees. Grease a large baking pan.

4. Place the dough balls on a greased surface and press to flatten. Roll and stretch the dough into very thin rounds about 10 inches in diameter.

5. Brush the dough rounds lightly with the oil in the baking pan and sprinkle with some of the cheese. Spread 1 tablespoon of the filling along one edge of the dough and roll up jelly roll style from the filling side. Starting from one end, curl up into a coil, the seam side in.

6. Place the coils in the larger baking pan, leaving a little space between the coils to allow for rising. Brush the tops lightly with oil and sprinkle with the remaining grated cheese.

7. Bake until golden brown, about 30 minutes. Drain on paper towels.

Borekas

SEPHARDIC PASTRY TURNOVERS

 ABOUT 30 TURNOVERS

Among the foods that the Turks brought with them from central Asia was a dumpling called *bugra* that evolved into an assortment of pastry turnovers collectively known as *borek* or *burek*. These pastries became a beloved part of Ottoman cuisine. Indeed, the position of head *borek* baker was one of the most important in the Ottoman imperial household. After arriving in the realm of the sultan, the Iberian Jewish exiles merged the *borek* with the similar Spanish *empanada* to create *borekas*, one of the most popular of Sephardic pastries.

Traditional *borekas* are made with the same pastry as *pastels* (see page 22), but more recent variations use phyllo dough and puff pastry. Almost anything can be used as a filling, but vegetable-cheese mixtures are the most prevalent. Cheese *borekas* are popular treats at Saturday and Sunday morning *desayuno* and at dairy meals on Shavuot (see page 315) and Hanukkah (see page 220). Meat fillings are popular for Friday night dinner; spinach, pumpkin, and winter squash for Rosh Hashanah (see page 126); and sweet nut for Purim (see page 316). Turnovers made from a cheese pastry and cheese filling are called *borekitas*.

1 recipe oil pastry (see page 42) or short pastry (see page 40)

1 recipe Sephardic pastry filling (see pages 45–47)

1 large egg beaten with 1 tablespoon water

Sesame seeds for garnish (optional)

1. Preheat the oven to 375 degrees.
2. Form the dough into 1-inch balls. On a lightly floured surface, roll the balls into 3-inch rounds, about ⅛ inch thick.
3. Place a heaping teaspoon of the filling in the center of each round. Fold the dough in half over the filling to form a half-moon and press the rounded edge with the tines of a fork to seal. (The *borekas* can be prepared ahead to this point and frozen. Do not defrost before baking; increase the baking time by about 10 minutes.)
4. Place the *borekas* on a baking sheet. Brush the tops with the egg wash and, if desired, sprinkle with sesame seeds.
5. Bake until golden brown, about 30 minutes. Serve warm or at room temperature; plain or with *tarator bi tahina* (sesame seed sauce).

Piroshki

UKRAINIAN PASTRY TURNOVERS
 ABOUT 30 PASTRIES

There is much confusion over a variety of Russian and Polish pastries all of whose names come from the Slavic word *pir* (feast). *Piroshki* (from the Russian *pirozhki*, singular *pirozhok*) are half-circle Ukrainian/Russian pastry turnovers. *Piroghi* (singular *pirog*) are large double-crusted Russian pies. Neither of these are the same as the Polish filled pasta rounds called pierogi.

Russians use various types of dough to make piroshki, but they are especially fond of yeast. For much of history, mashed turnip was the most popular filling for piroshki. With the popularization of the potato in the mid-nineteenth century, however, it became the most widespread filling, and turnips were relegated to relative obscurity. Potato, meat, liver (use chopped liver; see page 17), cabbage, mushroom, and kasha (see page 188) piroshki are commonly served as an accompaniment for soups or simply by themselves as an appetizer.

*1 recipe rich yeast dough
(see page 265), sour cream
pastry (see page 41),
oil pastry (see page 42), or
short pastry (see page 40)*
*1 recipe Ashkenazic pastry
filling (see pages 48–50; see
Note)*
1 egg white, lightly beaten
*1 egg yolk beaten with 1 tea-
spoon water*

1. Preheat the oven to 375 degrees. Lightly grease a large baking sheet.
2. On a lightly floured surface, roll out the dough ⅛ inch thick. With a glass or a biscuit cutter, cut into 2½- to 3-inch rounds.
3. Place a heaping teaspoon of the filling in the center of each round. Brush the edges with a little egg white and fold over to form a half circle, pinching the edges or pressing with the tines of a fork to seal. Reroll any scraps. (The piroshki may be prepared to this point up to a week ahead and frozen. Do not thaw before baking.)
4. Place the piroshki on the prepared baking sheet and brush the tops with the egg wash. Bake until golden brown, 20 to 30 minutes. Serve warm or at room temperature.

Note: Sweet fillings such as prune (use 2 cups prune jam) and carrot (use 2 cups soft carrot-ginger candy; see page 367) are used to make dessert piroshki. Apple-filled turnovers (use the filling from apple blintzes; see page 225) are called *punchekes*. Dessert piroshki are sometimes brushed with melted honey while still warm.

Knishes

EASTERN EUROPEAN FILLED PASTRIES
 ABOUT 8 LARGE OR 36 SMALL KNISHES

Krepish, a small filled pie, was the favorite pastry among the Franco-German Jews. In eastern Europe, this treat took on the name knish, from a Slavic cake roll called *knysz*, and became the preeminent Ashkenazic filled pastry. Popular fillings include potato, cheese, kasha (called *koshnikes*), cabbage, liver, and ground beef. Miniature knishes serve as attractive party fare, while larger knishes make a satisfying appetizer.

1 recipe oil pastry (see page 42)
  or short pastry (see page 40)
About 2 cups Ashkenazic pastry
  filling (see pages 48–50) or
  kasha (see page 188)
1 large egg beaten with
  1 teaspoon water

1. Preheat the oven to 375 degrees. Lightly grease a large baking sheet.
2. On a lightly floured surface, roll out the dough ⅛ inch thick. For large knishes, cut into 5-by-4-inch rectangles; for small knishes, cut into 3-inch rounds or squares.
3. Place about ¼ cup of the filling or kasha in the center of the large knishes, about 1 tablespoon in the small knishes. Bring the edges together in the center, pinching to seal.
4. Place the knishes seam side down on the prepared baking sheet and brush with the egg wash. Bake until lightly browned, about 30 minutes. Serve warm or at room temperature. (After cooling, the knishes can be frozen for several months. To reheat, cover loosely with foil and bake in a 375-degree oven until heated through, about 15 minutes.)

VARIATION
Knish Rolls (48 small or 24 medium knishes): Roll out the dough into a 16-by-12-inch rectangle about ⅛ inch thick. Cut the dough into four 12-by-4-inch rectangles. Spread about ¾ cup of the filling along a long edge of each dough rectangle. Fold the long edge over the filling and roll up jelly roll style, pinching the ends of the dough under the filling. Brush with oil or egg wash. Place the rolls on a greased baking sheet and cut slashes in the top at 1- or 2-inch intervals. Bake until lightly browned, about 30 minutes. Cut the knishes at the slash marks.

Fruma Gorenstein's Knishes, Los Angeles, 1985. *According to admirers, Fruma Gorenstein, a Russian-born Californian, makes the most delicious food in the world and her knishes melt in your mouth. She cooks only for Jewish organizations on a volunteer basis.*

Sambusak

MIDDLE EASTERN PASTRY TURNOVERS
ABOUT 30 TURNOVERS

*S*ambusak, which is mentioned in Iraqi sources of the tenth century, has long been the most popular pastry among the Jews of Iraq, Syria, Lebanon, and Calcutta. It appears to have originated in Persia and was probably introduced by the Arabs to Spain, where it was called *empanada*. For *sambusak bi loz* (nut *sambusak*), use 1 recipe *ma'amoul* nut filling (see page 331).

1 recipe *semolina pastry*
   (see page 43), oil pastry
   (see page 42), or short pastry
   (see page 40)
About ½ cup sesame seeds
1 recipe sambusak *filling (see*
   page 50–51)

1. Form the dough into 1-inch balls. Flatten slightly, then press the bottoms into the sesame seeds. Roll into 3-inch rounds.
2. Place a heaping teaspoon of the filling in the center of each dough round. Fold an edge over the filling to form a half-moon shape and crimp the rounded edge or press with the tines of a fork. (The pastries can be prepared ahead to this point and frozen. Do not thaw; increase the baking time by about 10 minutes.)
3. Preheat the oven to 375 degrees.
4. Place the *sambusak* on baking sheets. Bake until golden brown, about 20 minutes. Serve warm or at room temperature.

TAMARIND

*T*amarind (from the Arabic *tamar hindi*, "date of India") is a brown 2- to 6-inch-long pod encasing up to ten glossy seeds surrounded by a tart brown pulp. Before the introduction of lemons, tamarind served as one of the primary souring agents in Central and Middle Eastern cooking, a role it still serves in Syrian fare.

Tamarind is sold in Middle Eastern and Indian stores as concentrated pulp, in dried blocks that must be softened in liquid before using, and as a sauce called *temerhindi*. Equal amounts of prune butter and apricot butter may be substituted for the *temerhindi*.

Lahamagine

NEAR EASTERN SMALL MEAT PIZZAS
24 SMALL PIZZAS

Small meat pizzas, called *lahmacun* in Turkish and *lahamagine* or *lahm b'ajin* (meat with dough) in Arabic, are popular appetizers in Syria and many surrounding countries once under the domain of the Ottoman Empire.

1 recipe lean yeast dough (see page 264)

1 pound ground lamb or beef

1 medium yellow onion, finely chopped (about ½ cup)

¼ cup toasted pine nuts or chopped fresh parsley

1 to 2 tablespoons lemon juice or ¼ cup temerhindi (tamarind sauce; see opposite)

3 tablespoons tomato paste

¼ teaspoon ground cinnamon

Pinch of ground allspice

About 1 teaspoon salt

Ground black pepper to taste

Vegetable oil for brushing (optional)

1. Preheat the oven to 375 degrees. Sprinkle a large baking sheet with cornmeal, line with parchment paper, or lightly grease.

2. Punch down the dough. Divide into 24 equal pieces and roll out each piece into a ⅛-inch-thick round, 3 to 4 inches in diameter. Or roll out the dough and cut into 3- or 4-inch rounds. Place on the prepared baking sheet.

3. Combine lamb or beef, onion, pine nuts or parsley, lemon juice or *temerhindi*, tomato paste, cinnamon, allspice, salt, and pepper and spread a heaping tablespoon of the topping on each dough round, pressing down. (The pastries can be prepared ahead to this point and frozen. Do not thaw; increase the baking time by about 10 minutes.)

4. Bake the pies until lightly browned but not crisp, about 15 minutes. To keep the edges soft, brush with a little oil, if desired. Serve warm. (After cooling, *lahamagine* may be frozen and reheated in a 350-degree oven.)

VARIATION

Yeast Sambusak (Middle Eastern Yeast Turnovers): Place a heaping teaspoon of *sambusak* filling (see pages 50–51) in the center of each round. Fold in half to form a half-moon shape, pressing the edges to seal. Brush the tops with lightly beaten egg and bake as above. (*Note:* Meat-filled *sambusak* are also deep-fried in several inches of 375-degree vegetable oil to produce a very crisp pastry.)

YEMENITE SPICE

"**N**o form of Jewish cooking is more health-conscious than that of Taiman [Yemen]," declares Miriam Shurabi. "Medical studies on Yemenites who maintain our ancient diet show that we are usually free of the afflictions of Western society such as high blood pressure and diabetes."

Yemen stretches along the southwestern tip of the Arabian Peninsula. The first known Jewish settlement was established after the destruction of the Second Temple in 70 C.E. and, for centuries thereafter, Jews played a prominent role in the country's economy and politics, dominating the important spice trade that once flowed through the area.

The advent of Islam in the eighth century relegated Yemenite Jews to the lowest rung of the social ladder and poverty. Until the Ottomans gained control of the area in 1872, Yemenite Jews were forbidden to leave the country. From World War I to 1948, roughly one-third of Yemen's Jews, about sixteen thousand in total, left for Israel. With "Opera-tion Magic Carpet" (June 1949 through August 1950) nearly fifty thousand Yemenites were airlifted to Israel by the Israeli government.

"The common thread running through Yemenite recipes is that they are high in spice and low in fat and sugar. The fire in our dishes helps to cleanse the body," says Shurabi.

"Most Yemenite meals commence with bread accompanied with *chilbeh* [fenugreek relish]. The other favorite condiment is *z'chug*, a green chili and coriander mixture, or a red chili version called *shatta*. Tahini [sesame seed paste] is also popular. A spice mixture called *chawish* [dominated by cumin] is used to add flavor to dishes."

Shurabi notes, "Eggplant [which arrived from India, located directly across the Arabian Sea] is the favorite vegetable. *Memuleh* [stuffed

Opposite: **Yemenite mountain Jews clad in traditional clothing celebrate the Passover Seder.** *Because of their isolation, Yemenite Jews experienced fewer outside influences than any other community, and thus their culture remained truer to ancient Jewish practices. Yemenite matza is thicker and softer than that made by other communities.*

vegetables and fruits] are served both hot and at room temperature. Salads or cooked vegetable purees [there is often little distinction between the two in Yemenite cooking] accompany almost every meal. Yemenites love adding pine nuts to dishes for flavor and texture.

"Meat is usually served for lunch, rarely for dinner, as that is considered unhealthy," Shurabi continues. "Meat is generally prepared in the form of *chouia* [stews] and soups. Although Yemenites sometimes use chicken [always in a soup or stew], pigeons and squabs [usually stuffed and roasted or baked] are more prevalent. In Yemen, fish was a rare treat.

"A Yemenite Sabbath meal differs greatly from those of either Ashkenazim or Sephardim," explains Shurabi. "Since grape wine did not exist in Yemen, kiddush was recited over *araq* [fruit wines, not the more commonly known anise-flavored liqueur]. Flat breads called *lachuach* are used for the challah. We start all three Sabbath meals by nibbling from small bowls filled with *jaaleh* [a mixture of dried fruits, nuts, beans, and some-times small pieces of pepper-spiced roast meat]. Besides any health benefits, *jaaleh* helps to achieve the total of one hundred blessings traditionally recited each day, as we recite a blessing over each item before eating it. Meals end with spiced tea and bowls of *jaaleh*."

"There were no cakes or cookies in Yemen," Shurabi admits. "However, in Israel my family, like many other Yemenites, began serving pastries for dessert. Still, many contain no refined sugar. Fruit honey, not sugar, is used as a sweetener. It's healthier."

Subya

YEMENITE EGG LOAF
8 TO 10 SERVINGS

Subya is traditionally slow-cooked for Friday night dinner. The main course usually consists of chicken or beef soup (see page 57) containing chunks of meat and a vegetable such as pumpkin.

4 pieces of Yemenite flaky pastry
(see page 44)
3 large eggs
2 to 3 teaspoons black cumin
seeds

1. Preheat the oven to 250 degrees. Grease a large loaf pan.
2. Roll out the 4 pieces of dough to fit the loaf pan. Press 1 dough rectangle into the prepared pan, then top with 1 lightly beaten egg. Repeat layering, ending with a dough rectangle. Sprinkle with the cumin seeds.
3. Bake until golden brown, about 3 hours. Let the *subya* cool slightly or completely before cutting into slices.

Pastry Doughs

Masa Fina/Muerber Teig

SHORT PASTRY
ENOUGH PASTRY FOR ABOUT 30 (3-INCH) TURNOVERS OR
1 LARGE DOUBLE-CRUST PIE

The secret to this delicate pastry, the basis for an assortment of pies and turnovers, is the little pockets of fat in the dough that melt and release steam during baking, creating layers and producing a flaky crust. Using shortening produces a flakier pastry; oil produces a sturdier pastry. A little acid—vinegar, lemon juice, or sour cream—makes the dough easier to handle and the pastry more tender. Some cooks add one to two tablespoons sugar to the dough for sweet fillings.

2½ cups all-purpose flour

½ cup (1 stick) butter or margarine, chilled

¼ cup vegetable oil or 6 tablespoons vegetable shortening

1 teaspoon mild vinegar or lemon juice

1 teaspoon salt

About 5 tablespoons ice water or chilled seltzer

1. Place the flour in a large bowl or on a pastry board and make a well in the center. Place the butter or margarine and oil or shortening in the well and, using the tips of your fingers, a pastry blender, or two knives cutting scissors fashion, cut in the fat until the mixture resembles coarse crumbs.

2. Stir the vinegar or lemon juice and salt into the ice water or seltzer. Sprinkle the water, 1 tablespoon at a time, over a section of the flour. Gently mix with a fork to moisten. Push the moistened section aside and continue adding enough water to make a soft dough that just holds together. (The dough should be neither wet nor crumbly, as too much liquid and overmixing reduce tenderness.)

3. Place the dough on a lightly floured surface and knead briefly with the heel of your hand. Form into a ball, flatten slightly, cover with plastic wrap, and refrigerate for at least 30 minutes or up to 1 week. The dough can also be frozen for up to 3 months. (Chilling makes the dough easier to handle and more tender.) Let the chilled dough stand at room temperature until workable, about 1 hour, before rolling.

VARIATIONS

Masa mal Tomada/Teig (Flaky Pastry): Omit the oil or shortening and increase the amount of butter or margarine to 1 cup (2 sticks), or omit the butter or margarine and increase the shortening to ⅔ cup.

Masa Afrijaldada/Smeteni Teig (Sour Cream Pastry): Omit the vinegar or lemon juice and substitute 3 to 4 tablespoons sour cream for an equal amount of water, stirring the sour cream into the remaining water or 1 lightly beaten large egg. (*Note*: This is used by Sephardim for cheese tarts and by Ashkenazim for pastry strudels, piroshki, and filled cookies.)

Masa Aceite/Ail Teig

OIL PASTRY

ᐁ ENOUGH PASTRY FOR ABOUT 30 (3-INCH) TURNOVERS
OR 1 LARGE DOUBLE-CRUST PIE ᐃ

This simple, sturdy dough is used by Sephardim to make savory pies such as *pastels* (see page 22), turnovers such as *borekas* (see page 32), and pastries such as *huevos de Haman* (a pastry encasing a hard-boiled egg). Ashkenazim use it to make knishes (see page 34) and piroshki (turnovers; see page 33).

*½ cup plus 2 tablespoons
    vegetable oil*
*½ cup plus 2 tablespoons
    lukewarm water*
1 teaspoon salt
*About 2½ cups all-purpose
    flour*

1. Combine the oil, water, and salt in a large bowl. Add 1½ cups of the flour. Gradually stir in enough of the remaining 1 cup flour to make a soft dough that comes away from the sides of the bowl.

2. Form into a ball, flatten slightly, cover with plastic wrap, and let rest at room temperature for 30 minutes. Do not refrigerate.

VARIATION

Cheese Pastry: Add ¼ to ½ cup grated Swiss cheese, *kashkaval* (see page 30), or Parmesan cheese. (*Note:* This is used by Sephardim to make cheese turnovers called *borekitas* and other dairy pastries.)

Ajin Smead

MIDDLE EASTERN SEMOLINA PASTRY

 ENOUGH PASTRY FOR ABOUT 40 (3-INCH) TURNOVERS

This semolina dough is used to make an assortment of Middle Eastern cookies (such as *ma'amoul*; see page 330) and turnovers (such as *sambusak*; see page 36) with a distinctive crunch. If you do not have semolina or farina, you can use the short pastry (see Variation).

2 cups all-purpose flour
1 cup fine semolina or farina
Dash of salt
1 cup (2 sticks) butter or
*   margarine, softened*
About ½ cup lukewarm water

1. Combine the flour, semolina or farina, and salt. Beat the butter or margarine with a wooden spoon or an electric mixer until light and fluffy, 5 to 10 minutes.
2. Gradually work in the flour mixture. Add enough water to make a soft but not sticky dough. Cover and let stand at room temperature for at least 1 hour or overnight. The dough firms as it rests.

VARIATION
Middle Eastern Short Pastry: Omit the semolina and reduce the amount of water to ¼ cup.

SEMOLINA

Semolina, *smead* in Arabic, is the endosperm of durum wheat. It is available in Middle Eastern, Italian, and some health food stores in three forms: coarse grind; fine grind, sometimes labeled No. 1 quality, a slightly granular meal used to add crunch to pastries and cakes; and semolina flour, a powdery product used to make pasta and bread. Farina can be substituted for fine semolina meal in most baked goods. Semolina cooked in water and baked becomes hard, however, while farina remains soft.

Ajin

YEMENITE FLAKY PASTRY
9 PIECES OF PASTRY DOUGH

Yemenites continue to prepare many of their ancient dishes, which are rich in spices and flavor but low in sugar. In a manner reminiscent of puff pastry, this dough is rolled and folded to produce layers of butter in the dough that turn to steam during baking, resulting in a flaky pastry. A common way of using this dough is to bake balls of it alongside eggs in their shells in a slow oven overnight and to serve the eggs and pastry for Sabbath lunch. It is also used to make several other Yemenite Sabbath dishes, including *miloach* (flaky bread; see page 271) and *subya* (egg loaf; see page 40).

8¾ cups all-purpose flour

1 teaspoon single-acting baking powder

1 teaspoon salt

2½ cups water

1 large egg

1 cup (2 sticks) butter or margarine, softened

1. Combine the flour, baking powder, and salt. Add the water, the egg, and ½ cup of the butter or margarine and knead until smooth. Divide into 9 balls, cover, and let stand for 15 minutes.

2. Divide the remaining butter or margarine into 9 equal pieces. On a lightly floured surface, roll out each dough ball into a ¼-inch-thick rectangle. Spread each rectangle with a piece of butter or margarine.

3. Fold the bottom third of the rectangle over the center third, then fold the top third over. Roll out the dough into a ¼-inch-thick rectangle. Fold the bottom third of the rectangle over the center third, then fold the top third over. Repeat with the remaining eight rectangles. Cover and refrigerate for 20 minutes.

4. Repeat the rolling and folding once more. Cover with plastic wrap and refrigerate for at least 4 hours.

Gomo de Carne

SEPHARDIC MEAT FILLING

 ABOUT 2½ CUPS

Sephardim prepare many variations of meat filling, adding favorite flavors such as eggplant, spinach, chopped *huevos haminados* (brown eggs; see page 382), pine nuts, mint, dill, and cinnamon.

2 tablespoons olive or vegetable oil

2 medium yellow onions or leeks, chopped (about 1 cup)

1 pound ground beef or lamb

2 tablespoons matza meal or ½ cup mashed potatoes

1 large egg, lightly beaten

¼ cup chopped fresh parsley

About ½ teaspoon salt

Ground black pepper to taste

1. Heat the oil in a large skillet over medium heat. Add the onions or leeks and sauté until soft and translucent, 5 to 10 minutes.

2. Add the meat and cook until it loses its red color, about 5 minutes. Pour off the excess fat and let cool.

3. Stir in the remaining ingredients.

Gomo de Berenjena

SEPHARDIC EGGPLANT FILLING

❧ ABOUT 2¼ CUPS ☙

*1 large eggplant
   (about 1½ pounds)
2 tablespoons olive or vegetable
   oil
1 medium yellow onion,
   chopped (about ½ cup)
2 large eggs, lightly beaten
¼ cup matza meal or bread
   crumbs or 1 cup mashed
   potatoes
1 tablespoon chopped fresh
   parsley
About ½ teaspoon salt
Ground black pepper to taste*

1. Preheat the oven to 375 degrees.
2. Cut several slits in the eggplant. Place on a baking sheet and bake, turning once, until tender, about 30 minutes. Let stand until cool enough to handle. Peel the eggplant, removing all of the skin, then mash the pulp.
3. Heat the oil in a large skillet over medium heat. Add the onion and sauté until soft and translucent, 5 to 10 minutes.
4. Remove from the heat and stir in the eggplant and the remaining ingredients. If the mixture is too thin, stir in a little additional matza meal, bread crumbs, or mashed potatoes.

VARIATION

Gomo de Berenjena y Queso (Eggplant and Cheese Filling): Reduce the amount of eggplant to 1 medium (about 1 pound) and add ¾ cup farmer cheese or crumbled feta cheese and ¾ cup grated *kashkaval* (see page 30), Muenster, Gouda, Cheddar, or Swiss cheese.

HARD CHEESES

Hard grating cheese, called *grana* in Italian, has a granular texture. Parmesan, made from partially skimmed milk, is ideal for cooking or grating over foods. Romano, usually made with a combination of cow's and goat's milk, has a more piquant flavor than Parmesan. The best way to grate hard cheeses is with a metal grater; food processors tend to grind the cheese too finely. Grated Parmesan and Romano cheese evidence a stark decline in quality after three or four weeks, becoming rather dry and bitter. For salads, use freshly grated or shaved cheese.

Gomo de Queso

SEPHARDIC CHEESE FILLING

 ABOUT 2½ CUPS

1 cup grated kashkaval (see page 30), Muenster, Monterey Jack, or Swiss cheese

¾ cup crumbled feta, pot cheese, or farmer cheese, or ⅔ cup grated Parmesan cheese

1 cup mashed potatoes

2 large eggs, lightly beaten

About ½ teaspoon salt

Combine all of the ingredients.

VARIATIONS

Parmesan Filling: Omit the hard and soft cheeses and increase the amount of Parmesan cheese to 1¼ cups.

Feta and Parmesan Filling: Omit the hard cheese and use ½ cup crumbled feta cheese and ⅔ cup grated Parmesan cheese.

Gomo de Espinaca

SEPHARDIC SPINACH FILLING

ABOUT 2¼ CUPS

3 tablespoons olive or vegetable oil

1 medium yellow onion or 6 scallions, chopped (about ½ cup)

10 ounces frozen spinach, thawed and squeezed, or 1 pound fresh spinach or Swiss chard, washed, stemmed, and chopped

2 large eggs, lightly beaten

½ cup mashed potatoes or finely chopped walnuts

¼ cup chopped fresh parsley or dill

About ½ teaspoon salt

1. Heat the oil in a large skillet over medium heat. Add the onion or scallions and sauté until soft and translucent, 5 to 10 minutes. Let cool.
2. Stir in the remaining ingredients.

VARIATION

Gomo de Espinaca y Queso (Spinach and Cheese Filling): Substitute ¾ cup farmer cheese or crumbled feta cheese and ¾ cup grated *kashkaval* (see page 30), Muenster, or Swiss cheese for the potatoes or nuts.

Zeesih Kaesefullung

ASHKENAZIC SWEET CHEESE FILLING

❧ ABOUT 2½ CUPS ❧

Cheese-filled pastries are traditional for Shavuot (see page 315).

1 pound pot or farmer cheese
   (or 12 ounces pot cheese and
   4 ounces cream cheese)
1 large egg, lightly beaten
2 tablespoons sour cream
1 tablespoon matza cake meal
   or all-purpose flour
2 to 6 tablespoons sugar
½ cup raisins (optional)

Beat the cheese, egg, sour cream, cake meal or flour, and sugar until smooth. If desired, stir in the raisins.

Below: **Kiddush on Sabbath eve.** *Woodcut from Seder Zermirot U'Birchat Hamazon. Prague, 1514.* The Sabbath is ushered in with the lighting of candles and a cup of wine (kiddush), symbolizing joy and fruitfulness, and departs with a candle, a sniff of spice, and a cup of wine (havdallah). In the words of Isaac Bashevis Singer, "Our house was filled with the odor of burning wax, blessed spices, and with the atmosphere of wonder and miracles."

Fleischfullung

ASHKENAZIC GROUND BEEF FILLING

ABOUT 2½ CUPS

3 tablespoons schmaltz (see
   page 109) or vegetable oil
1 large yellow onion, chopped
   (about ¾ cup)
1½ pounds ground beef
2 tablespoons tomato sauce,
   ¼ cup chopped fresh parsley,
   or 1 tablespoon chopped
   fresh dill or 1 teaspoon dried
About ¾ teaspoon salt
Ground black pepper to taste

1. Heat the schmaltz or oil in a large skillet over medium heat. Add the onion and sauté until soft and translucent, 5 to 10 minutes.
2. Add the meat and cook until it loses its red color, about 5 minutes. Pour off the excess fat.
3. Add the tomato sauce, parsley, or dill, salt, and pepper and cook for 1 minute. Let cool.

Kartoffelfullung

ASHKENAZIC POTATO FILLING

ABOUT 2½ CUPS

3 medium potatoes
   (about 1 pound)
3 tablespoons schmaltz
   (see page 109) or margarine
2 medium yellow onions,
   chopped (about 1 cup)
1 large egg, lightly beaten
About 2 teaspoons salt
About ¾ teaspoon ground black
   pepper

1. Place the unpeeled potatoes in a large pot, add water to cover, and boil until fork-tender, about 25 minutes. While still warm, peel and mash.
2. Heat the schmaltz or margarine in a large skillet over medium heat. Add the onions and sauté until golden brown, about 15 minutes. Remove from the heat and stir in the potatoes, then the egg, salt, and pepper. Let cool.

VARIATIONS

Kartoffel un Kaesefullung (Potato-Cheese Filling): **Add 1 cup** farmer or pot cheese. Or add ½ cup farmer cheese and ½ cup grated Cheddar cheese.

Pastries mit Neshamos (with Souls): **Add 2 to 3 tablespoons** coarsely chopped *gribenes* (poultry cracklings; see page 109).

Krautfullung

ASHKENAZIC CABBAGE FILLING

ABOUT 3 CUPS

Cabbage-filled pastry is traditional for Sukkoth (see page 146).

1½ pounds green cabbage,
   coarsely chopped
   (about 6 cups)
3 tablespoons vegetable oil
1 medium yellow onion,
   chopped (about ½ cup)
2 tablespoons granulated or
   brown sugar or chopped
   fresh dill
About 1 teaspoon salt
Ground black pepper to taste

1. Place the cabbage in a large pot of boiling water, return to a boil, and parboil for 3 minutes. Drain, squeezing out the excess moisture.
2. Heat the oil in a large skillet over medium heat. Add the onion and sauté until soft and translucent, 5 to 10 minutes.
3. Add the cabbage, reduce the heat to low, and cook until soft, about 20 minutes. Stir in the sugar or dill, salt, and pepper. Let cool.

Sambusak Cheese Filling

ABOUT 2 CUPS

Cheese, the most common *sambusak* filling, is a traditional Shavuot (see page 315) dish. In Lebanon, cheese *sambusak* are commonly dipped into a spice mixture called *za'atar*.

2 cups finely grated Muenster,
   kashkaval (see page 30), or
   other hard white cheese
   (or 1 cup grated hard cheese
   and ¾ cup crumbled feta
   cheese)
1 large egg, lightly beaten

Combine the ingredients.

Sambusak Chickpea Filling

This filling is particularly beloved by Iraqi Jews, who commonly serve chickpea-filled pastries on Purim (see page 316).

2 tablespoons vegetable oil
2 medium yellow onions,
  chopped (about 1 cup)
About 1 teaspoon ground cumin
¼ teaspoon ground turmeric
About ¼ teaspoon salt
Ground black pepper to taste
2 cups cooked chickpeas, mashed

Heat the oil in a large skillet over medium heat. Add the onions and sauté until soft and translucent, 5 to 10 minutes. Stir in the cumin, turmeric, salt, and pepper. Add the chickpeas and cook until dry.

VARIATION

Sambusak B'Tawah (Iraqi Chickpea and Meat Filling): Reduce the amount of the chickpeas to 1 cup. Before adding the chickpeas, add 8 ounces ground chicken or beef and sauté until it loses its color, about 5 minutes.

Sambusak Meat Filling

2 tablespoons olive or vegetable
  oil
1 medium yellow onion,
  chopped (about ½ cup)
1 pound ground beef or lamb
¼ cup chopped fresh parsley
½ teaspoon ground allspice
½ teaspoon ground cinnamon
About ½ teaspoon salt
Dash of ground black pepper
¼ cup pine nuts (optional)

1. Heat the oil in a large skillet over medium heat. Add the onion and sauté until soft and translucent, 5 to 10 minutes. 2. Add the meat and cook until it loses its red color, about 5 minutes. Pour off the excess fat and let cool. Stir in the parsley, allspice, cinnamon, salt, pepper, and, if desired, pine nuts.

SOUPS

*And Esau said to Jacob: Let me swallow I pray
thee, some of this red, red (pottage) . . .*
—Genesis 25:30-34

In a medieval kitchen one would likely find a kettle on the back of the wood-burning stove or hanging to the side of an open fire. There meat trimmings, bones, vegetables, and other leftovers were simmered into a savory soup known in French as a *pot-au-feu* (literally "pot on the fire"). In most instances, these soups were not replaced but simply added to each day. In some Middle Eastern communities, it is still common for a pot of soup to be put on the fire early in the morning to simmer all day, thereby providing a quick, substantial dish not only for the family but also for unexpected guests, a not infrequent occurrence even in areas with telephones.

From the outset, soup has been an enduring part of Jewish cooking. Esau sold his birthright for a pot of red lentil pottage, and, today, most forms of Jewish cuisine still feature lentil soup. Many Lithuanians insist on serving the soup after the main course, so that if the Messiah arrives in the midst of the meal, the more substantial entrée will sustain them during their trip to Israel.

Opposite: "The Feast of the Tabernacles." Undated engraving by Moritz Daniel Oppenheim (1799–1882). *In place of a permanent roof, a layer of branches or other vegetation covers the top of the sukkah, so thin that the stars can be seen by those inside, thereby emphasizing the impermanence of life and the inspiration of nature.*

Goldena Yoiche

ASHKENAZIC CHICKEN SOUP
⊗ ABOUT 2 QUARTS ⊗

Since Talmudic times, chicken has been a traditional dish for weddings, a custom derived from a once-common saying at marriage ceremonies, "Be fruitful and multiply like chickens." Chicken soup has been a part of the Sephardic culinary repertoire since medieval times. Moses Maimonides (1135–1204), the Spanish philosopher, codifier, and physician to the vizier of Egypt, recommended poultry soup for the weak and sick. As such, *soupa de kippur* (chicken soup with orzo) or *soupa de gallina* (chicken soup with rice) is commonly served at the meal preceding the fast of Yom Kippur.

It was among eastern European Jews, however, that chicken soup, also called *goldzup* (the gold refers to the globules of fat floating on top of the soup, which many modern cooks remove), found its greatest appreciation. Soup provided an ideal way of using a tough aging hen that was no longer capable of laying eggs. By the late fifteenth century, chicken soup with noodles had replaced *vermesel* (fried/baked dough in honey; see *chremslach*, page 215) as the first course for Friday evening dinner. Thereafter in many Ashkenazic households, no Friday night, holiday, or wedding meal could begin without a bowl of golden chicken soup.

---

1 (4- to 5-pound) chicken,
   cut up
3 quarts cold water
2 medium yellow onions, sliced
3 medium carrots, halved
   crosswise
2 to 3 stalks celery, halved
   crosswise
1 small parsnip, quartered
6 sprigs fresh parsley
8 to 10 peppercorns or
   ¼ teaspoon ground black
   pepper
1 bay leaf
About 2½ teaspoons salt
3 sprigs fresh dill

1. Place the chicken in a large pot and cover with the water. Bring to a boil, reduce the heat to low, and simmer, occasionally skimming the foam from the surface, for 30 minutes.

2. Add the onions and simmer for 1 hour.

3. Add the carrots, celery, parsnip, parsley, peppercorns or pepper, and bay leaf, partially cover, and simmer until the chicken is very tender, at least 1 hour.

4. Add the salt and dill and simmer for 10 minutes. The chicken can be deboned, shredded, and returned to the soup or served separately. Serve hot with the vegetables and *knaidlach* (dumplings; see page 254), *kreplach* (filled pasta; see page 238), *lukshen* (noodles; see page 232), *mandlen* (soup nuts; see page 242), or rice.

Marag

CALCUTTA CHICKEN SOUP

6 TO 8 SERVINGS

The name of this soup, popular among the Jewish community of Calcutta, is appropriately a corruption of the Hebrew word for soup, *marak*, and the Persian and Indian word for chicken, *morgh*. Like most Calcutta Jewish fare, it is a synthesis of Iraqi and Indian cooking.

1 tablespoon vegetable oil
1 small yellow onion, chopped
    (about ¼ cup)
2 cloves garlic, minced
1 teaspoon minced fresh ginger
1 teaspoon ground turmeric
1 green cardamom pod
    (optional)
6 cups cold water
1 large chicken, cut into
    10 pieces
1 medium potato, peeled and
    cubed (optional)
About 1½ teaspoons salt
Ground black pepper to taste
Chopped fresh coriander or
    parsley for garnish

1. Heat the oil in a large pot over medium heat. Add the onion, garlic, and ginger and sauté until fragrant, 1 to 2 minutes. Stir in the turmeric and, if desired, cardamom. Add 1 cup of the water and cook until reduced to a very thick liquid.

2. Add the chicken, stirring to coat well. Cover and cook until most of the liquid is absorbed by the chicken, about 15 minutes.

3. Add the remaining 5 cups water and, if desired, the cubed potato. Bring to a boil, reduce the heat to low, and simmer until the chicken is tender, about 45 minutes. Season with the salt and pepper. Serve accompanied with rice and garnish with coriander or parsley.

VARIATIONS

Tomato Marag: Add 2 cups (1 pound) peeled, seeded, and chopped tomatoes with the 5 cups water.

Vegetable Marag: After cooking the chicken for 20 minutes, add 2 cups (1 pound) peeled, seeded, and chopped tomatoes, 1 cup cauliflower florets, 1 chopped carrot, ¼ cup sliced green beans, and ¼ cup green peas.

Avicas

SEPHARDIC WHITE BEAN AND BEEF SOUP

❧ 6 TO 8 SERVINGS ☙

In Salonika (today Thessaloníki), this thick bean soup was a ubiquitous Friday night entree accompanied with *pasteles* (meat pies), spinach-filled *borekas* (turnovers; see page 32) or *ojaldres* (phyllo triangles), and *yaprakes finos* (stuffed grape leaves). Leftover soup was often kept in the oven to simmer overnight, in the manner of a Sabbath stew, and then served for Sabbath lunch. By reducing the amount of water to 4 cups, *avicas* becomes a thicker version, sometimes called *fijones*, which is served as a side dish over rice or with bread to sop up the *caldo* (sauce). A vegetarian version, omitting the meat, is served during the week preceding Tisha b'Av (see page 209) and at dairy meals.

1 pound (about 2⅓ cups) dried
    navy or other white beans
¼ cup olive or vegetable oil
2 large yellow onions or leeks,
    chopped (about 1½ cups)
1½ pounds beef chuck or short
    ribs, cut into 2-inch pieces
7 cups cold water
4 cups (2 pounds) peeled,
    seeded, and chopped tomatoes,
    1 cup tomato sauce, or ¼ cup
    tomato paste
3 tablespoons chopped fresh
    parsley
About 1½ teaspoons salt
Ground black pepper to taste

1. Cover the beans with water, bring to a boil, reduce the heat to low, and simmer for 1 hour. Drain.
2. Meanwhile, heat the oil in a large pot over medium heat. Add the onions or leeks and sauté until golden.
3. Add the meat and the 7 cups water. Bring to a boil, reduce the heat to low, and simmer, skimming occasionally, for 45 minutes.
4. Add the beans and tomatoes, tomato sauce, or paste. Cover the pot and simmer until the meat and beans are very tender, at least 3 hours. Stir in the parsley, salt, and pepper. Serve with pita (see page 267) or other flat bread and lemon wedges.

VARIATIONS

Garvansos (Sephardic Chickpea Soup): Substitute 2 cups dried chickpeas for the beans. (*Note:* This was a common winter soup in many Sephardic communities.)

Makhloota (Middle Eastern Mixed Bean Soup): Reduce the amount of white beans to ½ cup and add ½ cup black beans, ½ cup chickpeas, ½ cup lentils, and, if desired, 2 teaspoons ground cumin.

Shorabit Ful Abiad wa Bourgul (Middle Eastern Bean and Bulgur Soup): Simmer ⅔ cup coarse bulgur in about 1½ cups water until tender (about 30 minutes), drain, stir into the cooked soup, and heat through.

Marak Temahni

YEMENITE BEEF SOUP

❧ 6 TO 8 SERVINGS ❧

Although Yemenites consider it unhealthy to serve meat for dinner, they make an exception for the Sabbath and festivals. Meat is generally prepared in the form of stews and soups that were, until recently, left to simmer all day in copper pots in the manner of European *pot-au-feu*. As elsewhere in the Middle East, lamb has long been the predominant meat. However, since the Yemenites immigrated to the West, beef has gained in popularity. This traditional Yemenite Friday night dish generally serves as the main part of the meal. When grains are added and the soup is cooked overnight for Sabbath lunch, this dish is called *harisa*. Since Yemenites prefer a spicy soup, they generally stir in a spoonful of *chilbeh* (fenugreek relish; see page 14).

2 pounds beef shank bones or feet, cut into 2-inch pieces (ask your butcher to do this; see Note)

3 medium carrots, cut into chunks

3 stalks celery, cut into chunks

2 medium yellow onions, sliced

5 sprigs fresh parsley

8 to 10 peppercorns

8 cups cold water

1 pound pumpkin or 2 large potatoes, peeled and cut into large chunks

About 2 teaspoons salt

Ground black pepper to taste

1. Combine the bones or feet, carrots, celery, onions, parsley, peppercorns, and water in a large pot. Bring to a boil, reduce the heat to low, cover, and simmer, occasionally skimming the foam from the surface, for at least 3 hours.

2. Strain, removing any meat from the shanks or feet and discarding the bones and pressing the liquid from the vegetables into the soup.

3. Add the pumpkin or potatoes, salt, and pepper and simmer until tender, about 30 minutes. Serve with hard-boiled eggs and *miloach* (Yemenite flaky bread; see page 271), *lahuhua* (Yemenite flat bread; see page 270), or pita bread (see page 267).

Note: The shank comes from the shin section of the leg and is suitable for stewing and braising. Substitute 1½ pounds cubed stewing beef and 2 to 3 soup bones for the shanks.

VARIATION

Regale (Yemenite Spicy Beef Soup): Add with the bones 1 cup pureed tomatoes, ½ cup chopped fresh coriander, 1 tablespoon paprika, 1 teaspoon ground cumin, and 6 green cardamom pods.

Gruenkernsuppe

GERMAN GREEN KERNEL SOUP
6 TO 8 SERVINGS

G*ruenkern* are husked and kiln-dried immature kernels of spelt. Primarily grown in Poland, *gruenkern* are rare in America, but they are found in some specialty food stores. Germans use the greenish-tan kernels in soups, stews, puddings, gruels, and fritters. This slow-simmered soup still begins Sabbath lunch in many German-Jewish homes.

1 cup green kernels (gruenkern)
2 pounds beef chuck or short-ribs, cubed
1 to 2 pounds soup bones
3 stalks celery, diced
2 medium carrots, diced
2 tablespoons oatmeal or 1 slice toasted rye bread
About 2 teaspoons salt
Ground black pepper to taste
10 cups cold water

1. Soak the green kernels in water overnight. Drain.
2. In a large pot combine the green kernels with the remaining ingredients. Bring to a boil, place on a *blech* (thin sheet of metal) over very low heat or in a slow crock-type cooker set on low, and simmer for 6 hours or overnight. Serve hot, garnished with chopped parsley and, if desired, accompanied with water challah (see page 280).

Kharcho

GEORGIAN BEEF AND RICE SOUP
6 TO 8 SERVINGS

K*harcho* is to the Georgians what borscht is to the Ukrainians across the Black Sea, the favorite soup and a mainstay of the diet. Typical of Georgian cooking, the presence of fresh herbs is very pronounced in this dish. Although Georgians generally use *tkhlopi* (sour plum leather) as the souring agent, tamarind concentrate (see page 36), or lemon juice can be substituted.

2 pounds beef marrow bones,
cut into 2-inch pieces (ask
your butcher to do this)

9 cups cold water

1½ pounds beef brisket or short
ribs, cut into 1-inch pieces

3 tablespoons sunflower or
vegetable oil

2 medium yellow onions,
chopped (about 1 cup)

3 cloves garlic, minced

3 tablespoons tomato paste

1 cup (8 ounces) peeled, seeded,
and chopped tomatoes

½ cup rice

1 sheet tkhlopi (sour plum
leather), 3 tablespoons plum
butter, 1 tablespoon
tamarind concentrate, or
¼ cup lemon juice

1 small whole chili or
½ teaspoon hot red pepper
flakes

½ teaspoon ground coriander

About 1 teaspoon salt

Ground black pepper to taste

½ cup ground walnuts
(optional)

¼ cup chopped fresh coriander

¼ cup chopped fresh parsley

¼ cup chopped fresh dill or
basil

1. Bring the bones and water to a boil in a large pot, reduce the heat to low, and simmer, skimming occasionally, for 4 hours. Discard the bones.

2. Add the beef pieces and simmer until nearly tender, about 2 hours.

3. Heat the oil in a large skillet over medium heat. Add the onions and sauté until golden, about 15 minutes. Stir in the garlic, then the tomato paste, and sauté until the paste begins to darken, about 3 minutes.

4. Stir the onion mixture into the soup. Add the tomatoes and rice, cover, and simmer for 15 minutes.

5. Add the plum leather, plum butter, tamarind concentrate, or lemon juice, chili or pepper flakes, ground coriander, salt, pepper, and, if desired, walnuts. Simmer, uncovered, until the rice is tender, 10 to 15 minutes.

6. Add the fresh coriander, parsley, and dill or basil and simmer for 5 minutes. Ladle into serving bowls and garnish with additional chopped fresh herbs. Serve with *deda puri* (Georgian flat bread) or pita bread (see page 267).

Note: Tkemali/tkhlopi is a tart dark-red plum used as a souring agent in Georgian cooking. Although the dried plum is not found in America, a fruit leather made from it is available at stores specializing in Middle Eastern products. The more readily obtainable tamarind concentrate (also available in Middle Eastern and Indian groceries) or lemon juice can be substituted.

Lagman

BUKHARAN LAMB, VEGETABLE, AND NOODLE SOUP

 6 TO 8 SERVINGS

Bukharans take advantage of the fresh produce of their region to make thick soups and stews called *vadzha*, which make a hearty winter lunch or dinner. During the summer, lighter fare such as yogurt soup is served. The favorite *vadzha* is this meat and vegetable version called *lagman* (the Bukharan word for "noodles").

¼ cup vegetable oil

1½ pounds boneless lamb or beef shoulder, cut into 1-inch cubes

2 medium yellow onions, chopped (about 1 cup)

2 to 3 cloves garlic, minced

1 to 1½ teaspoons ground cumin

1 teaspoon paprika

½ teaspoon ground coriander

About 1 teaspoon salt

Ground black pepper to taste

2 cups (1 pound) peeled, seeded, and chopped tomatoes

2 medium carrots, sliced

2 medium potatoes, peeled and cubed

2 medium frying (Italian) peppers or green bell peppers, seeded and sliced

1 cup diced black radishes or daikon (Asian radish)

½ cup cooked chickpeas

1 medium turnip, peeled and cut into chunks

2 quarts lamb or beef broth

1 pound medium or thin egg noodles, cooked (see page 232)

About ¼ cup chopped fresh coriander for garnish

About ¼ cup chopped fresh parsley or mint for garnish

1. Heat the oil in a large pot over medium heat. Add the meat and brown on all sides, about 15 minutes. Remove the meat.

2. Add the onions and sauté until soft and translucent, 5 to 10 minutes. Stir in the garlic, cumin, paprika, ground coriander, salt, and pepper. Return the meat to the pot and add the tomatoes, carrots, potatoes, peppers, radishes, chickpeas, and turnip.

3. Add the broth, bring to a boil, cover, reduce the heat to low, and simmer until the meat and vegetables are tender, about 1 hour.

4. Place a heaping handful of the noodles in each of 6 to 8 large serving bowls. Ladle the soup over the top and sprinkle with a little fresh coriander and parsley or mint. Serve with pita bread (see page 267) or other flat bread.

Opposite: **Bukharan Jews celebrating the Feast of the Tabernacles.** *For centuries, Bukhara was a part of the Persian Empire or under its cultural influence. Then the Shiite Safawids gained control of Persia in 1502, resulting in hostility between them and the Sunni Muslims of the Ottoman Empire and Central Asia. At this point, Bukharan Jewry began to develop its own distinctive character.*

Ab-Gush

PERSIAN LAMB SHANK SOUP

❧ 6 TO 8 SERVINGS ☙

The Persian word for cook is *ash-paz* (soup maker) and the word for kitchen is *ash-paz-khaneh* (room of the soup maker), reflecting the position of soup in Persian dining. There are two basic types of soup: *ash*, a vegetable-based soup that sometimes contains a little meat, and *ab-gush*, a meat stew. The following soup is one of the foundations of Persian cooking; a few of the many variations are given below. Chicken is substituted for the lamb for special occasions.

¼ cup vegetable oil

2 large yellow onions, sliced

1 teaspoon ground turmeric

3 to 4 lamb shanks or 3 pounds cubed lamb shoulder

10 cups cold water

2½ cups (20 ounces) peeled, seeded, and chopped tomatoes or 2 tablespoons tomato paste

½ to 1 teaspoon ground cinnamon

1½ to 2 cups cooked chickpeas (or 1 cup cooked chickpeas and 1 cup cooked white beans)

About 1 teaspoon salt

Ground black pepper to taste

1. Heat the oil in a large pot over medium heat. Add the onions and sauté until soft and translucent, 5 to 10 minutes. Stir in the turmeric. Add the shanks or shoulder and brown on all sides.

2. Add the water, tomatoes or tomato paste, and cinnamon. Bring to a boil, cover, reduce the heat to low, and simmer for 1½ hours.

3. Add the chickpeas, salt, and pepper and simmer until the meat is tender, about 30 additional minutes.

4. Remove the shanks from the soup and shred the meat. Return the meat to the soup and discard the bones. Serve with pita bread (see page 267) or other flat bread, or with dumplings such as *ghondi nokhochi* (chickpea dumplings; see page 257).

VARIATIONS

Ab-Gushe Adas (Persian Lamb and Lentil Soup): Substitute ¾ cup dried lentils for the chickpeas.

Ab-Gushe Beh (Persian Lamb and Quince Soup): Add 1 peeled, seeded, and cubed quince with the chickpeas.

Ab-Gushe Lapeh (Persian Lamb and Split Pea Soup): Substitute ¾ cup yellow split peas for the chickpeas.

Ab-Gushe Sib va Albaloo (Persian Lamb, Apple, and Cherry Soup): Add 4 to 5 peeled, cored, and chopped apples, ½ cup pitted sour cherries, 1 to 3 tablespoons sugar, and 1 tablespoon lemon juice with the chickpeas.

Fleishidik Borsht

EASTERN EUROPEAN BEET SOUP WITH MEAT
6 TO 8 SERVINGS

For centuries, Ukrainians made a soup from a type of parsnip called *borschtsh*. With the development of the beet root in the sixteenth century, Ukrainian cooks discovered that adding beets made a tastier soup than did using the parsnips alone. Soon, the beets completely supplanted the *borschtsh* while assuming its name. Ukrainian Jews brought their love for this old-world soup to America, where it was served in the many Jewish resorts that flourished in the Catskill Mountain region of eastern New York, giving rise in the 1930s to the nickname for the region—the Borscht Belt.

The original Ukrainian borscht was made with pork. Therefore, Jews substitute beef or, as in *kalt borsht*, omit the meat entirely. Some versions are made strictly with beets, while others feature a host of vegetables such as cabbage, carrots, celeriac, celery, cucumbers, and tomatoes. Polish Jews add a large amount of sugar, while most Ukrainians favor the original zesty version. Iraqis make a tarter version of beet soup called *cholo chamad,* and Calcutta Jews make a mint-and-ginger-flavored version called *khutta* ("sweet-and-sour" in Hindi). Borscht is commonly served with another mainstay of the eastern European diet, boiled potatoes.

2 pounds beef brisket, short ribs, or stewing meat, cubed
2 beef marrow bones
8 cups cold water
8 medium beets (about 2 pounds), peeled and diced
2 medium yellow onions, chopped (about 1 cup)
1 to 2 cloves garlic, minced
2 tablespoons tomato paste
3 to 6 tablespoons lemon juice, cider vinegar, or red wine vinegar
About 3 tablespoons granulated or brown sugar
About 1½ teaspoons salt
Ground black pepper to taste

1. Bring the meat, bones, and water to a boil in a large pot. Cover, reduce the heat to low, and simmer, occasionally skimming the foam from the surface, for 1 hour.
2. Add the beets, onions, and garlic, cover, and simmer for an additional 1 hour.
3. Stir in the tomato paste, lemon juice or vinegar, sugar, salt, and pepper and simmer until the meat is tender, about 30 minutes. Serve hot with boiled potatoes.

VARIATION

Russel Borsht: Substitute 3 cups *russel tzikel* (fermented beets; see page 154) for the plain beets, reduce the amount of water to 4½ cups, and add 3½ cups *russel* beet juice. (*Note:* Since *russel*, beet vinegar, is sour, you will need less or no lemon juice.)

Talpechal

COCHIN FISH SOUP

 6 TO 8 SERVINGS

According to local legend, the first Jews to settle on the Malabar Coast of southwestern India were fleeing Nebuchadnezzar's troops in 586 B.C.E. The first verification of a Jewish community existing in the area is a pair of copper plates inscribed in a Tamil dialect, recording seventy-two special privileges granted to the Jews by the local ruler. (Some scholars date these plates to as early as 379 C.E.; others to as recently as 1000.) Following the Portuguese purge of the Jewish community of nearby Cranganore in 1524, Sephardim made their way to the area. Emulating the Hindu caste system, the Jews of Cochin divided themselves into three distinct groups: *Paradesi* (Whites, literally meaning "foreigners"); *Meshuharim* (literally "emancipated"), descendants of freed slaves who converted; and *Kala* (Blacks), descendants of the original Jews who married dark-skinned natives. Over the centuries, Cochini Jews maintained contact with and married Jews across the Arabian Sea in Yemen and Iraq. They were also ardent Zionists and, beginning in the 1950s, began immigrating to Israel. Presently, more than five thousand Cochini Jews live in Israel, most on *moshavim* (cooperative settlements). Only a handful of elderly Jews remain on the Malabar Coast.

The cuisine of the Malabar Coast is very pungent, making use of native spices such as pepper and curry leaves. Coconut and tomatoes are used to temper the effect. Rice and lentils are the mainstay of the diet. Fish is the primary source of protein. This zesty soup is among the most popular dishes of the Black Jews of Cochin.

¼ cup coconut or vegetable oil

3 medium yellow onions, chopped (about 1½ cups)

3 to 4 cloves garlic, minced

1 teaspoon grated fresh ginger

1 cup (8 ounces) peeled, seeded, and chopped tomatoes or 3 tablespoons tomato paste

6 to 8 curry leaves (kari patta) or 2 teaspoons seeded and minced red or green chili

1 teaspoon ground coriander or cumin

About 1 teaspoon salt

Ground black pepper to taste

3 cups cold water or coconut milk (see page 207)

2 pounds firm-fleshed fish fillets, cut into large chunks

About 1 tablespoon lemon juice or cider vinegar

About 2 tablespoons chopped fresh coriander or parsley for garnish

1. Heat the oil in a large saucepan over medium heat. Add the onions and sauté for 2 minutes. Add the garlic and ginger and sauté until soft, about 5 minutes.

2. Stir in the tomatoes or tomato paste, curry leaves or chili, coriander or cumin, salt, and pepper and cook for 10 minutes.

3. Add the water or coconut milk and bring to a boil. Add the fish, return to a boil, reduce the heat to low, and simmer until just cooked through, about 10 minutes. Season with the lemon juice or vinegar. Garnish with the chopped coriander or parsley. Serve accompanied with rice.

Opposite: **Group of Cochini Jews.** *The Jews of the Malabar Coast of southwestern India, home of the peppercorn, maintained a spititual and mercantile relationship with Jewish communities across the Arabian Sea. Jews dominated both ends of the spice trade until Venetians usurped the Western end of this lucrative business in the thirteenth century.*

Meggy Leves

HUNGARIAN CHERRY SOUP

❧ 6 TO 8 SERVINGS ❧

Fruit soups and compotes, made from both fresh and dried fruit, are a favorite part of central European cooking. The most popular Hungarian variation is made from cherries. There are two types of cherries: sweet and sour (morello). Sweet cherries are primarily eaten fresh; sour cherries, which are smaller and paler, are used in cooking, baking, and liqueurs. One pound of fresh cherries yields about 2¼ cups pitted fruit. If using canned cherries, substitute the cherry juice for an equal amount of water. Since cherries make their appearance in early summer, this soup is a traditional Shavuot (see page 315) dish.

*2 pounds fresh or 40 ounces
    canned tart red cherries, pitted
4 cups water
½ to 1 cup sugar
1 (2-inch) cinnamon stick
Slice of lemon peel
Pinch of salt
1 cup dry red wine
About 2 tablespoons lemon juice
Sour cream or lemon slices for
    garnish*

1. Bring the cherries, water, sugar, cinnamon, lemon peel, and salt to a boil. Cover, reduce the heat to low, and simmer until the cherries are tender, about 15 minutes for canned cherries, about 30 minutes for fresh.
2. Strain the soup, discarding the cinnamon stick and lemon peel. Return the liquid to the pot. Reserve 1 cup of the cherries and puree the remaining cherries.
3. Stir the pureed cherries into the cooking liquid. Add the wine and lemon juice and return to a simmer. Stir in the reserved whole cherries. Let cool, then refrigerate for at least 4 hours. Spoon into soup bowls and garnish with dollops of sour cream or lemon slices.

VARIATION

Frucht Zup (Central European Fruit Soup): Reduce the amount of cherries to 1 cup, do not puree the fruit, and add with the cherries 1 cup each sliced peaches, sliced plums, and raspberries or strawberries.

Sopa de Lentejas/Linzen

RED LENTIL SOUP

6 TO 8 servings

According to tradition, Jacob made the red lentil pottage that his brother Esau so wanted, in memory of his grandfather Abraham, who had just died. "Why was it lentils? In the West [Israel] they say in the name of Rabbah ben Mari: Just as the lentil has no mouth [opening], so the mourner has no mouth. Others say: Just as the lentil is round, so mourning comes round to all the denizens of this world." (Talmud, Baba Bathra 16b). Therefore, lentil dishes are traditionally served at the *Seudat Havra'ah* (the meal of consolation following a funeral) and at the meal before the fast of Tisha b'Av (see page 209) often accompanied with cheese pastries such as *borekas* (see page 32).

Red lentils—also called Egyptian lentils, Persian lentils, and *massor dal*—are actually a reddish-orange color when hulled. They cook faster than green varieties and possess a pleasing earthy flavor. Since red lentils break down while cooking, they are best for pureeing and soups.

3 tablespoons vegetable or
   olive oil
2 medium yellow onions,
   chopped (about 1 cup)
2 to 3 cloves garlic, minced
1 pound (about 2 cups) red
   lentils, rinsed and drained
3 medium carrots, chopped
2 stalks celery, diced
8 cups beef broth, chicken broth,
   or water
1 bay leaf
About 2 teaspoons salt
Freshly ground black pepper to
   taste

1. Heat the oil in a large, heavy saucepan or Dutch oven over medium heat. Add the onions and garlic and sauté until soft and translucent, 5 to 10 minutes.

2. Add the lentils, carrots, celery, broth or water, and bay leaf. Bring to a boil, reduce the heat to low, and simmer until the lentils are tender, about 30 minutes.

3. Discard the bay leaf and season with the salt and pepper. Serve hot with pita bread (see page 267) or other flat bread.

FISH

Wherewith does one show delight in the Sabbath?
Rav Judah the son of Samuel ben Shilath said in the
name of Rav: With beets, a large fish, and garlic.

—TALMUD, SHABBAT 118b

Fish were singled out in Genesis with the blessing "Be fruitful and multiply and fill the waters in the seas . . ." and have served ever since as a Jewish symbol of fertility and prosperity. In the Talmud, fish took on mystical dimensions—as a reminder not only of the creation of life, but of the Messianic age to be ushered in by the Meal of the Righteous, featuring the Leviathan ("In that day the Lord with His great, cruel, mighty sword will punish Leviathan the elusive fish . . ." [Isaiah 27:1]). Besides the aforementioned symbolism, fish have a practical attribute: They do not require ritual slaughter and can be served at either dairy or meat meals. In addition, fish is delicious when served cold for Sabbath lunch. Thus, for millennia no Sabbath has been considered complete without it.

Opposite: **Friday Evening.** Isidor Kaufmann (1853–1921), 1920. *On the table are objects associated with the Sabbath—a wine goblet, a candelabra, and a challah cover. Although not intrinsically holy, these objects have a special role in the fabric of Jewish life, and an attempt is made to beautify these ritual objects for the "enhancement of the commandment."*

Jelatine di Pescado/Fische Gelee

JELLIED FISH

6 TO 8 SERVINGS

One of the oldest and most widespread forms of Sabbath fish, popular in nearly every Jewish community, is poached fish in jellied sauce. Cooking the fish with the bones and head produces moist, tender flesh and releases the fish's natural gelatin into the cooking liquid, thereby jelling it. Delicate whitefish and rich-flavored carp are favored by Ashkenazim and gelatinous striped bass by Sephardim, but any firm-fleshed fish, even salmon or trout, can be used. Sephardic versions incorporate a little lemon juice and sometimes substitute tomato juice for the cooking liquid. Since lemons were scarce in eastern Europe, Ashkenazim usually added vinegar for tartness.

6 to 8 (1-inch-thick) firm-fleshed fish steaks, such as carp, striped bass, whitefish, haddock, pike, or salmon (4 to 5 pounds total), head, bones, and tail reserved

About 2 tablespoons kosher salt

3 medium yellow onions, sliced

2 medium carrots, sliced

2 bay leaves

½ teaspoon peppercorns

Salt to taste

Lemon slices and fresh parsley sprigs for garnish

1. Sprinkle the fish steaks, head, and tail lightly with the kosher salt and place in the refrigerator for at least 1 hour. Rinse under cold water and drain. (This process helps to extract excess moisture from the fish and reduces any fishy smell or taste.)

2. Put the fish head, tail, and bones, onions, carrots, bay leaves, peppercorns, and salt in a large skillet or saucepan. Add enough water to cover. Bring to a boil, reduce the heat to medium-low, and simmer for 30 minutes.

3. Add the fish steaks and return to a boil. Cover, reduce the heat to low, and simmer until the fish is tender and loses its translucency, 15 to 20 minutes.

4. Remove the fish and strain the cooking liquid, reserving the carrots for a garnish. Discard the bones.

5. Boil the cooking liquid over high heat until reduced by half, about 15 minutes. Pour the liquid over the fish and refrigerate for at least 4 hours or overnight. Serve the fish with the jelled cooking liquid and garnish with the cooked carrots, lemon slices, and parsley sprigs.

VARIATIONS

Jelatine di Pescado (Sephardic Jellied Fish): Add the juice of 1 to 3 lemons with the fish. (*Note:* This Sabbath and festival dish is also called *pichtee.*)

Suz und Sauer Fische (German Sweet-and-Sour Fish): Add ½ cup wine vinegar, ½ cup brown sugar, ¼ to ½ cup raisins, and 3 to 4 whole cloves with the vegetables.

Zeesih Fische (Polish Sweet Jellied Fish): Add about ½ cup sugar with the vegetables. (*Note:* This variation is also called *Shabbos fische,* "Sabbath fish.")

FISH FACTS

When buying fresh fish, look for bright, clear eyes, bright red or pink gills, firm flesh, shiny skin, and a fresh, "nonfishy" odor. If the fish emits an odor or the skin is dull, look elsewhere. Steaks and fillets should be firm with no signs of drying around the edges.

- To prepare a whole fish, remove the scales, fins, and gills. The bones, head, and tail all add flavor to the fish during cooking and, therefore, it is usually best not to remove them, or to add them to the cooking liquid.

- Do not skin steaks, since it helps to hold the fish together during cooking. Steaks from the center of the fish, detectable from the opening at the top formed by the abdominal pocket, have more fat and a richer flavor than those from the ends.

- Fish needs less cooking than meat and poultry. Actually, fish is tender enough to eat raw, as we know from Japanese sashimi, since its connective tissue is much weaker than that of other animals. However, to destroy bacteria and parasites, it is generally advisable to cook fish.

- Fish is done when it reaches 130 to 150 degrees on an instant-read thermometer inserted in the thickest part. At this stage the flesh is still moist and will separate. After it reaches a temperature of 155 degrees, the proteins in the fibers begin to contract and press out the juices. Since the fish continues to cook after removing it from the heat, it is best to remove the fish when it registers 125 to 130 degrees.

Gefilte Fish

ASHKENAZIC GROUND FISH

ABOUT 22 MEDIUM FISH CROQUETTES

One of the prohibited forms of work on the Sabbath is *borer*, removing the inedible part of food from the edible part. Gefilte fish originated in Germany, probably in the fourteenth century, as a method of serving fish on the Sabbath without the problematic act of separating the bones from the flesh. Whether this dish is descended from the chopped fish dishes mentioned in the Talmud or was adapted from a local dish is uncertain, but, whatever the case, it became a popular Sabbath dish. Originally, the flesh was carefully removed from the fish, chopped, seasoned, and stuffed (*gefullte* in German) into the skin; then the fish was sewn up and baked. At some point, cooks began poaching the fish in a fish stock. Eventually, the process was simplified by eliminating the stuffing step. Although today few cooks still stuff the skin, the name remains.

In western and central Europe, gefilte fish was not the most popular Sabbath fish; that position was held by the various types of *fische gelee* (jellied fish; see page 70). In eastern Europe, however, gefilte fish became the most widespread form of Sabbath fish, partially because the added onions, matza meal, and other fillers stretched limited resources. The cooking liquid was often served as a soup during the following week.

Pike was the most prevalent freshwater fish in Germany and thus the type commonly used for making gefilte fish. In Poland, however, the more common carp was generally substituted. These two fish along with whitefish remain the favorites for this classic dish. Everyone who makes gefilte fish has his or her own preference for varieties and proportion of fish: Using more carp gives a stronger flavor, while using a larger portion of whitefish and pike gives a more delicate one. Some popular combinations are one-half part carp to one-quarter whitefish and one-quarter pike; two-fifths pike and two-fifths whitefish to one-fifth carp; one-half pike to one-half whitefish; and one-half carp to one-half pike. When these varieties are unavailable, substitute any firm-fleshed fish, such as halibut, haddock, cod, or even the unorthodox salmon.

The amount of sugar added to the fish depends on personal preference. In general, Jews from western Poland prefer a very sweet fish; Lithuanians add less sugar but a lot of ground black pepper. Some Polish Jews add a few onion skins to the cooking liquid to produce a brown-colored fish. Some Ukrainians add ground bitter almonds or a dash of almond extract to the fish. In Germany, gefilte fish was originally accompanied with vinegar and later mayonnaise, but in eastern Europe *chrain* (horseradish; see page 380) became the principal condiment.

*5 pounds whole fish, such as
carp, whitefish, yellow pike,
or any combination
(see step 1)*

*3 medium yellow onions,
chopped (about 1½ cups)*

3 large eggs, lightly beaten

¾ to 1⅓ cups ice water

*About 3 tablespoons matza
meal or challah crumbs*

1 to 5 tablespoons sugar

About 4 teaspoons salt

*About ½ teaspoon ground white
or black pepper*

FISH STOCK

2 quarts cold water

2 medium yellow onions, sliced

2 stalks celery, sliced

2 teaspoons salt

Dash of ground white pepper

1 tablespoon sugar

2 to 3 medium carrots, sliced

*Lettuce leaves for garnish
(optional)*

1. Fillet the fish, reserving the heads, tails, and bones for making the stock. (It is a good idea to have your fishmonger do this chore. You will end up with about 3 pounds of fish fillets, which yields about 6 cups of ground fish.)

2. In a food grinder or processor, finely grind the fish fillets with the onions. (You will have about 7½ cups of ground fish and onions.)

3. Transfer the ground fish mixture to a large wooden bowl and using a metal hand chopper such as a *mezzaluna*, add the eggs in a slow, steady stream. (This may be done in the food processor.)

4. Gradually add the water. (Use about ¼ cup of water for every pound of fish fillets. For a softer consistency, use more water; for a firmer consistency, use less water.) Stir in the matza meal or challah crumbs, sugar, salt, and pepper. (When done by hand, the entire mixing process will take about 15 minutes to ensure a soft fish.) Cover the mixture and refrigerate for at least 1 hour.

5. Meanwhile, prepare the stock. Place the fish heads, tails and bones in an 8-quart pot and add the water, onions, celery, salt, and pepper. Bring to a boil, reduce the heat to low, and simmer for 1 hour. Strain, discarding the solids. (The fish stock will be cloudy.) Return the stock to a boil.

6. Moisten your hands with cold water (do this often while shaping the fish). Roll the fish mixture into smooth rounds or ovals: Use 2 tablespoons for very small balls; ¼ cup for small; ⅓ cup for medium; or ½ cup for large. Gently drop the fish balls, one at a time, into the stock.

7. After all the fish balls have been added, return the stock to a boil. Reduce the heat to low, cover, and simmer, shaking the pot occasionally to prevent sticking, for 1 hour.

8. Add the 1 tablespoon sugar and the sliced carrots and simmer, uncovered, for 1 hour. Add more water if the stock threatens to reduce below the level of the fish.

9. Remove from the heat and let the fish cool in the stock. Transfer the fish and stock to a container and refrigerate overnight.

Members of Beth Lechem Aniyim on 100th Street in Manhattan distributing fish and other food to the poor for the Jewish New Year, 1930. *Most Jewish communities serve some form of fish at Rosh Hashanah dinner, a symbol of fruitfulness and of the Leviathan, the giant fish that according to legend is to be served at the feast following the arrival of the Messiah.*

CARP

Carp, a native of China, was first brought to France and Germany in the fifteenth century. Since this large, hardy, prolific fish does well in brackish water, it quickly adapted itself to ponds, streams, and lakes throughout Europe. Its lean, firm flesh made it a favorite for cooking. From Alsace to the Balkans, Jews were instrumental in spreading and breeding this newcomer; thus, it became associated with Jewish cuisine. Since anti-Semitism excluded European Jews from the guilds and farming, they were generally in the forefront of establishing new ventures and promoting new products ranging from carp to cornmeal to chocolate.

Carpe à la Juive au Persil

ALSATIAN CARP WITH GREEN SAUCE

6 TO 8 SERVINGS

For many centuries, the most popular Ashkenazic Sabbath fish dish was *fische gelee* (jellied fish; see page 70) or various versions such as carp in brown sauce, a sweet-and-sour gravy flavored with *einbren* (roux) or gingersnaps. *Larousse Gastronomique* (the French Bible of cooking) mentioned three Alsatian versions that had become part of the cooking repertoire of the non-Jews of the area: *carpe à la Juive au persil* (Alsatian Jewish carp with green sauce), a traditional dish at Alsatian Passover Seders; *carpe à la Juive aux raisins* (Alsatian Jewish sweet-and-sour carp), a traditional Rosh Hashanah dish; and *carpe à la Juive a l'Orientale* (Alsatian Jewish carp with almonds).

About 4 cups water
1 cup finely chopped fresh parsley
2 medium yellow onions, sliced
1 to 2 cloves garlic, minced
½ teaspoon peppercorns
6 to 8 (1-inch-thick) carp steaks (4 to 5 pounds total), head and tail reserved

1. Bring the water, parsley, onions, garlic, peppercorns, and fish head and tail to a boil in a large skillet or saucepan. Reduce the heat to medium-low and simmer for 30 minutes.
2. Add the carp steaks and return to a boil. Cover, reduce the heat to low, and simmer until the fish is tender and loses its translucency, 15 to 20 minutes.
3. Place the fish in a shallow dish and pour the cooking liquid over the top. (Some people discard the head and tail, but others like to eat these parts.) Refrigerate for at least 4 hours or overnight.

Hint: For the best flavor, carp should be freshly killed.

Pescado Helado

SEPHARDIC FISH IN TOMATO SAUCE

❧ 6 TO 8 SERVINGS ❧

Cooking fish in a thick, tart sauce is an ancient method for producing a moist, flavorful dish. *Agra* (sour grape sauce), the most ancient of these souring agents, is rarely used today. The arrival of tomatoes from the New World brought an additional flavor dimension, becoming the most popular sauce for this Friday night and festival dish, also called *pescado en salsa de tomat*. It is also served at the meal preceding the fast of Tisha b'Av (see page 209).

¼ cup olive or vegetable oil

1 medium yellow onion,
    chopped (about ½ cup)

4 cups (2 pounds) peeled,
    seeded, and chopped tomatoes

¼ cup chopped fresh parsley

½ cup water

Juice of 1 to 2 lemons

About 1 teaspoon salt

Ground black pepper to taste

6 to 8 (1-inch-thick) firm-
    fleshed fish steaks, such as
    carp, striped bass, whitefish,
    or haddock (4 to 5 pounds
    total), or 3 pounds fish fillets,
    such as snapper, sea bass,
    cod, flounder, sole, trout,
    grouper, haddock, or halibut

1. Heat the oil in a large skillet over medium heat. Add the onion and sauté until soft and translucent, 5 to 10 minutes. Add the tomatoes and parsley and simmer until the tomatoes break down into a sauce, about 20 minutes.

2. Stir in the water and lemon juice and simmer about 5 minutes. Season with the salt and pepper.

3. Add the fish to the skillet, spooning some of the sauce over the top. Simmer until the fish is tender and loses its translucency, about 8 minutes for thin fillets, 12 minutes for thick fillets, 15 to 20 minutes for steaks. To bake this dish, arrange the fish in a single layer in a large casserole, pour the tomato sauce over the top, and bake, uncovered, in a 375-degree oven until tender.

4. Remove the fish to a serving platter. Boil the cooking liquid until thickened, then pour over the fish. Serve warm or at room temperature.

VARIATIONS

Pescado con Prounes Agres (Sephardic Fish with Greengage Plums): Add 6 to 8 peeled, pitted, and chopped greengage plums with the tomatoes. Or substitute 24 to 30 peeled and chopped greengage plums for the tomatoes. (*Note:* A legend that Abraham sat under a plum tree following his circumcision led to the custom of serving fish in plum sauce, sometimes called *Abramela*, on Friday nights.)

Pescado con Ruibarbo (Sephardic Fish in Rhubarb Sauce): **After** the tomatoes break down, add 1 pound sliced rhubarb cooked in 3 cups water until soft (about 20 minutes) and 1 tablespoon honey or sugar.

Pesce all'Ebraica

ITALIAN SWEET-AND-SOUR FISH

6 TO 8 SERVINGS

Quite a few Jewish dishes—such as *carciofi arrosto* (fried artichokes, now called *carciofi alla Giudia,* see page 151), caponata (braised eggplant; see page 12), and *finocchio in tegame* (braised fennel; see page 168)—became an integral part of general Italian cooking. This ancient dish is served by many Italkim on the Sabbath, Rosh Hashanah, and the meal preceding Yom Kippur.

6 to 8 small whole pan-dressed fish, such as red snapper or trout, or 4 pounds firm-fleshed fish fillets, such as sole, flounder, cod, grouper, or haddock

½ cup olive oil

¼ cup wine or cider vinegar

About 1 tablespoon sugar or honey

½ cup raisins

⅓ cup pine nuts

3 tablespoons chopped fresh parsley

About ½ teaspoon salt

Ground black pepper to taste

1. Preheat the oven to 400 degrees. Oil a 13-by-9-inch casserole.
2. Arrange the fish in the bottom of the casserole. Combine the oil, vinegar, sugar or honey, raisins, pine nuts, parsley, salt, and pepper and pour over the fish.
3. Cover and bake for 15 minutes. Uncover and bake, basting occasionally, until the fish is tender and loses its translucency, about 20 additional minutes. Serve hot or at room temperature.

VARIATION

Sogliola di Rolatine (Italian Roulade of Sole): **Add** 1 cup bread crumbs to the oil mixture. Spread a little of the crumb mixture over the fillets, roll up from the narrow ends, and place in the baking dish. Add 1½ cups dry white wine and sprinkle with any remaining crumb mixture.

Mukhli ka Kari

Calcutta Fish Curry

6 to 8 servings

An important element in Indian cooking is the extensive number of inexpensive home-grown spices. No Indian cook would dream of using commercial curry powder, preferring to freshly prepare his or her own blend of *masala* (spices) and varying the ingredients to produce a milder or hotter curry depending on the dish. Ingredients are often added in various stages: Turmeric, which has to cook out the bitterness, is added near the beginning; sweet spices such as cardamom and cinnamon are added near the end. Breads are used to convey the curries to the mouth; yogurt and rice, to balance the intense flavors of the dishes; and relishes such as chutney, which accompany the meal, to stimulate and cleanse the palate.

3 pounds firm-fleshed fish fillets,
such as sea bass, red snapper,
bluefish, cod, flounder, sole,
trout, grouper, or halibut, cut
into 2-inch pieces
¼ cup olive or vegetable oil
2 medium yellow onions,
chopped (about 1 cup)
3 cloves garlic, minced
2 teaspoons minced fresh ginger
1 teaspoon ground turmeric
1 to 2 chilies, seeded and minced
4 cups (2 pounds) peeled,
seeded, and chopped tomatoes
½ cup water
1 tablespoon ground cumin
1 tablespoon ground coriander
seeds
2 teaspoons ground mustard
3 cardamom pods
2 whole cloves
About 1 teaspoon salt
Ground black pepper to taste

1. Soak the fish in cold water for 15 to 30 minutes. Drain and pat dry.

2. Heat the oil in a large skillet over medium heat. Add the onions and sauté until soft and translucent, 5 to 10 minutes. Add the garlic, ginger, turmeric, and chilies and sauté until fragrant, about 1 minute.

3. Add the tomatoes and water and simmer until the tomatoes break down into a sauce, about 15 minutes. Add the cumin, coriander, mustard, cardamom, cloves, salt, and pepper and simmer for about 5 minutes.

4. Add the fish to the skillet, spooning some of the sauce over the top. Cover and simmer, turning the fish once, until it is tender and loses its translucency, about 10 minutes. Serve with rice, pita bread (see page 267) or other flat bread, and yogurt.

Variation

Coconut Fish Curry: Add 1 cup grated coconut (or 8 ounces desiccated coconut) and 6 to 8 curry leaves (*kari patta*); and increase the water to 1 cup.

Kangi

BOMBAY FISH FILLETS IN ROMAINE

6 SERVINGS

According to a local tradition, the Bene-Israel of Bombay, the oldest and largest Indian Jewish community, dates back to a group of Jews fleeing Antiochus Epiphanes in 175 B.C.E. A storm wrecked their ship in the Indian Ocean and seven men and seven women managed to make it to the Konkan coast. The size of the community grew and their settlements spread along the Konkan coast. Over the centuries, Bene-Israel married native converts, producing a diversity of skin coloring in the community. The Bene-Israel had no contact with world Jewry or religious developments until the mid-1700s and were unfamiliar with the Talmud, rabbis, synagogues, or prayer books, all of which originated after their separation from the main body of Jewry. The Bene-Israel primarily made their livelihoods in the preparation and selling of sesame seed oil, thus earning them the name *Shanwar Teli* (Saturday Oilmen) among their Hindu neighbors—referring to their refusal to work on the Sabbath. In response to Nehru's anti-Zionist attitude, more than twelve thousand of the Bene-Israel immigrated to Israel during the 1950s and 1960s. Today, the Bene-Israel community in Israel numbers about fifty thousand, while only about forty-five hundred remain in India.

The Bene-Israel don't eat fish and dairy together, a practice that Indians believe to be unhealthy. This is a traditional Rosh Hashanah (see page 126) dish among many Indian Jews.

8 large romaine lettuce leaves	1. Preheat the oven to 400 degrees. Grease an 8- or 9-inch-square baking dish.
¼ cup chopped fresh parsley	
2 tablespoons chopped fresh mint	2. Blanch the romaine in boiling water until pliable. Drain. Arrange 2 of the leaves in the bottom of the baking dish.
2 tablespoons brown sugar	3. In a blender or food processor, puree the parsley, mint, brown sugar, lemon juice, vinegar, curry powder, salt, and pepper.
1 tablespoon lemon juice	
1 tablespoon cider vinegar	
1 teaspoon curry powder	4. Spread a heaping tablespoon of the spice mixture on each fillet. Place the fillets on the remaining 6 romaine leaves. Fold the stem end over the fish, tuck in the sides of the leaf, and roll up. Place, seam side down, in the baking pan. (The fish may be refrigerated for several hours until ready to cook.)
About 1 teaspoon salt	
½ teaspoon white pepper	
6 (4-ounce) firm-fleshed fish fillets, such as cod, flounder, grouper, halibut, bluefish, sea bass, or snapper	
	5. Bake until the fish is tender, about 30 minutes.

Tevzi

GEORGIAN POACHED FISH WITH POMEGRANATE SAUCE
 5 TO 6 SERVINGS

The rich land and gentle climate of Georgia yields a profusion of vegetables, herbs, and fruits, including pomegranates. Georgians use pomegranate juice and sauces to add a refreshing tartness to many dishes.

1 (3- to 4-pound) whole
  pan-dressed fish, such as red
  snapper, sea bass, or trout
Salt to taste
Ground black pepper to taste
5 tablespoons butter, melted, or
  vegetable oil
About 1 cup pomegranate sauce
  (see below)
¼ cup pomegranate seeds or
  chopped fresh parsley for
  garnish

1. Preheat the oven to 375 degrees. Set aside a baking dish large enough to fit the fish.
2. Sprinkle the fish with the salt and pepper and place in the baking dish. Drizzle with the butter or oil. Add enough water to almost cover the fish.
3. Place in the oven and poach, basting occasionally, until tender, about 35 minutes for 3 pounds, about 50 minutes for 4 pounds.
4. Transfer the fish to a serving platter and drizzle with the pomegranate sauce. Garnish with the pomegranate seeds or parsley. This is frequently served with fried eggplant slices.

Pomegranate Sauce

4 to 5 medium pomegranates
  (about 8 ounces each)
2 tablespoons minced yellow
  onion
2 tablespoons chopped fresh
  basil
2 tablespoons chopped fresh
  coriander
1 clove garlic, minced

1. Cut the fruit in half. Squeeze the juice into a strainer and discard the hard white kernels.
2. Boil the pomegranate juice until reduced almost by half. Add the onion, basil, coriander, and garlic. Let cool.

Kosher fish market in Gold Beach, Mississippi. *"These you may eat of all that are in the waters: Everything in the waters that has fins and scales . . . you may eat. But anything that has not fins and scales in the seas or rivers, of all that move in the waters, and of any living thing which is in the waters, they are an abomination to you."* (LEVITICUS 11: 9–11)

POMEGRANATES

The pomegranate is not actually a fruit but a tough, leathery, reddish brown skin covering a mass of small shiny red, pink, or clear fruit. The pomegranate, which probably originated in Persia, plays a significant role in Jewish literature and lore: It was one of the fruits brought back from Canaan by the spies sent by Moses; it is spoken of in glowing terms six times in "Song of Songs"; its shape was woven onto the robes of the high priest; brass pomegranates were a part of the Temple's pillars; and ancient Jewish coins pictured them. According to tradition, each pomegranate contains 613 seeds, corresponding to the number of commandments in the Torah.

OLIVE OIL

The olive's oil is easily pressed out and, unlike most other vegetable and seed oils, requires no further processing or refining. Olive oil, made in the Levant more than five thousand years ago, was one of the world's first oils. Eventually, it became the primary cooking fat of the entire Mediterranean region. Indeed, the very word *oil* is derived from the Latin word for this fruit, *olea*. Olive oil was used to anoint Aaron and his sons as priests (Exodus 29:7) as well as all the kings of Israel. In the Temple, olive oil was used in the candelabra and was mixed with flour for meal offerings.

Olive oil is generally classified by three grades, based upon the amount of acidity: Extra-virgin, virgin, and pure. Extra-virgin oil is cold-pressed from the first pressing; virgin oil is cold-pressed from the second or third pressing; and pure, a misleading term indicating that it is made only from olives, is chemically refined and deodorized to reduce acidity and impurities. The quality of olive oil, like that of wine, varies from year to year and according to growing conditions, quality of the fruit, and producer standards. Oils range from bitter to very pungent to fruity in flavor, yellow to vivid green in color, light to very thick in texture, and dull to intense in aroma.

Extra-virgin olive oil makes a superior choice for salads and soups. Since much of the flavor dissipates when subjected to heat, it is wise to use less expensive pure oil or virgin oil for frying. Besides imparting its own flavor, olive oil also serves as a flavor enhancer.

Pescado Frito

SEPHARDIC PAN-FRIED FISH FILLETS
6 TO 8 SERVINGS

Of the many ways that the Jews living on the Iberian Peninsula found to prepare fish, their favorite and most celebrated is *pescado frito*. This dish became a part of every Friday dinner, with the leftovers enjoyed cold the following day at *shalosh seudot* (the afternoon meal) and even for several days thereafter. The secret to this dish is frying in oil, which, unlike butter, remains liquid at room temperature, and thus the fish stays light and flavorful when served cold. Frying crisps the flour, seals in the juices, and cooks the fillets quickly. The coating prevents sticking, protects the fish from the heat, holds the tender flesh together, and gives it a darker color. The result is a firm, moist, flavorful fish.

The Sephardic method of frying fish caught the attention of many non-Jews. Fried fish was frequently served at Monticello by Thomas Jefferson, who discovered the dish during his tenure as ambassador to France. (See Marie Kimball, *Thomas Jefferson's Cook Book*, Richmond, Virginia: Garrett and Massie, 1949, p 77.) Sephardic Jews from Holland brought this dish to England in the sixteenth century and introduced it and the concept of frying in oil, rather than lard, to the British. A Jewish fishmonger by the name of Joseph Malin is credited with combining his fried fish with the fried potatoes of a neighboring Irish shop, creating in 1865 the classic British combination of fish and chips.

About ½ cup olive or vegetable
   oil
3 pounds firm-fleshed fish fillets,
   such as red snapper, haddock,
   sea bass, sole, flounder, or
   trout
Salt to taste
Ground black pepper to taste
2 large eggs beaten with
   2 tablespoons water
1 cup all-purpose flour or
   matza meal
Lemon wedges or agristada
   (egg-lemon sauce; see page
   374)
Chopped fresh parsley
   for garnish

1. Heat ¼ inch of oil in a large, heavy skillet over medium-high heat.
2. Sprinkle the fillets with the salt and pepper. Dip them into the eggs, then into the flour or matza meal. Do not let the dredged fillets stand for more than a few minutes, or the coating will turn gummy.
3. Fry the fish in a single layer until golden brown on both sides, 2 to 4 minutes per side for thin fillets; 5 to 7 minutes per side for thick fillets. Drain on paper towels. Serve warm or cold with lemon wedges or *agristada* and garnished with chopped parsley.

VARIATIONS

Pescado Marinte (Sephardic Marinated Fried Fish): Bring 1 cup vinegar, ½ cup water, 3 minced cloves garlic, ¼ teaspoon dried rosemary, and about 1 teaspoon salt to a boil in a large skillet. Add the fried fish and simmer for 1 minute. Transfer the fish and marinade to a nonreactive container (do not use iron, copper, or brass) and refrigerate overnight or up to 1 week.

Peshe en Saltsa (Greek Fried Fish with Walnuts): After frying the fish, add ½ cup vinegar and ½ cup water to the skillet, stirring to loosen any browned particles. Stir in ¾ cup matza meal and simmer until slightly thickened. Arrange the fried fish on top, cover, and simmer over low heat for 15 minutes. Transfer the fillets to serving plates, spoon the sauce on top, and sprinkle with 1 cup finely chopped walnuts. (*Note:* This was a traditional Passover entrée among the Jews of Salonika [today Thessaloníki].)

Hraimeh

NORTHWEST AFRICAN RED FISH
6 TO 8 SERVINGS

The cuisine of the Maghreb differs greatly from Egyptian and Libyan fare, which is much simpler, and from what Americans tend to lump together as Middle Eastern cuisine. Over the centuries a succession of influences—Phoenician, Berber, Roman, Jewish, Moorish, Turkish, Spanish, and, most recently, French—have affected the cooking of the region, producing a spicy but sophisticated cuisine. The following variation of poached fish steaks is a typical Sabbath eve dish among Moroccan, Tunisian, and Algerian Jews. It features a favorite seasoning combination of the region—garlic, cumin, chili, and paprika. The fish course is usually followed by soup, then couscous (see page 246) and an assortment of cooked vegetable salads.

¼ cup vegetable oil

1 large yellow onion, chopped (about ¾ cup)

6 to 8 large cloves garlic, minced

1 to 3 teaspoons seeded and minced red chili

¼ cup chopped fresh parsley

¼ cup lemon juice

3 tablespoons tomato paste

1 teaspoon paprika

¼ to 1 teaspoon ground cumin

About ½ teaspoon salt

¼ teaspoon ground black pepper

Pinch of ground coriander

Pinch of cayenne

2 cups water

6 to 8 (1-inch-thick) firm-fleshed fish steaks, such as whitefish, haddock, pike, halibut, grouper, or sea bass (4 to 5 pounds total)

1. Heat the oil in a large skillet or saucepan over medium heat. Add the onion, garlic, and chili and sauté until soft, 5 to 10 minutes.

2. Stir in the parsley, lemon juice, tomato paste, paprika, cumin, salt, pepper, coriander, and cayenne. Add the water and bring to a boil.

3. Add the fish, cover, reduce the heat to low, and simmer until the fish is tender and loses its translucency, 15 to 20 minutes. Let cool. Serve at room temperature accompanied with plenty of pita, *khboz* (see page 282), or whole wheat bread.

Samak

YEMENITE SPICY POACHED FISH

6 TO 8 SERVINGS

Yemenites maintain that the fire in their food helps to cleanse the body, a contention that is difficult to argue, since those who still heed the traditional dietary habits are generally free of many of the afflictions of Western society, such as high blood pressure, high cholesterol, and diabetes. This dish is spicy in the Yemenite style.

3 cups tomato juice
1½ cups water
1 large yellow onion, chopped
    (about ¾ cup)
¼ cup chopped fresh coriander
¼ cup chopped fresh parsley
3 tablespoons z'chug
    (Yemenite chili paste; see
    page 379)
3 tablespoons lemon juice
2 tablespoons vegetable oil
About 6 pounds firm-fleshed fish
    fillets, such as flounder, cod,
    or perch, cut into 3-inch pieces

1. Combine the tomato juice, water, onion, coriander, parsley, *z'chug*, lemon juice, and oil in a large saucepan and bring to a boil.
2. Add the fish and return to a boil. Cover, reduce the heat to low, and simmer until the fish is tender and loses its translucency, 5 to 10 minutes. Serve warm or at room temperature accompanied with pita (see page 267) or other flat bread, and *chilbeh* (Yemenite fenugreek relish; see page 14).

PARSLEY

Although most Americans think of parsley as simply a garnish, in areas such as the Middle East it serves as a seasoning in salads, soups, stews, and ground meat dishes. The more strongly flavored parsley roots are sometimes used in soup. Parsley, along with celery, is identified as the *karpas* served at the Passover Seder. Although the curly or French variety of parsley is the type most available in America, the more flavorful flat-leaf or Italian variety is preferable for cooking. The taste of dried parsley is objectionable, and it should not be substituted for the fresh herb.

POULTRY

And it came to pass at evening, that the quails came up and covered the camp.

—Exodus 16:13

Although chicken is far and away the predominant fowl on Jewish tables today, that was not always the case. In biblical times, most birds were caught wild, including quails, geese, ducks, and partridges. The most common fowl, and among the few domesticated species in the Near East, were doves and their close relatives, pigeons. (Young pigeons are called squabs.) Chickens are descended from a red jungle fowl of Southeast Asia that was domesticated more than forty-five hundred years ago but only became widespread in Israel during the Second Commonwealth period.

The Romans loved the taste of chicken and introduced it throughout their domain. However, after the collapse of the empire, chickens practically disappeared from much of Europe. In the medieval Franco-German Jewish communities, beef was the predominant Sabbath entrée; geese, the predominant fowl, were generally reserved for festivals, weddings, and other special occasions. The Jews of the Rhineland became particularly proficient at raising geese. Geese were customarily fattened through the summer and autumn, then slaughtered around Hanukkah. Not surprisingly, goose became a traditional Hanukkah dish.

In the revival of European cuisine that followed the first Crusade, chickens began to make a comeback. Still, it was only in the face of a meat shortage in Europe in the fifteenth

Opposite: **La Juif a l'Oie (The Jewish Poultry Inspector), nineteenth-century France.** *The Hebrew word* kosher *means "fit." The laws of kashruth, therefore, involve the fitness of food for the Jewish table. In order for even an acceptable fowl to be kosher, it must be free of injuries or diseases to the major organs and ritually slaughtered.*

century that chickens became common fare. Western European rabbis of that time wistfully noted that "chicken does not awaken the joy of the festival as does beef."

A different mentality prevailed in eastern Europe, where beef was always rather scarce. In the East, chicken served as the most important food animal for the Jews, although, for the majority, it was a luxury reserved for the Sabbath and special occasions. Many Jewish families kept at least a few chickens in their yard or in coops. When the hen had passed its egg-laying days, it went to feed the family. On Thursday or Friday, the chicken was taken to the *shochet* (ritual slaughterer). Afterward, the housewife or maid would defeather, *kasher* (make kosher by soaking in water and salting), and cook the chicken in honor of the Sabbath. No part of the bird was wasted: The feet, head, wing tips, and gizzards went into the soup pot to be transformed into a rich broth or braised with onions to make a fricassee; the fat was rendered into schmaltz; the skin was cooked to make *gribenes* (cracklings; see page 109); the liver was grilled, chopped with a little schmaltz and hard-boiled eggs, and used to fill doughs such as knishes and kreplach or perhaps mixed into a kugel; the neck was filled and roasted (*helzel*; see page 108); the feathers became stuffing for pillows, mattresses, and quilts; and, under extremely desperate circumstances, even the bones were ground up and fried.

Roast Chicken

Gayna al Horno/Gebratener Hindle

ROAST CHICKEN
4 SERVINGS

Serving hot food for Friday night dinner can be a problem—for according to tradition, all of the food has to be in the oven at least thirty minutes before sundown. By the time that the various family members return from the synagogue, recite the kiddush, ritually wash their hands, and say the *hamotzi* (blessing) over the bread, the entrée can cool or toughen. Therefore, various communities developed dishes that could slow-cook for a long time, providing a warm and flavorful dish on Friday night. Arguably the most popular of all Ashkenazic Friday night entrées is roast chicken, a dish that can be left to finish cooking after lighting the Sabbath candles. In the Germanic manner, the animal is cooked and served whole, rather than cut into pieces as favored by Sephardim. Although most Ashkenazim prefer the flavor of ungarnished roast chicken, Hungarians often flavor the chicken with marjoram, and Greeks with lemon and oregano. Romanians serve it with *mujdei* (garlic sauce), and Georgians with *bazha* (walnut sauce; see page 375) or *tkemali* (plum sauce).

At first glance, roasting a chicken appears to be a simple process, but because of the uneven character of the bird, it can actually be problematic. The lean white meat lying in an exposed mass over the breastbone becomes dry and stringy if cooked to more than 150 degrees, while the fatty, dark meat compacted on the legs and thighs needs to reach at least 160 degrees to remove its raw flavor and tenderize its connective tissue. And most people prefer a temperature of at least 180 degrees for dark meat.

In olden times, this dilemma was solved by roasting the bird on a spit, a method that proves impractical in most modern kitchens. Some cooks, in order to avoid the problem, simply cut up the chicken. However, a whole bird turns out more juicy and flavorful than one cooked in pieces. In order to more evenly roast the chicken, place it breast side down on a rack or bed of vegetables to begin, then turn it partway through the cooking process. Start the chicken at a relatively high temperature to produce a rich brown color and flavor, then reduce the temperature to allow for more even cooking. Very large chickens, like turkeys, do not require this initial high heat, since they brown amply during their lengthy cooking time. Very small chickens, on the other hand, cook so quickly that there is not sufficient time to brown at a reduced heat.

The size and flavor of a chicken varies greatly depending on its age. Young birds have little connective tissue and should be cooked quickly, since a long cooking time would toughen the muscle fibers. Older birds have more connective tissue and require a long, slow moist-cooking to tenderize.

1 (3- to 4-pound) whole chicken
Salt to taste
Ground black pepper to taste
2 tablespoons vegetable oil or
    margarine, melted
Chicken stuffing (see pages 91-
    93), optional

1. Preheat the oven to 425 degrees. Oil a rack (this prevents the skin from sticking) and place it in a shallow roasting pan. Or line the pan with a layer of cubed carrots, celery, potatoes, and onions.

2. Wash the chicken inside and out and pat dry. Sprinkle with salt and pepper, inside and out. If desired, loosely stuff the cavity. Rub the outside of the chicken with the oil or margarine. Tie the drumsticks loosely together to prevent them from extending, and tuck the wings under the body.

3. Place the chicken, breast side down, on the prepared rack or on top of the cubed vegetables in the pan. Do not cover the bird. Roast for 15 minutes.

4. Reduce the heat to 350 degrees. Turn the chicken breast side up, baste with the pan juices, and roast an additional 1 hour to 1 hour and 20 minutes, or until the thigh juices run

clear when poked with a fork and a meat thermometer inserted into the thickest part of the meat between the thigh and breast registers 170 degrees (figure 20 to 25 minutes per pound unstuffed; 30 to 40 minutes per pound stuffed). Let the chicken stand at room temperature for 10 minutes before carving.

Dajaaj al Riz

SYRIAN ROAST CHICKEN WITH RICE
6 TO 8 SERVINGS

Dajaaj al riz and similar dishes—such as *dajaaj al batata* (chicken with potatoes), *dajaaj al macaruna* (chicken with pasta), and *dajaaj al badinjan* (chicken with eggplant)—are popular on the Sabbath and festivals.

1 recipe roast chicken
  (see page 88)
1 cup chicken broth or water
1 teaspoon ground allspice
½ teaspoon ground cinnamon
About 1 teaspoon salt
3 cups cooked rice (about 1 cup uncooked)

1. Preheat the oven to 250 degrees.
2. Cut the roasted chicken into 8 to 10 pieces. Or bone the chicken, discard the bones, and shred the meat.
3. Remove the wire rack from the roasting pan and stir the broth or water, allspice, cinnamon, and salt into the pan juices. Stir in the rice, then bury the chicken pieces or shredded meat in the rice.
4. Cover and bake for at least 2 hours and up to 4 hours. This dish is traditionally served with a salad, *mechshe* (stuffed vegetables), and another vegetable dish such as black-eyed peas or lima beans cooked with veal cubes; *kibbe nebelsia* (Syrian fried stuffed torpedoes); or spinach seasoned with allspice and cinnamon.

Chicken Stuffings

Matzafullung

ASHKENAZIC MATZA STUFFING

 ABOUT 4 CUPS

4 cups (about 8 ounces)
  crumbled matzot
3 tablespoons vegetable oil or
  schmaltz (see page 109)
1 medium yellow onion,
  chopped (about ½ cup)
⅓ cup chopped celery
1 clove garlic, minced
About ½ cup chicken broth
1 to 2 large eggs, lightly beaten
2 tablespoons chopped fresh
  parsley
2 tablespoons chopped gribenes
  (poultry cracklings; see page
  109), 1 teaspoon grated
  orange zest, ¼ teaspoon
  paprika, or pinch of ground
  ginger (optional)
About 1 teaspoon salt
Ground black pepper to taste

1. Soak the matzot in warm water until soft but not mushy, about 3 minutes. Drain and squeeze out the excess liquid.
2. Heat the oil or schmaltz in a large skillet over medium heat. Add the onion, celery, and garlic and sauté until softened, about 10 minutes. Stir in the matza.
3. Remove from the heat and moisten with the broth. Stir in the egg. Add the parsley, *gribenes*, orange zest, paprika or ginger, and the salt and pepper. Let stand for 15 minutes to absorb the liquid.

VARIATIONS

Herbed Matza Stuffing: Add 1 teaspoon chopped fresh rosemary or ¼ teaspoon dried and 1 teaspoon chopped fresh sage or ¼ teaspoon dried.

Matza and Fruit Stuffing: Add to the sautéed onion 4 ounces (1 cup) chopped dried apricots, 4 ounces (¾ cup) chopped pitted prunes, 1 peeled, cored, and chopped apple, and 2 tablespoons raisins and cook until the fruit starts to become tender, 2 to 5 minutes.

Matza and Mushroom Stuffing: Add 1 cup sliced mushrooms to the sautéed onion and sauté until soft, about 5 minutes.

Brotfullung

ASHKENAZIC VEGETABLE-CHALLAH STUFFING

❧ ABOUT 4 CUPS ❧

2 tablespoons schmaltz (see page 109), oil, or margarine

1 medium yellow onion, chopped (about ½ cup)

½ cup thinly sliced celery

½ cup thinly sliced carrots

½ cup thinly sliced parsnips (optional)

4 ounces mushrooms, sliced

2 tablespoons chopped fresh parsley

About 1 teaspoon salt

¼ teaspoon ground black pepper

½ teaspoon dried thyme

⅛ teaspoon dried oregano

Pinch of dried sage

2 tablespoons dry white wine or chicken broth

4 cups challah cubes

1. Heat the schmaltz, oil, or margarine in a large skillet over medium heat. Add the onions, celery, carrots, and, if desired, parsnips and sauté until softened, about 10 minutes.

2. Add the mushrooms and sauté until soft, about 5 minutes. Add the parsley, salt, pepper, herbs, and wine or broth and cook, stirring, for 2 minutes.

3. Pour over the bread, tossing well. Let cool.

Jaj Mihshee

PERSIAN RICE STUFFING

 ABOUT 5 CUPS

¼ cup (½ stick) margarine or
   vegetable oil
1 large yellow onion, chopped
   (about ¾ cup)
½ pound ground lamb or beef
¼ cup pine nuts
About 1 teaspoon salt
½ teaspoon ground cinnamon or
   1 (2-inch) cinnamon stick
¼ teaspoon ground allspice
¼ teaspoon ground black pepper
½ cup rice
1 cup chicken broth
⅓ cup dried currants or raisins
   or 1 cup pomegranate seeds

1. Heat the margarine or oil in a large skillet over medium heat. Add the onion and sauté until soft and translucent, 5 to 10 minutes.

2. Add the meat and sauté until it loses its red color, about 5 minutes. Stir in the pine nuts, salt, cinnamon, allspice, and pepper. Add the rice and stir until translucent, about 3 minutes.

3. Add the broth, cover, reduce the heat to low, and simmer until the liquid is absorbed, about 15 minutes. Let stand covered for 5 minutes, then stir in the currants, raisins, or pomegranate seeds. Remove the cinnamon stick and let cool.

ALLSPICE

When Christopher Columbus arrived in the West Indies looking for peppercorns, the dried berries of the black pepper (*pimienta* in Spanish), he found the natives using the dried brown berries of a local myrtle tree (*Pimenta diocia*), which he misnamed *pimienta*, or *pimento*. Actually, it was one of the few spices native to the Western Hemisphere—called allspice in America and England and *toute epice* in France. Despite its confusing name, this spice is actually one spice, so named because it is reputed to possess the flavor and scent of a combination of cinnamon, cloves, and nutmeg. Some people also find a trace of pepper or ground ginger in this spice; others have trouble finding more than a note of cloves. Still, the name persists. Allspice has become an important seasoning in certain Middle Eastern cuisines, most notably Syrian and Persian.

Moist-Cooked Chicken

Kabbalists, noting that *gever,* the Hebrew word for "rooster," also means "man," viewed the link between men and chickens as mystical. From this connection developed the ninth-century Ashkenazic ritual of *kapparot* (expiations), whereby a person symbolically transferred his or her sins to a chicken on the day before Yom Kippur. Afterward, the chicken served as dinner for the family or was given to the poor. Although Sephardic authorities strongly disparaged this ritual because of its non-Jewish origins, many adopted the custom of serving chicken at the meal before the fast. Today, coins are generally substituted for the chicken as a donation to charity, but moist-cooked chicken remains the traditional Yom Kippur eve entrée.

Chukandar Khuta

COCHIN CHICKEN WITH BEETS
❧ 4 TO 5 SERVINGS ❧

The vibrancy of both the flavor and color of this popular Indian dish contrasts with the characteristic blandness of *gikochteh hindle* (Ashkenazic boiled chicken).

1 (3- to 4-pound) chicken, cut into 10 to 12 pieces
Chicken broth or water
4 medium beets (about 1 pound), cooked, peeled, and sliced
3 cups (1½ pounds) peeled, seeded, and chopped tomatoes
3 to 4 small green chilies
¼ to ⅓ cup fresh mint leaves
1 teaspoon sugar
Juice of 2 lemons
Salt to taste
Ground black pepper to taste

1. Put the chicken in a large pot and add enough broth or water to just cover. Bring to a boil, reduce the heat to low, cover, and simmer for 1 hour.

2. Add the beets, tomatoes, and chilies and simmer for 15 minutes.

3. Add the mint leaves and sugar and simmer for 10 minutes.

4. Just before serving, stir in the lemon juice and season with salt and pepper. Serve with rice.

Armico de Pollo

SEPHARDIC CHICKEN WITH TOMATO SAUCE

4 TO 5 SERVINGS

This dish, also called *gayna con tomat* and *poya en salsa* in Greece and *fricassada* (with the addition of a pinch of cinnamon) in Morocco, is a Sabbath and Sukkoth favorite. Since it is filling yet easy to digest, it is also traditional at the meal preceding Yom Kippur.

1 (3- to 4-pound) chicken, cut
    into 8 to 10 pieces
3 tablespoons olive or vegetable
    oil
1 medium yellow onion,
    chopped (about ½ cup)
1 to 2 cloves garlic, minced
½ cup water
4 cups (2 pounds) peeled,
    seeded, and chopped tomatoes
½ cup chopped fresh parsley
½ teaspoon sugar or honey
About 1 teaspoon salt
Ground black pepper to taste

1. Pat the chicken dry. Heat the oil in a large saucepan over medium-high heat. Add the chicken and brown on all sides, about 5 minutes per side. Remove the chicken.
2. Add the onion and garlic and sauté until soft and translucent, 5 to 10 minutes.
3. Add the water, stirring to loosen the caramelized bits from the bottom. Add the tomatoes, parsley, sugar or honey, salt, and pepper.
4. Return the chicken to the pot. Bring to a boil, cover, reduce the heat to low, and simmer until the chicken is tender and the sauce is thickened, about 50 minutes. Serve the chicken in the sauce accompanied with rice, noodles, or bulgur.

VARIATION

Pollo con Bamia (Sephardic Chicken with Okra): Soak 1 pound stemmed okra in 2 quarts water mixed with 2 tablespoons vinegar for 30 minutes and drain. Simmer the chicken for 20 minutes, add the okra, and simmer until the chicken and okra are tender, about 30 minutes.

BUKHARAN TREASURES

"In my family, my wife does most of the cooking," explains Yusuf Abramov, a short, squat fortyish resident of Jerusalem, "but I always make the *palov* [Bukharan rice pilaf]. My father taught me the intricacies of this dish just as his father taught him and I taught my sons."

Along the fabled Silk Road—starting in China, skirting the northern fringes of the Gobi Desert, passing through Baghdad, and ending in the eastern Mediterranean—a stream of caravans once bore the riches of the Orient to the West, engendering great wealth for legendary central Asian trading towns, most notably Samarkand, Tashkent, and Bukhara.

"According to local tradition," says Abramov, "Bukhara is the site of the biblical Habor [2 Kings 17:6], one of the places to which the Assyrians exiled the Ten Tribes. Another legend claims that the first Jews settled in the area following Cyrus's conquest

---

Above: **Bukharan Jews with one of their favored possessions, a tea service.** *Hot green tea is served at the end of every Bukharan meal as well as frequently in between. Visitors to an Uzbeki house are given the royal treatment and presented with a* dastarkhan *("offering tray") featuring an array of treats and accompanied by a samovar filled with green tea.*

of Babylon." Benjamin of Tudela noted that there were fifty thousand Jews living in Samarkand at the time of his visit in 1170, who, like the population as a whole, were prosperous, secure, and well educated. The golden age of central Asia came to an abrupt end in 1220, when Genghis Khan and his Mongol hordes devastated the region. In the fourteenth century, Tamerlane restored some of the region's glory. Beginning in 1864, with the encroachment of Russian control over the region, small groups of Bukharan Jews began making their way to Israel.

Yusuf Abramov's great-grandfather, a Bukharan merchant, maintained homes both in Bukhara and the Rechovot quarter of Jerusalem. He sent Abramov's grandfather to Israel to study. During World War I, the Turkish government appropriated the home in Jerusalem and Abramov's grandfather returned to Bukhara. Shortly thereafter, the Soviet takeover led to the confiscation of the family's central Asian holdings and Abramov's grandfather, now impoverished, returned to Jerusalem, where he temporarily joined the ranks of Bukharans who earned their livelihood as porters.

"The B'nai Israel [a term Bukharan Jews call themselves] possess a rich heritage," Abramov explains. "We were the court musicians to the emir. We were great poets. The most visible manifestations of our culture are our *kaltshaks* [brightly colored embroidered ceremonial caftans made from silk that are worn on top of layers of robes], which are similar to those once worn at the royal court. We have special white cotton robes for Yom Kippur. Today, we only wear these colorful costumes, except the *tyubeteika* [embroidered silk skullcap], on special occasions like weddings."

The food of central Asia, like the demographics of the people, bears the imprint of many cultures, including Turkic (pastries), Chinese (pasta and steamed dumplings), Persian (kebabs, *palov*, halvah, and flat breads), Mongolian, Indian, and Russian. Abramov explains, "Our main seasonings are onion, garlic, coriander, cumin, and red chilies, the latter used sparingly. An abundance of luscious fruits and vegetables are coaxed out of the soil by means of a series of ancient irrigation canals. Uzbekistan grows about one thousand types of melons that are justly renowned throughout the [former] Soviet Union. There are a dozen varieties of raisins. Mung beans are the favored legume, but chickpeas and lentils are also popular. Rice is the most costly grain and, therefore, a luxury item generally reserved for special dishes like *palov*. *Nan* [a flat bread] is served at every meal.

"Since much of central Asia was populated by nomadic shepherds, it's not surprising that lamb was the predominant meat of the region," Abramov notes. "As with other pastoral cultures, dairy products make up a significant part of the diet. *Kumys* [a sour yogurt] is part of most breakfasts. A summer lunch might consist of bread, hard cheese, a green salad, and fruit. A winter lunch usually features a hearty meat soup such as *lagman*. Dinner is the biggest meal of the day, centering on meat such as kebabs [grilled chunks of lamb] or *shaslyk* [roasted lamb]. Hot green tea is enjoyed at the end of every meal as well as frequently in between."

Tovuk Palov

BUKHARAN CHICKEN PILAF
4 TO 5 SERVINGS

This dish—a combination of chicken, rice, and fruit—reflects the Persian influence on Bukharan cooking. The Uzbeks grow an assortment of fruit, generally of immense proportions, including apples, apricots, cherries, figs, grapes, melons, mulberries, peaches, pears, plums, pomegranates, and quinces. Chicken and rice were historically regarded as luxury items and, therefore, *palov* is generally served for dinner, the biggest meal of the day, on holidays and other special occasions. Dessert consists of fresh fruit.

1 (3- to 4-pound) chicken, cut into 8 to 10 pieces
3 tablespoons vegetable oil
2 medium yellow onions, chopped (about 1 cup)
2 medium carrots, chopped
1 medium apple, peeled, cored, and cubed
1 medium quince, peeled, cored, and cubed
½ cup raisins
½ teaspoon ground cumin
¼ teaspoon ground cinnamon
Salt to taste
Ground black pepper to taste
2 cups chicken broth or water
1 cup rice

1. Pat the chicken dry. Heat the oil in a large saucepan over medium-high heat. Add the chicken and brown on all sides, about 5 minutes per side. Remove the chicken.

2. Add the onions and sauté until soft and translucent, 5 to 10 minutes. Add the carrots, apple, and quince, and sauté until slightly softened, about 10 minutes.

3. Return the chicken to the pot and stir in the raisins, cumin, cinnamon, salt, and pepper. Add the broth or water.

4. Bring to a boil, cover, reduce the heat to low, and simmer for 20 minutes. Add the rice, cover, and simmer until the chicken and rice are tender, about 30 minutes. Serve with flat bread and hot green tea.

Tabyeet

MIDDLE EASTERN SABBATH CHICKEN AND RICE

❧ 6 TO 8 SERVINGS ❧

Many similarities exist in the food of Syria, Iraq, and Lebanon, a blending of Persian, Arabic, Turkish, and Iberian influences. Rice and chicken are served on special occasions, including this dish based on a medieval Spanish Sabbath favorite of chicken stuffed with meat, but adding rice and Middle Eastern seasonings. This style of chicken, called both *tabyeet* (shelter) and *hamin* (hot), is customarily served with a meze (an appetizer assortment) for Sabbath lunch. Some people cook this dish for only a few hours over moderate heat and serve it on Friday night. Whole eggs are sometimes cooked in the stew in the Sephardic fashion; beans may be added; and some cooks remove the entire skin, stuff it, and cook it alongside the chicken. The result is a chicken that is very tender and rice that, in the Persian style, is fluffy in the center and crisp on the bottom.

3 tablespoons vegetable oil

½ teaspoon ground turmeric

1 (3- to 4-pound) chicken

6 cups water

2 cups (1 pound) peeled, seeded, and chopped tomatoes or 3 tablespoons tomato paste

¾ to 1 teaspoon ground allspice or cardamom

¼ teaspoon ground cinnamon

About 1 teaspoon salt

Ground black pepper to taste

3 cups rice

2 cups cooked chickpeas or fava beans (optional)

1. Heat the oil in an 8-quart pot over medium-high heat. Stir in the turmeric. Brown the chicken on all sides.

2. Add the water, tomatoes or tomato paste, allspice or cardamom, cinnamon, salt, and pepper. Bring to a boil, cover, reduce the heat to medium, and cook for 10 minutes. Remove the chicken.

3. Return the cooking liquid to a boil, add the rice, cover, reduce the heat to low, and simmer for 15 minutes. If the rice is too dry, add a little more water.

4. Spoon 1 cup of the rice mixture into the chicken's cavity. Place, breast side up, in the pot on top of the remaining rice, and, if desired, add the chickpeas or fava beans. Bring to a boil, tightly cover, place in a 200-degree oven, and cook overnight. Or bake in a 350-degree oven for 2 hours, reduce the heat to 250 degrees, bake for 2 to 3 additional hours, and serve for Friday night.

5. Debone the chicken and arrange the meat on a serving platter. Scrape the crispy rice from the bottom of the pot and serve with the stuffing and chicken.

Doro Wot

ETHIOPIAN CHICKEN STEW
4 TO 5 SERVINGS

Wot (stew) is the national dish of Ethiopia, commonly cooked in a clay vessel over an open fire. Vegetable stews are common during the week, although the wealthy add chicken for dinner. Meat, primarily goat, is generally reserved for special occasions. In the impoverished Ethiopian Jewish communities, even those who could not afford it during the week made a special effort to have a little chicken in their *Sanbat wot* (Sabbath stew). Customarily, diners use pieces of *injera* (Ethiopian pancake bread; see page 274) to scoop up the *wot* from a communal serving plate. For a more fiery *wot*, Beta Israelis frequently substitute 3 to 6 tablespoons *berbere* (Ethiopian chili sauce) for the dry spices.

6 large yellow onions, chopped (about 5 cups)
⅓ cup vegetable oil
2 to 4 cloves garlic, minced
1 teaspoon minced fresh ginger
1 cup water
1 cup tomato sauce
1 (3- to 4-pound) chicken, cut into 12 pieces
About 1 teaspoon salt
½ teaspoon ground cardamom
¼ teaspoon ground turmeric
⅛ teaspoon ground cinnamon
⅛ teaspoon ground cloves
⅛ teaspoon grated nutmeg
⅛ teaspoon ground black pepper
4 or 5 hard-boiled eggs, peeled

1. In a dry large skillet or saucepan over medium heat, cook the onions, stirring constantly, until they begin to soften, about 3 minutes.

2. Add the oil. When it begins to sputter, add the garlic and ginger and sauté until fragrant, about 1 minute.

3. Add ½ cup of the water and the tomato sauce. Bring to a boil and cook, stirring constantly, until the liquid is reduced to the consistency of heavy cream, about 8 minutes.

4. Add the chicken, tossing until well coated, 2 to 3 minutes.

5. Stir in the spices and the remaining ½ cup water. Reduce the heat to low, cover, and simmer, stirring occasionally, until the chicken is tender, about 30 minutes. Add a little more water if the liquid reduces too much.

6. With a toothpick, pierce numerous ½-inch-deep holes in the surface of each egg. Add the eggs to the *wot* and turn gently in the sauce. Serve with *injera* (see page 274) or other flat breads. *Wots* can be prepared a day ahead and reheated before serving.

Csirke Paprikás

HUNGARIAN CHICKEN PAPRIKASH

4 TO 5 SERVINGS

The nomadic Magyars who eventually settled in Hungary carried cauldrons called *bogracs* in which they slow-simmered stews over open fires. A *paprikás* is related to the better-known *gulyás* (goulash) but contains larger pieces of meat or poultry and a thicker sauce. As with many Hungarian dishes, the most distinguishing feature of this dish is the liberal use of paprika (a by-product of Ottoman occupation). Typical of Hungarian stews, the onions are first slowly cooked to bring out their full flavor. Although most Hungarians would insist on using schmaltz to ensure the best flavor and color, vegetable oil may be substituted. Chicken *paprikás* is usually served with *uborka salata* (cucumber salad) and *galuska* (Hungarian dumplings) or noodles.

¼ cup schmaltz (see page 109) or vegetable oil

2 medium yellow onions, chopped (about 1 cup)

About ¾ cup chicken broth or water

2 to 3 teaspoons sweet paprika (see paprika; page 119)

1 (3- to 4-pound) chicken, cut into 8 pieces

About 1 teaspoon salt

Ground black pepper to taste

2 medium tomatoes, peeled, seeded, and chopped

1 medium green bell pepper, seeded and chopped

1 medium red bell pepper, seeded and chopped

1. Heat the schmaltz or oil in a large saucepan or Dutch oven over medium heat. Add the onions and sauté until slightly softened, 2 to 3 minutes. Stir in ¼ cup of the broth or water, cover, reduce the heat to low, and simmer, stirring occasionally, for about 1 hour. (If the onions appear to be in danger of burning, add a little more liquid.)

2. Remove the pot from the heat and stir in the paprika. Arrange the chicken in the pot and add the remaining ½ cup broth or water, the salt, and pepper. Scatter the tomatoes and bell peppers over the top, cover, and simmer for 20 minutes.

3. Rearrange the chicken pieces, cover, and simmer until fork-tender, about 25 additional minutes. (The idea of *paprikás* is to cook the chicken in very little liquid so that the chicken actually fries in its own fat. However, if all of the liquid evaporates, add a little more to prevent burning but not enough to overly thin the sauce. If the sauce is too thin, remove the chicken and boil the sauce until thickened.) Serve with Hungarian dumplings, noodles, or rice.

Djadja Tagine

MOROCCAN CHICKEN STEW

6 TO 8 SERVINGS

A *tagine* refers both to a ceramic pot from the town of Tafarout, Morocco, that consists of a shallow roundish dish with a cone-shaped lid, as well as any food cooked in the pot. This dish, served at many holiday meals, is usually preceded by a small phyllo appetizer or *pastilla* (see page 26).

½ cup olive or vegetable oil

3 medium yellow onions, chopped (about 1½ cups)

About 1 teaspoon salt

1 teaspoon ground ginger

1 teaspoon ground coriander

½ teaspoon ground cinnamon or 1 (3-inch) cinnamon stick

½ teaspoon ground cumin

½ teaspoon ground turmeric

¼ teaspoon saffron threads, crumbled (optional)

2 (3- to 3½-pound) chickens, cut into pieces

1. In a large pot, combine the oil, onions, salt, and spices. Add the chicken, tossing to coat. Cover and cook over high heat for 15 minutes.

2. Add enough water to barely cover the chicken. Bring to a boil, cover, reduce the heat to low, and simmer, stirring occasionally, until very tender, about 45 minutes.

3. The cooking liquid should be a thick gravy. If too thin, uncover and cook until the sauce is reduced; if too thick, stir in a little water. Serve with couscous (see page 246) or rice.

VARIATIONS

Djadja bi Hummus (Moroccan Chicken Tagine with Chickpeas): Add 2 cups cooked chickpeas to the cooked chicken and heat through.

Djadja bi Mishmish (Moroccan Chicken Tagine with Apricots): Soak 1 cup apricots in water to cover until soft; drain. Add the apricots with the chicken.

M'rouzya Tagine (Moroccan Chicken Tagine with Prunes): Soak 1 pound pitted prunes in water to cover overnight; drain. After the chicken is tender, add the prunes and cook until the sauce is reduced.

Dajaaj

YEMENITE CHICKEN FRICASSEE WITH FRUIT AND NUTS

 4 TO 5 SERVINGS

Yemenites always use chicken cut up in a stew or a soup, which often contains chunks of a vegetable such as pumpkin. On the other hand, pigeons and squabs are usually cooked whole. Side dishes include *memulayim* (see page 144; verduras reyenados—stuffed fruits and vegetables) and cooked vegetable purees. Pine nuts and almonds provide texture and flavor. In this dish the raisins and nuts are cooked in the dish.

1 (3-pound) chicken, cut into 8 pieces
¼ cup vegetable oil
2 medium yellow onions, chopped (about 1 cup)
2 teaspoons ground cumin
2 teaspoons ground ginger
1½ teaspoons cayenne
1½ teaspoons ground turmeric
1 teaspoon ground coriander
1 teaspoon ground cinnamon
1 teaspoon z'chug (Yemenite chili paste; see page 379)
2 cups water
½ cup raisins
½ cup almonds
About ½ teaspoon salt

1. Pat the chicken dry. Heat the oil in a large skillet over medium-high heat. Brown the chicken—do not crowd the pan—on all sides, about 5 minutes per side. Remove the chicken.

2. Add the onions and sauté until soft and translucent, 5 to 10 minutes. Add the cumin, ginger, cayenne, turmeric, coriander, cinnamon, and *z'chug* and sauté for 1 minute.

3. Return the chicken to the skillet. Add the water, raisins, almonds, and salt. Bring to a boil, cover, reduce the heat to low, and simmer until tender, about 45 minutes. Serve the chicken in the sauce accompanied with rice.

Khoresh Morgh va Narenge

PERSIAN TANGERINE CHICKEN
4 TO 5 SERVINGS

For the twelve centuries following Cyrus the Great's victory over the Medes in 550 B.C.E. and his subsequent conquest of Babylonia, Persia was one of the world's most powerful military forces and influential culinary forces. Much of the food enjoyed in the Middle East, central Asia, and India, as well as that of Greece and Rome, can be traced to Persia. Persian cooking is marked by the subtle use of herbs and spices, *golab* (rose water), *farsi* (stuffed vegetables and fruits), *borani* (vegetables with yogurt), *tursi* (pickled vegetables), *shirini* (sweets including baklava, marzipan, and halvah), and the cooking together of meat and fruit to produce a sweet-and-sour flavor (unlike the Romans, who relied on vinegar and honey). Persians prefer their dishes tart, adding an abundance of pomegranates and citrus fruits. Tangerines are reserved for special occasions.

6 tangerines
3 tablespoons vegetable oil
1 (3- to 4-pound) chicken,
  cut into 8 to 10 pieces
2 medium yellow onions,
  chopped (about 1 cup)
¼ teaspoon saffron threads,
  crumbled
2 cups chicken broth or water
1 pound carrots, sliced
2 tablespoons lemon juice
About 1 tablespoon sugar
About 1 teaspoon salt
Ground black pepper to taste
1½ teaspoons dried mint

1. Remove the zest (orange part) from the tangerine peel and cut into julienne strips. Cover the zest with water, bring to a boil, drain, and discard the water. Separate the tangerines into sections.
2. Heat the oil in a large saucepan or Dutch oven over medium-high heat. Add the chicken and brown on all sides, about 5 minutes per side. Remove the chicken.
3. Add the onions and sauté until soft and translucent, 5 to 10 minutes. Return the chicken to the pot.
4. Dissolve the saffron in the broth or water. Add the saffron mixture and tangerine zest to the chicken. Bring to a boil, cover, reduce the heat to low, and simmer for 30 minutes.
5. Add the carrots, lemon juice, sugar, salt, and pepper and simmer until the chicken and carrots are tender, about 20 minutes.
6. Remove the chicken and vegetables to a warm platter. Add the tangerine sections and mint to the sauce and cook until heated through, about 5 minutes. Pour over the chicken. Serve with rice.

VARIATION
Omit the tangerines and sugar and add 22 ounces drained canned mandarin oranges and ½ cup orange marmalade with the carrots.

Murgi Kari

CALCUTTA CHICKEN CURRY
4 TO 5 SERVINGS

This dish, a Sephardic chicken stew with Oriental seasonings, exemplifies the synthesis of Iraqi and Indian cuisines found in Calcutta Jewish cooking. In India, chicken is the most expensive meat and therefore reserved for special occasions. Chicken curry is traditionally served on Friday nights, Rosh Hashanah, and other festivals, accompanied with *aloo makalla* (fried potatoes; see page 173) and *halba* (Indian fenugreek relish, similar to *chilbeh*, page 14).

1 (3- to 4-pound) chicken, cut into 8 to 10 pieces
3 tablespoons vegetable oil
2 medium yellow onions, chopped (about 1 cup)
2 large cloves garlic, minced
1 teaspoon minced fresh ginger
½ teaspoon ground turmeric
1 cup water
1 (3-inch) cinnamon stick
2 to 3 cracked green cardamom pods or 2 to 3 whole cloves
About 1 teaspoon salt
Ground black pepper to taste

1. Pat the chicken dry. Heat the oil in a large saucepan or Dutch oven over medium-high heat. Add the chicken and brown on all sides, about 5 minutes per side. Remove the chicken.

2. Add the onions and sauté until soft and translucent, 5 to 10 minutes. Add the garlic, ginger, and turmeric and sauté for 2 minutes.

3. Add the water, cinnamon, cardamom or cloves, salt, and pepper. Return the chicken to the pot. Bring to a boil, cover, reduce the heat to low, and simmer until tender, about 50 minutes. Serve with rice.

Gebratener Gans

ASHKENAZIC ROAST GOOSE

6 TO 10 SERVINGS

Although rare in America, geese were popular in European Jewish communities, particularly in Alsace, an area renowned for its goose liver, and central Europe. In much of Europe, roast goose was considered a traditional Hanukkah dish. Goose contains a great deal of fat, a problem solved by pricking the goose all over with a fork before roasting it. Larger geese tend to be tough, so it is better to purchase smaller birds. Figure 20 minutes roasting time per pound, unstuffed.

1 (8– to 12–pound) goose

*½ lemon or 1 orange, sliced
(optional)*

Salt

Pepper to taste

*½ teaspoon ground ginger
(optional)*

8 to 10 cups stuffing (optional)

1. Preheat the oven to 350 degrees.

2. Cut off any excess fat from the neck and body cavities. Rinse the goose well and pat dry. If desired, rub inside with the lemon or orange. Sprinkle lightly inside and out with salt and pepper. If desired, rub the ouside with the ginger. Prick the skin of the goose lightly all over with the tines of a fork or with a small metal skewer.

3. If desired, fill the body cavity loosely (stuffing will expand during cooking) with desired stuffing—fruit stuffings complement the rich, fatty meat of geese—or place 1 quartered onion, 1 orange, 1 apple, or 1 potato in the center. Fold the loose skin of the neck together and skewer or sew closed. Tie the legs together.

4. Set the goose on a rack in a shallow roasting pan, breast side down. Roast, uncovered, basting occasionally, for 1 hour. Discard the fat in the bottom of the pan.

5. Turn the goose breast side up and roast, basting occasionally, until the thigh juices run clear and the internal temperature of the thigh meat—thermometer not touching the bone—registers 180 degrees (about 20 minutes per pound).

For an 8- to 12-pound goose, the roasting time will be 1½ to 2 hours after turning upright—or 2½ to 3 hours total roasting time. Add 20 to 40 minutes for stuffed goose. Cover loosely with aluminum foil and let stand 15 minutes before carving. If desired, serve with braised cabbage and mashed potatoes or potato dumplings.

VARIATION

Duaz Fenjo (Persian Roast Goose): Brush the goose with the juice of 2 lemons. Substitute ½ teaspoon cinnamon or allspice for the ginger. Fill the goose with 6 cored and sliced medium apples, ½ cup blanched almonds, and 3 tablespoons granulated sugar. And 5 minutes before goose is tender, brush with ¼ cup honey, return to the oven, and continue roasting until glazed. (*Note:* This is a traditional Persian Rosh Hashanah main course.)

Below: **The Bar Mitzvah Speech (in Frankfurt, Germany).** Moritz Oppenheim (1799–1882). *Bar mitzvah ("son of the commandment") and bat mitzvah ("daughter of the commandment") are the ceremonial recognition of religious maturity, at age thirteen for a male and twelve for a female. The bar mitzvah ceremony was formalized by the fifteenth century, while the first record of a bat mitzvah is by Rabbi Joseph Chaim ben Eliyahu (1835–1909) of Baghdad in the nineteenth century.*

Miscellaneous Poultry

Helzel

ASHKENAZIC STUFFED POULTRY NECK

 6 TO 8 SERVINGS

Stuffed poultry neck, also called *gefullte gansehals* (stuffed goose necks), is another ancient Sabbath dish that utilizes items that might otherwise go to waste. *Helzel*, similar to kishke (stuffed beef casing), is stuffed with a flour or matza kugel batter and roasted alongside the poultry or by itself. Turkish Jews add a little chopped walnuts to the flour mixture, while Yemenites prepare a stuffing of cinnamon-accented ground beef. You can also substitute potato kugel batter (see page 205) for the classic stuffing.

2 to 3 large yellow onions,
*   sliced*
1 cup all-purpose flour
*   (or ½ cup flour and ½ cup*
*   matza meal or bread crumbs)*
¼ to ½ cup schmaltz
*   (see page 109), vegetable oil,*
*   or vegetable shortening*
1 medium yellow onion, grated
*   or minced (about ½ cup)*
1 clove garlic, crushed
½ teaspoon paprika
About ½ teaspoon salt
¼ teaspoon ground black pepper
Skin of 1 goose or turkey neck
*   or 2 large chicken necks*

1. Preheat the oven to 325 degrees. Scatter the sliced onions in a shallow roasting pan.

2. Combine the flour, schmaltz, oil, or shortening, grated or minced onion, garlic, paprika, salt, and pepper. Stuff loosely into the poultry neck.

3. Place the *helzel* on the bed of onions in the roasting pan. Roast, basting occasionally with the pan juices, until golden brown, at least 1½ hours. Or roast the *helzel* in the same pan as the poultry from which it came.

Schmaltz mit Gribenes

ASHKENAZIC RENDERED POULTRY FAT WITH CRACKLINGS
❧ ABOUT 2 CUPS ❧

As Jews moved north and east in Europe, many of the ingredients that had previously been an essential part of their larder became scarce or, more often than not, unobtainable. Whereas in the Mediterranean region, olive oil was ubiquitous, in northern Europe oil of any sort was expensive or unavailable. Since non-Jews in these areas generally used lard for cooking, Jews had to look toward kosher animal fats. Thus, schmaltz (rendered poultry fat) became to Ashkenazic cooking what olive oil was to Mediterranean cooking and what sesame oil was to Near Eastern cooking.

In Europe, geese were born in the spring, fattened over the summer and autumn, and generally slaughtered at the onset of winter before food became scarce. The fat was rendered and used to make pancakes and other fried Hanukkah dishes. Most of the jars were set aside to last through the winter and a special container was reserved for Passover.

Pieces of skin cooked with the fat are transformed into cracklings called *gribenes*. Stir these crispy, browned bits into chopped liver or chopped eggs, sprinkle them over a green salad, mashed potatoes, or chicken soup, or mix them into a potato kugel (see page 205) or *knaidlach* (dumpling; see page 254) batter. A whimsical Yiddish adjunct for dishes containing *gribenes* is *mit neshamos* ("with souls").

Five chickens yield about 1 pound of chicken fat. Save the fat in the freezer until you collect enough to make schmaltz. Schmaltz, liquid at room temperature and solid when cold, is used for frying as well as a flavoring agent. Although either vegetable oil or margarine can be substituted for schmaltz in recipes, they will not have the same rich flavor and texture.

1 pound (about 4 cups) chicken or goose fat
½ pound chicken or goose skin
½ cup water
1 medium yellow onion, chopped (about ½ cup)

1. Cut the fat into small pieces and the skin into ¼-inch strips. Cook the fat, skin, and water in a large skillet or saucepan over medium-low heat until the water evaporates and the fat is melted, about 35 minutes.

2. Add the onion and cook until the onion and skin turn golden brown, about 5 minutes. Remove the *gribenes* (browned pieces) with a slotted spoon. Store the schmaltz and *gribenes* separately in the refrigerator or freezer.

MEAT

Beef

For much of western European history, meat constituted a major part of the diet. Beef, generally as pot roasts and meat pies, was the predominant Sabbath entrée. Indeed, it was in thirteenth-century France and Germany that the Yiddish terms *fleishig* (meat), *milchig* (dairy), and *pareve* (neutral) first emerged. Sephardim, who used few dairy products besides cheese, did not develop similar terminology until modern times. It was also at this time that the position of *shochet* (ritual slaughterer) was first institutionalized (before then, any Jew versed in the ritual could slaughter an animal) and Ashkenazim began doing without the hindquarters. (The sciatic nerve and certain fats located in the hindquarter of an animal are forbidden and must be removed. Since the process of removing these parts is extremely complicated and time-consuming, Ashkenazim avoid the entire hindquarter, which includes the tenderloin and the rear leg of lamb.) This situation changed only in the fifteenth century, when Europe experienced a shortage of meat.

Such was not the case in eastern Europe, where, because of sparse grazing conditions and cooler temperatures, meat was always scarcer. And since most of the cattle in the region

Opposite: **Housewives in Bialystok carry pots of *cholent* to the bakery, circa 1932.** *Since the instructions to build the Sanctuary and prohibition of working on the Sabbath are juxtaposed in the Bible, those forbidden forms of work are the thirty-nine categories of work used to build the Sanctuary, including by inference cooking. Therefore, the* cholent *pots were placed in the oven before the onset of the Sabbath, providing a warm dish for Saturday lunch.*

were raised for the dairy industry and not slaughtered until very mature, much of the meat was tough. To further complicate the situation, beginning in the seventeenth century the authorities in many parts of eastern Europe imposed a *korobka* (steep tax) on kosher meat. As a result, eastern European Jews could rarely buy meat, particularly the more tender cuts. Instead, they made do with the tough, sinewy cuts from the lower part of a cow. Brisket, a cut with a lot of connective tissue and a very grainy texture, is the meat covering the breastbone. Below the arm lie the chuck short ribs called flanken. Eastern European Jews discovered that these tougher and cheaper cuts could actually be very flavorful. The trick lay in tenderizing the meat by slowly simmering it in water, a process that breaks down the connective tissue by converting the collagen to gelatin.

For a long time, American butchers, with the exception of kosher butchers, practically gave away these tougher cuts. Then, barbecuers learned how flavorful brisket and short ribs could be, and deli goers discovered the joys of corned beef and pastrami.

Gedempte Fleisch

ASHKENAZIC BOILED BEEF
10 TO 12 SERVINGS

Despite its name, this dish is not boiled but rather slow-simmered. Typical of eastern European cuisine, the meat is not browned before cooking but relies on paprika for color. If you prefer a more Western-style brisket, sear it on both sides in 2 tablespoons of hot vegetable oil, then add the onions and the remaining ingredients and proceed as directed.

1 (5-pound) beef brisket or
  short ribs
About 2 teaspoons salt
Ground black pepper to taste
Paprika to taste
2 large yellow onions, sliced
  (for a more colorful broth,
  do not peel)
1 bay leaf
About 7 cups boiling water
2 medium carrots, sliced

1. Sprinkle the meat liberally with the salt, pepper, and paprika. Scatter half of the onions in a large pot or roasting pan. Add the brisket, the remaining onion, the bay leaf, and enough boiling water to cover. (Adding boiling water seals the brisket, resulting in a more flavorful meat; cold water produces a more flavorful broth.)

2. Bring to a boil and skim the foam. Cover, reduce the heat to low, and simmer for 1½ hours.

3. Add the carrots, celery, and parsnip. Cover and simmer until the meat is fork-tender (there is only a slight pull on a fork when it is removed from the meat), about an additional

2 stalks celery, sliced

1 medium parsnip, sliced

1 hour for brisket; 30 minutes for short ribs. (At this point, the meat can be refrigerated for up to 3 days; skim the fat from the surface, slice the meat, and reheat in the cooking liquid.) 4. Let the brisket stand in the cooking liquid for 15 minutes. Remove the meat and slice diagonally against the grain (the muscle lines). Serve the meat moistened with the broth (serve the leftover broth as soup) and accompanied with the vegetables and noodles or potatoes. Serve with grated horse-radish or prepared mustard.

Variations

Tomato Brisket: Substitute 2 cups peeled, seeded, and chopped tomatoes and 2 cups dry red wine for the water.

Brisket mit Beblach (Brisket with Beans): Add 4 cups cooked dried navy or lima beans with the water. If desired, add ¼ cup brown sugar, ¼ cup molasses, and 2 teaspoons dry mustard.

Essig Fleisch (Ashkenazic Sweet-and-Sour Beef): When the meat is tender, add about ¼ cup lemon juice or vinegar and ¼ cup granulated or brown sugar. For a thicker sauce, stir in 4 to 5 crushed gingersnaps and cook for about 10 minutes. (*Note: Essig fleisch* is related to the German sauerbraten, except that the latter is marinated in a wine mixture for several days. Perhaps these sauces originated to mask any off flavors from poor-quality meat. The gingersnaps are a distinctive Teutonic touch.)

Russel Fleisch (Ukrainian Ashkenazic Beef with Fermented Beets): Reduce the amount of water to 3 cups and add 4 cups *russel* beet juice and 2 cups chopped *russel* beets (see page 154). After the meat is tender, add about ¼ cup sugar and a little lemon juice. For a thicker sauce, stir 1 cup of the hot cooking liquid into 2 lightly beaten eggs, stir it into the pot, and cook a few minutes until thickened. (*Note:* This Passover dish was an eastern European adaptation of *essig fleisch,* using *russel* as the souring agent and eggs as the thickener. The meat is served moistened with a little of the sauce, and the bulk of the sauce is served separately as borscht, providing two favorite Ukrainian dishes in one.)

Tzimmes

ASHKENAZIC STEWED BEEF AND VEGETABLES

8 TO 10 SERVINGS

The Yiddish writer Sholom Aleichem penned a tale of a *shadchan* (marriage broker) who said she was so well treated by the parents of a hopeful bride that "they serve me the best portions of meat and feed me tzimmes even on weekdays." Tzimmes is a late medieval slow-simmered stew whose origins lie in the medieval German practice of cooking meats with fruits and vegetables. The Yiddish name is derived from two German words for "eat"—*zum* and *essen*. Tzimmes, which has entered the English language, took on the meaning of a fuss—*machan un tzimmes fun* (to make a fuss out of)—undoubtedly because of all the chopping, stirring, and stewing involved in making the dish. Over the centuries, tzimmes developed symbolic meanings and emerged as a characteristic Ashkenazic Sabbath and festival dish. It is particularly popular for the harvest festival of Sukkoth (the vegetables and fruits serve as reminders of the earth's bounty) and for Rosh Hashanah (a sweetened stew is ideal for symbolically ushering in a sweet New Year).

Tzimmes recipes vary greatly: Some call for whole cuts of meat, others for cubed meat, and some are meatless; some are highly seasoned with cinnamon or a combination of spices, while others call simply for salt and pepper; some are savory, while others add fresh or dried fruits such as apples, raisins, apricots, peaches, and, most commonly, *flohmen* (prunes) for a touch of sweetness. Romanians use chickpeas and pieces of pumpkin, adding a Middle Eastern touch. Beans are common in the Balkans. Lithuanians often cook *knaidlach* (dumplings) on top of the stew, making a complete meal in one dish.

All tzimmes recipes include at least one root vegetable. Turnips, whose German name *ruben* is similar to the Hebrew word *ribboi* (increase), are one of the oldest tzimmes vegetables. Carrots, which are golden, sweet, and slice into coinlike rounds, are the most commonly used in eastern Europe. Sweet potatoes, which share many of the carrot's attributes, and white potatoes became popular after they were introduced from America. Other traditional vegetables include parsnips and rutabagas. Whatever the ingredients, tzimmes requires a long cooking time over low heat to blend the various flavors. The following version is first stewed and then baked as a casserole, resulting in a very thick gravy.

3 to 4 pounds boneless beef chuck or brisket or 4 to 6 pounds beef short ribs

1. Pat the meat dry. (The meat can be left whole or cut into 1½-inch cubes.) Heat the schmaltz or oil in a large ovenproof pot or Dutch oven over medium-high heat. Add the meat and brown on both sides, 5 to 10 minutes per side.

3 tablespoons schmaltz (see
    page 109) or vegetable oil
2 medium yellow onions, sliced
3 tablespoons all-purpose flour
1½ pounds carrots, sliced
5 medium sweet potatoes
    (about 2 pounds), peeled
    and quartered
3 medium white potatoes
    (about 1 pound), peeled and
    sliced
1 pound pitted prunes, dried
    apricots, dried peaches, or
    any combination
About ½ cup honey, granulated
    sugar, brown sugar, or any
    combination
½ teaspoon ground cinnamon
Pinch of ground cloves or
    ground ginger
About 1 teaspoon salt
Ground black pepper to taste

2. Add the onions and enough water to cover. Bring to a boil, cover the pot, reduce the heat to low, and simmer for 1 hour.

3. Preheat the oven to 350 degrees.

4. To make the *einbren* (see sidebar), stir the flour in an ungreased heavy skillet over low heat until lightly browned and nutty smelling. Do not burn or it will be bitter.

5. Remove the *einbren* from the heat and gradually stir in 1 cup of the cooking liquid. Stir into the meat.

6. Add the carrots, sweet potatoes, white potatoes, prunes, apricots, or peaches, honey or sugar, cinnamon, cloves or ginger, salt, and pepper. Cover and bake until the meat is tender, at least 2 hours and up to 5 hours. (The flavor of the tzimmes improves as it cooks.)

7. Uncover the pot and continue cooking, adding more water to prevent burning, until the meat is very tender and the top is golden brown, about 30 minutes. Cut the meat into chunks and serve with the vegetables.

VARIATIONS

Omit the *einbren* (browned flour). After the tzimmes has finished cooking, dissolve 1 tablespoon cornstarch in 2 tablespoons cold water, stir into the cooking liquid, and cook until thickened. For a thinner sauce, the cornstarch can be omitted.

Vegetarian Tzimmes: Omit the meat and reduce the baking time to about 1½ hours.

EINBREN

Einbren, a precursor to roux, is a browned flour. At one time, European housewives browned 1 to 2 cups of flour at once and stored it in a jar in a cool place and, when needed, added a little to gravies and stews as a thickener and for its nutty flavor.

Einbren has about half the thickening power of all-purpose flour.

AN ALSATIAN ACCENT

"**W**hen my children and grandchildren come to visit for *Shabbos,*" explains Liselotte Gorlin, a gourmet cook, native of Strasbourg, and a member of a family that traces its roots in the most eastern part of France as far back as 1700, "they expect *choucroute garnie* [Alsatian cured meats with sauerkraut], not *cholent,* for lunch."

The French province of Alsace lies between the Rhine River (the site of the original area called Ashkenaz) and the Vosges Mountains. Separated historically and geographically from France and Germany, it has long been claimed and influenced by both countries. After its acquisition by France in 1648, Alsace remained semiautonomous until the French Revolution. Following the absorption of Provence into France in 1481 and the subsequent expulsion of its Jews, Alsace remained the only part of modern France in which Jews resided until the arrival of Conversos from Iberia in the fifteenth century.

"In Alsace there is only a fine line between Jews and non-Jews on the surface," Gorlin reminisces about her homeland. "On the whole, the Jewish community was well established and the people economically secure. My father made his living selling livestock and geese [used to make the regional classic, foie gras], as did many other Jews in the area."

Alsatian cuisine reflects a strong German influence: Few spices besides cinnamon are used; cabbage is the predominant vegetable; noodles—Alsatians prefer them very thin—

and dumplings enjoy greater popularity here than in the rest of France; and foods are cooked in fat, particularly goose fat, not butter. The wines of the region—including the elegant Riesling, the spicy Gewürztraminer, and the fresh-floral Pinot Blanc—with their distinctive, delicate flavor, floral style, and medium dryness, more closely resemble German rather than French wines.

Alsatian Jewish cuisine, lacking the Slavic influences of eastern Europe, is closer to the original Ashkenazic fare. As in no other part of western Europe, Jewish cuisine has become an integral part of the general Alsatian cuisine: Many dishes even include the term *à la Juive* ("in the Jewish style"). Gorlin explains, "A typical Alsatian Shabbat dinner commences with fish such as *carpe à la Juive* and might also include chicken noodle soup and *boeuf au raifort* [boiled beef with horseradish] or chicken fricassee. Dessert generally consists of kuchen, *kugelhopf, tarte Alsacienne* [fruit tart], or chocolate mousse.

"Jewish holiday foods in Alsace differ from those common to eastern Europe," Gorlin continues. "Traditional Purim treats include doughnuts [which Alsatians claim to have invented] and aged sausages, which have been hung up like Haman, the villain of the Purim story. The Hanukkah feast centers on a large goose. At the Passover Seder, horseradish is eaten in whole pieces, not grated, and the green vegetables are dipped into vinegar instead of salt water."

Choucroute Garnie

ALSATIAN CURED MEATS WITH SAUERKRAUT
8 TO 10 SERVINGS

Choucroute garnie is a popular Alsatian Sabbath lunch, commonly accompanied with a lentil salad and followed by *kuchen* (coffee cake) or a fruit tart for dessert. Although the classic recipe uses an assortment of pork cuts and lard, Alsatian Jews substitute kosher meats and goose fat.

3 pounds fresh corned beef

2 pounds pastrami

6 pounds sauerkraut

2 tablespoons schmaltz (see page 109) or vegetable oil

2 medium yellow onions, chopped (about 1 cup)

4 cups Riesling or other dry white wine

10 juniper berries, 8 peppercorns, 2 whole cloves, and 2 bay leaves tied in cheesecloth (optional)

1 pound beef knockwurst or other highly seasoned sausage

8 to 10 beef frankfurters

16 to 24 small new potatoes, boiled

1. Partially cook the corned beef and pastrami in water to cover for about 1 hour. Drain.

2. Wash the sauerkraut in cold water several times to remove most of the salt. Drain and press out the liquid.

3. Heat the schmaltz or oil in a large ovenproof pot over medium heat. Add the onions and sauté until soft and translucent, 5 to 10 minutes. Add the sauerkraut, wine, and, if desired, bouquet garni and bring to a low boil.

4. Arrange the corned beef and pastrami on top of the sauerkraut, cover the pot, and simmer over low heat or bake in a 350-degree oven for at least 3 hours or overnight. (*Choucroute garnie* can be prepared a day ahead as it tastes even better reheated.)

5. About 1 hour before serving, add the sausage. About 15 minutes before serving, add the frankfurters and potatoes.

6. Place the sauerkraut on a serving platter and arrange the meats, sausages, and potatoes on top.

Marha Gulyás

HUNGARIAN BEEF GOULASH
6 TO 8 SERVINGS

In 800, Charlemagne made the land to the west of the Danube a tributary state and, in the process, its Jewish community, which had lived in the area since Roman times, was united with the Ashkenazim. The Ashkenazic influence was further enriched with the arrival of immigrants fleeing the Crusaders and other massacres in the West. At the end of the ninth century, a nomadic group called the Magyars settled in the area, introducing a culture that differentiated Hungary from its Teutonic and Slavic neighbors. The arrival of the Ottoman Empire in 1526 produced an important side effect, a major improvement in Hungarian cooking. Following the Ottoman retreat in 1687, Austria filled the power vacuum in Hungary and, during the following two centuries, further transformed the food. As a result of these various influences, Hungarian-Jewish cuisine evolved into the liveliest form of Ashkenazic cooking, as exemplified by this dish.

Goulash, the most famous of all Hungarian dishes, is also among the earliest, dating back to the Magyars' nomadic days when *gulyás* (shepherds) cooked stews in easily transportable cauldrons called *bogracs*. Eventually, *gulyás* came to mean any of the stews prepared by the shepherds. As is typical of Hungarian cooking, the meat is not browned. Goulash contains less liquid than most stews and the sauce is never thickened with flour. For *gulyásleves* (goulash soup), increase the liquid to about 10 cups.

¼ cup schmaltz (see page 109) or vegetable oil

1 large yellow onion, chopped (about ¾ cup)

1 to 2 cloves garlic, minced

1 to 3 tablespoons sweet paprika (see opposite page)

3 pounds boneless beef chuck or shoulder, cut into 1½-inch cubes

2½ cups (1 pound) plum tomatoes, peeled, seeded, and chopped

1. Heat the schmaltz or oil in a large pot over medium heat. Add the onion and sauté until lightly golden, about 15 minutes. Stir in the garlic. Remove from the heat and stir in the paprika.

2. Return to the heat and stir in the beef. Add the tomatoes, bell peppers, caraway, salt, pepper, and enough broth or water to almost cover the beef. Bring to a boil, cover, reduce the heat to low, and simmer, stirring occasionally, until the meat is nearly tender, about 1½ hours.

3. Add the potatoes and, if desired, marjoram. Cover and simmer until the meat and potatoes are tender, about 30 minutes. Skim any fat from the surface and check the seasonings. Serve over wide noodles.

2 medium green bell peppers,
    seeded and sliced or chopped
1 teaspoon caraway seeds
About 1 teaspoon salt
Ground black pepper to taste
About 4 cups beef broth, chick-
    en broth, or water
6 medium potatoes (about
    2 pounds), peeled and diced
½ teaspoon dried marjoram
    (optional)

VARIATION

Kolozsvari Gulyás (Goulash with Cabbage): Add about 1 pound (½ medium head) shredded green cabbage 10 minutes after adding the potatoes.

PAPRIKA

Paprika is made by grinding dried red capsicum chilies. Chilies made their way from their native South America to western Europe by way of the Spanish. The Ottoman Turks probably first discovered the ground form of pepper pods in their dealings with the Portuguese. In turn, the Turks introduced this brightly colored spice to Hungary during their occupation of the region that began in 1526. The Hungarians called the spice after the Slavic name for peppercorns, *paparka*. Since paprika was much less expensive than peppercorns, it quickly emerged as the predominant seasoning of Hungarian peasants and an essential part of Hungarian cuisine, used to make such classic dishes as *gulyás* (goulash) and *csirke paprikás* (chicken paprikash).

Unquestionably, the world's finest paprika comes from the country that favors it the most. Paprika ranges in intensity from sweet to hot, depending on the variety of pepper used and how it is ground. The mildest Hungarian paprika is called *rozsa* (noble sweet rose), made after the veins and seeds are removed. Hot paprika, called *koenigspaprika* (kings paprika) and *eros*, is made by grinding the veins and seeds along with the pods. *Feledes* is a mixture of sweet and hot paprika and has a slightly piquant flavor. The Spanish type of paprika, called *pimenton*, is coarser, darker, and more pungent than the Hungarian spice.

Paprika possesses a high sugar content that caramelizes when it comes into contact with direct heat. This characteristic is an asset when browning, which is why meat is often dusted with paprika before cooking. However, for the best flavor, add it near the end of cooking. Store paprika in the refrigerator to retain freshness.

Khoresh

PERSIAN BEEF SAUCE-STEW

 3 TO 4 SERVINGS

Before the advent of refrigeration, cooks had to find ways to preserve foods. In Persia, meat was cut into 1-inch cubes and sautéed in fat with spices. These meat cubes, called *geimeh*, were then stored in crocks in a cool place and, when needed, cooked in water to produce a saucelike stew called *khoresh*. The Moroccan tagine is an adaptation of this stew. Iranians continue to use this ancient process, making use of seasonal produce and fruit to create a vast array of *khoreshes*. These stews, in reflection of the Persian preference, tend toward the tart side and are always served with *chelou* (Persian crusty rice; see page 198).

3 tablespoons vegetable oil
1 pound boneless beef or lamb chuck, cut into 1-inch cubes
1 large leek or large yellow onion, chopped (about ¾ cup)
½ teaspoon ground cinnamon
¼ teaspoon ground turmeric
¼ teaspoon grated nutmeg
2 cups water
Juice of 1 lemon or lime
About 1 teaspoon salt
¼ teaspoon ground black pepper

1. Heat the oil in a 4-quart saucepan or Dutch oven over medium heat. Add the meat, leek or onion, cinnamon, turmeric, and nutmeg and sauté until the meat is browned, 5 to 10 minutes.

2. Add the water, lemon or lime juice, salt, and pepper. Bring to a boil, reduce the heat to low, and simmer—adding a little more water if too much liquid evaporates—until the meat is tender and the sauce is thick, about 1¼ hours. Serve with *chelou* (see page 198) or steamed rice.

VARIATIONS

Khoreshe Alu (Persian Beef and Prune Stew): After cooking the *khoresh* for 1 hour, add 24 prunes soaked in water to cover until soft and drained, and cook another 15 minutes. If desired, add 2 cups chopped fresh parsley, 1 cup chopped fresh chives, and ¼ cup chopped fresh mint before adding the water. (*Note:* Although Persians use a tart golden prune, you can substitute the sweeter black prune.)

Khoreshe Grach (Persian Beef and Mushroom Stew): Sauté 1 pound sliced mushrooms in 2 tablespoons vegetable oil until soft. After cooking the *khoreshe* for 1 hour, add the sautéed mushrooms and cook another 15 minutes.

Khoreshe Sabzi (Persian Beef Stew with Greens): **After adding the water, add 1 pound chopped fresh or 20 ounces frozen spinach and 1 cup finely chopped fresh parsley.**

Khoreshe Sib (Persian Beef and Apple Stew): **Sauté 4 sliced medium apples in 2 tablespoons vegetable oil until tender (about 5 minutes), and stir into the stew just before serving.**

Siga Wot

ETHIOPIAN BEEF STEW

5 TO 6 SERVINGS

Ethiopian Jews generally reserve meat *wots* for very special occasions.

5 large yellow onions, chopped (about 4 cups)

⅓ cup vegetable oil

2 to 3 cloves garlic, minced

1 teaspoon minced fresh ginger

1 cup tomato sauce

1 cup water

1½ pounds boneless beef or lamb chuck, cut into ½-inch cubes

1 teaspoon salt

½ teaspoon ground cardamom

¼ teaspoon ground turmeric

⅛ teaspoon ground cinnamon

⅛ teaspoon ground cloves

⅛ teaspoon grated nutmeg

⅛ teaspoon ground black pepper

1. In a dry large skillet over medium heat, cook the onions, stirring constantly, until they begin to soften, about 3 minutes.

2. Add the oil. When the oil begins to sputter, add the garlic and ginger and sauté until fragrant, 1 to 2 minutes.

3. Add the tomato sauce and ½ cup of the water. Bring to a boil and cook, stirring constantly, until the liquid is reduced to the consistency of heavy cream, about 8 minutes.

4. Add the meat, tossing until well coated, 2 to 3 minutes.

5. Add the remaining ½ cup water, the salt, and the spices. Reduce the heat to low, cover, and simmer until the meat is tender, about 1 hour. Add a little more water if the liquid reduces too much. Serve with *injera* (Ethiopian pancake bread; see page 274).

SABBATH STEWS

You shall kindle no fire throughout your habitations upon the Sabbath day.

—EXODUS 35:3

Iberian bean and chickpea stews were so identified with Jewish cooking that the Spanish Inquisition regarded anyone preparing such foods as suspect of practicing Judaism. The only defense Conversos (Jews who had outwardly converted to Catholicism, but secretly observed Jewish rituals) had against prying eyes was to replace the customary beef or lamb with pork, an item no traditional Jew would eat. Thus was born one of Spain's classic dishes, *cocida madrileno* (literally "boiled from Madrid"), a slow-simmered chickpea and pork stew. Today, in parts of Spain as well as Central and South America, in areas where there are no overt Jews, some housewives secretly prepare bean stews every Friday and let the dish cook overnight. These versions of *hamin* are a residual effect of the Inquisition's pursuit of Conversos even into the New World.

In a similar vein, several early French church leaders railed against members of their flock who ate Jewish foods, particularly slow-cooked bean dishes. As evidenced by the widespread popularity of cassoulet, their calls went generally unheeded.

The influence of these Sabbath stews was not limited to the Old World. Before reaching Plymouth Rock, the Pilgrims spent several years in Holland, where they came into contact with Sephardim who had immigrated to that country following the expulsion from Spain. Since the Pilgrims observed Sunday as a day of rest and refrained from cooking, they took a special interest in exotic dishes of the Dutch Jews, including *shkanah* (from an Arabic word meaning "hot"), a slow-simmered sweetened Sabbath bean stew. In America, the Pilgrims substituted maple syrup and bacon for the traditional molasses/honey and goose fat, placed the pot in the oven on Saturday night, and left the dish to simmer until after church services the following morning. Thus was born a classic American dish, Boston baked beans.

Left: **Medieval *cholent* pot.**
"He who delights in the Sabbath is granted his heart's desires."
(TALMUD SHABBAT 118a)

Hamin/Cholent

ASHKENAZIC SABBATH STEW

6 TO 8 SERVINGS

Cholent is the food of heaven. . . . Cholent is the kosher ambrosia.
—PRINZESSIN SABBAT ("THE SABBATH PRINCESS"),
HEINRICH HEINE

Although cooking is one of the thirty-nine categories of creative work forbidden on the Sabbath, hot food is treasured as an enhancement of the day. Indeed, "*tomnin et ha'hamin*" (cover the hot foods) is included in the Sabbath liturgy in a list of the activities that a person must do on Friday before nightfall. Hot dishes gained special importance in the eighth century when the Karaites, an anti-rabbinic sect, forbade the presence of any fire or hot food during their Sabbath. In the face of the intensity of this religious dispute, lighting the Sabbath candles and eating hot foods became acts of affiliation with the rabbis and Talmudic tradition. Thus, for millennia, Jewish cooks found ways of producing warm meals for Saturday lunch, which, according to Halakah (Jewish law), must be at least half cooked before the onset of the Sabbath.

During the course of history, there have been many of these Sabbath dishes—some are long forgotten, others are still served on Jewish tables weekly. Among the most popular of these dishes are slow-simmered bean stews called *hamin/hamim* (from *cham*, the Hebrew word for "hot") or *dafina/adafina* (from the Arabic word for "covered") by Sephardim and *schalet* (western Yiddish)/ *cholent* (eastern Yiddish)—from *chald*, the old French word for "warm"—by Ashkenazim. Only minor variations exist in the basic ingredients in these stews: Sephardim generally use chickpeas, fava beans, or large lima beans, while Ashkenazim prefer barley and small haricot beans. *Hamin* traditionally contains *huevos haminados* (brown eggs; see page 382); a calf's foot, which is removed and served separately as an appetizer, is often added; and it is often slightly sweetened with dates, quinces, apricots, or sweet potatoes. Sephardic versions are generally thinner than *cholent* and are traditionally separated into different dishes before serving: the cooking liquid in one bowl, the eggs in a second, the potatoes and beans in a third, and the meat in a fourth.

There are slight variations of this dish, the common denominator being a long, slow cooking time. After that, everything depends on the individual cook, who varies his or her *hamin/cholent* by adding a little of this or some of that. Some are made with large cuts of meat, others with pieces of beef, and some with chicken or goose. Many Hungarians like to add a whole tongue. *Cholent* may contain beans, barley, rice, potatoes, kasha (see page 188), or any combination of grains and legumes. It may be sweetened with honey or fruit or spiced with paprika and a bay leaf.

10 to 14 ounces (1½ to 2 cups) any combination dried navy, lima, pink, or kidney beans

1½ pounds beef or veal marrow bones

3 medium yellow onions, sliced

2 to 3 cloves garlic, minced

6 to 8 medium potatoes (2 to 2½ pounds), peeled and quartered

2 to 3 pounds beef short ribs, brisket, or chuck roast, cut into 2-inch cubes

¾ cup pearl barley (for cholent*)*

About 2 teaspoons salt

About ½ teaspoon ground black pepper

8 to 12 hard-boiled eggs in shell (for hamin*)*

1. Soak the beans in water to cover overnight. Drain.

2. In the order given, place the bones, beans, onions, garlic, potatoes, beef, and barley (for *cholent*) in a 6- to 8-quart pot. Add enough water to cover. (*Hamin* usually contains more liquid than *cholent*.)

3. Bring to a boil, cover, reduce the heat to medium-low, and simmer, skimming the foam from the surface, until the beans are nearly soft, about 1 hour.

4. Season with the salt and pepper. (Salt prevents the beans from softening properly and therefore is added after the beans are tender.) Add the eggs (for *hamin*) and more water if necessary. Tightly cover, place on a *blech* (a thin sheet of metal placed over the stove top) over low heat or in a 225-degree oven, and cook overnight (see Hint).

Hints: Cholent and *hamin* can be cooked on the stove for 1 hour as in step 3, then transferred to a Crock-Pot set on low to cook overnight.

Kishke or various dumplings are often cooked on top of the *cholent*, then cut into slices and served as a side dish. When the kishke mixture is cooked without the casing or an aluminum foil covering, it is commonly called *cholent kugel*. If using an unwrapped dough, bring the water to a boil before placing it in the pot.

Dafina

Moroccan Sabbath Stew

6 TO 8 SERVINGS

When the Sephardim arrived in northwest Africa following the expulsion, they merged their dishes with the native cuisine, exemplified by North African Sabbath stews known by various names in different parts of the country: *dafina/adafina* (Arabic for "covered"), *skhina* (from an Arabic word meaning "hot"), and *frackh* (Arabic for "happiness"). These stews reflect popular local seasoning combinations—cumin, cinnamon, paprika, and saffron—while dates or honey impart an interesting depth of flavor. Some versions add sweet potatoes, others a spoonful of minced red chili. Algerian *dafina* is usually accompanied with a *bobinet* (steamed beef sausage) or *megnina* (steamed beef and egg hash), while Moroccan stews usually contain a calf's foot, a whole tongue, or a *kouclas* (a dumpling similar to rudimentary Ashkenazic kugels). In the Sephardic tradition, all of these stews contain *huevos haminados* (brown eggs; see page 382). Moroccans also make a Sabbath stew from wheat berries and red chilies called *orissa*. The following is a basic Moroccan *dafina*.

8 ounces (about 1¼ cups) dried chickpeas

3 tablespoons vegetable oil

2 medium yellow onions, chopped (about 1 cup)

4 whole cloves garlic

1 pound beef or veal marrow bones

3 pounds beef brisket, short ribs, or chuck roast, cut into 4 pieces

12 to 16 medium potatoes (4 to 5 pounds), peeled, or ½ cup bulgur

5 to 6 pitted dates or 3 tablespoons honey

1 tablespoon paprika

1 teaspoon ground cumin

½ teaspoon ground cinnamon

¼ teaspoon ground turmeric or 6 saffron threads, crumbled

About 2 teaspoons salt

Ground black pepper to taste

1 recipe kouclas *(dumplings; see page 261)*

6 to 8 large eggs, in shell

1. Soak the chickpeas in water overnight. Drain.
2. Heat the oil in a 6- to 8-quart pot over medium heat. Add the onions and sauté until soft and translucent, 5 to 10 minutes.
3. Add, without mixing, the chickpeas, garlic, bones, meat, potatoes or bulgur, dates or honey, paprika, cumin, cinnamon, turmeric or saffron, salt, and pepper. Place the *kouclas* in the center of the *dafina* and arrange the eggs around it. Add enough water to cover.
4. Bring to a boil, cover, reduce the heat to medium-low, and simmer, occasionally skimming the foam, for 1 hour.
5. Tightly cover the pot, place on a *blech* (a thin sheet of metal placed over the stove top) over low heat or in a 225-degree oven, and cook overnight. Or transfer to a slow crock-type cooker set on low to cook overnight.
6. *Dafina* is traditionally separated into different dishes before serving: the chickpeas and cooking liquid in one bowl, the eggs in a second, the potatoes in a third, the meat in a fourth, and the dumpling in a fifth.

Veal

*Feasting on lambs from the flock, and on
calves from the stall.*
                 —AMOS 6:4

Today, veal, the meat of a calf less than three months old, is an expensive cut of meat. In Europe, however, it once cost much less than beef, since less feed and time is required to raise a calf than a cow. Veal breast, one of the most economical cuts of veal, is a festival favorite in Ashkenazic communities and a popular main course at many Seders and on Sukkoth. With a less pronounced flavor than beef, veal lends itself to a large variety of flavorful stuffings and sauces. Look for pinkish gray, fine-grained meat with soft fat.

SYMBOLIC FOODS

On Rosh Hashanah, the performance of symbolic acts is of special value in reflecting on the past and pondering the future. The Talmud (Keritot 6:A) states, "Since symbols are meaningful, everyone should eat the following on the New Year: gourds, black-eyed peas, leeks, beets, and dates." Each of these five foods was specified because of a similarity between its name and another word, thereby signifying a wish for the coming year. The Hebrew word for "gourd" (*kraa*) is similar to *yikaru* ("to be called out"), reflecting that our good deeds be called out at the time of judgment. The Aramaic word for "black-eyed peas" is *rubiya,* which also means "abundance" and "increase." The Hebrew word for "leek" (*karti*) is similar to *yikartu* ("to be cut off"), signifying that the Jews' enemies should be cut off. The word for "beet greens" (*selek*) is reminiscent of the prayer *she'yistalqu oyevainu* ("to remove our enemies"). Similarly, the Hebrew word for "date" (*tamar*) sounds like *yitamu* ("to be removed").

Lubiya M'sallat

SYRIAN BLACK-EYED PEAS AND VEAL
6 TO 8 SERVINGS

Veal (except for the sweetbread and brains) is generally ignored by Sephardim, with the exception of Syrians, who commonly serve it for the Sabbath and festivals. The Aramaic name for black-eyed peas, *rubiya* or *lubiya*, sounds similar to the Hebrew word for "many," and, therefore, dishes like this one are traditional Syrian Rosh Hashanah fare, representing fertility and success. Fava beans, green peas, and chickpeas are commonly substituted for the black-eyed peas, and a popular version, called *biza jurah*, is made with green peas and rice.

3 tablespoons vegetable oil
2 cloves garlic, minced
2 pounds boneless veal shoulder, cubed
2 cups water
3 pounds (4 cups) shelled fresh or 20 ounces frozen black-eyed peas
1 teaspoon ground allspice
½ teaspoon ground cinnamon or dried thyme
About 1 teaspoon salt
Ground black pepper to taste

1. Heat the oil in a large saucepan over medium heat. Add the garlic and sauté until lightly colored but not burned, about 2 minutes.
2. Add the veal and water. Bring to a boil, cover the pan, reduce the heat to low, and simmer for 30 minutes.
3. Add the black-eyed peas, allspice, cinnamon or thyme, salt, and pepper. Cover and simmer over low heat, adding more water if necessary, until the meat and beans are tender and most of the liquid is absorbed, about 1 hour. Or bake in a 350-degree oven, adding more water if necessary, for 2 to 3 hours. Serve with rice.

Gefullte Kalbbrust

ASHKENAZIC STUFFED VEAL BREAST

❧ 6 TO 8 SERVINGS ❧

Only the smaller seven ribs of the veal breast have sufficient meat to make a pocket for the stuffing, so the bones after the seventh rib are sometimes removed. It is easiest to have your butcher make a pocket in your veal breast. To cut a pocket yourself, place the veal, meat side up, on a flat surface. With a sharp, thin knife, cut a slit along the widest side of the breast, as close to the ribs as possible.

1 (4- to 7-pound) veal breast, cut with a pocket and the bones between the ribs cracked

Salt to taste

Ground black pepper to taste

1 recipe matza stuffing (see chicken stuffings, page 91), 1 recipe vegetable-challah stuffing (see chicken stuffings, page 92), or 1 recipe veal stuffing (see opposite page)

Vegetable or olive oil for brushing

4 medium carrots, cut into 1-inch pieces

4 stalks celery, cut into 1-inch pieces

3 large potatoes (about 1½ pounds), cut into chunks

1. Preheat the oven to 400 degrees.

2. Wash the veal and pat dry. Sprinkle the outside of the veal and inside the pocket with salt and pepper. Loosely fill the pocket with the stuffing and sew up or secure with skewers. Brush the veal with the oil.

3. Spread the vegetables in the bottom of a shallow roasting pan and place the veal on top. Or place the veal on a rack in the pan. Roast for 30 minutes.

4. Reduce the heat to 325 degrees and continue cooking until the meat is fork-tender and a meat thermometer registers 175 degrees in the thickest portion, about 2 hours, or 25 to 30 minutes per pound.

5. Let the meat stand at least 15 minutes before carving. Serve warm or at room temperature.

VARIATION

Braised Veal Breast: After roasting for 30 minutes, add 1 cup dry white wine or water, cover, and cook until tender.

Cima

ITALIAN VEAL BREAST STUFFING

❧ ABOUT 4 CUPS ☙

1½ pounds finely ground veal
   or chicken
1 cup chopped cooked spinach
1 cup cooked green peas or fava
   beans
2 large eggs, lightly beaten
2 tablespoons pine nuts or
   chopped pistachio nuts
2 tablespoons brandy or cognac
About 1 teaspoon salt
1 teaspoon chopped fresh thyme
   or ¼ teaspoon dried
1 teaspoon chopped fresh
   marjoram or ¼ teaspoon
   dried
½ teaspoon ground black pepper

Combine all of the ingredients.

Syrian Veal Breast Stuffing

❧ ABOUT 4 CUPS ☙

½ cup rice
1 pound ground beef
1 teaspoon ground allspice
1 teaspoon ground cinnamon
Salt to taste
Ground black pepper to taste
1 cup cooked green peas or
   fava beans

Soak the rice in hot water to cover for 15 minutes and drain. Add all of the remaining ingredients.

Lamb

Sheep flourish in the dry climate and mountainous terrain of the Middle East and the Mediterranean region and serve as the main source of meat (as well as provide milk, wool, and leather) in those areas. Sheep hold a special place in Jewish life and lore. Indeed, the Bible often uses them as a symbol for Israel and refers to both God and the leaders of Israel as shepherds. A host of Biblical figures—including all three patriarchs as well as Moses and King David—were shepherds. *Rachel,* the Hebrew word for "ewe," provided the name of one of the matriarchs. Sheep, not surprisingly, play an important role in Jewish ritual. Sounding the *shofar* (ram's-horn trumpet) serves as the central Rosh Hashanah rite. As an element in the Exodus story, lamb plays an important role in Passover festivities and is a traditional main course at many Sephardic Passover Seders. Since sheep do not fare well in the northern part of Europe, they are a rarity among Ashkenazim, who favor beef.

Lamb refers to any sheep under one year of age; older animals are called mutton. The younger the animal, the more tender the meat and delicate the flavor. When choosing lamb, look for meat that is a lighter red than beef, with a bright pink color, a fine-grained texture, bright white fat, and soft pinkish bones. A darker color indicates a more mature animal.

CORIANDER

And the house of Israel called its name manna; and it was like coriander seeds, white; and its taste was like wafers with honey.

—EXODUS 16:31

Coriander—also called Chinese parsley and cilantro—is a native of the Levant and one of the most ancient spices. It was one of the most important of all seasonings in ancient Israel, with the leaves, seeds, and roots each contributing a different flavor. The dried yellow-brown coriander seeds have a peppery-lemony flavor quite different from the slightly musty pepper flavor of fresh coriander leaves. Do not substitute coriander seeds for fresh coriander leaves. The seeds are sometimes toasted, particularly in Indian cooking, to bring out the flavor. Coriander seeds are used in Indian curries, Middle Eastern meatballs and stews, Moroccan roast lamb, German sausages, pickles, and a variety of baked goods.

Yakhnat

PERSIAN LAMB STEW
6 TO 8 SERVINGS

Lamb, specifically the fat-tailed sheep, is the predominate meat in Persian cooking. Meat is rarely cooked in large pieces; rather, it is cut into chunks. Typical of Persian cuisine, this dish uses less spices than stews of other Middle Eastern countries. Onions are a fundamental seasoning in this cuisine, while garlic is generally ignored.

¼ cup vegetable oil

3 pounds boneless lamb or beef shoulder, cubed

4 medium yellow onions, sliced

4 cups (2 pounds) peeled, seeded, and chopped tomatoes

½ cup chopped fresh coriander or parsley

About 1½ teaspoons salt

Ground black pepper to taste

1. Heat the oil in a large pot over medium heat. Add the meat and onions and sauté until the meat is browned on all sides, 5 to 10 minutes per side.

2. Cover and cook over medium heat, stirring frequently, for 30 minutes.

3. Add the tomatoes, coriander or parsley, salt, and pepper. Cover and simmer over low heat, adding a little water if necessary, until the meat is tender and the sauce is thick, about 30 minutes. Serve with rice.

VARIATIONS

Yakhnat Bamia (Persian Lamb and Okra Stew): **Add** 1½ pounds trimmed (do not cut the pods) okra with the tomatoes.

Yakhnat Hummus (Persian Lamb and Chickpea Stew): **Add** 4 cups cooked chickpeas with the tomatoes.

Yakhnat Lubya (Persian Lamb and Bean Stew): **Add** 4 cups lima or green beans with the tomatoes.

Masbahat Darveesh (Persian Lamb and Vegetable Stew): **Add** 1 eggplant cut into 2-inch cubes, 3 peeled and cubed medium potatoes, and 2 to 3 seeded and cubed medium green bell peppers with the tomatoes.

Osh Palov

BUKHARAN LAMB AND FRUIT PILAF

6 TO 8 SERVINGS

This Uzbek adaptation of the Persian *polo* is the region's favorite dish, served at all special occasions as well as simple family gatherings. The best *palov* makers, almost always men, are revered throughout the region. In the Uzbek manner, the rice is steamed on top of a stew called a *zirvak*. *Palov* is customarily cooked in a well-seasoned oval cast-iron pot called a *kazan*, but any oval, heavy-bottomed pot can be substituted. *Dezira*, a pinkish-tinged medium-grained variety, is the preferred rice. To make this dish, Uzbeks always use the meat and fat from a fat-tailed sheep, the fresher the better. The flavor is varied by adjusting the amount of spices (primarily cumin), meat, and vegetables in the *zirvak* (stew) or by mixing in assorted additions. Carrots and onions form the basis of all *zirvaks*. Adding apple, quince, and raisins is a popular Jewish variation.

2 cups medium-grain or long-grain rice

¼ cup vegetable oil

2 pounds boneless lamb shoulder, cut into 1-inch cubes

1 pound carrots, cut julienne style

3 large yellow onions, coarsely chopped (about 2½ cups)

2 teaspoons cumin seeds

½ teaspoon ground cinnamon

¼ teaspoon ground turmeric

1 large tart apple, peeled, cored, and diced

1 quince, peeled, cored, and diced

½ cup cooked chickpeas

½ cup raisins

1 head garlic, separated but the cloves left whole

Salt to taste

1. Soak the rice in water to cover for 30 minutes. Drain and set aside.

2. Heat the oil in a large, heavy-bottomed, preferably oval pot over medium heat. Add the lamb and brown on all sides, about 10 minutes. Remove the lamb.

3. Add the carrots and onions and sauté until softened, about 10 minutes. Stir in the cumin seeds, cinnamon, and turmeric.

4. Return the lamb to the pot. Stir in the apple, quince, chickpeas, raisins, garlic, salt, and pepper and ½ cup water. Cover, reduce the heat to low, and simmer, shaking the pan occasionally, until the meat is nearly tender, about 40 minutes.

5. Using the back of a spoon, press down on the meat mixture to flatten as much as possible. Sprinkle the rice over the top, then drizzle with the boiling water or broth. Press down on the rice without stirring it into the meat. Cover the pot and simmer for 15 minutes.

6. Using the handle of a wooden spoon, poke about 7 holes into the stew reaching to the bottom of the pan. Do not stir.

7. Cover the pan with a towel or several paper towels,

Ground black pepper to taste
½ cup water
3½ cups boiling water or
  chicken broth

return the lid, and simmer over low heat until the rice is tender and the liquid is absorbed, about 20 minutes. Remove from the heat and let stand for 10 minutes.

8. Transfer the rice to a serving platter, then spoon the meat mixture over the top. Serve accompanied with flat bread, Uzbek salads, and hot green tea.

Below: **Bukharan Jewish wedding.** *Following the wedding ceremony, guests are treated to an elaborate meal provided by the groom's parents. Festive events such as weddings are always accompanied by the playing of music and singing. So noted were Bukharan Jews for their musical abilities that Muslims frequently requested Jews to perform at their festivities as well.*

Codrero al Horno

SEPHARDIC ROASTED LAMB SHOULDER
6 TO 8 SERVINGS

A whole shoulder of lamb weighs 4 to 6 pounds; a boned shoulder weighs about 30 percent less, 3 to 4 pounds. Since bone conducts heat, the cooking time for boned lamb is actually longer. This dish is a Passover and Rosh Hashanah favorite in many Sephardic households, corresponding to the time when the largest supply of lamb is available.

1 (4- to 6-pound) shoulder of lamb, bone in
4 to 8 cloves garlic, slivered
About 3 tablespoons olive or vegetable oil
Salt to taste
Ground black pepper to taste

1. Preheat the oven to 325 degrees.
2. Cut slits in the surface of the lamb and insert a garlic sliver into each slit. Rub with the oil, salt, and pepper.
3. Place in a shallow roasting pan. Roast, basting occasionally, until the exterior is browned and the interior is slightly pink, about 15 minutes per pound or until a meat thermometer registers 145 degrees for rare, 1 to 1¼ hours; or 160 degrees for medium, 1¼ to 1½ hours. Let the roast stand 10 minutes before carving.

VARIATIONS

Greek Roast Lamb with Lemon-Egg Crust: Blend together 12 lightly beaten eggs, ½ to ¾ cup lemon juice, and salt and pepper to taste. Pour over the roasted lamb and place the lamb under the broiler. Broil until lightly browned but not rubbery, about 10 minutes.

Meshwi/Mischui (Moroccan Roast Lamb): With a mortar and pestle, crush together ½ cup chopped fresh parsley, 2 teaspoons ground cumin or 1 tablespoon cumin seeds, 2 to 3 teaspoons salt, 2 large cloves garlic, ½ teaspoon seeded and minced red chili or a dash of cayenne pepper, and, if desired, ½ teaspoon crumbled saffron threads. Rub over the lamb, drizzle with 1 cup (2 sticks) melted margarine, and roast as above, basting frequently. (*Note: Meshwi* is usually prepared from a whole lamb in a brick or mud oven, but this is impractical for most home kitchens.)

Klops

EASTERN EUROPEAN SWEET-AND-SOUR MEATBALLS

 ABOUT 18 MEDIUM MEATBALLS; 3 TO 4 SERVINGS

MEATBALLS

1 pound ground beef

1 small yellow onion, minced
(about ¼ cup)

¼ cup water

¼ cup matza meal or bread
crumbs

1 large egg, lightly beaten

About 1 teaspoon salt

Ground black pepper to taste

SAUCE

½ cup sugar

2 cups boiling water

1 cup (8 ounces) peeled, seeded,
and chopped tomatoes

1 medium onion, chopped
(about ½ cup)

1 teaspoon sour salt or 3 to 4
tablespoons lemon juice

About ½ teaspoon salt

Ground black pepper to taste

1. To make the meatballs: Combine the meat, onion, water, matza meal or bread crumbs, egg, salt, and pepper. Moisten your hands with water (to prevent sticking) and shape the meat mixture into 1-inch balls.

2. To make the sauce: Melt the sugar in a large saucepan over low heat until light brown. Gradually stir in the water. Add the remaining sauce ingredients and simmer for 5 minutes.

3. Add the meatballs, cover, and simmer over low heat, or transfer to a casserole and bake in a 300-degree oven, for 1½ hours.

Note: Sour salt is another name for citric acid crystals. They are used in some northern countries, where citrus fruits are rare, as a substitute for lemon.

Keftes de Carne

SEPHARDIC MEAT PATTIES
ABOUT 12 PATTIES

Grinding is an ancient way of tenderizing tougher cuts of meat. *Kufteh,* the Persian word for "pounded," refers to the original method of preparing ground beef, pounding it in a mortar and pestle until the texture is nearly smooth. Variations of the word *kufteh* referring to patties and meatballs can be found in most Middle Eastern cuisines, including *kefte* in western Asia, *kofte* in Turkey, *keftede* or *keftike* in Greece, *kioftes* in the Balkans, *koftas* in India, and *kifte* in Morocco. Most Middle Eastern cooks prefer ground meat with a smooth texture, in contrast to European-style ground meat, which is coarser. To achieve the desired texture, grind the meat well in a meat grinder, then knead it by hand for several minutes or process it in a food processor.

Kefte mi'leeye (Arabic for "fried patties") can be made from ground meat, poultry, fish, or vegetables. Some cooks stuff the patties with cooked rice. After browning, these patties are often simmered in a sauce and served as an appetizer, a side dish, or a main course.

1 pound ground lamb or beef or any combination

1 large egg, lightly beaten

1 medium yellow onion, chopped (about ½ cup)

About ¼ cup matza meal or bread crumbs

¼ cup chopped fresh parsley

½ to 1 teaspoon ground cumin

About 1 teaspoon salt

About ½ teaspoon ground black pepper

1 tablespoon chopped fresh dill (optional)

Olive or vegetable oil for frying

1. Combine the meat, egg, onion, matza meal or bread crumbs, parsley, cumin, salt, pepper, and, if desired, dill.

2. Shape the meat mixture into 2- to 3-inch-long, 1-inch-wide, and ½-inch-thick patties. (The patties can be prepared ahead and stored in the refrigerator overnight.)

3. Heat about ¼ inch oil in a heavy skillet over medium heat.

4. If desired, dredge the patties in 1 cup matza meal or flour, then dip in a lightly beaten egg. In batches, fry the patties until browned on both sides, 4 to 5 minutes per side. Drain on a wire rack. (The *keftes* can be prepared ahead, refrigerated or frozen, and reheated in a 350-degree oven for about 20 minutes.)

5. Serve the *keftes* as is or simmer in 1 cup chicken broth or a sauce (see opposite page) for 10 to 20 minutes. Serve accompanied with lemon wedges.

VARIATIONS

Carnatzlach (Romanian Meat Patties): Omit the cumin and dill and add 3 to 4 crushed cloves garlic and a dash of ground cloves. (*Note:* Smaller, thumb-shaped patties are called *mitite,* "miniature." Both of these garlicky dishes, derived from the *kefte,* reflect the Middle Eastern influence on Romania during a protracted Ottoman rule.)

Keftes de Patata y Carne (Sephardic Potato and Meat Patties): Reduce the amount of meat to ½ pound, add 2 cups mashed potatoes, and omit the cumin.

Keftes de Espinaca y Carne (Sephardic Spinach and Meat Patties): Reduce the amount of meat to ½ pound, add 1 pound cooked and chopped fresh or 10 ounces frozen spinach, and substitute ⅛ teaspoon grated nutmeg for the cumin. (*Note:* This is a traditional Rosh Hashanah dish.)

Kefte Lemon Sauce

1½ cups chicken broth or water
Juice of 1 lemon
Salt to taste
Ground black pepper to taste

After frying the *keftes,* pour off the excess oil from the skillet. Add the broth or water, lemon juice, salt, and pepper. Return the *keftes* to the skillet and simmer for 10 minutes.

Kefte Tomato Sauce

2 tablespoons olive oil
1 small yellow onion, finely chopped (about ¼ cup)
1 to 2 cloves garlic, minced
4 cups (2 pounds) peeled, seeded, and chopped tomatoes
Pinch of sugar
½ cup chopped fresh parsley
⅓ cup water
1 tablespoon lemon juice
Salt to taste
Ground black pepper to taste

1. Heat the oil in a medium saucepan over medium heat. Add the onion and garlic and sauté until soft, 5 to 10 minutes.

2. Add the tomatoes and sugar and cook, mashing the tomatoes, until a sauce forms, about 15 minutes.

3. Stir in the parsley, water, lemon juice, salt, and pepper. Add the fried *keftes* and simmer for 10 to 20 minutes.

VARIATION

Increase the amount of water to ¾ cup and substitute 1½ cups tomato juice for the tomatoes.

Koofta Kari

CALCUTTA CURRIED MEATBALLS

ABOUT 18 MEDIUM MEATBALLS; 3 TO 4 SERVINGS

Meatballs originated in the Near East and were spread by the Persians throughout central Asia. In many Jewish communities, meatballs—called *kopetas* or *keftes* in the Middle East, *albondigas* in Ladino, *klops* in Yiddish, *ghondi* in Persian, and *boulettes*, reflecting a French influence, in northwest Africa—became a popular Friday night and festival dish. Local seasonings produced interesting variations, including dill and mint in Greece, allspice in Syria, cumin in Morocco, mint in Tunisia, paprika and marjoram in Hungary, and a combination of mint, allspice, and hot paprika in Georgia. This recipe reflects the synthesis of Middle Eastern dishes with Indian seasonings.

MEATBALLS

1 pound ground beef, veal, or chicken

2 tablespoons bread crumbs or matza meal

1. To make the meatballs: Combine the meat, bread crumbs or matza meal, onion, egg, fresh coriander, ground coriander, cumin, turmeric, salt, and pepper.

2. Moisten your hands with water (to prevent sticking) and shape the meat mixture into 1½-inch balls.

1 medium yellow onion, finely
   chopped (about ½ cup)
1 large egg, lightly beaten
2 tablespoons chopped fresh
   coriander
2 teaspoons ground coriander
1½ teaspoons ground cumin
½ teaspoon ground turmeric
About ½ teaspoon salt
Ground black pepper to taste
About ¼ cup vegetable oil

SAUCE
2 medium yellow onions,
   chopped (about 1 cup)
1 cup water
2 teaspoons ground cinnamon
2 teaspoons ground coriander
2 teaspoons ground cumin
1 to 2 teaspoons chili powder
¼ teaspoon ground turmeric
2 tablespoons lemon juice or
   1 tablespoon temerhindi
   (tamarind sauce; see
   page 36)

3. Heat the oil in a large saucepan or Dutch oven over medium-high heat. In several batches, brown the meatballs on all sides, about 10 minutes per batch. Remove the meatballs.

4. To make the sauce: Add the onions to the pot and sauté until soft and translucent, 5 to 10 minutes. Add the water, cinnamon, ground coriander, cumin, chili powder, turmeric, and lemon juice or *temerhindi* and bring to a boil.

5. Return the meatballs to the pot, cover, reduce the heat to low, and simmer until cooked through, about 40 minutes. Serve with rice or pita (see page 267) or other flat bread.

Opposite: **Bene Israel family of Bombay.** *The Bene Israel, the oldest and largest Indian Jewish community, were separated from the main body of Judaism at least two thousand years ago. Although influenced by their Hindu neighbors, the Bene Israel maintained their Jewish identity and adhered to many Jewish rituals.*

MINT

Mint, an aromatic herb that may be indigenous to Israel, has been a part of Jewish cooking since biblical times. There are a number of mint varieties, of which spearmint is the most common in the kitchen. Apple mint and pineapple mint are also treasured in cooking, while peppermint is preferred for mint liqueurs. Mint, available fresh and dried, can best be described as refreshing. Although in the West mint is generally associated with lamb, in the Middle East it is added to ground meat, stews, vegetables, salads, sauces, and beverages.

Rollos

SEPHARDIC MEAT-FILLED POTATO CROQUETTES
  ABOUT 18 CROQUETTES

These potato-covered croquettes—called *pastelles* in Morocco, *urug batata* in Iraq, and *kobebas* in Egypt—are a popular Sephardic Passover treat adapted from the Middle Eastern *kibbe nebelsia* (stuffed torpedoes).

FILLING

3 tablespoons vegetable oil

1 medium yellow onion, chopped (about ½ cup)

1 pound ground beef or lamb

2 chopped hard-boiled eggs or 1 tablespoon pine nuts

3 tablespoons chopped fresh parsley

About ¾ teaspoon salt

Ground black pepper to taste

Vegetable oil for deep-frying

DOUGH

4 medium potatoes (about 1½ pounds)

¼ cup matza meal or ½ cup all-purpose flour

1 large egg, lightly beaten

About ¾ teaspoon salt

1. To make the filling: Heat the oil in a large skillet over medium-high heat. Add the onion and sauté until soft and translucent, 5 to 10 minutes. Add the meat and sauté until it loses its red color, about 5 minutes. Remove from the heat and stir in the eggs or pine nuts, parsley, salt, and pepper.

2. To make the dough: Place the unpeeled potatoes in a large pot, add water to cover, and boil until fork-tender, about 25 minutes. While still warm, peel and mash. (You should have about 2½ cups.) Combine with the remaining dough ingredients.

3. To assemble: Moisten your hands with water (to prevent sticking) and form the dough into 1½-inch balls. Poke a finger into the middle of each ball to form a hole. Work your finger in the hole while pressing the outside of the ball against your palm, hollowing it out to form a large cavity.

4. Fill the cavity with about 1 tablespoon of the meat mixture, then press the edges of the dough together over the filling, forming an oval or a ball. Or form the dough into balls, flatten into rounds, spoon 1 tablespoon of the meat mixture into the center of each round, and press the dough edges together over the filling. (*Rollos* can be prepared ahead to this point and stored in the refrigerator for up to 1 day.)

5. Heat about 2 inches oil in a heavy skillet over medium heat to 375 degrees.

6. In batches, fry the *rollos* until golden brown on all sides, about 4 minutes per side. Drain on paper towels.

VARIATIONS

VARIATIONS
Pastelles (Moroccan Meat-Filled Potato Croquettes): Omit the hard-boiled eggs and add ¼ teaspoon ground cinnamon.
Urug Batata (Iraqi Meat-Filled Potato Croquettes): Omit the hard-boiled eggs and add ¼ teaspoon ground turmeric.

Kufteh Sabzi

PERSIAN GREEN MEATBALLS

ABOUT 18 MEDIUM MEATBALLS; 3 TO 4 SERVINGS

Persians, who may have invented meatballs, make a large variety of them, which they add to most soups and stews and many rice dishes. Typical of Persian cooking, fresh herbs are used in abundance.

3 cups water
¼ cup yellow split peas
¼ cup rice
1 pound ground beef or lamb or any combination
2 cups chopped fresh parsley
1 cup chopped scallions
1 large egg, lightly beaten
About 1 teaspoon salt
¼ teaspoon ground turmeric
Ground black pepper to taste
About ¼ cup vegetable oil
2 cups tomato sauce
2 tablespoons lemon juice

1. Bring the water to a boil. Add the split peas and rice and cook until the peas and rice are tender, about 30 minutes. Drain.

2. Combine the split pea mixture, meat, parsley, scallions, egg, salt, turmeric, and pepper. Moisten your hands in water (to prevent sticking) and shape the meat mixture into 1½-inch balls.

3. Heat the oil in a large saucepan or Dutch oven over medium-high heat. In several batches, brown the meatballs on all sides, about 10 minutes per batch. Remove the meatballs.

4. Add the tomato sauce and lemon juice and bring to a boil. Return the meatballs to the pot, reduce the heat to low, and simmer until cooked through, about 40 minutes. Serve with rice or pita (see page 267) or other flat bread and pickles.

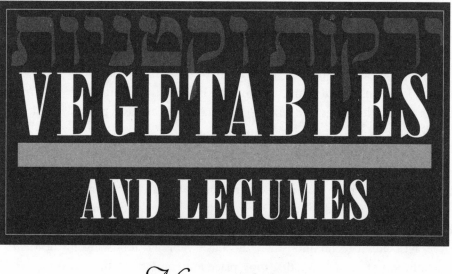

VEGETABLES
AND LEGUMES

Vegetables

And you shall eat the herbs of the field.
—GENESIS 3:18

In biblical times, a wealth of vegetables and herbs, many native to the region, grew wild in the "land of milk and honey." The Bible mentions around one hundred plants, and the Talmud several hundred more, including "the cucumbers and the melons and the leeks and the onions and the garlic" (Numbers 11:5), as well as artichokes, arugula, beets, cabbages, capers, celery, chard, coriander, cumin, fennel, gourds, hyssop, lettuce, mallow, mint, parsley, purslane, radishes, turnips, and watercress. By the Second Temple period, the cultivation of most of these vegetables was widespread. The Talmud, in emphasizing the wealth of Rabbi Yehudah ha-Nasi, the head of the Sanhedrin and compiler of the Mishnah, and reflecting the Israeli farmers' ability to grow these vegetables throughout the year, noted, "His table never lacked lettuce, cucumbers, and radishes in either summer or winter."

The Jews who settled in the lands of the Mediterranean found a mild climate compatible with the produce that they had known in Israel. Muslim Spain, Turkey, and many other parts of the medieval Muslim world possessed an extensive knowledge of

Opposite: **Pushcarts on Manhattan's Lower East Side, 1902.** *Many of the founders of America's major retail stores began their climb up the economic ladder as pushcart vendors.*

143

agriculture and built impressive irrigation systems that produced a wide variety of fruits and vegetables, some available year-round, others dried to last through the winter. Old standbys were joined by new arrivals from the East, including eggplants, cauliflower, spinach, and lemons. As a result, one of the hallmarks of Sephardic cuisine is the large number of vegetable dishes. Vegetables were rarely eaten raw; most were at least partially cooked or marinated in vinegar or lemon juice.

The situation was vastly different for Ashkenazim, for, because of the lack of agricultural and scientific knowledge in medieval Europe, fresh produce was sparse. Vegetables and legumes in the Franco-German communities consisted primarily of cabbage, parsnips, fava beans, split peas, and lentils. Dill was the principal herb and mustard the primary condiment. Although Charlemagne championed the planting of new vegetables and improved agricultural techniques, these advances vanished following his death. It was only with the infusion of knowledge that took place following the Christian conquest of Muslim Spain that agricultural and scientific knowledge improved in Europe and the quality and types of vegetables began to increase.

The people in eastern Europe continued to make do with a few hardy plants, and the diet consisted chiefly of starches. When Ashkenazim prepared vegetables such as carrots, beets, and parsnips, they were nearly always cooked until very soft and usually seasoned with onions, garlic, and salt. Ashkenazic salads, primarily made from radishes, beets, cucumbers, and cabbages, were few.

Verduras Reyenados

SEPHARDIC STUFFED VEGETABLES
13 STUFFED VEGETABLES

Stuffed vegetables—called *dolmeh* in Persian, *dolma* in Turkish, *dolmathes* in Greek, *mahshi* in Arabic, and *memulayim* in Hebrew—originated in the ancient Near East, probably Persia, as a way of using unused leaves: grape leaves—the by-products of vineyards—and the tough outer leaves of cabbages. Stuffing the leaves with meat or grains and simmering them in hot liquid until tender not only stretched limited resources but proved to be delicious. By the third century C.E., this humble dish had risen to the royal tables of the Persian court. The Ottoman Turks shared the Persian love for this dish and spread it throughout their empire, from the Maghreb to the Ukraine.

Although stuffed vegetables have been eaten by Middle Eastern Jews for more than a thousand years and were common in eastern Europe in the fourteenth century, it appears that Sephardim were introduced to this practice only after arriving in the Ottoman Empire. Still, the range of items stuffed by Sephardim includes artichokes, beets, cabbages, carrots, celery, chard stems, eggplants, grape leaves, onions, bell peppers, peppers, potatoes, quinces, radishes, summer squash, tomatoes, and turnips. Europeans, on the other hand, were generally limited in their options, primarily to cabbages, bell peppers, onions, and apples. The types of vegetables in this recipe may be altered according to individual preference and availability (e.g., use only bell peppers, onions, or tomatoes). This recipe is tart according to the Sephardic preference; for a sweet-and-sour sauce, add ¼ to ½ cup sugar or honey.

3 large bell peppers

3 medium yellow onions, peeled

3 large, firm tomatoes

2 medium zucchini or small eggplants (no longer than 8 inches), cut in half crosswise

3 tablespoons olive or vegetable oil

STUFFING

1½ pounds ground beef (or ¾ pound ground beef and ¾ pound ground veal)

½ cup rice or ⅓ cup matza meal or bread crumbs

1 medium yellow onion, chopped (about ½ cup)

1 large egg

¼ cup chopped fresh parsley or mint

About 1 teaspoon salt

¼ teaspoon ground black pepper

2 cups chicken broth, tomato juice, or water

2 to 4 tablespoons lemon juice

1. Slice the tops from the peppers, onions, and tomatoes. Scoop the pulp out of the vegetables, leaving a ¼-inch-thick shell. (A melon baller works well for scooping.) Discard the pepper seeds and vein; chop the onion, tomato, and zucchini or eggplant pulp.

2. Heat the oil in a large pot over medium heat. Add the onion pulp and sauté until soft and translucent, 5 to 10 minutes. Add the remaining chopped pulp and sauté until slightly softened, about 5 minutes.

3. Combine all of the stuffing ingredients and spoon into the vegetable cavities. (Any extra stuffing can be shaped into balls and cooked with the vegetables.) Arrange the stuffed vegetables upright on top of the sautéed vegetables in the pot.

4. Add the broth, tomato juice, or water and lemon juice. Cover and simmer over low heat or transfer to a casserole and bake in a 350-degree oven until tender, about 1 hour.

SUKKOTH

Four days after the fast of Yom Kippur falls the eight-day holiday (seven in Israel) of Sukkoth. This autumn festival historically represents the trek of the Israelites through the wilderness following the Exodus from Egypt. Sukkoth also has a nature connection, representing the final harvest of the agricultural year. In remembrance of the Lord's protection during the forty-year transitional period in the wilderness, a *sukkah* (booth) is constructed outside the home. The family dines and sometimes lives in the *sukkah* throughout the entire holiday, re-creating the experience of their ancestors. Most Sukkoth dishes reflect the harvest and the joyous nature of the holiday, incorporating a bounty of fruits and vegetables. Many of the dishes are prepared in the form of casseroles, which are easy to shuttle outside to the *sukkah*. The most common Sukkoth dishes are filled foods, particularly stuffed vegetables, symbolizing bounty, or mixed vegetable dishes.

Turshi

MIDDLE EASTERN PICKLED VEGETABLES

❧ 4 PINTS ❧

In the Middle East pickled vegetables are a popular appetizer. Use any of the following vegetables. To add a pink color to light-colored vegetables (such as cauliflower and turnips), add 1 fresh peeled and sliced beet.

CHOICE OF VEGETABLES

2 pounds small cucumbers

2 pounds halved or quartered green tomatoes

2 pounds green peppers, seeded and sliced

2 pounds carrots, sliced or cut into cubes

2 pounds celery, cut into cubes

2 pounds turnips, quartered

2 pounds blanched whole okra

1 cauliflower, cut into florets

1 head green cabbage, cut into chunks

PICKLING LIQUID

4 to 5 cloves garlic, halved

1 tablespoon pickling spices or sprinkle of hot red pepper flakes (optional)

4 cups water

½ cup distilled white or cider vinegar

3 tablespoons kosher salt

1. Fill sterilized widemouthed jars with the vegetable of choice and divide the garlic and, if desired, pickling spices or red pepper between the jars.

2. Bring the water to a boil in a large nonreactive saucepan over medium heat. (Do not use iron, copper, or brass.) Add the vinegar and salt and stir with a wooden spoon until the salt dissolves.

3. Add the hot liquid to the jars. Let cool and discard the garlic. Close the jars tightly. For crisp vegetables, refrigerate immediately and let sit at least 24 hours; for softer vegetables, leave in a cool, dark place for 2 days, then refrigerate.

Opposite: **Portuguese Jews in Holland celebrate the Feast of the Tabernacles in the** *sukkah.* Engraving by Bernard Picart, circa 1700. *In 1497, Portugal forcibly converted its Jewish inhabitants and forbade them to leave the country. Those* conversos *fortunate enough to escape reasserted their Jewish identities in less hostile locales such as Holland, France, Germany, Italy, and the Ottoman Empire.*

Guvetch

SEPHARDIC VEGETABLE STEW
6 TO 8 SERVINGS

This Turkish vegetable stew (also spelled *ghivetch* and *yuvetch*), named after the pottery in which it was originally cooked, is popular in areas influenced by the Ottoman Empire. It is a close relative of the better-known Provençal version, ratatouille.

5 tablespoons vegetable or
   olive oil
2 large yellow onions, sliced
1 clove garlic, minced
3 medium carrots, sliced
1½ pounds eggplant, cubed
1 pound green beans
4 small zucchini or other
   summer squash, cut into
   chunks
1 pound trimmed okra or
   sliced mushrooms
6 medium tomatoes, peeled,
   seeded, and chopped
2 medium green bell peppers,
   seeded and sliced
2 medium red bell peppers,
   seeded and sliced
½ cup water
About ½ teaspoon salt
Ground black pepper to taste
Pinch of sugar

1. Preheat the oven to 350 degrees.

2. Heat 3 tablespoons of the oil in a large saucepan over medium heat. Add the onions, garlic, and carrots and sauté until softened, 5 to 10 minutes.

3. Add the eggplant and sauté until slightly softened, about 5 minutes. Add the remaining vegetables in the order listed. Add the water, salt, pepper, and sugar.

4. Spoon into a large casserole and drizzle with the remaining 2 tablespoons oil. Cover and bake until very soft, about 1½ hours. Serve warm or at room temperature.

Inginaras con Limón

SEPHARDIC-STYLE ARTICHOKES

❧   8 SERVINGS   ❧

Thorns and thistles shall it [the ground] bring forth to you.
—GENESIS 3:18

Rashi, the leading Bible and Talmud commentator, explains that in the above quote the thorns and thistles, part of Adam's curse for eating the forbidden fruit, refer to "artichokes and cardoons, [plants] that can be eaten only by preparation." Artichokes are the flowers of thistle plants that grew wild in ancient Israel. They make their appearance in the early spring, thus are common on Sephardic and Italian Passover tables.

In the Balkans, sliced carrots or fava beans are commonly cooked in this dish, while Middle Eastern Jews add cubed veal or *kibbe mi'leeye* (fried stuffed torpedoes).

Juice of 3 lemons
8 large artichokes or 20 ounces
frozen artichoke hearts,
thawed
3 cups water
3 tablespoons olive or vegetable
oil
About 1 teaspoon salt
1 tablespoon chopped fresh
parsley or capers for garnish

1. If using fresh artichokes, add the juice of 1 lemon to a bowl of cold water. Cut the stem off the bottom of each artichoke. Pull off the tough outer leaves. Cut off the top third of the artichoke and trim off all of the dark green areas. Scoop out the fuzzy choke from the center. Leave the artichokes whole or cut into halves or quarters. Place in the lemon water to prevent discoloration. When ready to use, drain the artichokes.

2. Place the artichokes in a large saucepan. Add the water, juice of 2 lemons, oil, and salt. Bring to a boil, cover, reduce the heat to medium-low, and simmer until tender, about 30 minutes. Remove the artichokes with a slotted spoon.

3. Boil the cooking liquid until reduced by one-half. Pour over the artichokes and garnish with the parsley or capers. Serve warm or chilled as an appetizer or a side dish, with a little of the cooking liquid.

VARIATION
Sweet-and-Sour Artichokes: Add 2 to 3 tablespoons sugar or honey to the cooking liquid before reducing.

ARTICHOKES

Size is a matter of preference. The stalks and leaves of young artichokes are edible, but as they age only the fleshy base of the leaves and the heart are tender enough to eat. Choose artichokes with tightly closed inner leaves; spreading leaves are a sign of overmaturation. A bronze color on the outside of early spring artichokes is the result of frost and does not affect the taste. Do not cook artichokes in aluminum or iron pots—the pots will turn gray.

Carciofi alla Giudia

JEWISH-STYLE FRIED ARTICHOKES

6 TO 8 SERVINGS

Although the ancient Romans failed to appreciate the artichoke, typified by Pliny the Elder's statement that "artichokes are the most monstrous productions of the earth," Mediterranean Jews have been eating them for thousands of years. This dish originated among the Jews of Rome—*Giudia* was the name of the Roman ghetto—and is now served throughout Italy.

Juice of 1 lemon
6 to 8 small artichokes
Salt to taste
Ground black pepper to taste
Olive or vegetable oil for
*   deep frying*

1. Add the lemon juice to a bowl of cold water. Cut off about 1 inch from the top of each artichoke. Remove the loose, tough outer leaves around the bottom. Scoop out the choke, leaving the leaves and heart intact. Trim the dark green exterior from the bottom and stem, leaving the stem intact. Place the artichoke in the lemon water to prevent discoloration.

2. Holding each artichoke by the stem, place top side down on a flat surface, and press to loosen the leaves without breaking. Sprinkle with salt and pepper.

3. Heat at least 1½ inches of oil in a saucepan over medium heat. In batches, add the artichokes and fry, turning occasionally, until browned on all sides, about 20 minutes. During frying, occasionally sprinkle the tops of the artichokes with cold water, producing steam that helps to cook the interior.

4. Drain the artichokes on paper towels. Place top side down on a plate and let stand at least 1 hour.

5. Reheat the oil. Holding each artichoke by the stem, dip into the oil, pressing the leaves against the bottom of the pan. Serve warm or at room temperature.

Opposite: **Woman selling greens in an open-air market in the Bukharan quarter of Jerusalem, 1987.** *For millennia the semi-arid land of Central Asia was watered by a series of irrigation canals, yielding a medley of fruits and vegetables of immense proportions.*

ROMAN RISTORANTE

"The Jewish community of Rome is the oldest continuing one in Europe," notes Gennaro Boni of Piperno, a restaurant in the old Roman ghetto dating back to 1856 and owned by the Boni family since 1963. "Since the days of the emperors, while other Romans have come and gone, Jews have lived in Rome."

The first known Jews to visit Italy were members of a delegation sent to Rome by Judah Maccabee in 161 B.C.E. to conduct a treaty between Judea and Rome. Soon, Jews began settling in Rome and other Italian cities, especially in southern Italy and Sicily. Later, Ashkenazim—fleeing the massacres in the wake of the Black Death (1348–49) and the French expulsion (1394)—arrived in northern Italy. By the time of the Italian Renaissance in the fourteenth century, the Jewish population of Italy numbered about fifty thousand. Sephardim fleeing Spain arrived in Italy, while at the same time the Jews of Sicily and Sardinia, which were then under Spanish control, were forced from their homes. Nine years later, Spain acquired the kingdom of Naples, which at the time consisted of all of southern Italy, and expelled its Jews. Thereafter, Jewish life in Italy shifted to the northern and central states.

Before World War II, Italian Jewry (which numbered 47,485 in the 1931 census) was divided among seventy organized communities scattered throughout northern and central Italy. Only 29,000 Italkim survived the Nazis, and most of the small and intermediate-size Jewish communities disappeared. Following the war, refugees from other parts of Europe and North Africa doubled the Italian Jewish community, which today numbers about 50,000, more than half living in Rome.

"Roman Jewish food is simple fare utilizing inexpensive local ingredients," explains Gennaro Boni. A number of integral ingredients of modern Italian cooking were introduced to the country by the Jews. As late as the mid-1880s such current Italian staples as eggplant and fennel were, in the words of the Florentine cookbook writer Pellegrino Artusi (*La Scienza e L'Arte di Mangiar Bene*), "considered the vile food of the Jews." Boni adds, "Today, it is sometimes difficult to delineate between Jewish and Roman food. Although some Italian dishes attach such terms as '*alla Giudia*' and '*all'Ebraica*,' many other Jewish dishes are not so credited."

Since for much of its history Italy was fragmented into an assortment of independent states, it was only natural that differences in cuisine emerged. Boni explains, "In the north, which has generally been wealthier, they use much more meat than in the south. Northern food tends to be more subtly seasoned than the heavily spiced dishes so beloved in the south. Olive oil is the primary cooking fat of the south, while butter is rather common in the north. Pasta in the north generally contains eggs and tends to be fresh and flat [e.g., fettuccini and cannelloni]. In the south, pasta is almost always made strictly from semolina and water and is generally hard [e.g., spaghetti] and tubular [e.g., macaroni]. In the Po Valley of the far north, rice serves as the staple and pasta is used much less frequently. The area of the former Papal States, situated in the center of the country, enjoys the best of both worlds."

Italian Jewish fare bears a closer resemblance to Sephardic cuisine than to Ashkenazic. This is due in part to its Mediterranean origins and in part to the arrival of a sizable contingent of Sephardim. Boni notes, "An ancient method of preserving fish survives in the form of *baccala* [salt cod], used to make a variety of classic Jewish dishes, including *baccala fritto* [deep-fried cod fillets] and *pezzetti* [fish sticks]. From Sephardim, Italkim learned of *pesce fritto* [fried fish], *pesce marinato* [marinated fried fish], and other dishes."

Italian customs also vary from those of the Ashkenazim. For example, Italkim eat rice but refrain from dairy products on Passover. They also remove the sciatic nerve and use the hindquarter of animals. For special occasions, Italkim have adopted breads from both Ashkenazim (e.g., *pane del Sabato* [egg challah]) and Sephardim (e.g., *il bollo* ["sweet bread" similar to *roscas*]). Boni observes, "From the ghettos of Italy, especially Rome, come some of the most authentic of Jewish dishes. Since the laws of kosher restricted the use of meat sauces and cheese, Italian Jewish dishes tend to be more delicate than those of their non-Jewish neighbors. In the words of on old Italian saying, *Vesti da Turco e mangia da Ebreo* [dress like a Turk and eat like a Jew]."

Above: **The Ghetto of Venice.** *Conditions in Venice, the second-largest Jewish community in Italy, were generally better than in most parts of the country. Yet, it was the Venetians who in 1516 established the first ghetto (from* ghèto, *the Italian word for a foundry, next to which the Jewish area was located). Until the arrival of Napoleon, in 1800, Jews in every Italian city remained officially segregated, some living in terribly overcrowded conditions, especially in Rome.*

BEETS

The modern world knows the beet, a native of the Mediterranean region, primarily for its red root. The original vegetable, however, possessed thin white roots and large stalks and leaves, similar to its relative, chard. Early sources refer only to the consumption of the greens. Beet greens, primarily a late winter and spring vegetable, were so highly regarded in ancient Israel as well as Greece and Rome that efforts were made to grow them beyond their season. As a sign of his enormous wealth, legend records that King Solomon enjoyed beet greens throughout the summer. The Talmud made note of the beet green's nutritional and health benefits.

The common garden beetroot was developed in Italy in the sixteenth century and failed to make an impact on most of the culinary world until the eighteenth century. In northern Europe, however, where the beetroot was one of the few vegetables that could be stored throughout the winter, it became a staple of the diet and a common Ashkenazic Passover food. Because of their Aramaic name, *silka* ("to remove," as in enemies), beets are a traditional Rosh Hashanah food among both Sephardim and Ashkenazim. In Russia, Poland, the Baltic states, and Scandinavia, beets are used in a wide variety of dishes, including soups, relishes, preserves, and salads.

Russel Tzikel

RUSSIAN FERMENTED BEETS
ABOUT 8 CUPS OF LIQUID AND 4 CUPS OF BEETS

During the week following Purim throughout eastern Europe, beets were put into large earthenware crocks to ferment. By Passover, the mixture had been transformed into *russel* (the Slavic word for "brine"). The beets were ready to flavor soups, drinks, preserves, horseradish, kugels, and other traditional dishes, while the liquid was used as a vinegar.

5 pounds beets, peeled and cubed

1. Place the beets in a sterilized 1-gallon earthenware or glass crock and add enough cold water to reach 2 inches above the beets. Tie a layer of cheesecloth over the top to keep out any dust. Cover loosely and leave in a cool, dark place to ferment.

2. Every week skim the foam from the surface and stir. Make sure that the beets are always covered with water. If the fermentation process is working properly, each week the cloudy liquid will grow a darker shade of pink and, when ready in about 4 weeks, turn a clear, deep wine red. Store in the refrigerator.

Cuchunduria/Burekehsalat

BEET SALAD
ABOUT 1 QUART; 6 TO 8 SERVINGS

Vinegar is more common in Ashkenazic salads; lemon juice, in Sephardic versions.

7 medium beets
(about 2 pounds)
1 medium red or yellow onion,
thinly sliced

DRESSING
½ cup cider or white vinegar or
lemon juice
1 to 3 teaspoons sugar
About 1 teaspoon salt
Ground black pepper to taste
½ cup vegetable oil
2 tablespoons chopped fresh dill
or parsley for garnish

1. Trim the beets, leaving about 1 inch of the stem intact. Wash but do not scrub the beets. Do not pierce the skins, or the color will bleed.
2. Place the beets in a large saucepan and add water to cover. Bring to a boil, cover, reduce the heat to low, and simmer until tender, 30 to 45 minutes. Drain.
3. When the beets are cool enough to handle, peel them and cut them into ¼-inch-thick slices. (You will have about 4 cups.) Place the beets and onion slices in a large bowl.
4. Combine the vinegar or lemon juice, sugar, salt, and pepper. Whisk in the oil. Drizzle over the beets, cover, and let marinate for at least 3 hours. Garnish with the chopped dill or parsley.
Hint: Choose firm, deep red beetroots up to 2 inches in diameter. Larger beets tend to be woody.

VARIATION
Marinirte Burekeh (Ashkenazic Pickled Beets): Substitute ½ cup water or beet cooking liquid for the oil.

Sarmas de Kol/Holishkes

STUFFED CABBAGE

🙞 16 TO 18 LARGE CABBAGE ROLLS 🙜

Cabbage, one of the oldest cultivated plants, is the most important vegetable among Ashkenazim, who use it in sauerkraut, soups, noodle dishes, pastry fillings, and salads. The original cabbage, a native of Asia Minor, was a loose head of leaves—similar to kale—and very bitter, often requiring several boilings to be palatable. The now-familiar green cabbage, with a firm, mild head, evolved in Germany around the twelfth century.

Stuffed cabbage originated in the Near East as a way of using the tough outer leaves by simmering them in liquid. The result proved eminently tasty and began to spread. In the fourteenth century, the Tartars introduced this dish to the Russians and, about the same time, the Turks shared it with southern Europe. Thus, stuffed cabbage spread throughout eastern and central Europe, where it is known by an assortment of names—many based on the Russian *golubtsi* (little doves) or two Turkish words for "leaves," *yaprakes* and *sarmas*—including *holishkes* and *golabki* in Poland, *holoptsches/holubtsi* and *praakes* in the Ukraine, *yaprakes* and *dolmas de kol* in the Balkans, *sarmali* in Romania, *gefullte kraut* (literally "stuffed cabbage") in Germany, Austria, and Hungary, and *cavoli ripieni* in Italy. As with other well-traveled dishes, stuffed cabbage has many variations: Jews from Hungary, Italy, Romania, and Galicia prefer a savory sauce; Sephardim, a tart sauce made by adding a little lemon juice; and Jews from Poland, a sweet-and-sour sauce. Hungarians add sweet paprika or marjoram to the filling; Syrians, allspice and cinnamon; Persians, yellow split peas, cinnamon, and dill or mint; and Romanians, paprika, savory, and plenty of garlic. Stuffed cabbage, symbolizing abundance, became a traditional Ashkenazic Sukkoth and Simchas Torah dish.

1 large head green cabbage

STUFFING
*1½ pounds ground beef
(or ¾ pound ground beef and
¾ pound ground veal)
⅓ cup rice, bread crumbs, or
matza meal
1 medium yellow onion,
chopped (about ½ cup)*

1. Dip the cabbage into a large pot of boiling water until pliable enough to remove the leaves without breaking. Repeat until all of the leaves are removed.
2. Blanch 16 to 18 large cabbage leaves in the boiling water until supple enough to roll easily, about 2 minutes. Rinse under cold water, drain, and pat dry. Trim the tough center rib of each leaf.
3. Combine all of the stuffing ingredients.
4. Place about ¼ cup of the stuffing in the center of each large cabbage leaf. Fold the stem end over the stuffing, tuck in the sides of the leaf, and roll up.

1 large egg
¼ cup chopped fresh parsley
About 1 teaspoon salt
¼ teaspoon ground black pepper

SAUCE
1½ cups tomato sauce or juice
1 cup water
3 tablespoons vegetable oil
1 bay leaf
About 1½ teaspoons salt
Ground black pepper to taste

5. Shred the extra cabbage leaves and place in the bottom of a deep pot or baking dish. Arrange the cabbage rolls, seam side down, on top.

6. Combine the tomato sauce or juice, water, oil, bay leaf, salt, and pepper and pour over the cabbage rolls.

7. Cover, bring to a boil, reduce the heat to low, and simmer until the cabbage is very tender, at least 1½ hours. Or bake, covered, in a 325-degree oven for 1 hour, then uncover and bake 1 additional hour. Stuffed cabbage freezes well and is delicious reheated.

VARIATIONS

Sweet-and-Sour Sauce: Add ½ cup granulated or brown sugar or honey, ¼ cup lemon juice or vinegar, and, if desired, ½ cup raisins to the sauce.

Tart Tomato Sauce: Add the juice of 1 to 2 lemons with the tomato sauce and serve the cabbage with lemon wedges.

Sabbath Eve table in Eastern Europe. *In the words of the Yiddish writer Ahad Ha-Am, "It is not so much that the Jews have kept the Sabbath, but that the Sabbath has kept the Jews."*

Mehren Tzimmes

ASHKENAZIC GLAZED CARROTS

6 TO 8 SERVINGS

Since carrots grow even in poor soil, they became a staple of eastern Europe. Carrots are an important part of Rosh Hashanah tradition partially because of their name: in Yiddish, *mehren* ("multiply" or "increase") and in Hebrew, *gezer* (tear), indicating that any unfavorable decrees should be torn up. In addition, the carrot's sweetness fits in with the theme of the holiday. And carrots have an additional attribute—when sliced they resemble gold coins. Therefore, Ashkenazic cooks use this auspicious vegetable in any number of holiday dishes including tzimmes, soups, salads, puddings, cakes, jam, and candy.

Mehren tzimmes is a popular Ashkenazic side dish served with chicken and meat. This basic recipe can be enhanced in many ways: Add a pinch of ground ginger or cinnamon, substitute orange or lemon juice for part of the water, or stir in raisins or chopped dates.

3 tablespoons schmaltz (see page 109) or margarine
2 pounds carrots, sliced
1 cup chicken broth or water
½ cup honey or brown sugar (or ¼ cup each)
About 1 teaspoon salt
Chopped fresh parsley for garnish

1. Heat the schmaltz or margarine in a medium saucepan over medium heat. Add the carrots and sauté until lightly colored, about 5 minutes.

2. Add the broth or water, honey or brown sugar, and salt. Bring to a boil, cover, reduce the heat to low, and simmer until the carrots are tender but not mushy, about 25 minutes.

3. Uncover, increase the heat to medium, and cook, shaking the pan frequently, until most of the liquid is evaporated and the carrots are glazed, about 5 minutes. Garnish with the parsley. Tzimmes can be prepared ahead, stored in the refrigerator for up to 2 days, and reheated before serving.

Gadjar Kari

INDIAN CARROT CURRY

❧ 4 TO 5 SERVINGS ❧

This is a traditional Indian Rosh Hashanah dish.

¼ cup (½ stick) margarine or
vegetable oil
1 tablespoon cumin seeds
1½ teaspoons yellow mustard
seeds
1½ teaspoons ground turmeric
1 teaspoon ground cardamom
1 teaspoon curry powder
¼ teaspoon ground cloves
¼ teaspoon cayenne
1 pound carrots, sliced or cut
into chunks
1 medium banana, peeled and
sliced
¼ cup golden raisins
1 cup water
About 1 teaspoon salt
Ground black pepper to taste
Chopped fresh parsley or
coriander for garnish

1. Heat the margarine or oil in a large nonreactive pan (do not use iron, copper, or brass) over medium heat. Add the cumin seeds, mustard seeds, turmeric, cardamom, curry powder, cloves, and cayenne and sauté until fragrant, about 30 seconds.

2. Add the carrots and sauté until lightly colored, 3 to 5 minutes. Stir in the banana and raisins.

3. Add the water, salt, and pepper. Bring to a boil, cover, reduce the heat to low, and simmer until the carrots are tender but not mushy, about 20 minutes.

4. Uncover, increase the heat to medium, and cook, shaking the pan frequently, until most of the liquid is evaporated and the carrots and raisins are glazed, 5 to 10 minutes. Garnish with the parsley or coriander.

CARROTS

The carrot, a member of the same family as parsnips and parsley, is a native of central Asia. In Asia, carrots grow in a variety of colors—yellow, red, orange, and the two original colors, purple and white. The now-common orange variety probably emerged in Holland during the late Middle Ages.

Choose firm, well-formed roots. Avoid carrots that are split, blemished, or show signs of rotting at either end. The greens draw moisture from the roots and should be removed for storage.

Culupidia Frita

SEPHARDIC FRIED CAULIFLOWER

❧ 4 TO 6 SERVINGS ☙

Cauliflower, a name derived from the Italian *caulis floris* (cabbage flower), is a relative of cabbage. It was developed relatively late in history, appearing first in Asia Minor in the 1300s and soon finding its way to Muslim Spain. It was introduced to the rest of Europe only in the sixteenth century. During the following two hundred years, cauliflower was the rage of western Europe, favored on the tables of royalty and incorporated into a wide array of dishes. Its popularity has since waned except in such areas as India and the Mediterranean.

Sephardim serve cauliflower (*culupidia*) in many ways, including drizzled with a little olive oil and lemon juice, topped with *tarator bi tahina* (sesame seed sauce); pickled; stewed with other vegetables; and fried. It is also enjoyed with potatoes in a cheese sauce; in beef stews; in *fritadas* (omelets); in *keftes* (patties); and in tomato sauce. Fried cauliflower dipped in matza meal is a favorite Sephardic Passover dish.

1 medium head cauliflower, cut into florets
Olive or vegetable oil for frying
2 large eggs, lightly beaten
About 1½ cups all-purpose flour or matza meal

1. Place the cauliflower in a pot of lightly salted boiling water, cover, reduce the heat to low, and simmer until tender, about 15 minutes. Do not overcook or the cauliflower will be foul-smelling and mushy. Rinse under cold water and drain.
2. Heat about ½ inch oil in a large skillet over medium heat.
3. Dip the florets into the eggs, then into the flour or matza meal. In batches, fry the florets until golden brown on all sides, about 2 minutes. Remove with a slotted spoon and drain on paper towels. Serve warm.

VARIATION
Culupidia Frita con Limón (Sephardic Fried Cauliflower with Lemon): Place the fried cauliflower in a shallow pan, add ¼ cup lemon juice, and simmer until the liquid evaporates,

Apio

SEPHARDIC SWEET-AND-SOUR CELERY

 6 TO 8 SERVINGS

Originally *apio* was made from either celery or celeriac, but in recent times the more widely available celery has become the primary vegetable. In Turkey and parts of Greece, this dish, which uses the stalks, is served on the first night of Passover; the leaves are saved for the Seder plate.

2 cups water
Juice of 2 to 3 lemons
¼ cup vegetable or olive oil
1 to 2 tablespoons sugar
About 1 teaspoon salt
2 bunches celery, leaves removed
*   and cut into 1½-inch-long*
*   pieces, or 5 to 6 medium*
*   celeriac, peeled and cut into*
*   ¼-inch-thick slices*

1. In a large saucepan over high heat, bring the water, lemon juice, oil, sugar, and salt to a boil.
2. Add the celery or celeriac, reduce the heat to low, cover, and simmer until tender, about 20 minutes. Serve warm as a side dish or at room temperature or chilled as an appetizer.

VARIATION

Apio con Safanorias (Sephardic Celery with Carrots): Cut 1 pound thin carrots into 1½-inch-long pieces and cook with the celery. Or cut 1 pound carrots into ¼-inch-thick slices and cook with the celeriac.

CELERY AND CELERIAC

Celery originated in marshy areas along the shore of the eastern Mediterranean, where wild celery can still be found. The Romans were probably the first to cultivate celery, but they generally preferred the sharper flavor of the wild plants. Cultivated celery, which is crisp, sweet, and relatively free of strings, barely resembles its wild ancestor. Most American celery is the Pascal type, a pale green, crisp, and sweet variety. Celery found its way into Jewish ritual as an item on many Seder plates—which seems appropriate, as wild celery was found in Egyptian tombs dating back to the time of the Exodus.

Celeriac, also called celery root, is a variety of celery cultivated for its large knobby root. Although celeriac is sometimes served raw, it is most often cooked. Choose roots of one pound or less, as large roots tend to be woody. The fibrous skin must be removed.

Berenjena Frita

MIDDLE EASTERN FRIED EGGPLANT SLICES

6 TO 8 SERVINGS

Sephardim usually serve plain or marinated fried eggplant slices as part of a meze (appetizer table) or, when accompanied with a tomato sauce, as a side dish.

*2 large eggplants
  (about 1½ pounds each),
  cut crosswise into ¼- to
  ½-inch-thick slices
About 2 tablespoons kosher salt
About ½ cup olive oil*

1. Place the eggplant in a colander, sprinkle with the kosher salt, and let stand for 1 hour. Rinse the eggplant with water and press between several layers of paper towels until it feels firm. (The eggplant can be prepared ahead and stored in the refrigerator for up to 4 hours.)

2. Heat a thin layer of the oil in a large skillet over medium-high heat.

3. In several batches, add the eggplant slices (adding a little more oil with each batch) and fry, turning once, until golden brown and tender but not mushy, 3 to 5 minutes per side. Drain on paper towels. Serve warm or at room temperature.

VARIATIONS

Breaded Fried Eggplant: Before frying, dip the eggplant slices in 2 lightly beaten eggs, then dredge in 1 cup matza meal, cornmeal, or flour.

Badrijani Bazhashi (Georgian Eggplant in Walnut Sauce): Pour 2 to 3 cups *bazha* (walnut sauce; see page 375) over the fried eggplant and chill.

Badrijani Rebani (Georgian Eggplant with Basil): Combine ½ cup chopped fresh basil, ¼ cup chopped fresh parsley, 3 to 4 cloves minced garlic, and ⅓ cup wine vinegar and drizzle over the fried eggplant. Cool to room temperature and refrigerate, turning occasionally, for at least 1 hour or up to 2 days.

Borani Bademjan (Persian Sautéed Eggplant with Yogurt): Combine 2 cups plain yogurt, 2 to 3 cloves crushed garlic, and 1 tablespoon dried mint. Layer with the fried eggplant and chill.

Bruna Brinjal (Indian Fried Eggplant): Combine 1 teaspoon ground coriander and 1 teaspoon ground cumin and sprinkle over the warm eggplant slices.

EGGPLANT

Eggplant, a member of the nightshade family, is actually a large berry. The original eggplant was small, white, and egg-shaped, hence its name. However, since the white variety bruised easily, it was hybridized to create the more familiar purple color. The globe eggplant is the largest variety, with a thick, deep-purple skin and many large seeds. The Italian variety (also called baby and Tuscan) ranges from 2 to 4 inches long with a thinner, less intensely purple skin and smaller seeds. The Japanese variety (also called Oriental and Chinese) is long and slender with a thin, light purple skin.

Eggplant is a native of northern India where it has been cultivated for more than four thousand years. By the fourth century C.E., it had arrived in Persia and quickly became a favorite vegetable. In the thirteenth century, the Arabs introduced it to Spain and a little later to Sicily, where it became an important part of local Jewish cooking. The reception was very different, however, when the eggplant reached the Christian parts of Europe, where it was considered to be poisonous.

Eggplant, one of the most important vegetables in the Sephardic culinary repertoire, is found in casseroles, stews, salads, omelets, and pickles. It is used even as a pastry filling and for confections. It is cooked in a variety of ways: stuffed, fried, grilled, roasted (a method that adds no fat), and stewed. Not only does cooked eggplant have a rich flavor that is deliciously complemented by a large variety of ingredients, but it also soaks up seasonings and marinades so that their flavors meld into the eggplant's flesh.

Sphecha

SYRIAN STUFFED BABY EGGPLANT
❧ 6 SERVINGS ❧

S*phecha* are served on the Sabbath and festivals.

12 small (4 to 5 inches long)
  unpeeled eggplants
2 large eggplants (1½ to 1¾
  pounds each), peeled or
  unpeeled
Vegetable oil for frying

HASHU (MEAT STUFFING)
3 tablespoons vegetable oil
1 medium yellow onion, finely
  chopped (about ½ cup)
3 to 4 cloves garlic, minced
1 pound ground beef or lamb
¼ cup chopped fresh parsley
About ½ teaspoon kosher salt
1 teaspoon ground allspice
½ teaspoon ground cinnamon or
  ¼ teaspoon ground cumin
¼ teaspoon ground black pepper

SAUCE
3 tablespoons tomato paste
2 to 3 tablespoons lemon juice or
  1 tablespoon temerhindi
  (tamarind sauce; see page 36)
1 teaspoon ground allspice
¼ teaspoon ground cinnamon
Salt to taste
Ground black pepper to taste

1. Cut off the stem ends of the small eggplants. Using a melon baller or vegetable corer, scoop out the pulp, leaving the sides intact. Cut the large eggplants into ½-inch-thick slices.

2. Heat the oil in a large skillet over medium heat. In batches, fry the eggplant slices (not the hollow ones) until soft. Set aside.

3. To make the *hashu*: Heat the oil in a large skillet over medium heat. Add the onion and garlic and sauté until soft and translucent, 5 to 10 minutes. Add the meat and sauté until it loses its red color. Add the parsley, kosher salt, allspice, cinnamon or cumin, and pepper. Let cool.

4. Stuff the small eggplants with the *hashu*, leaving about 1 inch for expansion. (Any extra stuffing can be shaped into balls and cooked with the eggplants.) With the tines of a fork, prick 2 sides of each small eggplant to allow a little cooking liquid to seep in.

5. Arrange half of the fried eggplant slices in the bottom of a large pot. Add the small eggplants, stuffed side up. Top with the remaining eggplant slices.

6. Add the tomato paste, lemon juice or *temerhindi*, allspice, cinnamon, salt, and pepper. Add enough water to almost reach the top. Weigh down with a plate.

7. Cover, bring to a boil over medium-high heat, reduce the heat to low, and simmer until the sauce is nearly evaporated, at least 2½ hours. Or place in an ovenproof pot and bake in a 300-degree oven. Serve with rice.

VARIATION
Sweet-and-Sour Stuffed Baby Eggplant: After cooking for 1 hour, add ¾ cup distilled white or cider vinegar and ½ cup sugar to the sauce.

Badrijani Nigozit Satenit

GEORGIAN STUFFED EGGPLANT
8 SERVINGS

This appetizer typifies Georgian cooking, utilizing most of its favorite ingredients in a popular technique—spreading cooked vegetables with walnut sauce and rolling them up.

8 small (3 to 4 inches long) eggplants
About 3 tablespoons kosher salt

WALNUT SAUCE
1 cup walnuts
2 to 3 cloves garlic
1 teaspoon ground coriander
1 small yellow onion, finely chopped (about ¼ cup)
¼ cup chopped fresh coriander
¼ cup chopped fresh parsley
2 small stalks celery, finely chopped
1 to 3 tablespoons red wine vinegar
2 tablespoons fresh pomegranate seeds
1 teaspoon paprika or ½ teaspoon hot red pepper flakes
Salt to taste
Ground black pepper to taste

3 tablespoons vegetable or olive oil

1. Trim the ends of the eggplants and cut in half lengthwise. Sprinkle with the kosher salt, weigh down (to flatten), and let stand for 1 hour. Rinse and pat dry.
2. Meanwhile, in a food processor or a mortar and pestle, puree the walnuts, garlic, and ground coriander. Stir in the remaining sauce ingredients. Let stand at room temperature for at least 30 minutes. Check the seasonings. The sauce should have a spreadable consistency; if too thick, stir in a little water.
3. Heat the oil in a large skillet over medium heat. Fry the eggplants, turning once, until tender, about 15 minutes.
4. Place the warm eggplants skin side down on a flat surface, spread with the walnut sauce, and rull up jelly roll style. Cover and refrigerate several hours or overnight. Garnish with additional pomegranate seeds or chopped fresh parsley.

Saku

SEPHARDIC EGGPLANT AND MEAT CASSEROLE
 6 TO 8 SERVINGS

Eggplant-and-ground-meat casseroles are among the most popular ways of preparing this vegetable. Moussaka, the best known of these casseroles in America, is the Greek and Balkan version. Persians prepare a similar dish called *khorake bademjan*, without the cheese topping. *Saku* is the Sephardic version. Since ground beef is rarely used for an entrée in the Middle East, this is usually served as a side dish. *Saku*, easy to carry outside to the *sukkah* (see page 146), is served on Sukkoth often accompanying *armico de pollo* (chicken with tomato sauce; see page 95) and *fidellos* (thin noodles; see page 234).

2 medium eggplants
   (about 1¼ pounds each),
   peeled and cut crosswise into
   ½-inch-thick slices
About 2 tablespoons kosher salt
Olive or vegetable oil for frying

MEAT FILLING
3 tablespoons olive or vegetable
   oil
1 medium yellow onion,
   chopped (about ½ cup)
1 clove garlic, minced
1 pound ground beef or lamb
2 large eggs, lightly beaten
½ cup chopped fresh parsley
About 1 teaspoon salt
Ground black pepper to taste

1. Place the eggplant in a colander, sprinkle with the kosher salt, and let stand for 1 hour. Rinse the eggplant with water and press between several layers of paper towels until it feels firm. (The eggplant can be prepared ahead and stored in the refrigerator for up to 4 hours.)

2. Preheat the oven to 350 degrees. Grease a 13-by-9-inch baking dish.

3. Heat a thin layer of oil in a large skillet over medium heat. In batches, lightly brown the eggplant slices on both sides, 2 to 3 minutes per side. Set aside.

4. To make the meat filling: Heat the 3 tablespoons oil in a large skillet over medium heat. Add the onion and garlic and sauté until soft and translucent, 5 to 10 minutes.

5. Add the meat and cook, stirring frequently, until the meat loses its red color, about 5 minutes. Drain off the excess fat. Remove from the heat and stir in the eggs, parsley, salt, and pepper.

6. Arrange alternate layers of the eggplant and meat in the prepared dish, beginning and ending with the eggplant.

7. Bake until golden brown and heated through, about 45 minutes. Let the casserole stand 10 minutes before slicing. Serve with pita bread.

VARIATION

Engreyee (Syrian Eggplant Casserole): Add ½ teaspoon ground cinnamon and ½ teaspoon ground allspice to the meat mixture. Combine 5 cups coarsely chopped tomatoes, ¼ cup *temerhindi* (tamarind sauce; see page 36) (or 2 tablespoons apricot butter and 2 tablespoons prune butter), 1 tablespoon lemon juice, salt, and pepper and pour over the top of the casserole.

Below: **Procession of Portuguese Jews with** *etrogim* **(citrons) and** *lulavim* **(palm branches).** Engraving by Bernard Picart, circa 1700. *"You shall take for yourself the fruit of the goodly tree, branches of palm trees, and branches of the myrtle and willows of the brook"* (LEVITICUS 23:40).

Finocchio in Tegame

ITALIAN BRAISED FENNEL
❧ 6 SERVINGS ❧

This anise-flavored relative of dill and parsley, a native of the Mediterranean region, resembles celery with a bulbous base. It was a favorite in ancient Greece, where it was called *marathon,* after the famous plain where the Anthenians defeated the Persians in 490 B.C.E. Fennel was common in ancient Israel, where it grew wild in the countryside. Until recently it was considered a Jewish food in Italy, although it is now highly prized in Italian cuisine.

The crisp stalks are eaten raw in salads, added to sauces and soups, and baked; the seeds serve as a spice; and the leaves are used as an herb. Fennel bulbs differ between male and female: Those with rounded bulbs are male; flattened bulbs are female. Some cooks claim that female bulbs are more flavorful. Fresh fennel is available from October through April. Look for very white bulbs tinged with a little green. The leaves should show no brown.

3 large fennel bulbs
    (about 1 pound each)
2 tablespoons olive or
    vegetable oil
1 small yellow onion, chopped
    (about ¼ cup)
2 cups chicken broth or water
Salt to taste
Ground black pepper to taste

1. Rinse the fennel well. Cut off the root ends and leaves. Cut the bulbs in half lengthwise.
2. Heat the oil in a large skillet or heatproof casserole over medium heat. Add the onion and sauté until soft and translucent, 5 to 10 minutes.
3. Add the fennel, stirring to coat. Add the broth or water and bring to a boil. Cook, uncovered, over medium heat or bake in a 350-degree oven until tender, about 30 minutes. Season with salt and pepper.

VARIATION
Substitute ¼ cup vinaigrette for the salt and pepper.

Prasa

Sephardic Braised Leeks

 6 to 8 servings

8 to 10 medium leeks
  (about 2 pounds)
½ cup vegetable or olive oil
½ cup chicken broth, veal broth,
  or water
Salt to taste
Ground black pepper to taste
Chopped fresh parsley for
  garnish

1. Trim the leeks, discarding the dark green parts and roots. Thinly slice crosswise the white and light green parts. Wash in a bowl of cold water, changing the water several times, and drain.

2. Heat the oil in a large saucepan over medium heat. Add the leeks and sauté until softened, about 10 minutes.

3. Add the broth or water, salt, and pepper. Bring to a boil, cover, reduce the heat to low, and simmer until the leeks are tender, about 20 minutes. Garnish with the chopped parsley. Serve warm or at room temperature as a side dish to meat or poultry.

LEEKS

Leeks, the mildest members of the onion family, were one of the seven foods that the Israelites ate in Egypt and then yearned for during their wandering in the wilderness (Numbers 11:5). As such, they are a traditional Passover food. Since the Hebrew word for leek (*karti*) is similar to *yikartu* (to be cut off), signifying the wish that the Jews' enemies be cut off, these bulbs are also a long-standing Rosh Hashanah food. Sephardim have a special fondness for leeks, using them in soups, stews, omelets, meatballs, and savory pastries.

Leeks vary in size from less than ½ inch to more than 2 inches in diameter. There is no difference in flavor or texture between large and small bulbs. Leeks can be substituted for onions or scallions in most dishes. They can also be braised, sautéed, or grilled and served as a side dish, either hot or cold.

In most recipes, only the white and light green parts are used; the tough dark green part is usually discarded. Leeks grow underground and contain a large amount of dirt and sand between their layers, and therefore must be thoroughly cleaned. To wash, halve leeks lengthwise, place in a bowl of cold water to soak for at least 15 minutes and up to two hours, then rinse under cold running water.

Bamia con Domates

SEPHARDIC OKRA WITH TOMATOES

6 TO 8 SERVINGS

Okra, a relative of cotton, is probably a native of Ethiopia, where it has been grown for more than three thousand years. Okra was spread by the Arabs to Spain and western Asia and subsequently found its greatest popularity in the Balkans, the southern United States, and India. Okra exudes a mucilaginous juice, a trait common to all members of the mallow family and disliked by some people. The five-sided pods, which range from light to dark green in color, run from 3 to 7 inches in length; for best flavor, the pods should be less than 4 inches long. If your fingernail does not easily pierce the pod, it is too old. Store fresh okra in a plastic bag in the refrigerator.

These pods are a great favorite among Sephardim, who often pair them with tomatoes, as the acid in tomatoes counteracts okra's mucilaginous nature. Okra's stickiness is also reduced by soaking the okra in vinegar water or blanching it in hot water.

2 pounds okra
½ cup distilled white vinegar
2 quarts plus ½ cup water
¼ cup olive or vegetable oil
2 medium yellow onions,
  chopped (about 1 cup)
6 cups (3 pounds) peeled,
  seeded, and chopped tomatoes
  or 1 cup tomato sauce
2 tablespoons lemon juice
About 1 teaspoon salt
Ground black pepper to taste
Pinch of sugar

1. Trim the caps of the okra without cutting into the flesh. Combine the vinegar and the 2 quarts water. Add the okra and soak for 1 hour. Drain.

2. Heat the oil in a large skillet over medium heat. Add the onions and sauté until soft and translucent, 5 to 10 minutes. Add the tomatoes or tomato sauce and the ½ cup water and cook, stirring occasionally, until the tomatoes are soft, about 15 minutes.

3. Add the okra, lemon juice, salt, pepper, and sugar. Cover and simmer, stirring occasionally, until the okra is tender, about 30 minutes.

4. Uncover and cook until the sauce has thickened. Serve warm or at room temperature as a side dish or salad.

VARIATION

Bamia con Limón (Sephardic Okra with Lemon): Omit the tomatoes, add 4 minced cloves garlic and sauté with the onions, and increase the lemon juice to ½ cup and the water to 1 cup.

Retachsalat

EASTERN EUROPEAN RADISH SALAD
5 TO 6 SERVINGS

Radish salads have been a zesty part of Jewish cuisine since at least Talmudic times. The black radish, a long white root covered with a black or brown skin, is the most ancient type; the round, red-skinned radish did not appear until the sixteenth century. Able to keep through the winter, radishes were widely used in eastern Europe in preserves, sautés, relishes, and salads. Radishes were flavored with schmaltz (see page 109) during the winter, providing a Sabbath and Hanukkah appetizer (according to legend, radishes were a favorite food of the Maccabees). Sour cream is popular on Shavuot and during the summer. Cucumbers and other vegetables are often added to radish salads to tone down the radish's sharpness.

*1¼ pounds radishes, preferably
    black, coarsely grated or
    thinly sliced (about 3 cups)*
*1 medium onion or 6 scallions,
    chopped (about ½ cup)*
*6 to 8 tablespoons schmaltz (see
    page 109) or 1 cup sour cream*
*2 tablespoons distilled white or
    cider vinegar*
*About 1 teaspoon sugar
    (optional)*
Salt to taste
Ground black pepper to taste

Combine all of the ingredients and refrigerate for at least 1 hour.

TO PEEL AND SEED TOMATOES

Since tomato skins leave tough strings in the dish, the seeds impart a bitter flavor, and the juice produces a watery effect, many recipes call for peeling and seeding the tomatoes. To peel, cut an X at the bottom of each tomato and blanch in boiling water for about 15 seconds. Place in a bowl of ice water to stop the cooking. Remove the peel, cut in half, and press out the seeds.

The Joseph family in Rangoon, Burma, in 1938. *In the early nineteenth century, Jews from India and the Middle East settled in several Burmese towns. By the 1850s, the Jewish community of Rangoon was large enough to support a synagogue. Following the Japanese invasion of Burma during World War II, most Burmese Jews relocated to India or Israel. The Baghdad-born Josephs moved their family to Calcutta in 1942. Today, hardly any Jews remain in Burma.*

TURMERIC

Turmeric, a member of the ginger family, is an orange-colored rhizome native to southern Asia. After harvesting, the rhizome is boiled or steamed, then dried and ground. The resulting golden powder imparts a rich saffron-like color, although it lacks saffron's flavor. Turmeric adds a slightly bitter flavor to curry powder, pickles, soups, poultry, rice, and eggs. Do not overdo it, as turmeric can make a dish bitter. A general rule of thumb is to use ⅛ to ¼ teaspoon turmeric for every cup liquid. Turmeric is particularly popular in Indian, Moroccan, and Persian cuisine.

Aloo Makalla

CALCUTTA FRIED POTATOES

∾ 6 TO 8 SERVINGS ∾

The cuisine of Calcutta's Jews evidences fewer Indian influences than that of other Indian Jewish communities, partially because of their late arrival in the country. The Baghdadi Jews prepare such Middle Eastern dishes as *hamin* (Sabbath chicken stew; see page 123), *mahasha* (stuffed vegetables; see page 144), *koftas* (meat or vegetable patties; see page 136), *sambusaks* (pastry turnovers; see page 36), *kubba* (stuffed dumplings), and *kaak* (biscuit rings; see page 290–291). In addition, they added local dishes to their repertoire as well as adopted local ingredients and spices. Characteristic of this synthesis is the Baghdadis' *Shabbat roti* (Sabbath bread), a Middle Eastern flat bread sprinkled with *kala jeera/kelonji* (nigella, sometimes mistakenly called black onion seed).

Aloo makalla, the most famous Jewish dish in India, is served on Friday nights, festivals, and other special occasions. It is a synthesis of Middle Eastern and Indian sources. Indeed, its very name is a hybrid: *Aloo* is the Hindi word for "potatoes" and *makalla* is derived from the Arabic word for "fried." Although the Jewish community of Calcutta has practically disappeared, this dish survives among their descendants in Europe and Asia as well as among the non-Jews of Calcutta. *Aloo makalla* is traditionally served with *murgi kari* (pot roasted chicken; see page 105), *bhaji* (curried potatoes and vegetables), *khutta* (vegetable dishes), and *pilau* (rice pilaf).

---

3 pounds small potatoes, peeled and pricked with a fork
2 teaspoons salt
½ teaspoon ground turmeric
About 1 quart vegetable oil

1. Place enough water to cover the potatoes in a large pot. Add the salt and turmeric and bring to a boil. Add the potatoes, return to a boil, and parboil for 5 minutes. Drain and let cool.

2. Place the potatoes in a wok or large pot and add enough oil to cover. Bring to a boil over medium-high heat. Reduce the heat to low and simmer, shaking the pan occasionally, until the potatoes are crusty and lightly golden, about 1 hour. (At this point, the potatoes can be removed from the heat and allowed to sit, in the oil, for up to 3 hours.)

3. Increase the heat to medium-high and fry until the crust is very hard and golden brown, about 5 minutes. Drain on paper towels. Serve warm.

Testine di Spinaci

ITALIAN SPINACH STALKS
6 TO 8 SERVINGS

Testine, meaning "small heads," is an ancient Venetian Jewish method for preparing the usually discarded spinach stems. Sephardim prepare a similar dish, substituting lemon juice for the vinegar.

¼ cup olive or vegetable oil

1 to 2 cloves garlic, minced

2 pounds spinach stalks, washed and cut into 1-inch pieces

1 cup water

Salt to taste

Ground black pepper to taste

¼ cup red wine vinegar

1. Heat the oil in a large pot over medium heat. Add the garlic and sauté until lightly colored but not burned, 1 to 2 minutes.

2. Add the spinach, tossing to coat. Add the water, salt, and pepper. Cook, uncovered, until the stalks are tender and the water is evaporated, about 15 minutes.

3. Drizzle with the vinegar and cook until the liquid is evaporated. Cool, then refrigerate for at least 1 hour. Serve chilled or at room temperature as a relish.

Note: Eight pounds of fresh spinach yields about 2 pounds of stalks.

SPINACH

The derivation of the word *spinach* from the Persian word *isfanakh* (thorn), referring to the vegetable's prickly seeds, reflects its Persian origins. This leafy green appeared in the sixth century and was introduced to Spain by way of the Moors about four centuries later and quickly became a favorite among Sephardim. Spinach makes its appearance in early spring and is harvested into early summer; thus it became traditional Passover and Shavuot fare.

Although it does not fare well in hot temperatures, after the nights begin to cool again in late August or early September, farmers plant the fall spinach crop, which matures in time for Rosh Hashanah. In most Sephardic recipes, spinach is used interchangeably (both the name and the greens) with Swiss chard, long a traditional Rosh Hashanah food.

One pound fresh spinach yields about 8 cups chopped and 1¾ cups cooked.

Esfongos

SEPHARDIC SPINACH NESTS

❧ 6 TO 8 SERVINGS ❧

Spinach has a delicate, slightly bitter flavor that provides a base for many foods, including eggs, fish, veal, pasta, and cheese. *Esfongos/fongos* (from the Spanish *esponga,* "sponge") is popular at festive dairy meals such as Shavuot (see page 315).

2 pounds fresh spinach, washed, stemmed, and finely chopped, or 20 ounces frozen spinach, thawed and squeezed

4 large eggs

About 1 teaspoon salt

Ground black pepper to taste

2 cups grated hard cheese, such as kashkaval (see page 30), Muenster, or Swiss cheese (or 1 cup crumbled feta cheese and 1 cup farmer cheese)

½ cup mashed potatoes

Yogurt for garnish (optional)

1. Preheat the oven to 375 degrees. Grease a 13-by-9-inch baking dish or two 7-inch pie plates.
2. Combine the spinach, one of the eggs, salt, and pepper and spread into the prepared pan. With the back of a spoon, make 6 to 8 indentations in the spinach every 2 inches.
3. Combine the cheese and potatoes with the remaining 3 eggs and spoon into the indentations. Or stir the cheese mixture into the spinach to marbleize.
4. Bake until golden brown, about 35 minutes. Serve warm or at room temperature accompanied with yogurt.

VARIATION

After baking the casserole, crack an egg into each cheese-and-potato "nest," cover the pan, and return to the oven until the whites are firm, 3 to 5 minutes.

Silka

SEPHARDIC BOILED SWISS CHARD

 6 TO 8 SERVINGS

This relative of beets, sometimes called *blette,* is a popular vegetable in Syria and France, where the green leaves are used like spinach and the white stalks like celery. Since the Aramaic name of Swiss chard, *silka,* is similar to the word for "remove," it has become a traditional Rosh Hashanah dish in Syrian households. Syrians enhance this plain dish in numerous ways, including cooking it with chickpeas, black-eyed peas, or lentils and adding it to casseroles, omelets, soups, and stews.

The leaves do not require any added cooking liquid, since they release their own juices. The tougher stems, however, require cooking liquid: Cut into ½-inch pieces and cook in boiling water until tender, about 7 minutes.

3 tablespoons olive or
  vegetable oil
2 to 3 cloves garlic, minced
2 pounds Swiss chard or spinach,
  washed, stemmed, and leaves
  torn into 1-inch pieces
About ½ teaspoon salt
Ground black pepper to taste

1. Heat the oil in a large skillet or saucepan over medium heat. Add the garlic and sauté until lightly colored but not burned, about 2 minutes.
2. Add the Swiss chard or spinach leaves, cover, reduce the heat to low, and simmer until wilted, about 15 minutes. Season with the salt and pepper. Serve warm or at room temperature.

Legumes

[Shobi the son of Nahash] brought beds and basins and earthen
vessels and wheat and barley and meal and parched grain and beans
and lentils and parched pulse. —2 SAMUEL 17:28

The word *legume,* from the Latin *legere* (to gather), refers to the more than fifteen thousand species of vines, shrubs, and small bushes that produce a fruit leaf called a pod to encompass its seeds. Of these many and varied leguminous plants, only about twenty-two species—including beans, peas, lentils, alfalfa, and peanuts—are grown in any large quantity. Yet, in almost every part of the globe, the edible seeds of these legumes, also called pulses, have long supplied a major part of human dietary needs, following only grains in importance.

Ful

MIDDLE EASTERN FAVA BEAN SALAD
6 TO 8 SERVINGS

Ful is the Arabic word for "fava beans." This dish is also called *salat lubiya* (bean salad). Although fava bean salads, inexpensive and flavorful, are commonplace throughout the Near East and North Africa, the eggs are a distinctive Jewish touch. Serve *ful* as a salad, side dish, or part of a meze (appetizer assortment).

1 pound (about 2 cups) dried
   fava beans (see Note)
3 quarts water
⅓ cup olive or vegetable oil
About 1 teaspoon salt
Ground black pepper to taste
6 to 8 large eggs in shell,
   washed well
About ¼ cup lemon juice
⅓ cup chopped fresh parsley

1. Soak the beans in water to cover overnight. Drain.
2. Place the beans in a 4-quart saucepan and add the 3 quarts of water. Bring to a boil, cover, reduce the heat to medium, and simmer, stirring occasionally, for 30 minutes.
3. Stir in the oil, salt, and pepper. Add the eggs. Reduce the heat to low and simmer, stirring occasionally and adding more water if necessary, until the beans are very tender, about 2 hours.
4. Remove the eggs, peel, and chop or quarter.
5. Add the lemon juice and parsley to the beans, tossing to coat. Divide among serving bowls and top with the eggs. Serve warm or chilled.

Note: Dried fava beans are available in Middle Eastern groceries and some specialty food stores. Since fava beans are sometimes hard to find, dried white beans, large dried lima beans, or chickpeas can be substituted.

VARIATIONS

Ful Medames (Sephardic Baked Fava Beans): Cook the beans and eggs, covered, overnight over very low heat and serve on Sabbath morning for *desayuno* (breakfast; see page 29). (*Note:* When simmered overnight this dish becomes a Sabbath stew similar to *hamin.*)

Syrian Ful: Add 1½ teaspoons ground cumin and ¼ to ½ teaspoon hot red pepper flakes or a pinch of cayenne.

Yemenite Ful: Spoon 2 tablespoons *tarator bi tahina* (sesame seed sauce; see page 368) over each serving of beans.

FAVA BEANS

Fava (also called broad bean) is an ancient legume found at pre-pottery Neolithic B levels at Jericho. Before Columbus's voyage to the New World, fava served as the primary bean throughout the Middle East and Europe. With the arrival of American haricot beans (including kidney, white, green, and lima beans), the fava lost popularity. Although fava beans are practically unknown in America, they remain an important food source in the Mediterranean area. The significant role of beans in Sephardic cooking may be seen from their Spanish name, *judia,* which is also the Spanish word for Jewess.

Fava beans are found in fresh and dried forms. The 3- to 8-inch-long pods contain five to six beans that look like large lima beans and possess a nutty flavor and creamy texture. Young, tender 3- to 5-inch-long pods are usually cut into 1½-inch pieces and cooked with the beans; older, tougher pods are generally discarded. Choose soft, tender bean pods that have a velvety exterior and contain bright green beans. Avoid pods that are shiny and firm and beans that are tough and a yellowish green color. One and a half pounds of fava in the pods equals about ½ pound (about 2 cups) shelled beans.

Avas Frescas

SEPHARDIC FRESH FAVA BEANS

6 TO 8 SERVINGS

This dish, taking advantage of the new spring crop of beans, is traditionally served at Sephardic Passover Seders and is popular fare throughout the spring. Turkish Jews sometimes serve this with a yogurt-garlic sauce (1 cup plain yogurt mixed with 1 crushed clove garlic and salt), while Syrians season the beans with a little cumin or allspice or, for a more substantial dish, add veal or beef cubes.

3 tablespoons olive or vegetable oil

2 medium yellow onions or 8 scallions, chopped (about 1 cup)

2 pounds (about 2⅔ cups) fresh fava beans, shelled (pods reserved)

1½ cups chicken broth, beef broth, or water

¼ cup chopped fresh coriander, dill, or parsley

1 to 3 teaspoons sugar

Salt to taste

Ground black pepper to taste

1. Heat the oil in a medium saucepan over medium heat. Add the onions or scallions and sauté until soft and translucent, 5 to 10 minutes. Stir in the beans, pods (if tender), broth or water, herbs, and sugar.

2. Bring to a boil, cover, reduce the heat to low, and simmer until tender, 10 to 20 minutes for younger beans, 20 to 30 minutes for older beans. For older, larger beans, rub to loosen the skins, then discard the skins. Season with salt and pepper. Fava beans are commonly accompanied with rice.

VARIATIONS

Ful ib Carchof (Middle Eastern Fresh Fava Beans with Artichokes): Reduce the amount of fava beans to 1½ cups and add 1½ cups artichoke hearts.

Ful ib Riz (Middle Eastern Fresh Fava Beans with Rice): Before adding the beans, stir in 1 cup rice and sauté until well coated and lightly colored and increase the amount of broth or water to 2 cups.

Opposite: **Portuguese Jews in Holland celebrate the Passover Seder.** Engraving by Bernard Picart, circa 1700. *"And you shall tell your son in that day, saying: It is because of that which the Lord did for me when I came forth out of Egypt."* (EXODUS 13:8)

Fijones Frescos

SEPHARDIC BLACK-EYED PEAS WITH TOMATOES

6 TO 8 SERVINGS

Syrians often cook veal, tongue, or *kibbe mi'leeye* (fried stuffed torpedoes) with these beans.

3 tablespoons olive or vegetable
   oil
2 medium yellow onions,
   chopped (about 1 cup)
3 to 4 cloves garlic, minced
2 cups water
3 pounds fresh black-eyed peas
   (4 cups shelled) or 20 ounces
   frozen black-eyed peas
3 cups (1½ pounds) peeled,
   seeded, and chopped
   tomatoes, 8 ounces tomato
   sauce, or 3 tablespoons
   tomato paste
About 1½ teaspoons salt
Ground black pepper to taste

1. Heat the oil in a large saucepan over medium heat. Add the onions and garlic and sauté until soft and translucent, 5 to 10 minutes.

2. Add the water and bring to a boil. Add the peas and tomatoes, tomato sauce, or paste, cover, reduce the heat to low, and simmer, adding more water if necessary, until tender, about 45 minutes for fresh, about 30 minutes for frozen. Season with the salt and pepper. Black-eyed peas are generally served over rice.

VARIATION

Substitute 1½ cups dried black-eyed peas for the fresh beans. Soak overnight in water to cover, increase the water to 3 cups, and increase the cooking time to about 1¼ hours.

BLACK-EYED PEAS

Black-eyed peas, also called cowpeas, are actually beans. These cream-colored oval seeds are so named because of a pronounced black spot on the inner rim. They are available fresh and dried. Black-eyed peas were cultivated in Ethiopia about four thousand years ago and had arrived in Judea by at least 1500 B.C.E.

They are popular among Sephardim, particularly those from Turkey and Syria. Since their name in Aramaic, *rubiya/lubiya,* sounds similar to the Hebrew word for "many" and therefore suggests fertility and success, black-eyed peas is a popular Sephardic Rosh Hashanah food.

Vadas

CALCUTTA LENTIL FRITTERS

6 TO 8 SERVINGS

In no other cuisine do lentils and other legumes play such a prominent role as in Indian. Although green lentils are the most common variety in the United States, the red variety—also called Egyptian lentils, Persian lentils, and *massor dal*—is more popular in Asia. Yellow lentils—called *toovar dal* or *arhar dal* in India—are kidney-shaped yellowish brown pigeon peas with an earthy flavor.

Indians love savory snacks, including *samosas* (pastry turnovers), *koftas* (meat and vegetable balls), and *pakoras* (vegetable fritters). These fritters, also called *piaju,* reflect the synthesis of Middle Eastern and Indian cooking produced by the Jews living in Calcutta, who substituted legumes such as lentils and split peas for the chickpeas common to falafel.

*8 ounces (about 1 cup) red
  lentils (or ½ cup red lentils
  and ½ cup yellow lentils)*
1 teaspoon ground black pepper
¾ teaspoon cayenne
½ teaspoon ground cumin
About ¾ teaspoon salt
*½ to 1 teaspoon minced fresh
  ginger or green chili*
*2 tablespoons chopped fresh
  coriander*
Vegetable oil for deep frying

1. Soak the lentils in water to cover overnight. Rinse and drain.
2. In a food processor or blender, puree the lentils with the pepper, cayenne, cumin, and salt. Stir in the ginger or chili and coriander.
3. Heat about 2 inches of oil over medium heat to 365 degrees.
4. In batches, drop the batter by heaping teaspoonfuls into the oil and fry until golden brown on all sides, about 5 minutes. Drain on paper towels. Serve warm.

VARIATION

Filorees (Calcutta Green Pea Fritters): Substitute 1 cup split green peas (*chunna ka dal*) for the lentils and omit the cumin.

Mengedarrah

MIDDLE EASTERN LENTILS AND RICE
✸ 6 TO 8 SERVINGS ✸

The combination of legumes and grains is found in nearly every culture. This simple lentils-and-rice dish is popular throughout the Middle East, called *megadara/mujadara* in Syria, Lebanon, and Greece and *koshari* in Egypt. A similar dish called *kedegeree* or *kitchiri* is popular in India. The Iraqi version, called *kitchree,* is seasoned with cumin and turmeric and topped with fried eggs. Yemenites call it *enjadara* and mix in pine nuts. The Persian version, called *adas polo,* is prepared with the customary crispy-rice bottom. Bukharans substitute split mung beans for the lentils, reflecting a Chinese influence.

Lentils, along with hard-cooked eggs, are the most ancient Jewish symbols of mourning. Both of these foods share a spherical shape with "no mouth" (opening), symbolic of mourners who are required to be silent. In addition, they serve as symbols of fertility and of man's mortality (life is round like a wheel). Therefore, *mengedarrah* is traditionally eaten during the week before Tisha b'Av and in a house of mourning. It is also popular on happy occasions such as Shavuot, when it is topped with yogurt and served with *huevos haminados* (brown eggs, see page 382).

1 pound (about 2 cups) green
   or red lentils
¼ cup vegetable or olive oil
2 medium yellow onions,
   chopped (about 1 cup)
2 cups rice
4½ cups water
About 1½ teaspoons salt
Ground black pepper to taste
Fried onions or yogurt for
   garnish

1. Rinse the lentils and soak in water to cover for at least 2 hours. Drain. (Although there is no need to soak lentils as with beans, soaking in warm water for several hours or overnight helps to bring out the lentil's flavor and maintain its shape during cooking.)

2. Heat the oil in a medium saucepan over medium-high heat. Add the onions and sauté until golden brown, 10 to 15 minutes. Stir in the rice and sauté until well coated, about 1 minute.

3. Add the lentils, water, salt, and pepper. Bring to a boil, cover, reduce the heat to low, and simmer until tender and the water is absorbed, about 30 minutes.

4. Remove from the heat and let stand covered for 5 minutes. Stir with a fork to fluff. Transfer to a large serving platter and scatter fried onions over the top or serve with yogurt.

Kik Wot

ETHIOPIAN SPLIT PEA STEW

6 TO 8 SERVINGS

In meat-scarce Ethiopia, stews made from dried legumes have long been the most common food. These stews are always well seasoned with spices in the manner of Indian curries. For a more fiery *wot,* add 1 to 3 tablespoons *berbere* (Ethiopian chili powder).

9½ cups water

2 cups yellow or green split peas

3 medium yellow onions, chopped (about 1½ cups)

½ cup vegetable oil

2 to 3 cloves garlic, minced

1½ teaspoons minced fresh ginger

About 1 teaspoon salt

⅛ teaspoon ground cardamom

⅛ teaspoon ground allspice

⅛ teaspoon ground turmeric

1. Bring 8 cups of the water to a boil. Add the split peas (there should be enough water to completely cover the peas) and cook until the peas begin to get mushy, 30 to 40 minutes. Drain.

2. In a dry large skillet over medium heat, cook the onions, stirring, until they begin to soften, 2 to 3 minutes. Add the oil, garlic, and ginger and sauté until fragrant, 2 to 3 minutes.

3. Add ½ cup of the water and the salt and spices and cook, stirring constantly, until the onions are soft, about 5 minutes.

4. Add the split peas and remaining 1 cup water. Partially cover, reduce the heat to low, and simmer until the sauce has thickened, about 30 minutes. Adjust the seasonings. Serve with *injera* (Ethiopian flat bread; see page 274) and salads.

SPLIT PEAS

It was not until the sixteenth century that varieties of peas were developed that could be eaten fresh. Until then, they were always dried. Split peas are so named because they split in half during drying. For thousands of years, these green or yellow seeds were prepared as a pottage, similar to *kik wot,* and once served as a staple of European cooking. Several cultures, most notably Persian and Indian, use split peas in expanded roles such as fritters, stews, and stuffings.

Hummus/Nahit

COOKED CHICKPEAS

ABOUT 6 CUPS

Nahit are traditionally served by eastern European Jews at a *shalom zachar,* a party held on the first Friday night after the birth of a male, in honor of his upcoming *bris.* Chickpeas were one of the earliest Purim foods, as these dried seeds served as a reminder of Esther, who, in order not to eat unkosher food while living in the king's palace, followed a vegetarian diet of grains and beans.

1 pound (about 2½ cups) dried
   chickpeas
Salt to taste
Ground black pepper to taste

1. Wash the chickpeas well in water. Soak for 24 to 48 hours in cold water in the refrigerator. Or, for quick cooking, cover the chickpeas with boiling water and soak for 12 hours. Drain. (Chickpeas double their weight during soaking.)

2. In a large pot with plenty of room for expansion, add enough water to cover the chickpeas by 2 inches. Bring to a boil, cover, reduce the heat to low, and simmer until tender, about 2 hours. Drain. Season with salt and pepper.

Notes: One cup dried chickpeas yields about 3 cups cooked. One 20-ounce can of chickpeas equals about 2 cups cooked chickpeas.

If the water in your area is very hard, add about ¼ teaspoon baking soda to the soaking liquid.

CAYENNE

Cayenne is a powder made by grinding red cayenne chilies and sometimes other hot chilies. When savory dishes lack flavor, add a little cayenne. But use sparingly, as it can be fiery. Add to cheese dishes, egg dishes, corn bread, and chowders.

Falafel

MIDDLE EASTERN CHICKPEA FRITTERS
ABOUT 24 BALLS

The chickpea, one of the earliest-known cultivated plants, is believed to be a native of northern Persia. However, its exact origins cannot be definitely ascertained, since it was already widespread before recorded history. Chickpeas were grown in the Hanging Gardens of Babylon and found in ancient burial mounds in Switzerland. The yellow, roundish, nutty-flavored chickpea is actually not a pea but a legume that grows two to a pod. Chickpeas have long played a prominent role in Jewish cooking. Ashkenazim generally eat them mixed with ground black pepper, while Sephardim often add them to various dishes, including couscous, *cocide, dafina* (Sephardic *cholent*), and soups. Chickpea flour—called *besan* in India and *nachochi* in Iran—is popular in those countries in fritters, as a thickener, and as a binding agent.

Fritters made from legumes originated in Egypt, many claim among the Copts. Far and away the most popular of these fritters are made from chickpeas. These spicy croquettes, peddled by street vendors and kiosks throughout the Middle East, are the Oriental equivalent of fast food. Serve falafel as an appetizer or stuff in pita bread with Israeli salad and *tarator bi tahina* (sesame seed sauce; see page 368).

8 ounces (about 1¼ cups) dried chickpeas

1 medium yellow onion, chopped (about ½ cup)

2 to 3 large cloves garlic

2 tablespoons all-purpose flour or 6 tablespoons dried bread crumbs

2 tablespoons chopped fresh parsley or coriander

About 1 teaspoon ground cumin

1 teaspoon salt

¼ teaspoon ground black pepper

¼ teaspoon baking powder

1 teaspoon ground coriander or ¼ teaspoon cayenne

Vegetable oil for deep frying

1. Cover the chickpeas with cold water and let soak overnight in the refrigerator. Drain.

2. In a food mill, meat grinder, or food processor, grind together the chickpeas, onion, and garlic. Stir in the remaining ingredients, except the oil, and chill for at least 1 hour.

3. Heat about 2 inches of oil to 365 degrees.

4. Shape the chickpea mixture into 1-inch balls. In batches, fry, turning occasionally, until golden brown on all sides, about 5 minutes. Drain on paper towels.

Hint: If you have no means of grinding the chickpeas, they can be cooked until soft, then mashed.

VARIATION

Tamiya (Egyptian Fava Bean Fritters): Substitute ½ pound dried fava beans for the chickpeas.

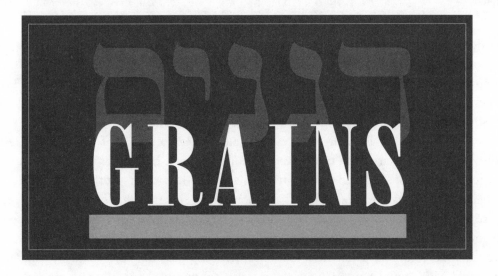

GRAINS

*I will give the rain of your land in its season, the
former rain and the latter rain, that you may gather
in your grains, and your wine, and your oil.*
—DEUTERONOMY 11:14

*A land of wheat and barley, and vines, and fig trees,
and pomegranates; a land of olive oil and honey.*
—DEUTERONOMY 8:8

Grains, wine, and olive oil formed the basis of the diet and the economy of ancient Israel. (In recognition of their importance, these three items were incorporated into Sabbath and festival rituals as challah, kiddush, and lights.) The principal grains in biblical times were barley and several varieties of wheat.

Barley, possibly a native of Israel and one of the seven species associated with the land's blessing, is one of the world's most ancient cultivated grains; only millet (tiny, bright yellow seeds most commonly used today in birdseed) may surpass it in antiquity. Barley is mentioned throughout the Bible and, at one time, played a major role in Jewish life and ritual. Barley's value was generally half that of wheat (2 Kings 7:1), and therefore it served as the bulk of the common person's as well as the army's diet (2 Samuel 17:28), since it grew under poor conditions. Indeed, the importance of barley in biblical times can be seen from the injunction that the valuation of a field was to be determined according to the

Opposite: **Mill, engraving, Venice 1593.** *The flour for making matza is safeguarded to prevent contact with moisture and, therefore, fermentation. "Passover flour" is supervised from the time of milling. Shmurah ("guarded") matza has been watched from the moment of harvest. The water for making matza must stand for at least twenty-four hours.*

187

measurement of barley that could be sown in it (Leviticus 27:16). Similarly, when the Bible (Judges 7:13–14) recorded an ancient Midianite's dream, the symbol of his Israelite opponents was the most widely cultivated crop in Israel at that time—barley. In Temple times, it was the first sheaf of barley that served as the *omer* offering on the second day of Passover, corresponding to the beginning of the barley harvest.

Shortly after the Roman conquest of Israel, wheat, a native of the Fertile Crescent, emerged as the primary grain of the land. Among the Jews, barley was thereafter reduced to being poor man's food and animal fodder. For the masses of southern Europe, barley remained the primary source of bread and porridge, a situation that changed only with the increased availability of other grains—wheat, rye, oats, and corn—in the sixteenth century. In the wake of the improved technology and refined milling methods that followed the Industrial Revolution, wheat flour became increasingly accessible, eventually emerging as the most widely used type of flour. In most of the world, barley is now generally over-looked as a food and primarily used to make beer and whiskey. Sephardim and western Europeans practically ignore barley in their cooking. Eastern Europeans, on the other hand, use it in such hearty fare as *cholent,* kugel, and thick soups called *krupnik* in Poland and *kolish* in the Ukraine.

Kasha

EASTERN EUROPEAN BUCKWHEAT GROATS

 ABOUT 3½ CUPS; 4 TO 6 SERVINGS

Toasting gives the groats a strong, nutty flavor that goes well with robust meats.

1 large egg, lightly beaten	1. Stir the egg into the kasha and let stand for 5 minutes.
1 cup kasha (buckwheat groats)	2. Cook in a dry 1-quart saucepan over medium-low heat,
2 cups boiling chicken broth or	stirring constantly, until each grain is separated, about 3
water	minutes.
2 tablespoons schmaltz	3. Remove from the heat and stir in the broth or water,
(see page 109) or margarine	schmaltz or margarine, and salt.
About ½ teaspoon salt	4. Pour into a medium saucepan, cover, and simmer over

4. Pour into a medium saucepan, cover, and simmer over low heat until tender, about 15 minutes. Fluff with a fork. If the kasha appears too liquid, cook, uncovered, for several minutes until dry. (Kasha can be kept warm in a 225-degree oven for several hours.)

Kasha Varnishkes

EASTERN EUROPEAN BUCKWHEAT GROATS AND NOODLES
6 TO 8 SERVINGS

One of the favorite eastern European side dishes is *kasha varnishkes,* traditionally served on Hanukkah and Purim as well as on many not-so-special occasions. Use this onion-flavored recipe, omitting the noodles, for stuffing such traditional Jewish dishes as knishes, kreplach, blintzes, and roast poultry.

8 ounces (2 cups) bow-tie noodles, plaetschen *(noodle squares), or small shells*

2 tablespoons schmaltz (see page 109) or margarine

2 medium yellow onions, chopped (about 1 cup)

1 recipe kasha (see page 188)

1. Cook the noodles in a large pot of lightly salted boiling water until tender, about 10 minutes. Drain.
2. Heat the schmaltz or margarine in a medium saucepan over medium heat. Add the onions and sauté until soft and translucent, 5 to 10 minutes.
3. Stir in the kasha and noodles and simmer over low heat, or transfer to a casserole and bake in a 350-degree oven, until heated through, about 10 minutes. *Kasha varnishkes* is commonly served with brisket or other robust meats.

KASHA

Kashk is an ancient Persian dish of cracked barley or wheat as well as a more recent Persian grain pudding. The dish reached the Slavic regions of eastern Europe and Russia by way of central Asia, where it became kasha, referring to any grain—such as buckwheat, oats, and millet—used to make porridge. In Russia, these porridges became a staple of the diet and were served at all important occasions, including the signing of peace treaties, thus providing the source of an ancient Russian saying used to describe an implacable enemy: "You can't make kasha with him." Eastern European Jews, however, used the term *kasha* specifically for husked and toasted buckwheat groats. Since Jewish immigrants popularized buckwheat in America, the English usage of kasha took on the Jewish connotation.

Buckwheat, a native of central Asia and a relative of sorrel and rhubarb, is a sturdy plant that grows well in cooler climates. Until the widespread cultivation of the potato in the mid-nineteenth century, buckwheat served as the mainstay of the diet in eastern Europe. Kasha still remains popular among Ukrainian and Polish Jews, served as a side dish with either meat or dairy dishes or used as a stuffing for such foods as poultry, blintzes, and knishes.

Bazargan

SYRIAN BULGUR AND TAMARIND SALAD
❧ ABOUT 4 CUPS; 6 TO 8 SERVINGS ❧

Although many Americans have been exposed to tabbouleh (bulgur and tomato salad), Middle Easterners prepare many variations of bulgur salad, including this Syrian-Jewish dish. Serve as a side dish to grilled or roasted meat or poultry or as a dip with pita bread.

2 cups boiling water
1 cup fine or medium bulgur
¼ cup olive or vegetable oil
2 tablespoons lemon juice
¼ cup chopped fresh parsley
4 to 6 tablespoons temerhindi
  (tamarind sauce; see page
  36) or 3 tablespoons prune
  butter and 3 tablespoons
  apricot butter
½ cup finely chopped walnuts,
  almonds, or pistachios
2 tablespoons tomato paste or
  ketchup
About 1½ teaspoons salt
½ teaspoon ground cumin
Dash of hot red pepper flakes or
  cayenne

1. Pour the water over the bulgur and let stand for 20 minutes. Drain and let stand for another 20 minutes. Fluff with a fork.
2. Stir in the remaining ingredients and let stand for several hours. *Bazargan* keeps in the refrigerator for several weeks. Serve chilled or at room temperature.

VARIATIONS
Fruited Bulgur Salad: Omit the *temerhindi* and tomato paste, increase the amount of lemon juice to 6 to 8 tablespoons, and add ⅓ cup chopped dates, ¼ cup chopped dried apricots or currents, ¼ cup chopped fresh mint or 1 tablespoon dried, and ⅛ teaspoon cinnamon.
Bulgur and Pepper Salad: Finely chop half a green bell pepper, half a red bell pepper, and half a yellow bell pepper. Add in step 2.

Rebechini di Jerusalem

ITALIAN FRIED POLENTA SANDWICHES

 8 TO 10 SERVINGS AS A SIDE DISH, OR ABOUT 40 APPETIZERS

Italian Jews often serve these polenta sandwiches as part of the antipasto at special occasions. Fry the scraps in the hot oil and serve as an appetizer or a side dish.

4 cups freshly cooked mamaliga
(see page 192)
About ½ cup anchovy paste
About ½ cup all-purpose flour
2 large eggs, lightly beaten
Vegetable oil for deep frying

1. Spread the *mamaliga* onto a greased baking sheet to a ⅛-inch thickness. Let cool. Cut into about eighty 1½- to 2-inch rounds.
2. Spread half of the rounds with a little anchovy paste and top with the remaining rounds. Dredge in the flour, then dip in the egg.
3. Heat about 1 inch of oil over medium heat to 365 degrees.
4. Deep-fry the sandwiches, turning once, until golden brown on both sides. Drain on paper towels. Serve warm.

BULGUR

Bulgur, an important ingredient in Middle Eastern cooking, is whole-wheat kernels that have been steamed or boiled, then dried and cracked. The partial processing removes very little of the kernel's protein, vitamins, and minerals. When rehydrated by soaking in liquid, bulgur nearly triples in volume. Bulgur is available in three granulations: fine (also labeled No. 1), medium (also labeled No. 2), and coarse. Fine- and medium-grain bulgur can generally be substituted for each other and can be prepared by simply soaking; the coarse type requires a brief cooking period. Do not substitute cracked wheat (cracked uncooked wheat berries) for bulgur.

Mamaliga

ROMANIAN CORNMEAL MUSH

ABOUT 7 CUPS; 6 TO 8 SERVINGS

For thousands of years the mainstay of the southeastern European diet consisted of porridges made from various grains—most notably barley, millet, spelt, and wheat—called *puls* by the Romans. After cornmeal was introduced to Europe in the sixteenth century, peasants from the Balkans to Georgia found it a cheaper and tastier replacement for the traditional grains. Thus, this hearty cornmeal porridge—called polenta (derived from "barley flour") in Italy, *puliszka* in Hungary, *kulesha* in the Ukraine, *ghomi* in Georgia, and *mamaliga* in Romania— became a staple food in much of eastern Europe.

Making *mamaliga* became a morning ritual for housewives, complete with its own traditions, equipment, and techniques, including a large copper pot, a special long-handled wooden stick for stirring (when thickened, the *mamaliga* bubbles and spits, so it is advisable to be at arm's length), and a method of cutting the thick mixture with a string. For the past three centuries, Romanian housewives have risen early, boiled water in a huge pot set over an open fire, gradually added the right amount of cornmeal by the handful, frantically stirring to prevent lumps, then continued to stir the mixture over low heat until thickened. This traditional method of making *mamaliga* takes more than an hour and is so tiring that the very word has become a popular Romanian term for a person with no energy.

Since *mamaliga* can be used with either dairy or meat dishes, it is ideal for any meal. Coarse cornmeal was used for everyday *mamaliga,* while finer cornmeal was usually reserved for special occasions. On Shavuot, Jews of northern Italy and Romania served white cornmeal *mamaliga,* symbolizing purity.

7 cups water

About 2 teaspoons salt

2 cups medium-grind cornmeal
  (or 1⅓ cups coarse cornmeal
  and ⅔ cup fine cornmeal)

1. In a large pot, bring the water to a boil. Add the salt. In a slow, steady stream, using a long-handled wooden spoon or whisk, stir in the cornmeal, stirring well to prevent lumps. (It can take up to 10 minutes to add all of the cornmeal.)

2. Reduce the heat to very low and simmer, stirring constantly, until the mixture thickens and begins to pull away from the sides of the pot, about 30 minutes.

3. Remove from the heat. Dip the wooden spoon into cold water and use it to scrape the *mamaliga* from the sides and toward the center of the pot.

4. Place over medium heat and let stand without stirring until the steam loosens the *mamaliga* from the bottom of the pot, 1 to 3 minutes.

5. Spoon the *mamaliga* into serving bowls or pour onto a large wooden board or serving platter, spread into a rectangle about 1 inch thick, and cut into portions. (The traditional method for cutting warm *mamaliga* is to place a taut thin string—or try a piece of dental floss—underneath, then quickly pull the ends toward each other.) Serve plain as an accompaniment to spicy foods or top with butter, sour cream, grated cheese, gravy, or tomato sauce. *Mamaliga* keeps in the refrigerator for at least 3 days.

VARIATION

Mamaliga can be made with less work on your part: After stirring the cornmeal into the water, cover, place on top of a double boiler set over simmering water, and cook, stirring every 10 minutes, until thickened and smooth, about 1¼ hours.

CORNMEAL

Cornmeal is ground whole corn ranging in texture from fine to coarse. The difference between yellow and white cornmeal is the color, the yellow variety containing a larger amount of beta-carotene. Otherwise, there is no perceptible difference in taste or texture between dishes made from either color meal.

Most commercial cornmeal is milled by electric-run rollers, a method that creates heat and subsequently destroys the germ. Bolted cornmeal is crushed by metal machines and then sifted to remove most of the bran and germ. Degerminated cornmeal is also crushed by machine, but the bran and germ are removed before crushing. Stone-ground (also called water-ground) cornmeal is crushed by water-powered mill stones, a process that retains the germ and bran (as no heat is produced). Stone-ground cornmeal tends to be coarser than the mass-produced kind. Although cornmeal without the germ (the oil) has a longer shelf life, it lacks much of the flavor. Store degerminated dried corn products in a cool, dry place. Store stone-ground products in the freezer.

ROMANIAN RHAPSODY

"I remember going to my grandmother's house every Sunday while growing up," reminisces Stan Zimmerman, owner of Sammy's Famous Romanian Restaurant, located on Manhattan's Lower East Side (although the restaurant features classic Jewish fare, it is not kosher). "She made great, wholesome food. I wanted a place that would re-create those meals."

According to local legend, the first Jews arrived in the northern part of the Balkan Peninsula during the reign of King Xerxes of Persia. Yet, its Jewish community remained a small one until the arrival of an influx of refugees fleeing the Byzantine Empire. A progression of other refugees further increased the Jewish population of the northern Balkans: Hungarians relocating after their expulsion in 1367, Sephardim who arrived with the Ottoman Empire, Polish Jews fleeing the Chmielnicki massacres of 1648, and Russians fleeing czarist persecution.

Romanian Jewish cooking reflects pronounced local and foreign roots. "Romanian cooking is primarily peasant fare, different from its neighbors through the generous use of spices and garlic, plenty of garlic," declares Zimmerman. "Standard Ashkenazic dishes include *knaidlach* [dumplings], kugels [baked puddings], *cholent* [Romanian *cholent* often contains goose flesh], and *barches* [braided challah]. Broiling and grilling over charcoal [reflecting a Middle Eastern influence] are the favorite ways of cooking meat. Most prominent are garlicky meat patties such as the four-inch-long *carnatzlach* and the smaller thumb-shaped *mitite* [both derived from the Middle Eastern kebab]. Arguably Romania's most well known meat specialty is pastrami [smoked dry cured beef brisket or plate, also derived from Turkish cooking].

"We use schmaltz instead of butter," Zimmerman notes. "We place pitchers of schmaltz on the table to spread on bread or mix into chopped eggs, chopped liver, black radishes, or mashed potatoes. And of course there are the *gribenes* [poultry cracklings]."

Romania's climate is particularly favorable for grains and legumes. Although non-Jewish Romanians eat little pasta, Romanian Jews commonly use broad noodles. "Unquestionably, the staple of the Romanian kitchen is cornmeal, generally prepared as a mush called *mamaliga*."

Conspicuous in the Romanian pantry is eggplant, a rarity in Hungarian and Polish kitchens. "Other popular Romanian vegetable dishes [all derived from the Turks] include *ghiveciu* [a vegetable stew], *brynza* [cucumber, tomato, and feta cheese salad], and *sarmali* [stuffed cabbage]."

Romanian pastry evinces a strong Hungarian influence, with its strudel, *rugelach, palacsinta* [Hungarian sweet crepes], and honey cake. *Fladni* is a traditional Rosh Hashanah dish. *Kindi* [wrapped pastries] are popular Purim treats. A Sabbath breakfast might contain sweet cheese turnovers and poppy seed horns.

Baked Mamaliga with Cheese

❧ 6 TO 8 SERVINGS ❧

4 cups freshly cooked mamaliga
(see page 192)
About 2 cups shredded
kashkaval (see page 30),
Cheddar, Muenster, or
Monterey Jack cheese,
1 cup crumbled feta cheese,
or ⅔ cup grated Parmesan
cheese
3 to 4 tablespoons butter

1. Preheat the oven to 350 degrees. Grease a 2-quart casserole.
2. Add the cheese to the *mamaliga,* stirring until smooth. Pour into the prepared pan. Dot with the butter.
3. Bake until golden brown, about 30 minutes. Cut into slices.

Fried Mamaliga

❧ 6 TO 8 SERVINGS ❧

4 cups freshly cooked mamaliga
(see page 192) or mamaliga
with cheese (see above)
About 3 tablespoons butter or
olive oil

1. Pour the *mamaliga* into a greased loaf pan or onto a greased baking sheet. Chill until firm, at least 4 hours.
2. Cut the *mamaliga* into ½-inch-thick slices.
3. Heat the butter or oil in a large skillet over medium heat. Fry the *mamaliga* until golden brown on both sides. Serve with sour cream or yogurt.

PERSIAN PANACHE

The relationship between Persia and the Jews began in 538 B.C.E., when Cyrus the Great conquered Babylonia and granted the Jews permission to return to Judea and rebuild the Temple. The emergence in 226 C.E. of the Sasanian dynasty, whose leaders were Zoroastrians, led to intense persecutions. Relief arrived in 642, when the Arabs conquered Persia, ending twelve hundred years of Persian dominance in western Asia. The position of Persian Jewry deteriorated again with the emergence of the Safawid dynasty in 1502 and the introduction of Shiism as the state religion. When the Islamic revolution of

1979 restored clergy control of the country as well as discrimination and persecution, those Jews able to escape the country fled.

"Fruits and vegetables are very important in Persian cooking and ritual," explains Talat Cohanim. "*Dolmeh* ["stuffed vegetables," a dish that the Persians probably created] is one of the most popular ways of preparing vegetables. *Dolmeh beh* [stuffed quince] and *dolmeh sib* [stuffed apple] are popular Sukkoth appetizers. Cold *dolmehs,* especially grape leaves, are popular for Shabbat lunch. Black-eyed peas with tongue is a traditional Rosh Hashanah dish. During Rosh Hashanah dinner, we cut off a piece of leek and throw it over our shoulders while reciting a blessing that our enemies should disappear. During the Passover Seder, everyone takes a bunch of scallions and lightly hits all the other people around the table while reciting *Dayenu* ["Enough," a Passover song].

"Citrus fruits and pomegranates are essentials, as the Persians prefer slightly tart dishes. Persian *charoseth* is made from a wide variety of fruits—dates, raisins, apples, bananas, and any kind of fresh fruit—and all kinds of nuts—almonds, walnuts, and pistachios. Since we didn't eat dairy foods on Passover, we

---

Opposite: **A Kurdish Jewish family in traditional costume, Jerusalem, 1995.**
Before the establishment of the State of Israel, about 25,000 Jews lived in Kurdistan—a region currently divided among Iraq, Iran, and Turkey. According to a local legend, Kurdish Jews are descended from the Ten Tribes who were exiled to this area—"Halah and Harbor by the river of Gazan" (II Kings 17:6)

made huge bowls of *charoseth* and served the leftovers for breakfast during the holiday.

"*Panir* [feta] is the favorite form of cheese," Cohanim notes. "Since you couldn't buy kosher cheese in the stores, my mother made her own at home. *Mast* [yogurt] accompanies many dairy meals.

"Meat is rarely cooked in large pieces; rather, it is cut into chunks to make kebabs, *khoreshes* [saucelike stews], and stews or ground to make meatballs, dumplings, and stuffings. Chicken is also very popular. A typical Shabbat dinner consists of *ghondi nochodi* [ground-chicken-and-chickpea-flour dumplings] in chicken soup, a main course of chicken, and always rice. For Shabbat lunch, we often serve *haleem* [Sabbath stew] made from meat or chicken and wheat berries with hard-boiled eggs on top."

Since the events of the Book of Esther occurred in Persia, Purim has special meaning to Persian Jews. Cohanim recalls, "On Purim eve at the end of the Fast of Esther, people would bring all kinds of *kukus* [vegetable omelets]—such as herbs, spinach, squash, and potato—and *halvas* [grain confections] flavored with cardamom, rose water, and saffron to the synagogue in memory of their dead relatives. After services everyone shared the feast. Like the Muslim custom, we also serve *halva* and *kuku* at a house of mourning.

"Although Persians love elaborate sweets, often to the point of excess, the recent trend has been toward lighter desserts such as fresh fruit or fruit compote; the more extravagant fare is generally reserved for special occasions."

Chelou

PERSIAN CRUSTY RICE

 6 TO 8 SERVINGS

The more than 7,000 varieties of rice fall into three basic categories: short-grain, medium-grain, and long-grain. Each category contains varying amounts of two primary starches, amylose and amylopectin. Amylose does not gelatinize during cooking, so the larger the proportion, the drier the kernels. Amylopectin does gelatinize during cooking, so the larger the proportion, the stickier the kernels. Long-grain rice contains the largest proportion of amylose starch, allowing it to cook without becoming heavy and sticky and clumping together. Medium-grain rice maintains its shape during cooking, softening on the outside while remaining firm on the inside. Short-grain (pearl or glutinous) rice has a large amount of amylopectin starch and a small amount of amylose—the grains cling together and the rice has a creamy texture.

The Persians invented many new ways of preparing their favorite grain, including a two-part cooking method called *chelou*. First the rice is soaked and partially cooked, and then it is steamed, producing fluffy, separate grains and a crisp bottom crust known as a *tahdiq* (literally "bottom of the pan"). When meats, vegetables, fruits, or herbs are cooked with the rice, the dish is called a *polo*. Chicken *polo*, chicken being reserved for special occasions, is traditionally served on Rosh Hashanah; *shirin polo* (sweet rice), at festive occasions. Since contact with Persia was limited during the past several centuries, *polo* is generally obscure in the West, while two of its adaptations—the Turkish pilaf and Indian pilau—are very well known.

3 cups long-grain rice	1. Wash the rice in lukewarm water, then soak it in cold water to cover for at least 2 hours or overnight. Drain and rinse under cold running water.
8 cups water	
2 tablespoons salt	
¼ cup vegetable oil	2. Bring the 8 cups water and salt to a boil over medium heat. Add the rice and cook, stirring occasionally to prevent sticking, for 10 minutes. Drain and rinse under cold running water.
¼ teaspoon ground turmeric	
2 tablespoons chicken broth or water	
2 medium potatoes or yellow onions, cut into ¼-inch-thick slices (optional)	3. Heat 2 tablespoons of the oil in a large saucepan over high heat. Stir in the turmeric, then the broth or water.
	4. Gradually add the rice, mounding in the center. Using the handle of a wooden spoon, poke a deep hole into the center of the rice. Drizzle with the remaining 2 tablespoons

oil. (Placing the rice in the oil produces a crisp bottom. If you do not want a crust on the rice, arrange the potato or onion slices in the pan before adding the rice.)

5. Place a kitchen towel or several layers of paper towels over the top of the pan. Cover with the lid and cook over medium heat until steaming, about 10 minutes.

6. Reduce the heat to low and simmer until the rice is tender and the bottom crisp, at least 20 minutes and up to 1 hour. (When the rice is ready, a cloud of steam emerges when the lid is lifted.) Fluff the rice with a fork. For easy removal of the crust, place the pot in a sink of cold water and let it stand for several minutes. Serve the warm rice and crust with a stew or *khoresh* (sauce-like stew; see page 120).

VARIATIONS

Polo (Rice with Meat or Vegetables): In step 4, spread half of the parboiled rice into the pot; spread 2 cups filling—such as cooked lentils, beans, peas, shredded chicken, or meatballs—over the rice, leaving the edges uncovered; and top with the remaining rice.

Reshteh Polo (Persian Rice with Noodles): Stir 8 ounces cooked thin egg noodles and, if desired, ½ cup raisins into the parboiled rice in step 4.

RICE

Rice was brought westward from eastern Asia to Persia at least three thousand years ago, where it quickly became so beloved that no meal was considered complete without its presence. Contact with the Persian Empire brought rice to Israel at the onset of the Second Temple period, and Jews became almost as passionate about it as the Persians, considering its whiteness a symbol of purity. By Roman times, Israeli rice had become an important export of which the Jerusalem Talmud (Demai 2:1,22b) boasts, "There is none like it outside Israel." Suggestions in the Talmud (Berachot 6:1,10b) for the blessing over this grain includes Simeon ha-Chasid's proposal, "who has created delicacies to delight the soul of every living being." In the eighth century, the Arabs introduced rice to Spain, where it became an important part of Sephardic cooking.

KUGELS,
PUDDINGS, AND PANCAKES

Kugels and Baked Puddings

Americans generally associate the term *pudding* with a sweet, soft-textured dish, but for much of history it referred to savory grain mixtures. Indeed, *poding,* the source of the word *pudding,* was an Old English sausage similar to the Slavic kishke (stuffed derma). *Kishke* (as well as *kasha*) was derived from *kashk,* a Persian term for cracked barley and wheat that became applied to a Persian grain pudding. (Later, *kashk* inspired *lakshah,* a Persian noodle dish, which spread to eastern Europe, where it became *lukshen,* the Yiddish word for noodles, and possibly the inspiration for noodle kugel.) *Kashk* also evolved into *kutach,* a bread pudding made with sour milk, salt, and oil that was a favorite food of Babylonian Jews. Many Jews living in Israel, who generally preferred legumes to starches, detested *kutach,* as witnessed by the numerous disparaging remarks about it in the Jerusalem Talmud. Yemenites still prepare a form of *kutach* called *ghininun*—sometimes substituting cottage cheese for the milk—which is baked overnight for Sabbath lunch. Since at least the seventh century, Jews in the Arab world have eaten *harisa* (called *kashak* by Persians), a Sabbath pudding made from cracked wheat or semolina and meat.

It was among the residents of the Rhineland, however, that baked puddings found their greatest appreciation. Early records of Franco-German Jewry reveal that they prepared a flour

Opposite: **A California family gathers in a *sukkah* during the Feast of the Tabernacle, 1908.** *"In booths (sukkahs) you shall dwell, seven days . . . That your generations may know that in booths I made the children of Israel dwell when I brought them out of the land of Egypt"* (LEVITICUS 23:42).

201

batter or bread batter, the latter called *weck schalet* (*weck* is German for "bread roll"), an inspired way of using stale bread. The batter was spread on top of the *schalet* (Sabbath stew) to seal in the moisture or, perhaps inspired by the dumplings of their non-Jewish neighbors, dropped in a round mass into the center of the stew to simmer overnight, absorbing flavor from the cooking liquid. The pudding was then served warm alongside the stew for Sabbath lunch. Eventually, Franco-German housewives began cooking these puddings in a small round covered dish placed inside the stew pot. At first, the pudding was known by the same name as the Sabbath stew, *schalet*. However, in order to differentiate between the two, some people began calling it *schaletkugel* (derived from *koogel*, German for "ball"), a reference to the round shape of the dumplinglike pudding. Eventually, kugel became the generic name for baked puddings, while *schalet* was sometimes applied to sweetened puddings.

Today, items ranging from apples to zucchini serve as the basis for kugels. The common denominator among these puddings is an absence of water and the use of fat and eggs to bind the batter. Traditional kugels as well as innovative new forms remain popular Ashkenazic dishes, served on the Sabbath, on festivals, and at life-cycle events.

Birne Schalet

ALSATIAN PEAR AND PRUNE KUGEL

5 TO 6 SERVINGS

¼ cup vegetable oil

1 cup (2 sticks) margarine, softened

¾ cup sugar

1¾ cups all-purpose flour

1 cup white wine

About ¼ teaspoon salt

Dash of ground cinnamon

6 large pears, cored and quartered (peeling is optional)

1 small bread roll, soaked in water and crumbled

8 ounces (about 1½ cups) pitted prunes

1. Preheat the oven to 350 degrees. Heat the oil in an oven-proof pot or deep casserole.

2. Beat together the margarine and ¼ cup of the sugar until light and fluffy. Add the flour, wine, salt, and cinnamon. Stir in the pears and bread.

3. Pour the batter into the pot. Bake, uncovered, until golden brown, about 1 hour. Let cool and remove the kugel from the pot; set the pot aside.

4. Preheat the oven to 200 degrees.

5. Simmer the prunes in water to cover until soft but not mushy, about 15 minutes. Drain.

6. Sprinkle the remaining ½ cup sugar into the same pot or casserole, arrange the prunes on top, and return the kugel to the pot. Cover, place in the oven, and bake at least 4 hours or overnight. Serve warm.

Kugel Yerushalmi

HASIDIC CARAMELIZED NOODLE PUDDING

10 TO 12 SERVINGS

The Chmielnicki massacres in Poland in 1648, the apostasy of the false messiah Shabbetai Tzvi in 1666, the subsequent partition of Poland, and other problems shook the Jewish communities of eastern Europe. Some Jews found an answer in the freedom offered by the Enlightenment (*Haskala* in Yiddish). Others turned to Kabbalistic healers and miracle workers. One of these holy men was Israel ben Eliezer, commonly called the Ba'al Shem Tov (Master of the Good Name). By the time of his death in 1760, he had created a full-fledged religious movement known as Hasidism and, within a generation, the bulk of the Jews in central Poland, Galicia, and the Ukraine were Hasidim.

Beginning in the late 1700s, groups of Hasidim began moving to the Holy Land in order to live a more fully religious life. They brought with them the traditions of eastern Europe, including their manner of dress and foods. It was among the Hasidim of Jerusalem that this distinctive noodle kugel, which features a tantalizing contrast of pepper and caramelized sugar, was popularized.

1 pound thin noodles or vermicelli
⅔ cup vegetable oil
¾ cup sugar
About 1 teaspoon salt
½ to 1½ teaspoons ground black pepper
6 large eggs, lightly beaten

1. Bring a large pot of lightly salted water to a boil. Add the noodles and cook until tender, 5 to 8 minutes. Drain and set aside.
2. Preheat the oven to 350 degrees. Grease a 13-by-9-inch baking dish or a large tube pan.
3. Heat the oil in a large saucepan over low heat. Add the sugar and stir until dissolved. Stop stirring and cook until dark brown but not burned, about 10 minutes.
4. Immediately add the noodles, stirring to coat evenly. Remove from the heat and season with the salt and pepper. Let cool until lukewarm, at least 15 minutes, then add the eggs. Adjust the seasonings.
5. Spoon the noodle mixture into the prepared baking dish. Bake until golden brown and crispy—about 1 hour for the baking dish, about 1½ hours for the tube pan. Serve warm or at room temperature with roast chicken, meat, or *cholent*.

Lukshen un Kaese Kugel

ASHKENAZIC SWEET NOODLE AND CHEESE PUDDING

4 TO 6 SERVINGS

Although bread puddings remained popular Sabbath fare until modern times, inventive cooks devised many variations. During Passover, matza was substituted for the bread. In the early Middle Ages, Germans began adding honey and sometimes cinnamon, nuts, and fruit to their puddings, and Jews emulated this practice. In the seventeenth century, when sugar became affordable in Europe, it became a common sweetener in kugels and led to even more variations. By the sixteenth century, rice kugel, influenced by the Ottoman invasion, had appeared in eastern Europe. However, since rice was expensive, it was generally reserved for special occasions. About this time, cooks also began replacing the bread with *lukshen* (noodles), producing what arguably became the most popular form of baked pudding, *lukshen kugel*.

In the dairy-rich Baltics, cheese was commonly added to the kugel. Ashkenazim use only cottage-type or cream cheeses in kugels, however, never hard cheese or the stringy mozzarella-type popular in Italy and the Balkans. There are nearly as many variations of dairy noodle kugel as there are cooks. Whichever variation you prefer, this creamy dish is commonly served at dairy meals such as Shavuot and Hanukkah. The recipe can be doubled and baked in a 13-by-9-inch baking dish.

8 ounces medium or broad noodles

¼ cup (½ stick) butter

2 large eggs, lightly beaten

About ½ cup sugar

½ teaspoon vanilla extract

About ½ teaspoon salt

8 ounces pot cheese or small-curd cottage cheese

1 cup sour cream or 4 ounces cream cheese

½ cup raisins

Ground cinnamon for garnish

1. Preheat the oven to 350 degrees. Grease an 8-inch-square (2-quart) baking dish.

2. Bring a large pot of lightly salted water to a boil. Add the noodles and cook until tender, about 8 minutes. Drain. Place the noodles in a large bowl, add the butter, and stir until the butter is melted.

3. Beat together the eggs, sugar, vanilla, and salt. Stir in the pot or cottage cheese and sour cream or cream cheese. Stir into the noodles. Add the raisins.

4. Pour into the prepared baking dish. Sprinkle with the cinnamon. Bake until golden brown, about 45 minutes. Serve warm or at room temperature as a side dish or dessert.

VARIATIONS

Custard Noodle Kugel: Increase the number of eggs to 4 and add ¾ cup milk.

Pareve Sweet Noodle Kugel: Omit the cheese and sour cream and increase number of the eggs to 4 or 5. (*Note:* The more eggs, the softer the kugel.)

Galician Salt and Pepper Kugel: Omit the cheese, sour cream, and sugar, increase the number of eggs to 3 or 4, and add ground black pepper to taste.

Kartoffel Kugel

ASHKENAZIC POTATO PUDDING
6 TO 8 SERVINGS

There are many variations of potato pudding: Some use grated raw potatoes, others mashed cooked potatoes. Some add *russel* (fermented grated beets), sautéed mushrooms, or chopped liver; others add sugar and ground almonds to make a dessert. And *potatonik* is a combination of yeast bread and potato kugel. The following version has a crisp crust and a moist, soft interior. The recipe can be doubled and baked in a 13-by-9-inch baking dish.

½ cup schmaltz (see page 109) or vegetable oil

6 medium or 4 large russet potatoes (about 2 pounds), peeled

2 medium yellow onions, chopped (about 1 cup)

3 large eggs, lightly beaten

About 1 teaspoon salt

Ground black pepper to taste

¼ cup gribenes (poultry cracklings; see page 109) or grated carrot (optional)

About ⅓ cup matza meal or all-purpose flour

1. Preheat the oven to 375 degrees. Heat an 8- or 9-inch-square baking dish in the oven.

2. Coat the bottom and sides of the baking dish with ¼ cup of the schmaltz or oil and return to the oven until very hot, about 15 minutes.

3. Place the potatoes in a large bowl of lightly salted cold water. (This keeps them from discoloring.) Grate the potatoes into the onions, stirring to mix.

4. Stir in the eggs, remaining ¼ cup schmaltz or oil, salt, pepper, and, if desired, *gribenes* or carrot. Add enough matza meal or flour to bind the batter.

5. Pour into the heated dish and bake until golden brown, about 1 hour. Although this is best when warm, the leftovers can be served at room temperature.

Babanatza

GREEK SEMOLINA AND RAISIN PUDDING
9 TO 12 SERVINGS

In Greece, this treat was often served for *shalosh seudot* (the afternoon meal, literally "third meal") or following the Sabbath.

2 cups dark raisins
12 large eggs
1 to 1½ cups sugar
¾ cup honey
1½ cups fine semolina or farina
1½ to 2 cups coarsely chopped almonds or walnuts
2 to 3 medium apples, peeled, cored and chopped (optional)

1. Soak the raisins in water to cover overnight. Drain. Grind or puree the raisins.

2. Preheat the oven to 325 degrees. Grease a large baking dish.

3. Beat the eggs until light. Add the sugar and honey and beat until thick and creamy, about 5 minutes. Stir in the raisins, semolina or farina, nuts, and, if desired, apples.

4. Pour into the prepared baking dish—the batter should be no more than 2 inches deep. Bake until golden brown, about 1½ hours. Let cool.

VARIATION
Passover Babanatza: Substitute 1½ cups matza meal or 12 crumbled matzot (about 6 cups) for the semolina.

Stove-Top Puddings

Kheer

INDIAN RICE PUDDING
 6 TO 8 SERVINGS

Cardamom-flavored rice puddings are popular Indian treats. This coconut milk version is a traditional Rosh Hashanah dessert.

2 cups water
1 cup rice
5 cups coconut milk
1¼ cups sugar
6 cardamom pods or ½ to 1
*   teaspoon ground cardamom*
Pinch of salt
1 teaspoon vanilla extract

1. Bring the water to a boil in a medium saucepan. Add the rice, cover, reduce the heat to low, and simmer until the liquid is absorbed, about 18 minutes.

2. Add the coconut milk, sugar, cardamom, and salt. Simmer, uncovered and stirring frequently, over medium heat until thickened, about 20 minutes.

3. Remove from the heat and stir in the vanilla. Pour the pudding into 6 to 8 serving bowls. Serve warm or chilled.

TO MAKE COCONUT MILK

1. Bring 2 cups of water to a low boil. Stir in 2 cups of grated fresh coconut or unsweetened desiccated coconut, remove from the heat, and let cool to room temperature, stirring occasionally, about 2 hours.

2. Puree in a food processor or blender. Strain through a fine cheesecloth. Store in the refrigerator. Makes about 2 cups.

Sutlach

MIDDLE EASTERN RICE FLOUR PUDDING

 6 TO 8 SERVINGS

A Turkish Jewish wedding feast—weddings were customarily held on Friday afternoon with the wedding feast serving as Sabbath dinner—traditionally features seven courses. The first course is *sutlach,* also called *mahallebi,* a rich, rose-flavored rice pudding, symbolizing a sweet life for the newlyweds. Next comes an ancient symbol of fertility, fish, followed by *siete en boca* (tiny sugar-coated almond pieces), *ojaldres de carne* (meat-filled phyllo triangles), and *albondigas de meyoyo* (calf's-brain meatballs). The *meneado* (main course) is left to the discretion of the cook but always contains almonds (considered an aphrodisiac). The final dish, served only to the couple, is pigeon.

Sutlach (*sut* means "milk" in Turkish) is also served in many Sephardic households at special dairy meals, including Shavuot (called "the Feast of Roses") and the meal following Yom Kippur. For *desayuno* (Sabbath breakfast; see page 29), many mothers write their young children's names or initials with ground cinnamon on top of individual cups of pudding.

6 tablespoons rice flour or
*   cream of rice*
⅓ to ½ cup sugar
4 cups milk
1 tablespoon rose water or
*   1 teaspoon vanilla extract*
Ground cinnamon and/or
*   chopped nuts for garnish*

1. Combine the rice flour or cream of rice and sugar in a large saucepan. Stir in a little of the milk to make a smooth paste. Gradually stir in the remaining milk.

2. Bring to a boil over medium heat, stirring constantly. Reduce the heat to low and simmer, stirring frequently, until the pudding thickens, about 15 minutes.

3. Remove from the heat and stir in the rose water or vanilla. Pour into 6 to 8 serving bowls and sprinkle with the cinnamon and/or nuts. Serve warm or chilled.

Hint: To make your own rice flour, process 1 cup white rice in a blender until powdery.

VARIATIONS

Baked Sutlach: Pour the thickened pudding into a greased casserole to a depth of 3 inches and bake at 325 degrees until the top is golden brown, about 40 minutes.

Loz Sutlach (Middle Eastern Almond Rice Flour Pudding): Substitute ¼ teaspoon almond extract for the rose water and stir in ¾ cup ground blanched almonds.

Dodail (Cochin Rice Flour Pudding): Substitute 3 cups coconut milk (or 3 ounces cream of coconut dissolved in 3 cups water) for the milk.

TISHA B'AV

On the ninth day of the month of Av in the year 586 B.C.E., Babylonian forces entered Jerusalem and torched Solomon's Temple and much of the city. The emperor Nebuchadnezzar, emulating the Assyrian practice of removing the upper and middle classes of a society and replacing them with those from a distant country as a way of minimizing political unrest, deported much of the Jewish population to Babylonia. On the ninth day of the month of Av in 70 C.E., after three years of revolution, Roman forces breached the walls of Jerusalem and burned the Second Temple. Sixty-two years later, a second insurgency met a similar fate as, once again on the ninth day of Av, the Roman legions defeated the rebel leader Bar Kokhba at the fortress of Betar. Thus, the most somber span of the Jewish calendar is a three-week period of semi-mourning stretching from the seventeenth day of the month of Tammuz, a minor fast day marking the beginning of the siege of Jerusalem by Babylonian forces in 586 B.C.E., to Tisha b'Av (the ninth day of the month of Av), commemorating the national disasters that occurred on this day, including more recently the expulsion of the Jews from Spain in 1492.

From the first day of Av, Jews traditionally do not eat meat, except on the Sabbath; a few abstain during the entire three-week period. Accordingly, cooks prepare an assortment of dairy and vegetarian fare during this time of year. The meal before the fast also consists of dairy foods and usually contains dishes made from lentils and eggs, both ancient Jewish symbols of mourning.

Halva di Gris

MIDDLE EASTERN SEMOLINA PUDDING
6 TO 8 SERVINGS

Although Westerners are most familiar with halvah as a sweetened sesame confection, the name actually refers to a variety of sweetened cooked grain confections popular throughout central Asia and the Middle East. Ironically, although halvah originated in the Middle East and Ashkenazim only recently became familiar with the sesame variation, the word entered the English language by way of Yiddish, as the confection was common in Jewish delis.

The semolina in this firm pudding, also called *halva aurde sujee,* is toasted in fat, then steamed to plump the grains. It is popular in Iran and central Asia, where it is served at most celebrations, particularly Purim (see page 316) and Hanukkah (see page 220). Raisins (about ¾ cup) are simmered in the sugar syrup for Tu b'Shevat (see page 213). Greek Jews make a version using milk for Shavuot (see page 315), Hanukkah, and other dairy meals.

3 cups water (or 1½ cups water and 1½ cups milk)

1½ cups sugar

1 cup (2 sticks) butter or margarine

1½ cups coarse or fine semolina (not semolina flour)

½ teaspoon ground turmeric

½ to 1 cup coarsely chopped almonds, pistachios, walnuts, or any combination (optional)

1 teaspoon rose water or vanilla extract

1 teaspoon ground cinnamon or ½ teaspoon ground cardamom

1. Bring the water and sugar to a boil. Reduce the heat to very low, cover, and let stand while preparing the semolina.
2. Melt the butter or margarine in a medium saucepan over medium-high heat. Stir in the semolina and turmeric. Reduce the heat to low and cook, stirring constantly, until golden brown, about 20 minutes. If using the nuts, add them halfway through the toasting.
3. Return the syrup to a boil, then slowly stir into the semolina. (Be careful, since the mixture will splatter.)
4. Cook over low heat, stirring constantly, until the liquid evaporates and the mixture comes away easily from the sides of the pan, about 5 minutes. Stir in the rose water or vanilla and cinnamon or cardamom.
5. Remove from the heat, cover with a damp cloth, replace the lid, and let stand for at least 30 minutes. Serve warm or at room temperature. Spoon the halvah into serving dishes or press into a large mold or several small molds, let cool, and invert onto serving plates.

VARIATIONS

Indian Raisin-Coconut Semolina Halvah: Cook 3 tablespoons raisins, 3 tablespoons grated coconut, and 1 teaspoon grated orange zest with the sugar syrup.

Halva aude Birinj (Persian Rice Confection): Substitute 1½ cups rice flour or cream of rice for the semolina and increase the amount of rose water to 1 tablespoon.

***Below:* Purim costumes.** Amsterdam, 1723. *On Purim, children as well as many adults dress up in costumes, a custom that originated in Italy at the end of the fifteenth century, inspired by the masked entertainers of the* commedia dell'arte.

Kofyas

MIDDLE EASTERN SWEETENED WHEAT BERRIES
 ABOUT 9 CUPS; 6 TO 8 SERVINGS

Wheat berries are unprocessed whole wheat with only the outer husk removed. Their nutty flavor and chewy texture are delicious alone or mixed with other grains. They are available in health food and Middle Eastern stores. It is advisable to purchase grains from a source with a high turnover in order to assure freshness. Store in the refrigerator or freezer. Add wheat berries to salads, soups, stews, casseroles, and puddings.

Since wheat berries resemble teeth, Sephardim customarily serve them at a party to honor a baby's first tooth. Sweetened and mixed with fruits and nuts, they become a holiday dish—called *kofyas* in Turkey, *assurei* (from an Arabic word for "ten") or *koliva* in Greece, and *korkoti* in Georgia—for Tu b'Shevat (see page 213) and Rosh Hashanah (see page 126). A similar Turkish pudding made from cracked wheat or bulgur is called *prehito* (see page 214) or *moostrahana*.

1 pound (about 2 cups) whole-wheat berries
8 cups water
About 1½ cups sugar or honey
1 to 2 teaspoons ground cinnamon
2 cups raisins or dried currants (or 1 cup raisins and 1 cup chopped dates)
2 cups chopped mixed nuts (any combination of walnuts, almonds, pistachios, and pine nuts)
Pomegranate seeds for garnish (optional)

1. Soak the wheat berries in water to cover overnight. Drain. (Without presoaking, the cooking time can take up to 5 hours.)
2. Bring the wheat berries and 8 cups water to a boil, reduce the heat to medium-low, and simmer, uncovered, until tender but still slightly chewy, about 2 hours. (For a firmer texture, add salt to the cooking liquid.) Drain.
3. Add the sugar or honey and cinnamon and stir over medium-low heat until the sugar or honey melts, about 2 minutes. (The wheat berries harden a bit when the sugar is added.)
4. Remove from the heat and stir in the fruit and nuts. Serve warm, at room temperature, or chilled. Mound the *kofyas* on a serving plate, and, if desired, garnish with the pomegranate seeds. (*Kofyas* is commonly garnished with similarly shaped pomegranate seeds.)

VARIATION

Sleehah (Syrian Anise-Flavored Wheat Berries): Add ¼ cup anise seeds (*shimra* in Arabic) before cooking the wheat berries or add ½ cup anise liqueur and, if desired, 1 teaspoon rose water with the fruit and nuts.

TU B'SHEVAT

Tu b'Shevat (the fifteenth day of the month of Shevat) is a minor holiday sometimes referred to as the Jewish Arbor Day. The Talmud refers to the day as Rosh Hashanah l'Ilanot (New Year for Trees). In Israel by early February, most of the year's rain has fallen, the sap has started to flow again, and the branches have begun to show the first signs of budding. In agricultural-based ancient Israel, this was a meaningful occasion accompanied with singing and dancing.

Sephardim, who lived in warm locales, manifest a deep devotion for the day, which they call Las Frutas (The Fruit). On the day of Tu b'Shevat, Sephardic families customarily visit relatives, where they are served a feast. The children, who are given a vacation from school for the day, are encouraged not only to partake of the spread, but also to take *bolsas de frutas* (bags of fruit) home with them.

The primary influence on Sephardic Tu b'Shevat practices was the community of Kabbalists who made their home in sixteenth-century Safed. This group of mystics maintained a profound regard for this minor

holiday and developed a new liturgy and rituals for the day. An expanded version of those prayers was collected in an eighteenth-century work called "Peri Etz Hadar" ("Fruit of the Goodly Tree"), describing a Tu b'Shevat Seder (ceremonial meal). This ceremony, based on the Passover Seder, contains such rituals as drinking four cups of wine—each wine a different type—and sampling at least twelve (some increase the number to fifteen, corresponding to the numerical value of *tu*) fruits and nuts, especially those associated with Israel or mentioned in the Bible: *bokser* (carob), dates, raisins or grapes, figs, citrons, apples, pears, pomegranates, quinces, olives, almonds, walnuts, and pistachios. Iraqi Jews further expanded on the concept, increasing the number to a minimum of one hundred fruits and vegetables.

Although there are few specific Tu b'Shevat dishes, a common custom is to serve entrées containing fruit and grains—particularly wheat and barley—mentioned in the Bible.

Prehito

SEPHARDIC BULGUR PUDDING
6 TO 8 SERVINGS

This pudding, called *moostrahana* in Turkey and *belella* in the Middle East, is a traditional Tu b'Shevat (see page 213) and Sukkoth (see page 146) dish.

1 cup medium bulgur
3 cups water
Pinch of salt
½ cup sugar or honey
1 cup coarsely chopped walnuts
*   or almonds*
½ cup dried currants or raisins
¼ cup chopped dates (optional)
1 teaspoon ground cinnamon

1. Combine the bulgur, water, and salt in a medium saucepan. Bring to a boil, reduce the heat to low, and simmer, stirring occasionally, until the liquid is absorbed and the bulgur is tender, about 30 minutes. If necessary, continue cooking uncovered until the liquid is absorbed.

2. Remove from the heat and fluff with a fork. Stir in the remaining ingredients.

3. Spoon into a 9-inch-square baking dish and refrigerate until chilled.

VARIATION

Baked Prehito: Before transferring to the baking dish, add 1 lightly beaten egg, and bake in a 350-degree oven for 40 minutes.

Chremslach

ASHKENAZIC MATZA MEAL PANCAKES IN HONEY
❧ ABOUT 36 (1-INCH) PANCAKES ❧

In his work *De re conquinaria libri decem* (Cuisine in Ten Books), the Roman epicure Apicius (died 37 C.E.) included a recipe for preparing the popular Roman dish *vermiculos* (Latin for "little worms"): "Cook the finest flour in milk to make a stiff paste. Spread it on a dish, cut it into pieces, that, when fried in fine oil, cover with pepper and honey." This dish, called *iytree* in the Talmud, was adopted by Jews from Judea to the Rhineland. During the Middle Ages, however, the original dish disappeared from the Italian culinary repertoire and the name *vermicelli* was applied to long, thin threads of dough boiled in water.

Beginning in the twelfth century, numerous Franco-German rabbis mentioned the custom of eating fried or baked strips of dough in honey called *vermesel* or *verimslish* at the start of the Friday evening meal. At some point, the name changed to *gremsel* and later, when the dish reached eastern Europe, it became *chremsel.* Eventually, the dish itself changed, taking on the meaning of various fritters and pancakes. In France and Germany, the term *vermesel* also evolved into *frimsel,* the western Yiddish word for noodles. By the late fifteenth century, chicken soup with *frimsel* replaced *vermesel* as the first course for Friday evening dinner. Although Ashkenazim no longer prepare the original *vermesel,* both these Passover pancakes and *teiglach* (honey dough balls; see page 348) hark back to this ancient dish.

1 cup matza meal
¼ cup chopped almonds
1 to 6 teaspoons sugar
1 teaspoon ground cinnamon
Pinch of ground ginger
About ½ teaspoon salt
1 cup water or sweet wine
4 large eggs, lightly beaten
Vegetable oil for frying
1½ cups honey

1. Combine the matza meal, nuts, sugar, cinnamon, ginger, and salt. Stir in the water or wine and eggs. Let stand until thickened, about 10 minutes.

2. Heat a thin layer of oil in a large skillet over medium heat. In batches, drop the batter by teaspoonfuls and fry until browned on both sides. Drain on paper towels.

3. Add the honey to the skillet and bring to a boil over medium heat, stirring frequently (the honey may boil up).

4. Return the *chremslach* to the skillet, tossing to coat. Store the *chremslach* in the honey syrup.

Bimuelos de Massa/Matse Chremslach

MATZA FARFEL PANCAKES
ABOUT 24 (3-INCH) PANCAKES

Pancakes made from crumbled matza or matza meal are familiar Passover breakfast and supper fare in both Sephardic and Ashkenazic communities. They can be enhanced in a variety of ways: Fill with jam or fruit; stir in chopped fruit, nuts, or cheese; or bathe in a honey syrup. For a crisper pancake, decrease the number of eggs. Sephardic *bimuelos* are traditionally served with *arrope* (raisin syrup; see page 371), *dulce* (fruit preserves), or yogurt. Ashkenazic *chremslach* are topped with honey, *varenyah* (jam), cinnamon-sugar, or sour cream.

4 cups crumbled matza
About 3 cups boiling water
4 large eggs, lightly beaten
About 1 teaspoon salt
Pinch of ground black pepper
3 tablespoons butter, margarine,
  or schmaltz (see page 109)

1. Soak the matza in the water until soft but not mushy, about 1 minute. Drain and squeeze out the excess moisture.
2. Stir in the eggs, salt, and pepper.
3. Melt the butter, margarine, or schmaltz in a large skillet over medium heat. In batches, drop the batter by heaping tablespoonfuls and fry until golden brown on both sides, 1 to 2 minutes per side.

VARIATIONS

Matse Brei (Ashkenazic Fried Matza): Add the matza mixture to the skillet all at once and fry, pressing down the center occasionally, until golden brown on both sides, about 4 minutes per side. To turn the *matse brei* without fear of breaking it, cover the skillet with a large dish, invert it, then slide the pancake back into the skillet to finish cooking.
(*Note: Matse brei,* from the Yiddish *briehn* [soak], is a cross between a pancake and an omelet made by moistening matza farfel in eggs. This dish has provided many an Ashkenazic Passover breakfast over the years. The basic *matse brei* recipe developed many variations, including the addition of milk, sweeteners, cheese, onions, sliced mushrooms, fruit, and other ingredients. Although for *matse brei* purists these variations smack of heresy, others can enjoy the diversity.)
Bimuelos de Massa con Muez (Sephardic Matza Pancakes with Nuts): Dip the hot pancakes into cooled sugar syrup (see page 372), then into finely chopped walnuts.

Matse-Kaese Chremslach (Ashkenazic Cheese Farfel Pancakes): Add 3 to 4 tablespoons farmer or cottage cheese.

Matse Kleis/Matse Pletzel (Ashkenazic Savory Matza Pancakes): Add 4 chopped medium yellow onions sautéed in ¼ cup schmaltz (see page 109) or margarine until lightly golden.

Pizzarelle (Italian Matza Farfel Pancakes): Add ⅓ cup raisins or dried currants, ⅓ cup chopped walnuts or almonds, 1 tablespoon grated orange or lemon zest, and 3 to 6 tablespoons leftover *charoseth* (Passover fruit paste). Bring 1 cup honey, ¼ cup water, and 1 tablespoon lemon juice to a boil and drizzle over the pancakes.

Tzukel Chremslach (Ashkenazic Fruit and Nut Matza Pancakes): Add 2 to 4 tablespoons sugar, ¼ cup chopped walnuts or almonds, ¼ to ½ cup raisins and/or grated apples, 1 teaspoon grated lemon zest, and ½ teaspoon ground cinnamon.

Atayef

SYRIAN FILLED PANCAKES

 ABOUT 36 PANCAKES

Syrian Jews enjoy these filled pancakes on Hanukkah and special occasions.

Vegetable oil for frying and deep frying
1 recipe atayef *batter (see below)*
1 recipe atayef *filling (see below)*
About 1½ cups sugar syrup (see page 372), cooled

1. Preheat a griddle or large skillet over medium heat. Lightly grease with oil.
2. In batches, drop the batter by tablespoonfuls to form 3-inch pancakes and fry until bubbles appear on the tops. Do not fry the tops. Remove the pancakes and cover with a clean kitchen towel to keep moist.
3. Place 1 teaspoon of filling in the center of the uncooked side of each pancake and fold in half to enclose the filling, pressing the edges together to seal. Or top each pancake with a second pancake. (The *atayef* may be prepared ahead to this point and frozen. Do not thaw before frying; increase the cooking time.)
4. Heat about 2 inches oil to about 375 degrees.
5. In batches, deep-fry the pancakes, turning once, until golden brown on both sides, 2 to 3 minutes. Remove with a slotted spoon and drain on paper towels. Drizzle the warm pancakes with the cooled sugar syrup.

Yeast Atayef Batter

1 teaspoon active dry yeast
2⅔ cups lukewarm water
1 tablespoon sugar
1 large egg
2 tablespoons butter or margarine, melted
Pinch of salt
2 cups all-purpose flour

1. Dissolve the yeast in ¼ cup of the water. Stir in 1 teaspoon of the sugar and let stand until foamy, about 5 minutes.
2. Add the remaining water, remaining sugar, egg, butter or margarine, and salt. Gradually stir in the flour to make a smooth batter. Cover and let rise at room temperature for about 1½ hours. Stir.

Baking Powder Atayef Batter

1¼ cups all-purpose flour
1 tablespoon sugar
1¾ teaspoons double-acting
   baking powder
½ teaspoon salt
1¼ cups water (or ¾ cup yogurt
   and ½ cup milk)
1 large egg, lightly beaten
2 tablespoons vegetable oil

Sift together the flour, sugar, baking powder, and salt. Blend together the water, egg, and oil. Stir into the flour mixture. Or process all of the ingredients in a blender until smooth.

Atayef Cheese Filling

8 ounces drained ricotta or
   small-curd cottage cheese
¼ to ½ cup sugar (optional)

Combine all of the ingredients.

Atayef Nut Filling

1 cup chopped walnuts or
   pistachios
2 to 3 tablespoons sugar
½ teaspoon rose water
½ teaspoon orange blossom
   water

Combine all of the ingredients.

VARIATION
Add ½ teaspoon ground cinnamon and substitute 2 teaspoons water for the rose water and orange blossom water.

HANUKKAH

Hanukkah ("dedication" in Hebrew) commemorates the rededication of the Temple following the successful revolt of the Maccabees against Antiochus and the Syrian-Greek forces in 165 B.C.E. As the priests began the task of purifying the Temple, they found only one small vial of untainted olive oil fit for use in the candelabra. Although there was only enough oil to last for one day, the lamp continued to burn for eight days, until undefiled oil became available.

Fried foods and dairy foods are the source of most Hanukkah dishes. Fried foods represent the miracle of the oil. Every Jewish community has in its culinary ranks at least one fried pastry for Hanukkah.

The association of Hanukkah with dairy foods is more complicated, one due to a misunderstanding of Judith, one of the books of the Apocrypha. The narrative tells of Nebuchadnezzar, king of Assyria, sending his general, Holofernes, to conquer Judea. The Assyrians laid siege to Bethulia, a fortified town on the outskirts of Jerusalem. In order to save her town, Judith, a young widow, went to Holofernes, who, taken by her beauty, asked her to his tent. Judith fed him cheese to induce thirst and then plied him with wine. When the general fell into a drunken stupor, Judith cut off his head with his own sword. Learning of the death of their leader, the Assyrians panicked and fled. Although this legend predates the Greek period by many centuries, during the Middle Ages it became associated with the Hasmonean revolt. Judith was even believed to be the daughter of Judah Maccabee ("The Hammer") and Holofernes an agent of the Syrian-Greeks. Nonetheless, to commemorate Judith's heroism, dairy dishes, commemorating the cheese that she fed to Holofernes, became popular Hanukkah fare.

FRESH CHEESES

For millennia, farmers used the milk remaining after skimming the cream to make a homemade cheese aptly called "cottage." Creamed cottage cheese is cottage cheese mixed with a creaming mixture made from milk or cream called a dressing. Low-fat cottage cheese contains a lower-fat dressing.

Dry-curd cottage cheese is plain drained curd (without the added dressing of creamed cottage cheese). Pot cheese (also called baker's cheese and hoop cheese) is similar to dry-curd cottage cheese, except that not all of the whey is drained off. Farmer cheese is drained (pressed) cottage cheese mixed with a little cream.

Zeesih Kaese Latkes

ASHKENAZIC SWEET CHEESE PANCAKES

ABOUT 30 (3-INCH) PANCAKES

Latke—derived from *elaion,* the Greek word for "olive oil"—is an Ashkenazic term for pancakes, particularly those served on Hanukkah. Cheese, the original form of latke, combines the two primary Hanukkah foods—dairy and fried. Ashkenazim and Sephardim enjoy these delicate pancakes for dairy meals on Hanukkah and Passover.

1 pound cottage, pot, or ricotta cheese

4 large eggs

About ¾ cup all-purpose flour or matza meal

2 tablespoons butter, melted, or sour cream

1 to 2 tablespoons sugar or honey

½ teaspoon vanilla extract or ground cinnamon

½ teaspoon salt

Vegetable oil or butter for frying

1. In a food processor or blender, puree the cheese, eggs, flour or matza meal, butter or sour cream, sugar or honey, vanilla or cinnamon, and salt until smooth. Or beat the eggs with an electric mixer until thick and creamy, then beat in the cheese and the remaining batter ingredients.

2. Heat a large skillet or griddle over medium heat. Lightly grease with oil or butter.

3. In batches, drop the batter by heaping tablespoonfuls and fry until bubbles form on the tops and the bottoms are lightly browned, 2 to 3 minutes.

4. Turn and fry until golden brown, 1 to 2 minutes. (The pancakes may be kept warm by placing in a single layer on a baking sheet in a 200-degree oven.) Serve accompanied with sour cream, yogurt, maple syrup, flavored butter, jam, cinnamon-sugar, or fresh fruit.

VARIATION

Lighter Cheese Pancakes: Separate the eggs; beat the egg whites until stiff but not dry, and fold into the batter.

Kartoffel Latkes

ASHKENAZIC POTATO PANCAKES
ABOUT 24 MEDIUM PANCAKES

In eastern Europe, cheese, the basis of the original latke, was a luxury item during the winter months. Since butter was often unavailable at this time of year and oil was very expensive, schmaltz (rendered poultry fat) was the primary fat. Thus, pareve items such as flour and buckwheat were commonly substituted for the cheese. After potatoes, cheap and available, gained respectability, they became the most popular form of Hanukkah pancake and the potato latke became the preeminent Ashkenazic Hanukkah dish.

*6 medium russet potatoes
(about 2 pounds), peeled*
*1 medium yellow onion, finely
chopped (about ½ cup)*
2 large eggs, lightly beaten
*About 3 tablespoons matza
meal or all-purpose flour*
About 1 teaspoon salt
¼ teaspoon ground black pepper
Vegetable oil for frying

1. Grate the potatoes, coarsely or finely, into a bowl of lightly salted water. (This removes the starch and keeps the potatoes from darkening.) Drain and press out the moisture. Stir in the onion, eggs, matza meal or flour, salt, and pepper.
2. Heat about ¼ inch oil in a large skillet over medium-high heat to about 360 degrees.
3. In batches, drop the batter by heaping tablespoonfuls or ⅓ cupfuls into the oil and flatten with the back of a spoon. Fry until golden brown on both sides, 3 to 5 minutes per side.
4. Drain on paper towels. (The latkes can be kept warm by placing in a single layer on a baking sheet in a 200-degree oven.) Serve with applesauce, jam, or sour cream.

POTATOES

Sunday potatoes, Monday potatoes, Tuesday and
Wednesday potatoes, Thursday and Friday potatoes,
and for the Sabbath a special treat—a potato kugel!

—YIDDISH FOLK SONG

The potato is such an intrinsic part of eastern European Jewish cooking that it is difficult to believe that it is actually a relatively recent addition to the Jewish pantry. However, both the white and sweet potato, two unrelated tubers, are indigenous to the Andes Mountains of South America, where they were cultivated almost five thousand years ago by the Incas. The first mention of the white potato, a member of the nightshade family, in a European source was by a Spanish expedition to northern Peru in 1537. When this tiny tuber finally reached Spain around 1588, it was considered a little truffle (*taratufli* in Latin, hence its German and Yiddish name, *kartoffel*). The Spanish called it *patata*—a corruption of the Indian words *papas* (sweet potato) and *batata* (tuber).

For centuries, Europeans regarded the white potato either as a source of leprosy or poisonous. Only in the face of abject poverty did it become an important part of the diet, most notably in Ireland. The potato subsequently proved vital in France when famine and hunger swept the country in the wake of the Revolution. The Germans soon joined the bandwagon and by the end of the eighteenth century were using these tubers to make potato flour and a variety of dishes,

such as dumplings, salads, soups, and pancakes. The potato took longer to gain acceptance in eastern Europe. Indeed, it was not until a series of crop failures in Russia and Poland in 1839 and 1840 that potatoes were for the first time planted in large numbers in that part of the world. Within a short period, these hearty tubers emerged as the staple of the eastern European diet, replacing buckwheat and legumes.

Following the partition of Poland between Austria, Prussia, and Russia in 1795, the Jewish population of Russian Poland numbered about 1.25 million. By the census of 1897, that number, despite massive Jewish emigration, had grown to about 5 million (15 percent of the total population of Poland). Not coincidentally, this Jewish population explosion, a rate more than twice that of their non-Jewish neighbors, corresponded to the availability and emerging popularity of the potato in eastern Europe.

Eastern European Jews adopted the potato dishes prepared by their coreligionists from Germany as well as inventing their own dishes, including knishes, kreplach, *potatonick* (potato bread), and the basis for an inexpensive and filling, yet tasty, kugel.

Blintzes

ASHKENAZIC THIN PANCAKES

 ABOUT 16 (5-INCH) OR 12 (6-INCH) PANCAKES

These thin pancakes, called *blinchiki* in Russian and *bletlach* (leaves) in Yiddish, originated in the Ukraine and are relatively modern descendants of the ancient Russian buckwheat pancakes known as *blinis*. As with other filled foods, blintzes provide a great way of transforming leftovers into a special dish or stretching scarce resources. They are commonly filled with fresh cheese, mashed potatoes, kasha (see page 188), ground beef, chopped liver, and fruit.

Ashkenazim serve cheese blintzes, topped with sour cream or fruit sauce, on Shavuot and Hanukkah, during the week before Tisha b'Av, and on other occasions where it is customary to eat dairy dishes. Ashkenazim have an additional rationale for serving blintzes on Shavuot: Two blintzes placed side by side resemble the two tablets that Moses received on Mount Sinai.

4 large eggs, lightly beaten
1 cup milk or water (or ½ cup
milk and ½ cup water)
2 tablespoons butter or
margarine, melted, or
vegetable oil
About ½ teaspoon salt
1 cup all-purpose flour
Vegetable oil or butter for frying
1 recipe blintz filling (see pages
225–26) or Ashkenazic
pastry filling (see pages
48–50)

1. Whisk together the eggs, the milk or water, the butter, margarine, or oil, and the salt. Gradually whisk in the flour to make a smooth, thin batter with the consistency of heavy cream. Strain if there are any lumps. (The batter can be prepared in a blender or food processor.) Let the batter stand in the refrigerator at least 30 minutes or overnight.

2. Heat a thin layer of oil or butter in a 6-inch heavy skillet (nonstick is best) over medium heat. Pour in about 2 tablespoons batter, tilting the pan until the batter coats the bottom; pour the excess back into the bowl. Fry until the edges begin to brown, about 30 seconds.

3. Flip the blintz onto a clean cloth or a plate lined with waxed paper, browned side up. Stack the blintzes between pieces of waxed paper. (The pancakes can be prepared ahead and stored in the refrigerator for up to 5 days or in the freezer for up to 1 month. Return to room temperature before filling.)

4. Place a blintz, browned side up, on a flat surface and spoon a heaping tablespoon of the filling in the lower center. Fold the sides over the filling, fold the bottom edge

over, then roll up to form a package. Repeat with the remaining blintzes.

5. Heat 1 tablespoon butter or margarine in a large skillet over medium heat. Fry the blintzes until golden brown on both sides, about 2 minutes per side. (The blintzes can be prepared ahead, frozen, and reheated in a 325-degree oven for about 20 minutes. Do not defrost before baking.) Serve warm.

Apple Blintz Filling

¼ cup (½ stick) butter or
    margarine
6 medium apples, such as
    Golden Delicious, Macoun,
    or Granny Smith (about 2
    pounds), peeled, cored, and
    diced
About ⅓ cup granulated or
    brown sugar
1 teaspoon ground cinnamon or
    ½ teaspoon grated lemon zest
½ cup raisins or ¼ cup chopped
    walnuts (optional)

1. Melt the butter or margarine in a large skillet over medium heat. Add the apples and cook, stirring occasionally, until tender but not mushy, 10 to 15 minutes.

2. Add the sugar, increase the heat to medium-high, and cook, stirring, until golden brown, about 5 minutes. Stir in the cinnamon or zest and, if desired, raisins or nuts.

Cherry Blintz Filling

½ to ¾ cup sugar

2 tablespoons cornstarch or
   potato starch

⅛ teaspoon ground cinnamon or
   pinch of ground cloves

3 cups pitted sour cherries

½ cup cherry juice or water

1 tablespoon lemon juice

Combine the sugar, starch, and cinnamon or cloves. Add the cherries, cherry juice or water, and lemon juice, tossing to coat. Cook over medium-low heat, stirring frequently, until thickened and clear, about 10 minutes.

Sweet Cheese Blintz Filling

1 pound farmer, pot, or cottage
   cheese or any combination

1 large egg

2 to 6 tablespoons sugar

1 tablespoon butter, melted, or
   sour cream

1 teaspoon vanilla extract,
   ground cinnamon, orange
   zest, or lemon zest

½ teaspoon salt

Combine all of the ingredients.

VARIATION

Turos Toltelek (Hungarian Cheese Filling): Increase the number of eggs to 3, separate the eggs, and add the egg yolks and ¼ cup golden raisins. Beat the egg whites until stiff but not dry and fold into the cheese mixture.

Toltott Palacsinta

HUNGARIAN WHIPPED-CREAM-FILLED CREPES

❧ 16 FILLED PANCAKES ❧

16 blintzes (see page 224)

1 cup heavy cream

About ¾ cup confectioners' sugar

½ to 1 cup chopped walnuts or almonds (optional)

Chocolate syrup for garnish (optional)

1. Fry the blintzes until golden on both sides.

2. Whip the cream with the confectioners' sugar until stiff peaks form. If desired, fold in the chopped nuts.

3. Fill the warm crepes with the whipped cream and roll up. If desired, drizzle with the chocolate syrup and top with more chopped nuts.

VARIATION

Gyumolcsiz Palacsinta (Hungarian Jam-Filled Crepes): Substitute about 2 cups of your favorite jam (e.g., lekvar, raspberry, strawberry, or apricot) for the whipped cream. If desired, flambé in a little matching fruit liqueur. Or place in a greased baking dish, top with 2 cups sour cream, and bake in a 325-degree oven until heated through, about 12 minutes.

PASTA
AND DUMPLINGS

Love is grand, but love with **lukshen** *is even better.*
—OLD YIDDISH PROVERB

By the first century, the northern Chinese were eating boiled strips of dough, what they call *mein* and what we call noodles (the word *noodle* is derived from the German *nudel*, an enriched grain mixture that was shaped into long rolls and force-fed to geese). At the same time, Westerners were eating strips of dough—called *laganon* by the Greeks, *vermiculos* (Latin for "little worms") by the Romans, and *iytree* (from *itriyah*, a Persian word meaning "string," and a word used in modern Hebrew for noodles) by the Jews. These dough strips, however, were fried in oil, then bathed in either honey or *garum* (fish sauce). It was many centuries before records of strips of dough boiled in water made an appearance in Europe.

Noodles had spread from China to central Asia and then to Persia by at least the seventh century and possibly earlier. The Babylonian Talmud (Berachot 37b) mentioned a dish of boiled dough called *rihata* (derived from the Persian *itriyah*), a word from which the modern Persian term for noodles (*reshteh*) developed. The Arabs introduced pasta to Spain around the tenth century, and it quickly found a prominent place in the Sephardic kitchen. Common forms of Sephardic pasta include *alatria* (vermicelli), *escolacha* (noodle dough pressed through a stainer), *fidellos* (coiled thin noodles), *fidikos* (tear-shaped strips), and

Opposite: **Woman Making Matza Balls.** Alphonse Levy, France, circa 1900. *Perhaps the most glaring difference between Ashkenazic and Sephardic cooking is the role of cooked dough dishes such as dumplings and kugels: In Ashkenazic Jewish communities these dishes formed the bulk of the diet, while they are rarely found among the Sephardim, who had access to fresh vegetables that were rarely available in the north.*

229

kelsonnes (filled pasta). Sephardim still use the word *macaron* as the overall term for cooked flour doughs. In the American vernacular, *macaroni* has been narrowed to include only the curved tubular varieties, while *pasta* has assumed *macaroni*'s role as the catchall term for this simple dough.

The first record of pasta in Italy appeared in an Italian cookbook ca. 1260, including recipes for vermicelli (by this point, the word had taken on its current meaning of thin threads of boiled dough) and *tortelli* (filled pasta). Therefore, pasta was certainly being eaten in Italy well before Marco Polo (ca. 1254–1324), who is erroneously credited with bringing the dish back from China. However, it is uncertain as to whether pasta—originally the name of a barley gruel sprinkled with salt derived from the Greek *pastos* (sprinkled)—developed independently in the West or reached Europe from China by way of Persia.

The first mention of boiled doughs in a European Jewish source appeared in *Messeket Purim*, a parody written by the Italian rabbi Kalonymous ben Kalonymous (1286–1328), who included macaroni and *tortelli* in a list of 30 dishes served at a Purim feast. (Among the other dishes listed are pheasant, quail, partridge, venison, pancakes, tarts, gingerbread, and chicken soup.) Considering the frequent interactions among the Jewish communities of Italy, France, and Germany, pasta had probably reached the Rhineland by at least the thirteenth century. Earlier Franco-German dough dishes—such as *vermesel* (fritters and pancakes) and *krepish* (meat-filled dough)—were fried or baked.

It is uncertain whether eastern Europeans learned of pasta from the Tartars (Mongolian tribes who overran the area beginning in 1240 with the sacking of Kiev), the Persians, or the Italians. Whatever the case, by the end of the fifteenth century, noodles had become a mainstay of the central European and Polish diet. Also by this time, *frimsel* had supplanted the antiquated *vermesel* as the western Yiddish word for noodles, as did *lukshen* in eastern Europe. The Yiddish *lukshen* and the Slavic *lokshyna* were derived from a Persian noodle dish called *lakshah* (from *kashk,* a Persian term for "cracked barley and wheat" that also gave rise to such well-known dishes as kasha and kishke), which spread to the Balkans, then to eastern Europe.

Fila/Lukshenteig

Egg Noodle Dough

About 1 pound dough

Noodles made from soft wheat flour customarily contain eggs, since those using water tend to become soggy when cooled. Pasta made from semolina, which is sturdier than regular flour, usually contains only water. However, semolina flour does not absorb liquid well and is best mixed in large machines. Therefore, home cooks must add some white flour, which results in a softer, starchy pasta. Homemade egg noodles, on the other hand, tend to produce results superior to store-bought varieties.

2¼ cups all-purpose flour, preferably unbleached

3 large eggs

½ teaspoon salt (optional)

1. Place the flour on a large wooden board or in a large bowl and make a well in the center. Place the eggs and, if desired, salt in the well and with the tips of your fingers or the tines of a fork, lightly beat the eggs.

2. Gradually work the flour into the eggs, always working from the sides of the flour to prevent it from sticking to the board/bowl, to form a firm dough. (Variations in the size of the eggs, moisture in the flour, and humidity in the air can slightly alter the measurements. Sift any unincorporated flour and reuse.)

3. Place the dough on a lightly floured surface and knead until smooth, 5 to 10 minutes. Wrap in plastic wrap and let rest at room temperature for 30 minutes.

VARIATION

Lower-Cholesterol Pasta: Reduce the number of eggs to 1 and add about ⅔ cup lukewarm water.

Lukshen mit Puter

ASHKENAZIC NOODLES WITH BUTTER
8 TO 9 CUPS COOKED PASTA

Noodles are tasty, filling, handy, versatile, and inexpensive. And they offer an additional advantage for the kosher kitchen: They can be served with either meat or dairy. Therefore, from at least the fifteenth century, noodles were served daily in many central European and Polish households. A general rule of thumb is to serve 4 ounces of pasta for a main course and about 2 ounces for an appetizer or side dish. Another practical rule is the wider the noodle, the heartier the sauce; the narrower the noodle, the more delicate the sauce.

1 recipe egg noodle dough
  (see page 231)
About 1 tablespoon salt
6 to 8 tablespoons butter or
  margarine
Ground black pepper to taste

1. Cut the dough in half. On a lightly floured surface, roll out each half into a thin rectangle. Let stand until the dough begins to feel dry but is still supple, about 10 minutes. (Drying times vary according to the thickness of the dough and climatic conditions.)

2. Roll up jelly roll style from a short side. Cut into strips: ⅛-inch-wide for thin noodles, ¼-inch-wide for medium, or ½-inch-wide for wide.

3. Unroll the dough strips, place in a single layer on a lightly floured surface or drape over a broom handle, and let stand until dry, at least 1 hour. (Drying prevents the noodles from clumping together while cooking.) Store the noodles in an airtight container or a plastic bag at room temperature for up to 1 day. For longer storage, dust several baking sheets with flour, arrange the noodles in a single layer on the sheets, place in the freezer until solid, at least 1 hour, transfer to plastic bags, and store in the freezer for up to 2 months. Do not thaw before cooking.

4. Bring 6 quarts of water to a rapid boil. Add about 1 tablespoon salt, then the noodles, and cook until tender but still firm, or al dente (Italian for "to the tooth"), about 5 minutes if the dough is thin and very fresh (*pasta fresca*), about 10 minutes if dry (*pasta secca*) and thick. Drain in a colander.

5. Toss the noodles with the butter or margarine and season with salt and pepper.

Variations

Dios Metelt (Hungarian Noodles with Walnuts): Omit the salt and pepper, add 1 cup coarsely chopped walnuts, and sprinkle with confectioners' sugar.

Makos Metelt (Hungarian Poppy Seed Noodles): Omit the salt and pepper, add ¾ cup poppy seeds and ¼ cup sugar to the noodles, and cook over low heat until heated through, about 3 minutes.

Topfenhaluska (Ashkenazic Noodles with Curd Cheese): Add 1 pound farmer, pot, or drained cottage cheese. (*Note:* Mixing a starch with dairy products is common in central and eastern Europe, a way of supplementing the other's nutrients.)

Kaposztas Teszta

HUNGARIAN NOODLES WITH CABBAGE

6 TO 8 SERVINGS

Hungarians prepare a similar dish substituting 3 shredded kohlrabi for the cabbage.

1 small green cabbage (about
  1½ pounds), shredded
About 2 tablespoons salt
¼ cup (½ stick) butter,
  schmaltz (see page 109), or
  vegetable oil
2 medium yellow onions,
  grated (about 1 cup)
Pinch of paprika or
  ½ teaspoon caraway seeds
1 pound wide noodles, cooked
  (see page 232)
Ground black pepper to taste

1. Sprinkle the cabbage generously with the salt and let stand for 1 hour. Drain and squeeze out the excess moisture. (This liquid is rather bitter.)

2. Heat the butter, schmaltz, or oil in a large skillet or saucepan over medium heat. Add the onions and sauté until soft and translucent, 5 to 10 minutes.

3. Add the cabbage and paprika or caraway, cover, reduce the heat to low, and simmer, stirring occasionally, until the cabbage is tender, about 30 minutes.

4. Add the noodles and heat through, about 5 minutes. Season with salt and pepper.

Fidellos (Tostados)

SEPHARDIC THIN NOODLES

6 TO 8 SERVINGS

*F*idellos or *fideyos* ("little tears") are coiled thin noodles available in Middle Eastern grocery stores. Fine twisted noodles or vermicelli make acceptable substitutes. Sephardim have a unique way of preparing these noodles, frying the raw pasta before cooking.

⅓ cup vegetable or olive oil
1 pound fidellos (coiled thin noodles) or vermicelli
4 cups chicken broth or water
About 1 teaspoon salt
Ground black pepper to taste

1. Heat the oil in a large skillet or Dutch oven over medium-high heat. In batches, add the raw noodles and fry until lightly browned. Drain on paper towels.
2. Bring the broth or water, salt, and pepper to a boil. Stir in the noodles, cover, reduce the heat to low, and simmer, stirring occasionally, until tender and the liquid is absorbed, about 15 minutes. Serve warm.

VARIATION
Fidellos con Domates (Sephardic Noodles with Tomatoes): **Add ¼ cup tomato sauce or 2 cups peeled, seeded, and chopped tomatoes with the water.** (*Note:* Syrians commonly add rice to this dish.)

Fila con Queso

SEPHARDIC NOODLES WITH CHEESE

6 TO 8 SERVINGS

Unlike Italian pasta-and-cheese dishes, this Sephardic version, called *pastichio* by the Greeks, uses eggs as the thickening agent rather than a starch such as flour or cornstarch.

1 pound medium noodles, macaroni, ziti, or spaghetti, cooked, rinsed under cold water, and drained

1 cup grated kashkaval *(see page 30) or other sharp cheese*

1 cup heavy cream or milk

4 large eggs, lightly beaten

Salt to taste

Ground black pepper to taste

1. Preheat the oven to 375 degrees. Grease a large baking dish.

2. Combine all of the ingredients and pour into the prepared pan.

3. Bake until set and golden brown, about 30 minutes.

VARIATION

Omit *kashkaval* and add 24 ounces farmer cheese and 8 ounces softened cream cheese. Or add ¾ cup cream cheese, ¾ cup crumbled feta cheese, and ¼ cup grated *kashkaval* cheese.

 A FEW PASTA FORMS

Fingerhuetchen (Ashkenazic Thimble Noodles): Roll out the pasta dough to a ⅛-inch thickness and fold the dough sheet in half. Using a floured thimble, cut out small dough rounds, cover, and let dry for 30 minutes. Deep-fry in hot vegetable oil until golden brown, about 1 minute, and drain on paper towels. (*Note:* Serve these pasta puffs, also called *oofhalaifers,* as a soup garnish.)

Quadrucci (Italian Miniature Pasta Squares): Roll out the pasta dough to a ⅛-inch thickness. Cut into ¼-inch squares, cover, and let dry for

30 minutes. (*Note:* Many Italians traditionally serve these noodles in chicken or beef broth to begin the meal following Yom Kippur.)

Farfalle (Bow Ties): Roll out the pasta dough to a 1/16-inch thickness. Using a fluted pastry wheel, cut into bow-tie shapes, cover, and let dry for 30 minutes.

Plaetschen (Eastern European Small Pasta Squares): Roll out the pasta dough to a ⅛-inch thickness. Cut into ½-inch squares, cover, and let dry for 30 minutes.

Manty

BUKHARAN STEAMED FILLED PASTA
 ABOUT 40 DUMPLINGS

The cooking method for this steamed dish, derived from the wonton, reflects the strong Chinese influence on Uzbek cuisine, while the filling reflects the Persian influence. These dumplings are served on Purim and other festive occasions. Although *manty* are customarily eaten plain, they can be accompanied with a dipping sauce or added to a chicken soup. Wonton skins may be substituted for the noodle dough.

1 pound ground lamb or beef chuck

1 medium yellow onion, finely chopped (about ½ cup)

About ½ teaspoon salt

½ teaspoon ground cinnamon (optional)

1 recipe egg noodle dough (see page 231)

¼ cup chopped fresh parsley or dill for garnish

1. Combine the meat, onion, salt, and, if desired, cinnamon.

2. On a lightly floured surface, roll out the dough ⅛ inch thick. Cut into 3-inch rounds.

3. Place a heaping teaspoon of the meat mixture in the center of each round. Bring the dough edges together over the filling, pinching the top and twisting to form a small pouch. (The dumplings may be prepared ahead to this point and refrigerated or frozen until ready to use. To freeze, place on a floured baking sheet, freeze until solid, transfer to plastic bags, and seal. Do not thaw before cooking; increase the cooking time by about 2 minutes.)

4. Place an oiled bamboo steamer in a wok and add water to reach about 1 inch from the bottom of the steamer. Or place an oiled colander in a large kettle and add water to reach about 1 inch from the bottom of the colander. Arrange the dumplings in the steamer, cover, and steam until the dough is tender and the filling is no longer pink, about 15 minutes. Sprinkle with the parsley or dill and serve warm.

VARIATION

Gushe Barreh (Persian Filled Pasta): Cook the dumplings in boiling water as for kreplach (see page 238). (*Note:* These dumplings are customarily served in chicken soup for Sabbath dinner. Persians usually sprinkle the dumplings and soup with ½ cup chopped fresh parsley, 2 teaspoons dried mint, and ½ teaspoon ground cinnamon.)

Masconod

ITALIAN PASTA ROLLS

❧ ABOUT 20 ROLLS ❧

This ancient Jewish dish bears an obvious similarity to the better-known cannelloni ("little channels"). *Masconod* is a common festival dish in Italian households.

1 recipe egg noodle dough (see page 231)
2 cups grated Parmesan cheese
1 teaspoon ground black pepper

1. Cut the dough in half. On a lightly floured surface, roll out each half into a thin rectangle. Let stand until the dough begins to feel dry but is still supple, about 10 minutes.
2. Cut the pasta into 4- to 5-inch squares.
3. Bring 6 quarts of lightly salted water to a rapid boil. Add the pasta and cook until tender but still firm, about 5 minutes. Drain in a colander.
4. Preheat the oven to 350 degrees. Grease a large casserole.
5. Combine the Parmesan cheese and pepper. Place the pasta squares on a flat surface and spread a heaping tablespoonful of the cheese mixture along one edge of each square or over the entire pasta. Roll up jelly roll style.
6. Place the rolls, seam side down, in a single layer in the prepared casserole. Sprinkle with any excess cheese. Bake until golden brown, about 30 minutes. Serve warm.

Kreplach and Varenikes

ASHKENAZIC FILLED PASTA
☙ ABOUT 32 (3-INCH) DUMPLINGS ☙

A popular Ashkenazic dish in the twelfth century was *krepish,* consisting of a sheet of dough wrapped around a piece of meat, which was then fried or baked. The name of this dish was derived from the Old French *crespe* (curled, wrinkled), which also gave rise to the name of the French crêpe. It appears that meat was the only filling used for *krepish* in western Europe, as Rabbi Isaac ben Moses of Vienna (1180–1260) made a point of noting that "Jews in the Slavic lands also made *krepish* with cheese."

After pasta reached the Ashkenazim, *krepish* developed into filled pasta triangles, while filled pasta rounds and sometimes fruit kreplach were called *vareniki* (possibly derived from *varenje,* a Persian word for "fruit conserve," indicating its origins) in the Ukraine and pierogi in Poland. Since kreplach provided a tasty way of using up leftovers or stretching scarce resources, fillings such as cabbage, kasha, and potato emerged. After a meat shortage befell Europe in the sixteenth century, fruit and nut fillings became popular.

Since these dumplings require some effort to prepare, kreplach are generally reserved for special occasions and three specific holidays: Yom Kippur eve, Hoshanah Rabbah, and Purim. Mystics compared the wrapping of dough with the divine envelopment of mercy and kindness demonstrated on Yom Kippur. Hoshanah Rabbah (the seventh day of Sukkoth) is regarded as the day on which the verdicts of judgment that were decided on Yom Kippur are sealed. Therefore, traditional Yom Kippur eve foods are served on Hoshanah Rabbah. In Kabbalistic tradition, Yom Kippur is compared with another, seemingly unrelated holiday—Purim. The similarity in names was seen as no coincidence and a parallel was drawn between the physical lots of Purim cast by Haman and the metaphysical lots of Yom Kippur. Indeed, the great Kabbalist Yitzchak Luria referred to the Day of Atonement as *Yom ke-Purim,* "a day like Purim."

The kreplach's triangular shape assumed a special symbolism representing the three Patriarchs—Abraham, Isaac, and Jacob; the three groups that constitute the Jewish people—Kohain, Levite, and Israelite; the three parts of the Bible—Torah, Prophets, and Writings; and, on Purim, the three-cornered hat worn by Haman. Thus, since the early seventeenth century, meat-filled kreplach have traditionally been served in chicken soup at the meal preceding Yom Kippur, on Hoshanah Rabbah, and at the Purim feast. Cheese kreplach are a popular Shavuot treat.

*1 recipe egg noodle dough
(see page 231)*
*About 2 cups Ashkenazic pastry
filling (see pages 48–50),
cherry filling (see page 226),
or fruit preserves*

1. Divide the dough in half. On a lightly floured surface, roll out each piece into a rectangle about ⅛ inch thick. Cut into 3-inch squares for kreplach or 3-inch rounds for *varenikes*. Reroll any dough scraps.

2. Place a heaping teaspoon of the filling in the center of each dough piece. Brush the dough edges with a little water to moisten and fold over to form a triangle or half-moon, pressing out any air. Pinch the edges or press with the tines of a fork to seal. Place on a lightly floured surface, cover with a towel, and let stand until the dough begins to feel dry but is still supple, about 30 minutes. (The pasta may be prepared ahead to this point and refrigerated or frozen until ready to use. To freeze, place on a floured baking sheet, freeze until solid, transfer to plastic bags, and seal. Do not thaw before cooking; increase the cooking time by about 5 minutes.)

3. In several batches, drop the pasta into a large pot of lightly salted boiling water. Reduce the heat to medium and cook, stirring occasionally to prevent sticking, until the kreplach are tender but not mushy, about 20 minutes. With a slotted spoon, remove the pasta and drain.

4. Add meat-filled kreplach to chicken soup or fry in a little schmaltz or vegetable oil until golden brown, 2 to 3 minutes, and serve as an appetizer or side dish. Serve cheese-filled kreplach with butter, sugar, sour cream, or fruit sauce or toss them with 1 cup bread crumbs browned in ¼ cup (½ stick) butter. Serve fruit-filled kreplach with cinnamon-sugar, sour cream, or a fruit sauce.

Kelsonnes

SEPHARDIC CHEESE-FILLED PASTA

ABOUT 30 (2-INCH) DUMPLINGS, 6 TO 8 SERVINGS

This version of cheese ravioli is a popular Shavuot (see page 315) treat among many Sephardim. Unlike the classic Italian ravioli, the cooked *kelsonnes* are usually mixed with noodles and baked. Or omit the noodles and fry the dumplings in a little butter. An ancient Roman-Jewish version called *calzonicchi* uses a calf's-brain filling; a spinach filling, taking advantage of the early spring crop, is traditional for Purim (see page 316).

1 recipe egg noodle dough (see page 231)
1 pound Muenster cheese, finely grated, or farmer cheese
2 large eggs
Dash of salt
8 ounces wide noodles, homemade (see page 232) or store-bought
½ cup plus 2 tablespoons (1¼ sticks) butter
Plain yogurt for garnish

1. Divide the dough in half. In a pasta machine or on a lightly floured surface, roll out each dough piece, turning occasionally to prevent sticking, into a 1/16-inch-thick rectangle about 15 by 9 inches.

2. Combine the cheese, eggs, and salt. On one of the rectangles, evenly space teaspoonfuls of the cheese mixture at 2-inch intervals. Brush the dough around the filling with cold water.

3. Cover with the second rectangle, pressing around the mounds of filling to remove any air. With a pastry wheel, knife, or biscuit cutter, cut into 2-inch squares or rounds. Crimp the edges with the tines of a fork to seal.

4. Place on a lightly floured baking sheet, cover with a towel, and let dry for 1 hour. (The *kelsonnes* may be prepared ahead to this point and refrigerated or frozen until ready to use. To freeze, place the *kelsonnes* on a floured baking sheet, freeze until solid, transfer to plastic bags, and seal. Do not thaw before cooking; increase the cooking time by about 2 minutes.)

5. Bring a large pot of lightly salted water to a boil. In several batches, add the *kelsonnes*, stirring gently to prevent sticking. Reduce the heat to medium and simmer until the *kelsonnes* rise to the surface and are tender, about 10 minutes. Remove with a slotted spoon. (The *kelsonnes* can be prepared ahead to this point, then rinsed under cold water and covered until ready to bake.)

6. Preheat the oven to 300 degrees.

7. Cook the wide noodles in lightly salted water until tender. (They can be cooked with the last batch of *kelsonnes*.) Drain.

8. Combine the *kelsonnes* and noodles and gently toss with the ½ cup butter. Transfer to a 13-by-9-inch baking dish and dot with the 2 tablespoons butter. Cover and bake for 30 minutes.

9. Uncover and bake until golden brown, about 10 minutes. Serve warm accompanied with yogurt.

Below: **An eighteenth-century kitchen.** *From the thrice-repeated Biblical injunction "You shall not boil a kid in its mother's milk" derives a restriction on cooking or mixing meat and dairy products together.*

Mandlen

ASHKENAZIC SOUP NUTS

5 TO 7 DOZEN "NUTS"

Although in German the word *mandlen* means "almonds," there are no nuts in these deep-fried pasta pieces—the name refers to their shape and nutty flavor. *Mandlen* have a particular significance for the Sabbath as a symbol of the manna, a connection based on the similarity of both the names and shapes. Serve as a soup garnish.

3 large eggs, lightly beaten
2 tablespoons schmaltz
*   (see page 109) or vegetable*
*   oil*
½ teaspoon salt
About 2 cups all-purpose flour
Vegetable oil for deep frying

1. Combine the eggs, schmaltz or oil, and salt. Stir in 1 cup of the flour. Gradually stir in enough of the remaining flour to make a soft dough that is not sticky.

2. Shape the dough into ¼- to ½-inch-thick ropes and cut the ropes into ¼- to ½-inch pieces.

3. Heat at least 1 inch of oil to about 375 degrees.

4. In batches, fry the *mandlen* until puffed and golden brown on all sides. Remove with a slotted spoon and drain on paper towels. Or spread the dough pieces on a greased baking sheet and bake in a 375-degree oven, shaking the pan occasionally, until golden brown, about 20 minutes. Let cool. Store in an airtight container at room temperature.

Farfel

Ashkenazic Egg Barley

❧ About 3 cups ❧

This traditional Ashkenazic pasta—known as barley farfel and egg barley—was once made from barley or a combination of grains. Although the modern version contains only wheat, the pasta shapes are still the size of barley grains, hence its English name. Round farfel is traditionally served on Rosh Hashanah as an accompaniment for chicken soup—farfel symbolizing both fertility and the wish that our misdeeds should be *farfellen* (Yiddish for "fallen away"), the round shape symbolizing that the coming year should be well rounded. Do not confuse barley farfel with crumbled matza pieces called matza farfel. For toasted farfel, toast the dried farfel in a 350-degree oven until evenly browned, 15 to 20 minutes, and substitute for regular farfel in any recipe.

*1 recipe egg noodle dough
(see page 231)*

1. Roll the dough into a thick log. Let stand at room temperature until stiff but not completely dry, about 1 hour.
2. Grate the dough into barley-sized bits. Spread on a baking sheet to dry. Store in an airtight container.
3. Bring a large pot of water to a boil. Add the farfel and cook until tender, about 10 minutes. Drain.

THE MOROCCAN MYSTIQUE

"The cuisine of northwestern Africa [Morocco, Algeria, and Tunisia] differs greatly from what Americans tend to lump together as Middle Eastern," notes Levana Levy Kirschenbaum, a native of Casablanca, Morocco. "Over the centuries a succession of influences [the native Berber, Phoenician, Roman, Jewish, Moorish, Spanish, Turkish, and most recently French] all affected the cooking of the region. Moroccan cuisine does not use yogurt, grape leaves, *kibbe* [a ground meat mixture], and many other common Near Eastern mainstays. Moroccan cooking relies on the character and combination of ingredients, not on condiments. It relies on a liberal mix of seasonings to produce delightful nuances of flavor, aroma, and color that more closely resemble Indian than Middle Eastern cuisine."

According to legend, Jews first reached the Maghreb (Arabic for "setting sun") during the reign of King Solomon. This idea is not so far-fetched, since Carthage (located near modern Tunis), the ancient power of northwest Africa, was founded by Israel's friendly northern neighbor, Phoenicia, and Jewish traders and sailors sometimes accompanied their allies on sea voyages. The first evidence of a Jewish presence in the Maghreb is tombstones dating to the second century C.E.

"While the size of portions are generally small, a Moroccan meal almost always contains a large number of dishes," Levana explains. "Many Moroccan dishes are one-pot meals, meat or poultry combined with vegetables, broth, and seasonings. A staple of the Moroccan diet is couscous [fine-grain pasta], one of the world's great foods. Soup is served almost every day. Vegetables, in great variety, are eaten at every meal. Frozen, canned, and processed foods are unheard of. A meal is not considered a meal unless it contains something hot. A common sight on Moroccan beaches is the pressure cooker and burner, ensuring hot food for the family outing."

Levana notes, "Because of the long and large Jewish presence in the area, Moroccan Jewish cooking is deeply intertwined with that of the country as a whole. Jews and Arabs of Morocco eat basically the same foods, allowing conversion to kosher with little or no substituting. Fish was a Jewish specialty in Morocco. Our Arab neighbors constantly approached my mother for her fish recipes. The distinctive elements of Jewish cooking are the presence of sweet-and-sour dishes and the use of more garlic and less cumin.

"Those who have sampled Moroccan cooking appreciate its greatness."

Couscous

After the defeat of Carthage at the close of the Third Punic War in 146 B.C.E., northwestern Africa fell under Roman rule and soon became the grain belt of the empire, supplying much of its wheat. The Romans were not interested in semolina, part of the endosperm of durum wheat, since its high cellulose content resulted in tough breads. Semolina's sturdiness proves an asset in certain dishes, however, because it remains firmer than other flours during cooking. North Africans used the neglected semolina to create one of the world's classic dishes, couscous.

The term *couscous* refers to the small pasta granules as well as to the various stews that are served with them. Although many Maghrebi cooks insist on making their own couscous from semolina flour, couscous grains are available at Middle Eastern markets, health food stores, and some supermarkets. There is an instant couscous—prepared by adding boiling water—that can be used, but it is not as light and fluffy as the steamed variety. Couscous can be served as a main course or a dessert; it can be fiery or sweet; it can contain an assortment of meats, poultry, or fish or it can be vegetarian. Every cook boasts slightly different variations of the stews that accompany this dish, adding a distinctive combination of spices, vegetables, fruits, and other seasonings.

Maghrebi cooks take great care in preparing couscous. The pasta granules are washed, drained, then diligently stirred with the fingers for up to 30 minutes to moisten the granules and remove any lumps. In North Africa, both the grains and the stew are traditionally made in a *couscousière,* a vessel with a stewing pot on the bottom and a steamer on top. As the couscous cooks, it absorbs the flavors of the stew below. A steamer or colander set over a large, deep pot can be substituted for the *couscousière.* After steaming, the granules are customarily fluffed up and heaped onto a deep-sided serving platter. The vegetables and/or meat are arranged on top of the couscous and the broth from the stew is poured over the dish to moisten the grains. Savory stews are generally accompanied with a fiery chili paste called *harissa,* which should be used sparingly by neophytes. Although Westerners find it more comfortable to eat couscous with a spoon, the traditional method is to use pieces of flat bread to scoop up some of the granules and stew.

Moroccan, Tunisian, and Algerian Jews serve couscous every Friday night, on festivals, and at all special occasions. It is usually accompanied with several salads.

Couscous

NORTHWEST AFRICAN STEAMED PASTA
ABOUT 9 CUPS

2 cups cold water
1 pound (2½ cups) couscous
1 tablespoon vegetable oil
1 cup water mixed with about 1
   teaspoon salt

1. Sprinkle the cold water over the couscous, drain, and let stand for 15 minutes. Drizzle with the oil and stir with a fork or your fingers to separate the granules.

2. Spoon the couscous into a sieve or colander, place over boiling water or stew, cover, and steam for 10 minutes. (If the holes in your steamer are too large to hold the couscous, line it with cheesecloth.)

3. Spoon the couscous into a large dish. Sprinkle with the salt water and stir with a fork to separate the granules.

4. Return the couscous to the steamer, cover, and steam until heated through and tender but not mushy, about 20 minutes.

5. Heap the couscous onto a warm serving platter and stir with a fork to separate the granules.

HARISSA

MOROCCAN CHILI PASTE
ABOUT 1⅓ CUPS

In a food processor or blender, puree 10 to 12 seeded and chopped red chilies (such as California), 4 cloves garlic, and 1 teaspoon kosher salt. Add 2 to 3 tablespoons olive oil to make a thick sauce.

Couscous aux Sept Legumes

COUSCOUS WITH SEVEN VEGETABLES

6 TO 8 SERVINGS

For Rosh Hashanah, which falls on the first day of the seventh month of the Jewish calender, Moroccans traditionally serve a stew containing seven symbolic vegetables: carrots, which represent sweetness; onions, which are one of the foods that the Jews remembered eating in Egypt; turnips, an ancient root vegetable that resembles coins when sliced; celery/celeriac, which is one of the greens used at the Passover Seder; squash or pumpkins, which contain many seeds and therefore are symbols of fertility and plenty; cabbage, which, according to the Talmud, "is good for sustenance as well as for health"; and chickpeas or beans, which are symbols of abundance. As the diners eat each type of vegetable, they recite a special prayer.

6 cups chicken broth or water

6 medium carrots, cut into chunks

3 medium yellow onions, quartered

2 turnips, peeled and quartered

2 stalks celery, sliced

1 (3-inch) stick cinnamon or 1 teaspoon ground cinnamon

½ to 1 teaspoon ground cumin

½ teaspoon ground turmeric

About 1 teaspoon salt

Ground black pepper to taste

1 butternut squash or small pumpkin, peeled and cut into 2-inch pieces, or 3 medium zucchini, sliced

½ head green cabbage, shredded

2 cups cooked or canned chickpeas or fava beans

1 tablespoon chopped fresh coriander or parsley

1 pound (2½ cups) couscous, steamed (see page 246)

1. Bring the broth or water to a boil. Add the carrots, onions, turnips, celery, cinnamon, cumin, turmeric, salt, and pepper. Cover, reduce the heat to low, and simmer for 30 minutes.

2. Add the squash, cabbage, and chickpeas or fava beans. Cook until tender, about 20 minutes. Add the coriander or parsley. To produce a thicker sauce, smash some of the chickpeas or squash into the stew. Discard the cinnamon stick.

3. Spoon the couscous onto a large deep-sided platter or into individual serving bowls. Make a well in the center and fill the well with the vegetables. Pour some of the broth over the couscous. Serve warm.

VARIATIONS

Chicken Couscous: Before adding the vegetables, simmer 1 cut-up chicken in the 6 cups water for 30 minutes. Shred the chicken, returning it to the pot and discarding the bones, and proceed as above.

Lamb Couscous: Before adding the vegetables, simmer 1 pound lamb shoulder cut into 1½-inch pieces in the 6 cups water for 1 hour and proceed as above.

Couscous Hiloo

COUSCOUS WITH DRIED FRUITS AND NUTS

6 TO 8 SERVINGS

This sweetened couscous is a traditional Moroccan Hanukkah dessert.

½ cup sugar

½ to 1 teaspoon ground cinnamon

¼ cup butter or margarine, melted

1 pound (2½ cups) couscous, steamed (see page 246)

¾ cup raisins

¾ cup chopped pitted dates

¾ cup chopped dried apricots

¾ cup chopped blanched almonds

¾ cup chopped walnuts or ⅓ cup pine nuts

About 1 cup almond milk (see below)

Additional ground cinnamon for garnish

1. Stir the sugar and cinnamon into the butter or margarine.
2. Pour over the couscous, tossing to coat. Stir in the raisins, dates, apricots, almonds, and walnuts or pine nuts. Gradually add enough of the almond milk to moisten the couscous.
3. Mound the couscous on a large platter and garnish with cinnamon.

LECHO DE ALMENDAS

SEPHARDIC ALMOND MILK

ABOUT 1 CUP

Soak ⅓ cup whole or slivered blanched almonds in 1 cup water for at least 4 hours. In a blender, puree the almonds and water until smooth. Strain through several layers of cheesecloth.

Dumplings

Kartoffel Kloese

ASHKENAZIC MASHED POTATO DUMPLINGS

ABOUT 36 MEDIUM OR 18 LARGE DUMPLINGS

Because of the climatic and soil conditions in eastern Europe, fresh vegetables and meat were rare and, as a result, starches such as dumplings, noodles, kugels, and breads constituted the bulk of the diet. Therefore, it is not surprising that Yiddish contains a number of synonyms for dumplings: *knaidlach* (*knaidel,* like the French *quennelle,* is derived from *knodel,* a southern German word for "dumpling"), *knedlicky* (the Czech version of *knodel), klopse, kloese, halkes* (from the Slavic *halushky), gomboc* (a Hungarian word), and *papanush* (a Romanian word).

Beginning in the mid-nineteenth century, potato dumplings became popular fare and Ashkenazim developed many variations: Dumplings can be made from grated raw potatoes or mashed potatoes, can be sweet or savory, and can be plain or contain a filling. The secret to light dumplings is to keep the amount of flour to a minimum. Potato dumplings are commonly topped with sautéed bread crumbs and served as a side dish with pot roast.

6 medium russet potatoes
(about 2 pounds)
2 large eggs
1 tablespoon vegetable oil
About 1 teaspoon salt
About ¼ teaspoon ground white
or black pepper
Dash of grated nutmeg or
2 teaspoons grated onion
About 2 cups all-purpose flour
or 1½ cups matza meal
(or 1 cup flour and ½ cup
matza meal or semolina)
About ½ cup margarine

1. Place the unpeeled potatoes in a large pot, add water to cover, and boil until fork-tender, about 25 minutes. Or bake in a 425-degree oven for about 1 hour. While still warm, peel and rice or mash the potatoes. (You should have about 4 cups.) Let cool. (If the potatoes are warm, they will absorb too much flour and be heavy.)

2. Combine the potatoes, eggs, 1 tablespoon oil, salt, pepper, and nutmeg or onion. Stir in the flour or matza meal until the dough is no longer sticky and holds together. (Too much flour produces heavy dumplings; too little flour produces mushy dumplings.)

3. On a lightly floured surface, knead the dough briefly until smooth. Do not overknead, or the dumplings will be heavy. Dust your hands with flour and shape the potato mixture into ½- or 1-inch balls. (The dumplings may be

prepared to this point, arranged in a single layer on a baking sheet, and refrigerated for up to 4 hours or, packed in plastic bags, frozen for up to 2 months. Do not thaw before cooking; slightly increase the cooking time.)

4. Bring a large pot of lightly salted water to a boil. In batches, add the dumplings, stirring to prevent sticking. Return to a boil and cook until the dumplings rise to the surface, about 10 minutes for medium dumplings, about 15 minutes for large dumplings. Remove with a slotted spoon. (The dumplings may be prepared a day ahead, stored in cold water, and reheated.)

5. Brush the dumplings with the ½ cup margarine and keep warm in a 300-degree oven while preparing the remaining dumplings. Serve plain, topped with gravy or tomato sauce, or with a stew.

VARIATIONS

Potato-Cheese Dumplings: Add 8 ounces cottage cheese, and increase the number of eggs to 3 and the amount of oil or margarine to ¼ cup.

Shlishkes: Roll the dough into ½-inch-thick ropes, cut into ¾-inch pieces, and cook as for potato dumplings. Melt ¼ cup butter or margarine in a large skillet, add 1 cup bread crumbs, and sauté until golden. Stir in the cooked *shlishkes*. (*Note:* These dumplings, once a common buffet item at Ashkenazic celebrations, are similar to the Italian *gnocchi di patate* but are firmer and lack the ridges.)

Opposite: **Baking of Matzot.** Engraving, circa eighteenth century. *To eliminate any possibility of leavening, both Ashkenazim and Sephardim roll out the dough very thin, perforate it to prevent the formation of air bubbles, then bake it until very crisp. The entire matza-making process—from exposure to moisture until the start of baking—must take place in less than eighteen minutes.*

Gefullte Kloese

ASHKENAZIC FILLED POTATO DUMPLINGS

ABOUT 16 DUMPLINGS

*1 recipe mashed potato
  dumplings (see page 249)
1 recipe dumpling filling
  (see below)*

1. Dust your hands with flour or matza meal and shape the potato mixture into 1-inch balls. Flatten the balls into thin patties. Place a spoonful of the filling in the center of each patty and press the edges together to enclose the filling. Reform into balls.

2. Cook as for mashed potato dumplings. For dessert dumplings, sprinkle the dumplings with cinnamon-sugar and/or ¾ cup bread crumbs sautéed in 3 tablespoons butter or margarine.

Apfelfullung

APPLE FILLING

*1 large apple, peeled, cored,
  and grated
¼ cup coarsely chopped almonds
  or walnuts
3 tablespoons granulated or
  brown sugar
½ teaspoon ground cinnamon
½ teaspoon grated lemon zest*

Combine all of the ingredients.

Note: This filling is also used to fill matza dumplings.

Fleischfullung

MEAT FILLING

*3 tablespoons schmaltz (see
page 109) or vegetable oil*
½ pound ground beef
*1 small yellow onion, chopped
(about ¼ cup)*
Dash of ground cinnamon
Salt to taste
Ground black pepper to taste

Heat the schmaltz or oil in a large skillet over medium-high heat. Add the meat and onion and sauté until the onion is soft, about 10 minutes. Stir in the cinnamon, salt, and pepper.

Szilvas Gomboc

HUNGARIAN PLUM FILLING

*About 16 pitted Italian plums,
pitted fresh apricots, or pitted
prunes*
*About 16 sugar cubes or ⅓ cup
cinnamon-sugar (optional)*

If desired, stuff each fruit with a sugar cube or 1 teaspoon cinnamon-sugar. Place a plum, apricot, or prune in the center of each dumpling.

Lekvarfullung

PRUNE-JAM FILLING

About 1 cup lekvar (prune jam)

Spoon about 1 tablespoon prune jam into the center of each dumpling.

Matse Knaidlach

ASHKENAZIC MATZA BALLS

≈ ABOUT 16 DUMPLINGS **≈**

During the eight days of Passover, eastern European housewives had to find ways of feeding their families using the limited ingredients permitted and available. *Matse knaidlach* are one of their crowning triumphs. Using matza meal in place of flour and adding eggs results in a light dumpling. Adding fat produces a more tender dumpling. The key to cooking *knaidlach* is to avoid crowding the dough balls in the pot and to simmer, not boil, them in liquid. Too rapid a heat will cause the soft dough to disintegrate or the eggs to toughen. Do not remove the lid during cooking, or the dumplings will be heavy.

Basic *knaidlach* possess little intrinsic flavor. But plain doughs are just the starting point: Serve them in soups; flavor them with herbs, sugar, almonds, or fruit; fill the centers with meat, *gribenes* (poultry cracklings; see page 109), or fruit; cook them with fruits such as prunes; or top them with butter or gravy for a hearty side dish. The dough can also be cooked directly in a soup or stew—a dumpling cooked in *cholent* or tzimmes is called *Shabbes ganif* (Sabbath thief) because it absorbs flavors from the liquid.

4 large eggs, lightly beaten
¼ cup schmaltz (see page 109)
  or vegetable oil
About 1 teaspoon salt
¼ teaspoon ground black pepper
1 cup matza meal
¼ cup club soda, seltzer,
  chicken soup, or hot water

1. Beat together the eggs, schmaltz or oil, salt, and pepper. Stir in the matza meal, then the liquid. Cover and refrigerate for at least 1 hour or up to 2 days.
2. Using moistened hands, form the matza mixture into 1-inch balls.
3. Bring 2 quarts of lightly salted water to a rapid boil. Drop in the *knaidlach,* one at a time, and stir to prevent sticking. Cover, reduce the heat, and simmer until tender, about 40 minutes—do not uncover during cooking. Remove with a slotted spoon. (The *knaidlach* can be frozen for up to 3 months and added to boiling soup.)

VARIATION
Flaumen (Prune) Knaidlach: Soak 1½ pounds pitted prunes in water to cover overnight, add 2 slices lemon, simmer until tender, and add sugar to taste. Place the uncooked *knaidlach* in a greased 3-quart baking dish, add the prune mixture, and bake, covered, in a 350-degree oven for about 30 minutes.

Mobile Passover kasherer, Lodz, Poland. *Because of the various dietary regulations of Passover, the holiday fare naturally differs from that of the rest of the year. Over the centuries, creative cooks found ways to adapt some of their everyday dishes to the special requirements of Passover. Modern manufacturing, combined with an unprecedented boom of products under kosher supervision, has led to a wide array of Passover dishes.*

Khenaghi

GEORGIAN WALNUT MATZA BALLS
18 TO 24 DUMPLINGS

These Passover dumplings incorporate the Georgian favorite, walnuts.

2 cups finely ground walnuts
½ cup matza meal
4 large eggs, lightly beaten
1 small yellow onion, finely
    chopped (about ¼ cup)
2 tablespoons chopped fresh
    oregano or parsley
Salt to taste
Ground black pepper to taste
2 large egg whites

1. Combine the walnuts, matza meal, whole eggs, onion, oregano or parsley, salt, and pepper. Beat the egg whites until soft peaks form. Fold into the walnut mixture.
2. Using moistened hands, shape the walnut mixture into 1½-inch balls.
3. Bring a large pot of lightly salted water to a boil. Add the dumplings, stirring to prevent sticking, and cook until tender, about 10 minutes. Remove with a slotted spoon. Serve warm in chicken soup or at room temperature with *narsharab* (pomegranate sauce; see below) or *bazha* (walnut sauce; see page 375).

Narsharab

GEORGIAN POMEGRANATE SAUCE
ABOUT 1 CUP

2 cups pomegranate juice
2 tablespoons chopped fresh
    coriander
1 clove garlic, crushed
Pinch of salt

Boil the pomegranate juice until reduced in half, about 15 minutes. Add the coriander, garlic, and salt and let cool.

Ghondi Nokhochi

PERSIAN CHICKPEA DUMPLINGS

❧ ABOUT 12 DUMPLINGS ❧

These unique dumplings are a common Persian Rosh Hashanah (see page 126) and holiday dish served in chicken soup.

1½ cups ground toasted
   chickpeas (nokhochi)
1 pound ground veal or chicken
2 medium onions, finely
   chopped (about 1 cup)
¼ cup chopped fresh parsley
   (optional)
1 tablespoon vegetable oil
½ teaspoon ground cardamom or
   cinnamon
¼ teaspoon ground turmeric
Salt to taste
About 3 tablespoons water
About 2 quarts chicken soup
About 1 cup cooked chickpeas
   (optional)

1. Combine all of the ingredients except the chicken soup and cooked chickpeas, adding enough water to make a firm dough that holds together. Refrigerate until easy to handle (about 2 hours). Using moistened hands, form the batter into 1- to 1½-inch balls.

2. Add the dumplings to the boiling chicken soup, reduce the heat to low, cover, and simmer for 20 minutes. If desired, add the cooked chickpeas to the soup.

Kubba

Iraqi Stuffed Dumplings
About 36 dumplings

Kubba, a distortion of the Persian word *kebab* (meat), has taken on an additional meaning in Arabic, "dome," the shape of meatballs. These meat-stuffed dumplings, similar to the Arabic *kibbe,* are found in most Iraqi Sabbath and festival soups or stews. Traditionally, the ingredients are prepared with a mortar and pestle, but a food processor makes the task immeasurably easier.

DOUGH
2 cups fine bulgur
About ¼ teaspoon salt

FILLING
3 tablespoons olive or vegetable oil
1 medium yellow onion, finely chopped (about ½ cup)
8 ounces ground beef or lamb
2 to 3 tablespoons pine nuts
2 tablespoons chopped fresh parsley
⅛ to ¼ teaspoon ground allspice
About ½ teaspoon salt
Ground black pepper to taste

2 quarts chicken or vegetable soup
Chopped fresh coriander or parsley for garnish

1. To make the dough: Soak the bulgur in water to cover for 1 hour. Drain. In a food processor or with a mortar and pestle, grind the bulgur into a smooth paste. Season with the salt. If necessary, add enough water to hold the bulgur together.

2. To make the filling: Heat the oil in a large skillet over medium heat. Add the onion and sauté until soft and translucent, 5 to 10 minutes. Add the meat and sauté until it loses its red color, about 5 minutes. Drain off any excess fat. Stir in the remaining filling ingredients. Let cool.

3. Using moistened hands, form the dough into 1-inch balls. Push a forefinger into the middle of a dough ball and hollow it out to form a cone-shaped cylinder.

4. Spoon about 1 teaspoon of the filling into the hole, then press the dough around it to enclose. Flatten slightly. (The *kubba* can be refrigerated for several hours.)

5. Bring the chicken or vegetable soup to a low boil. In batches, add the *kubba* and cook over medium heat until they rise to the surface, about 2 minutes. Remove with a slotted spoon.

6. Return all of the *kubba* to the soup, cover, and simmer over low heat for about 40 minutes. Serve the soup with the dumplings and garnish with the chopped coriander or parsley.

Variations

Fried kubba: Deep-fry the *kubba* in hot oil until golden brown on all sides. Serve as for boiled *kubba*.

Kubba Solet (Iraqi Semolina Kubba): Omit the bulgur and mix 2 cups semolina or farina, ½ cup bread crumbs, salt, pepper, and about ¾ cup water to make a smooth dough. Or reduce the amount of bulgur to 1 cup and add 1 cup semolina.

Below: **Jewish wedding in Dushanbe, Tadzhikstan, 1980.** *Jews have lived for thousands of years in Central Asia. The earliest mention of Jews living in the region was the Talmud Avodah Zorah 31b, which mentions how Samuel bar Bisna refused to drink the wine of Margiana, now located in nearby Turkmenia. The mountainous region of Tadzhikstan is located on the Afghan, Uzbekistan, and Chinese borders.*

Kubba Kari

CALCUTTA STUFFED DUMPLINGS
❧ ABOUT 36 DUMPLINGS ❧

During Passover, many Middle Eastern Jews substitute rice for the bulgur or semolina usually used to make the shells for *kubba*. The Iraqi and Syrian Jews who settled in Calcutta used this rice shell and added Indian spices to the filling. *Kubba kari* in chicken soup is frequently served at the end of a festival meal.

DOUGH

2 cups rice

4 cups warm water

About 1 teaspoon salt

FILLING

8 ounces ground lamb or chicken

1 medium yellow onion, grated (about ½ cup)

1 (¾-inch) piece fresh ginger, grated

1 clove garlic, minced

1 tablespoon chopped fresh coriander

½ teaspoon ground turmeric

About ½ teaspoon salt

Ground black pepper to taste

Marag (Calcutta chicken soup; see page 55)

1. To make the dough: Soak the rice in the warm water overnight. Drain and pat dry. In a food processor, grind the rice and salt until smooth. (The dough can be stored in the refrigerator for up to 1 day.)

2. Combine all of the filling ingredients.

3. Form heaping tablespoonfuls of the rice mixture into ¼-inch-thick rounds. Spoon about 1 teaspoon of the filling into the center of each round and bring the ends over to enclose the filling. Or form like Iraqi stuffed dumplings (see page 258).

4. Add the *kubba* to the soup and simmer until tender, about 30 minutes. Serve the soup with the dumplings.

VARIATIONS

Reduce the amount of rice to 1½ cups and add 8 ounces finely ground chicken breast to the dough mixture.

Fried Kubba: Deep-fry the *kubba* in hot vegetable oil until golden brown on all sides.

Kouclas bi Khobz

MOROCCAN BREAD DUMPLING
ABOUT 2 CUPS

1 cup bread crumbs
1 large yellow onion, chopped
   (about ¾ cup)
3 large eggs
¼ cup chopped fresh parsley
2 tablespoons all-purpose flour
Salt to taste

1. Combine all of the ingredients. Wrap loosely in a piece of cheesecloth or aluminum foil and tie securely.
2. Cook in *dafina* (Moroccan Sabbath stew; see page 124).

Kouclas bi Ruz

MOROCCAN RICE DUMPLING
ABOUT 3 CUPS

1 cup rice
4 ounces ground lamb or beef
½ cup ground walnuts
½ cup chopped fresh parsley
2 large eggs, lightly beaten
1 teaspoon ground cinnamon
1 teaspoon ground mace
1 teaspoon grated nutmeg
About ½ teaspoon salt
Ground black pepper to taste

1. Combine all of the ingredients. Wrap loosely in a piece of cheesecloth and tie securely.
2. Cook in *dafina* (Moroccan Sabbath stew; see page 124).

BREADS

And bread that sustains man's heart.
—Psalms 104:15

By applying the Whorfian hypothesis, which states that the subjects most important to a specific culture occur most frequently in the language, we can see the special place held by bread in Jewish life. The Bible contains about a dozen names for various shapes and types of bread, including matza (unleavened flat bread), challah (rolled loaves), *kikkar* (a round flat loaf), *rakik* (thin wafers), *ugah* (cakes of bread baked on a heated rock or ashes), *revuchah* (a dough made with hot water and oil), *levivah* (pancake breads), *lechem hapanim* (shewbread), *solet* (semolina bread), *pat* (a piece of bread), and *lechem* (also used as a general term for food). No Sabbath or festival meal is complete without bread, and it is central to two Jewish holidays: Not only is leavened bread forbidden during Passover, but it is the only food the Bible associates with the festival of Shavuot—"From the land upon which you live, you shall bring two loaves of bread as a wave offering" (Leviticus 23:17).

Sephardim historically ate more bread than Ashkenazim, who preferred their starch in the form of noodles, dumplings, gruels, kasha, and, later, potatoes. This disparity was partially due to the superior quality of Middle Eastern bread, which was primarily made from wheat, often from white flour. European loaves, on the other hand, tended to be coarse because of the use of barley, which was widespread until the fourteenth century, or rye, which served as the primary form of bread in northern Europe until the seventeenth century.

Opposite: A Yugoslavian refugee bakes bread the old-fashioned way in a brick oven in Santa Maria de Leuca, Italy, 1945. *Home baking became easier after Charles Fleischmann, a Hungarian-Jewish immigrant, began offering compressed yeast cakes in Cincinnati, Ohio, in 1876. In the 1930s, Fleischmann's introduced the now-essential active dry yeast.*

Masa de Pan/Vorteig

LEAN YEAST DOUGH
ABOUT 1½ POUNDS DOUGH

From only a handful of ingredients—flour, water, yeast, and salt—emerges the staff of life. With the addition of fat, eggs, sweeteners, spices, fruits, whole grains, and other ingredients, the flavor and character of the loaf is transformed into any of a myriad of possibilities. This basic dough is used to make a wide variety of breads, including the flat bread that has been eaten daily in the Middle East for thousands of years as well as such well-known descendants as pita and pizza.

1 package (about 2½ teaspoons) active dry yeast or
1 (.6-ounce) cake fresh yeast
1⅓ cups warm water (105 to 110 degrees for dry yeast, 80 to 85 degrees for fresh yeast)
1 teaspoon sugar or honey
2 teaspoons table salt or 4 teaspoons kosher salt
About 4 cups unbleached all-purpose flour

1. Dissolve the yeast in ¼ cup of the water. Stir in the sugar or honey and let stand until foamy, 5 to 10 minutes.
2. Using a wooden spoon, an electric mixer, or your hand, add the remaining water, salt, and 2 cups of the flour. Stir in the remaining flour, ½ cup at a time, until the mixture holds together.
3. On a lightly floured surface, knead the dough until smooth and elastic, 5 to 10 minutes.
4. Place the dough in a greased bowl, turning to coat. Cover with a towel or plastic wrap and let rise until double in bulk, about 1½ hours. (The dough has risen sufficiently when the indentations remain when touched with two fingers.)
5. Punch down the dough.

FOOD PROCESSOR METHOD

1. Combine the dry ingredients in the work bowl of a food processor fitted with a dough or metal blade. With the machine on, add the dissolved yeast mixture.
2. With the machine on, gradually add warm water until the dough forms a ball that cleans the sides of the bowl. Process around the bowl about 25 times. Let the dough stand for 5 minutes to allow the flour to absorb the liquid.
3. Process around the bowl about 15 times, adding more water if necessary to make a soft but not sticky dough. Be

careful not to overprocess, as the heat of the machine's engine may overheat the dough and the bread will rise unevenly.

4. Continue with step 4 above.

Note: This method can be used for any yeast dough in lieu of hand mixing and kneading. Add egg and oil, when applicable, along with dissolved yeast mixture.

VARIATIONS

Rich Yeast Dough: Add 1 egg and 2 to 3 tablespoons oil and increase the sugar to 1 tablespoon.

Whole-Wheat Yeast Dough: Reduce the amount of white flour to 2 cups and add 2 cups whole-wheat flour.

FLOUR

Barley rivals wheat as one of the oldest cultivated grains, but wheat has no competition when it comes to importance. Wheat's uniqueness lies in a special protein called gluten, the substance that gives flour the elasticity to rise and keep its structure under heat. Few grains possess gluten and none, except wheat, have enough to produce the light texture that we associate with bread.

There are two types of wheat used in baking: hard (spring) wheat and soft (winter) wheat. Hard wheat (high-gluten) flour, the type used by most commercial bread bakers, produces the lightest, firm-crumbed loaf. However, since this type of flour is often not easily obtainable, unbleached all-purpose flour, a mixture of hard and soft wheat, makes a suitable substitute. Cake flour,

pastry flour, and self-rising flour should never be used in bread making. Whole-wheat flour (containing bran and germ) can be substituted for part of the white flour but, since it has proportionately less gluten than white flour, any bread made from whole wheat has a denser, heavier texture.

An exact amount of flour cannot be given in bread recipes, since the moisture content of flour varies greatly, as does that of the atmosphere. The moister the flour, the more flour the dough will need. Unless otherwise indicated, measure flour for bread by dipping a gradated measuring cup into the canister, filling it above the rim, and leveling the top with a flat instrument such as the back of a knife.

Flat Breads

For millennia bread making was a difficult chore, one whose result was never entirely certain. The baker mixed flour, usually coarse, and water with a reserved portion of the previous day's dough in a large wooden kneading trough (see Exodus 12:34). The use of a starter was a major advance, as before this bakers relied on unpredictable airborne yeast to raise their dough. After a strenuous kneading, the dough was left to rise (occasionally it failed to live up to expectations) overnight.

The baker rose well before dawn to prepare the thin loaves of bread, which were originally baked directly on the coals of a campfire (thus the meaning of Proverbs 20:17, "Bread obtained by deceit is sweet to a man, but afterwards his mouth shall be filled with gravel") or on a heated stone. Many bedouin in the Middle East still prepare their bread in this manner. With the invention of the clay oven, the bread was baked by pressing the thin loaves against the inner wall, a method still used in some parts of the Middle East.

It was in Egypt that bread-baking methods were first refined and many of the techniques still in use today were first developed. The Egyptians, who created numerous types and forms of bread, took their breads very seriously. Indeed, Pharaoh had his chief baker executed in response to a pebble found in a loaf of bread (Genesis 40:22). However, flat breads remained the staple throughout most of the Middle East.

Above: **Iranian Jewish girl holding loaves of Persian bread in Teheran, 1952.** *The country of Persia (modern-day Iran) has been connected in many ways with the Jews ever since Cyrus the Great conquered Babylonia and granted the Jews permission to return to Israel in 539 B.C.E. The reforms of two important Jewish officials of the Persian court—Nenemian, appointed sarrap of Judah in 445, and Ezra the Scribe—laid the foundations for the future religious, social, and cultural character of the Jewish people.*

Pita (Khobiz)

MIDDLE EASTERN POCKET BREAD
❧ MAKES ABOUT 12 SMALL BREADS ❧

One of the most well known flat breads is the round, hollow loaf called *pita* (pocket) in Greek and *khobiz* in Arabic. To produce the traditional pocket, rounds of soft dough are baked in a very hot oven. The water inside turns into steam, which then puffs up and separates the bread into two layers. Fill the pita with falafel, kebabs, or salads or serve as an accompaniment to *tarator bi tahina* (sesame seed sauce; see page 368) or other dips.

1 recipe lean yeast dough (see page 264)

Fine semolina, cornmeal, or flour for sprinkling

1. Divide the dough into 12 equal pieces. Shape each piece into a ball, cover, and let stand for about 15 minutes. For large pita, divide the dough into 4 pieces and roll out each piece into about a 9-inch round.

2. Sprinkle 2 baking sheets with semolina, cornmeal, or flour. Flatten each dough ball and roll out into a ⅛- to ¼-inch-thick round, 5 to 6 inches in diameter. Place on the baking sheets, cover, and let stand until puffy, about 30 minutes.

3. Position a rack in the lower third of the oven. Preheat the oven to 475 degrees.

4. Bake the pitas—do not open the oven during the first 5 minutes—until puffed and the bottoms begin to brown, 5 to 10 minutes. Cool on a rack, then store in plastic bags to soften. If storing for more than 2 days, freeze.

VARIATIONS
Peda (Middle Eastern Herb Flat Bread): Brush the dough rounds with olive oil, then sprinkle with a seasoning such as sesame seeds, poppy seeds, thyme, cumin, *mahlab* (ground cherry pits), or a combination of spices.

Naan (Indian Flat Bread): Brush the dough rounds with lightly beaten egg and sprinkle with chopped scallions (about 1 scallion per round) or onions, kosher salt, and, if desired, cumin seeds (about ⅛ teaspoon per round) or black sesame seeds.

Lavash

CENTRAL ASIAN FLAT BREAD
 6 VERY THIN BREADS

This thin peasant bread, called *yufka* in Turkey, is ubiquitous at Caucasian meals in Georgia, Armenia, and Azerbaijan. Soft *lavash* is used to wrap a variety of fillings; crisp *lavash* is used as a cracker.

1 recipe lean yeast dough (see page 264)

1 egg beaten with 1 tablespoon water (optional)

Sesame seeds or poppy seeds (optional)

1. Preheat the oven to 475 degrees. Heat a baking stone or large heavy baking sheet in the oven, about 15 minutes.

2. Divide the dough into 6 pieces. Cover and let stand for 15 minutes.

3. On a lightly floured surface, roll out each piece into a very thin rectangle; each sixth will be about 12 by 10 inches. (The dough rectangles can be sprinkled with flour and stacked.) Prick the dough all over with the tines of a fork. If desired, brush with the egg wash and sprinkle with sesame or poppy seeds.

4. Slide the dough onto the preheated baking stone or sheet and bake until lightly browned, about 5 minutes.

5. For soft bread, cover the warm *lavash* with a damp cloth and let stand for 20 minutes. For crisp bread, transfer to a wire rack and cool. Store the *lavash* in an airtight container.

Mufleta

MOROCCAN PANCAKE BREADS
ABOUT 40 TINY BREADS

Moroccan Jews serve these breads for the holiday of Mimouna (see below).

1 recipe lean yeast dough (see page 264)

1. Divide the dough into about 40 balls. Place the balls on a greased surface and flatten.
2. Heat an ungreased skillet or griddle.
3. Cook the dough rounds, turning once, until golden brown on both sides and cooked through. Cover the *mufletas* with a cloth until serving. Serve with butter, honey, and jam.

MIMOUNA

At the conclusion of Passover, Moroccans celebrate a unique holiday of brotherhood and peace called Mimouna. The word *mimouna* is an Arabic variation of the Hebrew word *emunah* (faith), appropriate for the onset of spring. In addition, the day following Passover is the anniversary of the death of Moses Maimonides' father, Rav Maimon. After sunset on the last day of Passover, Moroccan Jews traditionally throw open their doors and hold a community-wide open house. Arab neighbors join in, bringing the Jews their first *chametz* (leavened grain) in the form of cakes and milk, which they refrain from drinking on Passover. Crowds of Jews and Arabs then roam from house to house wishing each other the blessing *terb'hou u'tsa'adu* (happiness and prosperity) and sampling from the tables laden with goodies. The following day is celebrated with family picnics, where tents are pitched in recognition of the biblical phrase, "How goodly are thy tents O Jacob." Recently, Mimouna festivities have gained increasing popularity in Israel among other Jewish communities.

Lahuhua

YEMENITE FLAT BREAD

ABOUT 20 (5-INCH) BREADS

Yemen was until recently an isolated and impoverished land, which is reflected in the region's breads, such as the flat, multilayered *miloach* and the pitalike *salufe,* both baked on the walls of clay ovens similar to those of ancient times. *Lahuhua,* a pancake bread reminiscent of the first breads, was originally baked on hot rocks. This recipe has been updated to use a skillet. These spongy, bubbly loaves are traditionally served with soups, stews, and spicy condiments. The following is a version using yeast.

1 package (about 2½ teaspoons) active dry yeast

3 cups warm water (105 to 110 degrees)

1 tablespoon sugar or honey

¼ cup vegetable shortening or margarine, melted

½ teaspoon table salt or 1 teaspoon kosher salt

3½ cups unbleached all-purpose flour

1. Dissolve the yeast in ¼ cup of the water. Stir in 1 teaspoon of the sugar or honey and let stand until foamy, about 5 minutes.

2. Blend in the remaining water, remaining sugar or honey, shortening, and salt. Stir in the flour.

3. Cover and let rise in a warm, draft-free place for 1 hour. Stir down, cover, and let rise for another hour.

4. Pour 3 to 4 tablespoons batter into a medium unheated nonstick skillet. (If you do not have a nonstick skillet, heat a regular skillet over medium-low heat and coat the bottom with a little oil.)

5. Place over medium heat for 1 minute. Reduce the heat to low and cook until the bottom is golden brown and the top bubbly, 3 to 4 minutes. Do not cook the top side.

Opposite: A Yemenite woman bakes unleavened bread by slapping thin loaves against the sides of an earthen oven in the Hashid Refugee camp in Aden in 1949 as her family awaits their transfer to Israel. Yemenite breads also include lahuhua, *a griddle bread, and the pita-like* salufe, *which is still baked on the walls of clay ovens.*

Miloach

YEMENITE FLAKY BREAD
9 BREADS

Miloach is served by Yemenite Jews at both Sabbath dinner and breakfast and at the meal to break a fast, accompanied with *z'chug* (chili paste; see page 379), *chilbeh* (fenugreek relish; see page 14), hard-boiled eggs, and assorted salads.

1 recipe Yemenite flaky pastry (see page 44), followed through Step 1.

1. Roll out each piece of dough into a ¼-inch-thick round.
2. Heat a large nonstick skillet or griddle over medium heat. (If you do not have a nonstick skillet, heat a regular skillet and coat the bottom with a little butter or margarine.) Fry the rounds until golden brown on both sides, about 4 minutes per side. Let cool. *Miloach* freezes well, stored between sheets of waxed paper.

ETHIOPIAN EATING

"Because of poverty and the recent famine, many Westerners believe that Ethiopian dining is a contradiction in terms," observes David (Dawet) Solomon, a native of Gondar, Ethiopia. "However, the Beta Esrael possess a simple but tasty cuisine making use of sparse resources."

For more than two millennia, the land lying to the west of the Red Sea served as home to a group of black Jews known to the Ethiopians by the derogatory term of *Falasha* ("wanderers" in Geez), but calling themselves Beta Esrael ("House of Israel"). Although several medieval Jewish travelers mentioned black Jews living in eastern Africa, their existence was first confirmed to the Western world in a 1790 report by the Scottish explorer James Bruce. Most scholars believe that the Beta Esrael are descendants of native Agau tribes converted to Judaism by contact with Jews living in Arabia or with Jewish refugees who arrived in the area by way of either Egypt or Arabia following the destruction of the first Temple. The Beta Esrael maintained their independence and their own kings and queens until being defeated in the 1620s by Emperor Susenyos. They were then banished to the Gondar region adjacent to the Sudanese border and subjected to centuries of persecution and aggressive proselytizing efforts.

With the overthrow of Emperor Haile Selassie in 1974 and the subsequent civil war, a growing number of Beta Esrael made their way to Israel by way of Sudanese refugee camps. Then, in 1984 and 1985, the Israeli government airlifted about fifteen thousand Beta Esrael to Israel in an action called Operation Moses. Subsequently, in 1991 during Operation Solomon, most of the surviving fourteen thousand Beta Esrael were flown to Israel. Remaining behind in the hills of Ethiopia were only a few old people, unable or unwilling to make the journey.

"For much of the past two millennia," David Solomon states, "Ethiopian Jewry was cut off from contact with other Jewish communities and, therefore, developed differently than the main body of Judaism. To be sure, we remained faithful to the *Orit* [the Bible and some books of the Apocrypha, which until recently were known to them only in the Geez translation] and we share many of the traditional Jewish beliefs and customs [including kashruth, circumcision, ritual slaughter, the calendar, Shabbat, and the biblical holidays]. However, until recently the Beta Esrael had no knowledge of the Talmud, although we possessed a number of traditions similar to the Talmud.

"The *mesgid* [synagogue] was literally the center of our villages," Solomon notes. "Livestock was slaughtered by the local *kes* [priest], then salted and rinsed to make kosher. However, meat was generally reserved for special occasions. Unlike non-Jewish Ethiopians, Beta Esrael do not eat raw meat. All dairy products were produced from cow's milk; goats and sheep were raised for meat and wool only.

"Ours is a peasant cuisine, simple but flavorful," explains Solomon. "Ethiopian spice mixtures reflect an Arabic influence. Ethiopians ate two major meals—breakfast and dinner. In between, we snacked on roasted corn kernels and seeds. The menu is varied by the basic ingredients of the *wot*. Vegetable *wots*

Above: **A young mother in the Ibenet distribution camp near Libo, Ethiopia, bakes *injera* (flat bread) near the family's grass hut.** *The ascendancy of Christianity in Ethiopia spelled persecution for the Beta Israel, who fled en masse to the area aound Lank Tana in the north of the country. The Beta Israel lived in relative obscurity, primarily in villages and rural areas, making their livelihood as farmers and craftsmen.*

are common breakfast fare; if affordable, meat, chicken, and fish *wots* were made for dinner. Chicken was occasionally roasted over an open flame, a dish usually reserved for the Sabbath."

The *Sanbat* [Sabbath] is a very special part of the Ethiopian Jew's week. As the biblical laws are often observed quite literally, no heating of food is done for the Sabbath. The meals are prepared in advance with everything ready before sundown on Friday and all food served at room temperature. Solomon notes, "The Beta Esrael usually serve small, round rolls called *dabos* at Sabbath meals. Since Ethiopian Jews lacked wine for kiddush, they used *tallah* [a beer fermented by gesho leaves]. In Israel, many Beta Esrael now use wine."

Injera

ETHIOPIAN PANCAKE BREAD
ABOUT 16 BREADS

Injera, flat breads prepared on a griddle or in a skillet, form a major part of every Ethiopian Jew's diet. The most common form of this bread is made from teff, literally "lost" in Amharic, referring to the tiny size of the finely ground grains, which are related to millet. Other types of *injera* are made from red, black, or white millet called Ethiopian wheat. Water is added to the teff and the batter is allowed to stand until fermented, a stage that imparts a sour flavor as well as creates holes during cooking. The thick *injera* batter is then fried on round trays or skillets. It is usually made in large batches and stored for up to a week in woven grass sacks.

The *injera* is arranged on a communal plate and a *wot* (stew) is then spooned on top of it. Each person pulls off a piece of *injera* while scooping up some of the *wot*, then folds it between his or her fingers. Silverware is unnecessary.

8 cups unbleached all-purpose flour
1 teaspoon baking soda
½ teaspoon active dry yeast
3 cups water
7 cups club soda, at room temperature

1. Combine the flour, baking soda, and yeast. Stirring constantly with a spoon or your hands, add the water in a slow steady stream. Stir in the club soda and continue to stir until the batter is smooth. If there are lumps, strain. (The batter can also be prepared in batches in a blender.) Let the batter stand for 10 minutes.

2. Heat a 10- to 12-inch skillet, preferably one with a nonstick surface, over medium heat. (If you do not have a nonstick skillet, heat a regular skillet and coat the bottom with a little oil.)

3. Pour ½ cup batter onto one side of the skillet and quickly tilt so the batter evenly covers the bottom of the pan.

4. Cook, uncovered, until the top is spongy and dotted with tiny air bubbles and the bottom is firm but not colored, about 1 minute.

5. Using a spatula or your fingers, carefully lift the *injera* out of the pan—do not cook the top side. Lay the *injera* on a plate or linen towel to cool. Repeat with the remaining batter. Serve with a meat or vegetable stew.

Sabbath Loaves

*When you enter the land into which I will bring you, and
when you eat of the bread of the land, you shall set aside a
portion unto the Lord. Of the first of your dough, you
shall set apart* **challah** *as a gift.*

—Numbers 15:18–21

You shall take **solet** *[fine semolina flour] and bake twelve*
challot, *two-tenths of a measure for each* **challah.**

—Leviticus 24:5

The Bible used the term *challah* (rolled loaves) in reference to two types of bread: the portion of bread given to the priests and the shewbread (twelve flat unleavened loaves, representing the twelve tribes of Israel, that were placed weekly on a gold-plated table in the Temple's sanctuary). Since the destruction of the Temple, neither of these biblical forms of challah can be fulfilled, although a one-ounce piece is customarily removed from bread dough and burned in place of the priest's portion. After the Temple period, the home table symbolically replaced the altar and the Sabbath loaves the shewbread. Therefore, many of the customs surrounding the Sabbath loaves stem from the Temple rituals or from another type of biblical bread, the manna.

Sabbath bread is traditionally made from white flour, once the province of the wealthy, since a prominent symbol for the Sabbath is that of a queen, and it is only appropriate that the Sabbath loaves should be bread fit for royalty. A tradition common to every Jewish community is to cover the Sabbath bread with a cloth, usually an embroidered one, recalling how the manna was protected by layers of dew. Two loaves are placed on the Sabbath and festival table to represent the double portion of manna gathered for the Sabbath. After reciting the kiddush (the prayer of "sanctification") over a glass of wine, *hamotzi* is recited over the bread. Ashkenazim slice the challah with a knife, while most Sephardim break the bread with their hands, as a knife may serve as an object of violence and war and therefore was not permitted in the Temple sanctuary. In certain Sephardic communities, pieces of the Sabbath bread are tossed, not handed directly, to the diners, reflecting that the real source of food is the Lord, not the host. Challah is traditionally served with a sprinkling of salt, an allusion to the altar of the Temple, where salt was a mandatory component of the sacrifices.

The earliest form of Sabbath bread, and the type still used in most Middle Eastern communities, was round flat bread. These loaves are generally served unembellished, although some are sprinkled with poppy or sesame seeds. Sephardim generally use plain rectangular loaves, similar to their weekday breads, but for the festivals some make intricate shapes, including spirals, books, and flowers.

Until the fifteenth century, Ashkenazim also used their weekday rectangular or round loaves for the Sabbath. Then many German Jews adopted a new form of Sabbath bread, an oval, braided loaf modeled on a popular Teutonic bread. This new form of Sabbath bread was commonly called *berches* or *barches*—possibly a corruption of the Yiddish word *broches* (blessings) or the German word *bercht* (braid). In some places, the Sabbath bread took on the biblical name *challah*. Eventually, this braided loaf with the latter name made its way eastward, becoming the most prevalent form of Sabbath bread among eastern Europeans.

In eastern Europe, the braided challah loaf was further embellished, the shape and appearance usually reflecting Jewish legend and lore, most notably the biblical manna. Eggs and sometimes saffron were added to the dough to simulate the yellow color of the manna. Sweeteners were symbolic of the manna's taste, which, when pounded into cakes, was like honey. Seeds were sprinkled over the dough, as the manna fell in the form of coriander seeds. Many Sephardic authorities questioned whether the *hamotzi* (blessing over the bread) could properly be recited over enriched loaves, since adding large amounts of eggs and sweetener actually transformed the finished product into a cake—this was not so far-fetched, as some eastern Europeans used part of the egg challah dough to make babka and other yeast cakes. Nonetheless, for the past four centuries, the aroma and flavor of egg challah has been a central part of the eastern European Sabbath.

Eier Challah

EASTERN EUROPEAN EGG BREAD
1 VERY LARGE, 2 LARGE, OR 3 MEDIUM LOAVES

The large amount of eggs, fat, and sugar gives this much-beloved bread a rich flavor, a golden color, a soft crust, and a tender, fine crumb (the inner part of the bread). The larger the amount of eggs and oil, the softer the bread. Challah for Rosh Hashanah and Sukkoth is traditionally kneaded with raisins or chopped dried fruits, a symbol of sweetness and the harvest. Use leftover challah (if there is any) to make French toast, bread pudding, or stuffing.

A braided loaf suggests a special occasion and is the most popular form of Ashkenazic Sabbath bread. Very large braided challahs, served at festive occasions such as weddings, are called *keylitch*.

*2 packages (about 5 teaspoons)
  active dry yeast or
  1 (1-ounce) cake fresh yeast
2 cups warm water (105 to
  110 degrees for dry yeast,
  80 to 85 degrees for fresh
  yeast)
½ to ¾ cup sugar or honey
3 to 4 large eggs
½ cup vegetable oil
1 tablespoon table salt or
  5 teaspoons kosher salt
About 8 cups unbleached
  all-purpose flour
1 egg beaten with
  1 tablespoon water
About 3 tablespoons poppy seeds
  or sesame seeds (optional)*

1. Dissolve the yeast in ½ cup of the water. Add 1 teaspoon of the sugar or honey and let stand until foamy, 5 to 10 minutes.

2. Add the remaining water, the remaining sugar or honey, eggs, oil, salt, and 3 cups of the flour. Stir in the remaining flour, ½ cup at a time, until the mixture holds together.

3. Place on a lightly floured surface and knead until smooth and elastic, about 10 minutes. Place in a greased large bowl, turning to coat. Cover loosely and let rise at room temperature until double in bulk, about 1½ hours, or in the refrigerator overnight.

4. Punch down the dough and let rest for 10 minutes. Shape the challah—for shaping techniques, see below. (At this point, the loaves can be frozen for up to 3 months. Remove from the freezer, place on a baking sheet, cover, and let rise for about 6 hours.)

5. Place the shaped loaves on a greased baking sheet or in a greased loaf pan, cover, and let rise at room temperature until double in bulk, about 45 minutes, or in the refrigerator for up to 2 days.

6. Meanwhile, position a rack in the center of the oven. Preheat the oven to 350 degrees.

7. Brush the challah with the egg wash, being careful not to drip any onto the baking sheet, and, if desired, sprinkle with the poppy or sesame seeds. (The egg produces a soft, shiny crust and helps the seeds to adhere to the surface.) Bake until golden brown and hollow-sounding when tapped, about 35 minutes for medium challahs, about 45 minutes for large ones. Transfer to a wire rack to cool.

Wedding canopy. Engraving, Venice, 1593. *Jewish weddings traditionally take place under a canopy supported by four poles. This custom developed during the Middle Ages when weddings were mostly celebrated outdoors under the canopy of heaven. The wedding canopy was created to separate the ceremony from the surroundings.*

CHALLAH SHAPES

Festival loaves, many originating in the Ukraine, often possess special shapes. Traditional Rosh Hashanah forms include rounds (symbolizing continuity, with no beginning and no end), spirals (symbolizing the ascent to heaven), and crowns (symbolizing the King of the universe). A bird shape, an allusion to the verse in Isaiah 31:5, "As hovering birds, so will the Lord of hosts shield Jerusalem," was customary at the meal preceding Yom Kippur. A key shape (symbolizing the gates of heaven) was prepared for the Sabbath following Passover, and five- or seven-rung ladder challahs (symbolizing the ascent to heaven) for Shavuot. Ukrainian Jews developed the custom of shaping the challahs for the meal before the Yom Kippur fast into images of ascension: birds (Isaiah 31:5), symbolizing that all sins should fly away and that one's prayers soar to the heavens; or ladders, reminiscent of Jacob's dream (Genesis 28:10–22).

Three-Strand Braided Challah

❧ 3 MEDIUM LOAVES ☙

1 recipe eier *challah (see page 276)*

1. Divide the dough into 3 equal pieces, then divide each piece into 3 equal pieces. Roll into 1-inch-thick ropes.
2. Pinch together the ends of 3 ropes. With the pinched side away from you, place the right-hand piece *(a)* over the center piece *(b)* and bring the left-hand piece *(c)* over piece *a.* Bring piece *b* over piece *c.* (Piece *a* is now on the left-hand side and piece *c* is on the right-hand side.)
3. Bring piece *a* over piece *b,* then *c* over *a.* Continue this pattern until all of the dough rope is braided, then pinch the ends together. Repeat in the same fashion with the remaining ropes.

Spiral Challah

❧ 3 MEDIUM LOAVES ☙

1 recipe eier *challah (see page 276)*

1. Divide the dough into 3 equal pieces. Roll each piece into a 3-inch-thick rope with one end tapered.
2. Place the thicker end of each rope in the center of a greased baking sheet and coil the dough around it in a spiral fashion, tucking the tapered end into the center or under the bottom.

Keter

CROWN LOAVES

❧ 3 MEDIUM LOAVES ☙

1 recipe eier *challah (see page 276)*

1. Divide the dough into 3 large pieces, 3 medium pieces, and 3 small pieces. Shape into smooth balls.
2. Place the large balls on a greased baking sheet and flatten slightly. Place a small ball on top of each large ball. Roll each medium ball into a rope and wrap around each small ball, pinching the ends to seal.

Bulkalach

ASHKENAZIC CHALLAH ROLLS

❧ ABOUT 40 (3-INCH) ROLLS ☙

Bulke is the Slavic-Yiddish word for "roll"; *zemmel* is the Germanic-Yiddish equivalent. Although rolls are also formed into simple round shapes, these knotted rolls make a more attractive presentation. For braided rolls, use three 4- to 5-inch-long dough ropes and braid as described in Three-Strand Braided Challah (see page 279).

1 recipe eier *challah (see page 276)*

1. Divide the dough into 1½-inch balls and roll each ball into a 6-inch-long rope about ¾ inch thick. Twist one end of the rope over the other (you will have a small hole in the center), pull one end through the hole, then press the ends together to seal.

2. Place the rolls about 1½ inches apart on a greased baking sheet. After rising, bake for about 20 minutes.

Vasser Challah

GERMAN WATER BREAD

❧ 2 LARGE LOAVES ☙

Most Americans think of challah as the rich egg bread of eastern Europe, but German Jews prefer a leaner loaf. The oblong bread strip running down the center of this challah symbolizes the ascent to heaven. Loaves made with a starter use half the amount of yeast, are more flavorful and denser, and remain fresh longer—which is important, since breads that contain no fat dry out relatively fast. Use any stale bread to make bread crumbs or croutons.

SAUERTEIG (STARTER)
1¼ teaspoons active
    dry yeast
1 cup warm water (105 to
    110 degrees)

1. To make the starter: Combine the yeast, ¼ cup of the water, and the sugar or malt in a nonmetallic bowl and let stand until foamy, 5 to 10 minutes. Using a wooden spoon, stir in the remaining water and the flour until smooth (traditionally 100 strokes).

1 teaspoon sugar or barley malt syrup (see Note)

1 cup unbleached all-purpose flour

TEIG (DOUGH)

2 cups lukewarm water (about 80 degrees)

1 tablespoon table salt or 1½ tablespoons kosher salt

About 6½ cups unbleached all-purpose flour

1 egg white beaten with 1 teaspoon water

About 3 tablespoons poppy seeds

2. Cover with plastic wrap and let stand at room temperature until bubbly, at least 4 hours and up to 24 hours. (The longer it stands, the tangier the flavor. When ready, the starter can be kept in the refrigerator for up to a week.)

3. To make the dough: Combine the starter, water, and salt. Stir in the flour, 1 cup at a time, until the mixture holds together.

4. On a lightly floured surface, knead until smooth and elastic, about 10 minutes. Place in a greased bowl, turning to coat. Cover with a towel or plastic wrap and let rise until double in bulk, about 1½ hours.

5. Punch down the dough and remove two 1½-inch pieces. Divide the remaining dough in half, shape into ovals, and place on a greased baking sheet. Roll the small pieces into 2 long ropes and arrange lengthwise down the center of the ovals. Cover with a towel and let rise at room temperature until double in bulk, about 1 hour.

6. Meanwhile, position a rack in the center of the oven. Preheat the oven to 400 degrees.

7. Brush the loaves with the egg white and sprinkle with the poppy seeds. (Egg whites give breads a crisper crust as well as help the seeds to adhere.) Bake until golden brown and hollow-sounding when tapped, about 45 minutes. Transfer to a wire rack to cool.

Note: Barley malt syrup is available at most health food stores.

VARIATION

Berches (Braided Water Bread): Braid the dough as for egg challah (see page 279). Or divide the dough into 4 equal pieces, shape 2 pieces into large ovals, divide each of the remaining 2 pieces into thirds, roll into ropes, braid as above, and arrange the braids on top of the ovals.

Khboz

MOROCCAN ANISE BREAD
 2 MEDIUM LOAVES

The Moroccans enliven even meager fare with the liberal use of seasonings. They enhance this loaf, also called *ksra,* with anise. It is traditionally served on Rosh Hashanah—the rounded shape representing the cycle of the year—but is also enjoyed by many Moroccans on the Sabbath. Almonds and rose water are sometimes added for Shavuot and Sukkoth.

1 package (2½ teaspoons) active
  dry yeast or 1 (.6-ounce)
  cake fresh yeast
1⅓ cups warm water
  (105 to 110 degrees for
  dry yeast, 80 to 85 degrees
  for fresh yeast)
1 teaspoon sugar or honey
1 tablespoon vegetable oil
2 to 3 teaspoons anise seeds
2 teaspoons table salt or
  4 teaspoons kosher salt
About 4 cups unbleached
  all-purpose flour
1 egg white beaten with
  1 teaspoon water
3 tablespoons sesame seeds

1. Dissolve the yeast in ¼ cup of the water. Add the sugar or honey and let stand until foamy, 5 to 10 minutes.
2. Add the remaining water, oil, anise, salt, and 2 cups of the flour. Gradually stir in the remaining flour until the mixture holds together.
3. On a lightly floured surface, knead the dough until smooth and elastic, about 10 minutes. Place in a greased bowl, turning to coat. Cover loosely with a towel or plastic wrap and let rise at room temperature until double in bulk, about 1½ hours, or in the refrigerator overnight.
4. Punch down the dough and divide in half. Shape each piece into a ball, cover, and let rest for about 10 minutes.
5. Sprinkle a large baking sheet with cornmeal or fine semolina or grease the baking sheet. Flatten each dough ball into a 6-inch round. Some cooks flute the outer edge, others leave it plain. Place the rounds on the prepared baking sheet, cover, and let rise at room temperature until double in bulk, about 1 hour.
6. Preheat the oven to 375 degrees.
7. Prick the dough around the sides with the tines of a fork or a toothpick. Brush the tops of the loaves with the egg white and lightly sprinkle with the sesame seeds.
8. Bake until golden brown and hollow-sounding when tapped, about 30 minutes. Transfer to a wire rack to cool.

VARIATION
Whole-Wheat Khboz: Substitute 1 cup whole-wheat flour for an equal amount of the white flour.

Kubaneh

YEMENITE OVERNIGHT BREAD

8 TO 10 SERVINGS

Yemenites serve this slow-cooked bread with a kugel-like texture for Saturday lunch. In Israel, this recipe is made with a special 8-inch-round pot with a flat bottom and a flat fitted top. If you do not have a *kubaneh* pot, substitute a 3-quart saucepan or ovenproof ceramic casserole and cover with heavy-duty aluminum foil.

1 recipe lean yeast dough (see page 264)
½ cup (1 stick) margarine or butter, melted

1. Preheat the oven to 200 degrees.
2. Form the dough into 1½-inch balls. Roll the dough balls in the melted margarine or butter to coat and arrange in a *kubaneh* pot or 3-quart saucepan or casserole.
3. Cover the *kubaneh* pot with its lid or the saucepan or casserole with aluminum foil. Cook over medium-low heat until the dough balls begin to expand, about 15 minutes.
4. Invert the *kubaneh* pot, saucepan, or casserole onto a baking sheet. Place in the oven and bake overnight. Or invert the pot onto a *blech* (a metal sheet that covers the stove top) and cook over low heat overnight. *Kubaneh* is traditionally served at Sabbath lunch with *chilbeh* (Yemenite fenugreek relish; see page 14) and hard-boiled eggs.

ANISE

Aniseed, the licorice-flavored seed of the anise plant, is one of the most ancient spices. It once grew wild throughout Israel and Egypt and remains one of the most popular flavoring agents in Europe and the Middle East. Star anise (Chinese anise), which possesses a similar flavor, is a different spice.

In both whole or ground form, anise is used in baked goods, confections, and medicine. Strong anise-flavored liqueurs abound in the Mediterranean, including Middle Eastern *araq*, Greek *ouzo*, Turkish *raki*, and French *pastis*, as well as the milder anisette.

Miscellaneous Breads

Bagels

EASTERN EUROPEAN BREAD RINGS

❧ 12 LARGE BAGELS ❧

As a boy, my favorite chore fell on Sunday mornings, when I walked the several blocks to the home of Mrs. Lottie Kanner, an elderly eastern European immigrant, to pick up a bag of warm, aromatic bagels made from her secret recipe. I would hurry to the small room attached to the back of her house and watch as she deftly shaped the dough rings, dropped them into a large tub of boiling water, scooped them out, and rushed them into the oven. They remain by far the best bagels I have ever tasted, and that is not simply nostalgia.

Mrs. Kanner was continuing a practice common in eastern Europe, where, to supplement the family income, some housewives prepared batches of bagels in their homes and their husbands or children peddled them in the streets. The bagel followed only rye bread as the most common bread among eastern European Jews. These round dough rings commonly accompanied men to work and students to school, providing a handy and filling lunch.

A popular legend claims that bagels were invented in 1683 by a non-Jewish Viennese baker, who called the ring-shaped breads *buegel* (stirrup) to honor the role of a Polish prince and his cavalry in a victory over the Turks. However, they are mentioned in the records of the Kraków Jewish community dating seventy-three years earlier (the citation affirms that bagels are an appropriate gift for pregnant women). The name of this doughnut-shaped bread, therefore, may be from *bougal*, a Middle High German word for "ring," or *beigen*, a Yiddish word for "bend," pointing to a Teutonic origin.

The bagel's uniqueness comes from being boiled in water before baking, a step that produces its crisp crust and moist, chewy interior. The dough and baking method are identical to that of the original pretzel (a German word derived from the Latin *pretiola*, meaning a "small reward"), which dates back to at least the seventh century. Thus, the soft pretzel, or a common ancestor, is probably the forerunner of the bagel. Sephardim make a similar bread called *escaladadas*, a name derived from the Spanish *escalder* (to scald).

Eastern European Jewish immigrants brought their favorite weekday breads—including bagels, bialys (onion rolls), and *pletzels/zemels* (flat breads)—to America at the end of the nineteenth century. Although *pletzels* and *zemels* remained in relative obscurity, bagels eventually became one of the country's most popular breads. By 1915 New York City bagel bakers had formed Local #338 and boasted three hundred members. Bagel stores now exist in most towns, even those with no Jewish population, and bagels are found in most grocery stores. In America, Jews began serving sliced bagels with a *shmir* (smear) of cream cheese and lox (the fish probably served as a substitute for meat, which, according to the dietary laws, is inappropriate with cheese), toppings that were not paired with bagels in Europe. This combination is now common fare not only at Jewish life-cycle events but at breakfasts and lunches across the continent.

1 package (2½ teaspoons) active dry yeast or 1 (.6-ounce) cake fresh yeast

1⅓ cups warm water (105 to 110 degrees for dry yeast, 80 to 85 degrees for fresh yeast)

2 tablespoons sugar or barley malt syrup (see Note)

1½ teaspoons table salt or 1 tablespoon kosher salt

About 4 cups high-gluten or bread flour

3 quarts water

2 tablespoons sugar, barley malt syrup, or honey

1 egg white beaten with 2 teaspoons water (optional)

1. Dissolve the yeast in ¼ cup of the water. Stir in 1 teaspoon of the sugar or malt and let stand until foamy, 5 to 10 minutes.

2. Add the remaining warm water, the remaining 5 teaspoons sugar or malt, the salt, and 2 cups of the flour. Gradually add the remaining flour until the mixture holds together.

3. Place on a lightly floured surface and knead until smooth and elastic, about 10 minutes. Place in a greased bowl, turning to coat. Cover loosely with plastic wrap or a towel and let rise at room temperature until double in bulk, about 1½ hours, or in the refrigerator overnight.

4. Punch down the dough and knead until smooth. Divide into 12 equal pieces. Cover and let stand for 10 minutes.

5. Roll each piece into a ball and flatten slightly. Poke a finger through the center of each ball and work the dough to form a smooth ring. Or roll each piece into a ¾-inch-thick rope and pinch the ends together.

6. Place the dough rings on a lightly floured surface, cover with a towel, and let stand at room temperature until puffy, about 20 minutes.

7. Preheat the oven to 425 degrees. Lightly sprinkle 2 large baking sheets with cornmeal or grease the baking sheets. Bring the 3 quarts water and 2 tablespoons sugar, malt, or honey to a low boil.

8. Gently lower the bagels into the water, 2 to 3 at a time—the bagels should not touch. (The bagels should sink to the bottom, then almost immediately rise to the surface. If they have proofed too little, they will not rise for several minutes; if they have proofed too long, they will not sink. No matter,

your bagels will still be quite tasty.) Simmer for 3 minutes, then turn and simmer until puffed up, about 2 minutes. Turn again and simmer for 1 minute. Remove with a slotted spoon and drain.

9. Place the bagels on the prepared baking sheets. For a crisper crust, brush the tops with the egg wash. Bake until golden brown and crisp, about 25 minutes. Let cool on a wire rack.

Note: Barley malt syrup, which gives bagels a special sheen and subtle flavor, is available at most health food stores.

VARIATIONS

Seeded Bagels: After brushing the dough rings with the egg wash, sprinkle each bagel with about ½ teaspoon poppy, caraway, or sesame seeds.

Cinnamon-Raisin Bagels: Add 1½ teaspoons cinnamon and 1 cup raisins.

Egg Bagels: Add 2 large eggs and reduce the amount of water to 1 cup. (*Note:* Adding eggs to the dough, a luxury in eastern Europe, keeps the bagels softer for much longer than the standard lean dough.)

Maali

ROMANIAN CHEESE-CORN BREAD

8 TO 10 SERVINGS

There are many versions of this Romanian cornmeal bread: Some use yeast as the leavening or baking powder, some use feta cheese instead of cottage cheese, and others substitute schmaltz and chicken broth for the dairy ingredients. *Maali* tastes best warm from the oven, but it is also served cold for Sabbath brunch.

1 cup yellow cornmeal
6 tablespoons granulated sugar
* or brown sugar*

1. Preheat the oven to 350 degrees. Grease a 9-by-5-inch loaf pan.

2. Sift together the cornmeal, sugar, flour, baking powder,

1 tablespoon all-purpose flour

2¼ teaspoons double-acting
   baking powder

½ teaspoon salt

2 cups sour cream

2 cups small-curd cottage cheese

½ cup (1 stick) butter or
   margarine, softened, or
   ½ cup vegetable shortening

3 large eggs, lightly beaten

and salt. Beat together the sour cream, cottage cheese, butter, and eggs. Stir in the dry ingredients.

3. Pour into the prepared pan, tapping the pan to remove any air bubbles. Bake until the bread is golden brown and pulls away from the sides of the pan, about 1 hour.

———

Below: **Kosher bakery on Manhattan's Lower East Side, with huge loaves of rye and pumpernickel, circa 1900.** *Between 1881 and 1911, many Jews—1,372,189, to be exact—primarily from Eastern Europe, immigrated to the United States through the port of New York, the majority getting their start in the tenements of the Lower East Side. Area shops such as this bakery reflected the tastes of the Jewish residents.*

Kawrinbroyt

ASHKENAZIC RYE BREAD
2 MEDIUM OR 3 SMALL LOAVES

In the centuries following the Ashkenazim's arrival in Poland and the Baltic states, dark bread served as the staple of the Ashkenazic diet until the popularization of the potato in the mid-nineteenth century. For many eastern European Jews, most meals consisted of rye bread, also called *rozoverbrot,* spread with butter or *podsmeteneh* (a mixture of sour cream and sour milk) or accompanied with pickled cucumbers. Among the poor, white flour was generally reserved for the Sabbath or sometimes only for the festivals. Sour rye bread, because of its popularity among Ashkenazim, is commonly known as Jewish rye.

*2 packages (about 5 teaspoons)
    active dry yeast or
    1 (1-ounce) cake fresh yeast*
*2 cups warm water (105 to
    110 degrees for dry yeast,
    80 to 85 degrees for fresh
    yeast)*
*¼ to ⅓ cup granulated sugar or
    brown sugar*
*¼ to ⅓ cup unsulfured
    molasses or dark corn syrup*
*2 to 4 tablespoons vegetable
    shortening or margarine,
    melted*
*1 tablespoon table salt or
    1½ tablespoons kosher salt*
*1 to 2 tablespoons caraway
    seeds or fennel seeds
    (optional)*
2 cups rye flour
*About 4 cups unbleached
    all-purpose flour*

1. Dissolve the yeast in ½ cup of the warm water. Stir in 1 teaspoon of the sugar and let stand until foamy, about 5 minutes.
2. Blend in the remaining water, remaining sugar, molasses or corn syrup, shortening or margarine, salt, and, if desired, caraway or fennel seeds. Stir in the rye flour. Add the white flour, ½ cup at a time, until the mixture holds together.
3. On a lightly floured surface, knead the dough until smooth and elastic, about 10 minutes. (The dough will be slightly sticky—be careful not to add too much flour while kneading, or the loaf will be too heavy.) Place in a greased bowl, turning to coat. Cover loosely with a towel or plastic wrap and let rise at room temperature until double in bulk, about 1½ hours, or in the refrigerator overnight.
4. Sprinkle a large baking sheet with cornmeal or grease the baking sheet. Punch down the dough, knead briefly, and divide in half or into thirds. Shape into loaves or rounds and place on the prepared baking sheet. Cover loosely and let rise until double in bulk, about 1 hour.
5. Preheat the oven to 350 degrees.
6. For a crisper crust, dissolve the cornstarch in the water and brush over the loaves. Bake until browned and hollow-sounding when tapped on the bottom, about 40 minutes. Transfer to a wire rack to cool.

GLAZE:

2 tablespoons cornstarch
¼ cup water

VARIATIONS

Pumpernickel Bread: Reduce the amount of white flour to 3 cups, substitute 3 cups pumpernickel flour (or 2 cups dark rye flour and add 1 cup bran) for the light rye flour, and add ¼ to ⅓ cup molasses and 1 tablespoon unsweetened cocoa powder or carob powder.

Raisin Pumpernickel Bread: Prepare as for pumpernickel bread. Add 1½ cups raisins or add 1 cup raisins and ¾ cup coarsely chopped walnuts. (*Note:* The residents of seventeenth-century Westphalia, Germany, merged the two words *pumper* (lumbering) and *nickel* (dwarf) as a term of derision meaning a fool or bumpkin. Later the word was applied to a heavy, dark, slightly sour rye bread.)

RYE

Rye originated in central Europe and was already cultivated as far north as Great Britain during the Iron Age, but it was unknown to most of the rest of the ancient world. When it eventually moved south, it was not enthusiastically received by the people, who preferred wheat and barley. The Greeks and Romans basically ignored it and the Egyptians make no mention of it. There is no evidence that Jews came into contact with rye before their arrival in Germany.

Because of this rye's ability to grow in colder climates and under poor conditions, it became the primary grain throughout much of northern Europe. In addition, its tendency to spread often brought it into wheat fields in northern Europe. Despite the farmers' best efforts, they could not totally weed out the invading grain. As a result, the two grains were frequently harvested together and the seeds planted together or ground into flour together. Thus nature created a rye-wheat mixture called *maslin,* which remained the primary form of flour in northern Europe and Russia until about 1700. Later, when methods were devised to keep the grains separate, people had already developed a taste for rye bread and purposely combined the flours.

There are four basic grades of rye flour—light, medium, dark, and pumpernickel. Light rye contains no bran and is therefore very pale in color. Dark rye contains all of the bran and therefore its flavor and color are more intense. Medium rye is a mixture of light and dark ryes. Pumpernickel is a dark rye with added bran.

Biscochos de Levadura

SEPHARDIC BREAD RINGS
ABOUT 48 RINGS

Sephardic housewives are renowned for their baking skills. An ancient and distinctive feature of Sephardic cuisine is crisp ring-shaped baked goods called *biscochos* or *roskitas di gueve* ("little screws"; these are different from the large doughnut-shaped sweet yeast bread called *roscas*). Many Sephardim serve these refreshing rings, or a sweetened version, at the meal following Yom Kippur, for the Sabbath morning *desayuno* (breakfast; see page 29), and at other special occasions. They are generally prepared in a large batch so that plenty will be available for unexpected company.

1 package (2½ teaspoons)
   active dry yeast or
   1 (.6-ounce) cake fresh yeast
1¼ cups warm water
   (105 to 110 degrees for
   dry yeast, 80 to 85 degrees
   for fresh yeast)
1 teaspoon sugar or honey
¼ cup vegetable oil or melted
   vegetable shortening
1 tablespoon anise liqueur or
   1 to 2 teaspoons ground
   anise seeds
1 teaspoon table salt or
   2 teaspoons kosher salt
About 4 cups unbleached
   all-purpose flour
1 large egg, lightly beaten
About ½ cup sesame seeds

1. Dissolve the yeast in ¼ cup of the water. Stir in the sugar or honey and let stand until foamy, 5 to 10 minutes.
2. Add the remaining water, oil or shortening, anise, salt, and 2 cups of the flour. Gradually add the remaining flour until the mixture holds together.
3. Place on a lightly floured surface and knead until smooth and elastic, about 10 minutes. Place in a greased bowl, turning to coat. Cover loosely and let rise at room temperature until double in bulk, about 1½ hours.
4. Preheat the oven to 400 degrees. Lightly grease several large baking sheets.
5. Punch down the dough and divide into 1-inch balls. Roll the balls into 4-inch-long ropes about ½ inch thick. Bring the ends together to form a ring, pinching to seal. Dip the top of the rings into the egg, then into the sesame seeds.
6. Place, sesame side up, on the prepared baking sheets, leaving about 1 inch between the rings. Bake until lightly colored, about 10 minutes.
7. After all of the rings are lightly colored, reduce the heat to 250 degrees, return the rings to the oven, and bake until golden brown and crisp, about 20 minutes. Transfer to a wire rack and let cool completely. *Biscochos* keep in an airtight container at room temperature for several weeks.

VARIATIONS

Reshas (Sephardic Pretzels): Loop the ends of the dough ropes over the middle to produce a pretzel shape.

Sweet Biscochos/Kaak: Add about ½ cup sugar.

Kaak (Middle Eastern Bread Rings): Add ½ teaspoon ground coriander or cumin (or ¼ teaspoon each) and ½ teaspoon *mahlab* (ground cherry pits).

Yutangza

BUKHARAN STEAMED BUNS

 18 TO 24 BUNS

This is another example of the impact of Chinese cooking, where steaming bread is common, on central Asia. Bukharan Jews served these rolls on special occasions.

1 recipe lean yeast dough
 (see page 264)
Melted butter or margarine
 for brushing
Chopped fresh coriander
 for garnish

1. Divide the dough into 18 to 24 equal pieces. Form into balls, cover, and let stand for 10 minutes.

2. On a lightly floured surface, roll out the dough into thin rounds. Brush with melted butter or margarine and sprinkle with coriander. Bring the edges together to meet in the center, then reform into balls. Cover and let rise until double in bulk, about 30 minutes. (Raising the buns on 3-inch pieces of waxed paper makes for easy moving to the steamer.)

3. Place the buns about 1 inch apart in an oiled Chinese steamer or a flat-bottomed metal steamer over medium heat. Cover and steam until puffed and cooked through, about 15 minutes. Transfer to a wire rack to cool.

Khachapuri

GEORGIAN CHEESE BREAD
8 TO 10 SERVINGS

Georgians love breads and, over the course of history, adopted the doughs of many cultures into their culinary repertoire. For centuries, a favorite Georgian treat was to take plain flat bread hot from the oven and wrap it around a chunk of cheese. The combination of fresh bread and melting cheese proved irresistible. Then, at some point, an inspired baker took this union a step further, baking the cheese inside the bread, thereby producing the Georgian national dish, *khachapuri*. Originally, *khachapuri* were baked on the sides of a *tone* (a brick oven similar to the Indian tandoor) or over an open fire in a pottery dish called a *ketsi*. The first *khachapuri* were made from bread dough, but eventually other doughs such as phyllo, puff pastry, and flaky pastry were adapted to this dish. There is even a version that resembles a small pizza.

Georgian Jews, unable to eat cheese breads at meat meals, introduced bean and potato fillings. Subsequently, these innovations were adopted by their non-Jewish neighbors, although cheese maintained its position as the favorite *khachapuri* filling. Today, *khachapuri* are sold at special cafés throughout Georgia, and proficient home cooks prepare their own breads for special occasions.

1 recipe lean yeast dough or rich yeast dough (see page 264)

1 recipe khachapuri *filling (see opposite page)*

1 egg beaten with 1 tablespoon water

1. Preheat the oven to 375 degrees. Grease a 9- to 10-inch ovenproof heavy skillet, springform pan, or other round baking pan at least 1½ inches deep.

2. On a lightly floured surface, roll out the dough into a ¼-inch-thick round about 22 inches in diameter. Ease the dough into the prepared pan, letting the excess drape over the sides.

3. Spread the filling evenly over the dough. Gather the dough edges together to meet in the center, pleating as evenly as possible into folds. Twist the dough ends that meet in the center to form a knob. Cover with a towel and let rise for 30 minutes.

4. Brush the top of the dough with the egg wash. Bake until golden brown, about 1 hour. Transfer the *khachapuri* to a wire rack and let cool for at least 10 minutes. Cut into wedges and serve warm or at room temperature.

Khveli

KHACHAPURI CHEESE FILLING

ABOUT 5 CUPS

To make this filling, Georgians use a string cheese called *suluguny*. Since this type of cheese is unavailable in the West, the following combination of cheeses is used to replicate its texture and flavor.

2½ cups grated mozzarella
  cheese
1½ cups crumbled feta cheese
¾ cup farmer or small-curd
  cottage cheese
1 large egg, lightly beaten
2 tablespoons butter, softened
About ½ teaspoon salt

In a food processor or with an electric mixer, beat all of the ingredients until smooth.

Hint: To grate soft cheeses such as mozzarella more easily, place in the freezer for about 20 minutes.

VARIATION

Omit the mozzarella and increase the amount of feta cheese to 3 cups and the farmer cheese to 1 cup. Or omit the feta cheese and farmer cheese and add 2½ cups grated Muenster, white Cheddar, or Monterey Jack cheese.

Lobiani

KHACHAPURI BEAN FILLING

ABOUT 5 CUPS

1 pound (about 2½ cups)
  dried red beans
¼ cup olive or vegetable oil
3 medium yellow onions,
  chopped (about 1½ cups)
¾ cup chopped fresh coriander
  or ½ teaspoon hot red pepper
  flakes
About 1 teaspoon salt
Ground black pepper to taste

1. Cover the beans with water by several inches. Bring to a boil, reduce the heat to medium–low, and simmer until very tender, about 1½ hours. Drain. Mash or puree the beans.
2. Heat the oil in a large skillet over medium heat. Add the onions and sauté until golden, about 15 minutes.
3. Add the beans and cook, stirring frequently, until dry, 5 to 10 minutes. Remove from the heat and stir in the coriander or pepper flakes, salt, and pepper. Let cool.

Sweet Breads and Yeast Cakes

Pandericas/Feine Hefeteig

SWEET YEAST DOUGH

❧ ABOUT 2½ POUNDS DOUGH; 2 LARGE OR 3 MEDIUM LOAVES ☙

The Ladino term *pandericas* (literally "bread of the rich") refers to the large amount of eggs, fat, and sugar used to make this dough, once the province of the wealthy or reserved for special occasions. This rich yeast dough serves as the basis for a wide variety of *bolas* (Sephardic cakes, from the Spanish for "ball," referring to balls of yeast dough) and kuchen (Ashkenazic cakes). Hungarians use it to make such treats as *arany galuska* (Hungarian "dumpling" coffee cake) and *darazsfesek* ("wasps' nest" coffee cake). Czechs top it with fruit to make *kolacky*. Georgians form it into round loaves called *nazuki*. Moroccans add anise seeds to make small, flat breads called *fackasch*. Italians, influenced by the Sephardim, use olive oil for the fat and add anise seeds and lemon zest to make oval loaves called *il bollo,* which are customarily served on Sukkoth (the rich dough is apropos for the festival of the harvest; see page 146) and at the meal following Yom Kippur. In Turkey, they add a little pepper and shape the dough into triangles to make *boyicos.* Dough pieces of 2½ ounces or under refer to rolls and buns—called *panisico dulces* by Sephardim, *bobkes* or *pultabulkas* by Ashkenazim. Larger pieces refer to breads or coffee cakes—*pan dulce* in Ladino, *kuchen* in Yiddish.

Sweet doughs are prepared in the same manner as the lean doughs used for bread, but are softer and stickier. Eggs give a rich flavor, a golden color, a tender, fine crumb (the inner part of bread), and a soft crust. Fat produces a rich flavor, a soft texture, and a tender crumb and acts as a preservative to keep the bread soft. Sweeteners not only provide the yeast with food but also add flavor, produce a more tender crumb and deep brown crust, and keep the bread softer longer. Too much sweetener, however, creates a sticky dough, inhibits the yeast's ability to grow, and produces a crust that is too dark. This recipe may be doubled or tripled.

1 package (2½ teaspoons)
  active dry yeast or
  1 (.6-ounce) cake fresh yeast
1 cup warm water
  (105 to 110 degrees for
  dry yeast, 80 to 85 degrees
  for fresh yeast)
½ cup sugar
½ cup vegetable oil, melted
  margarine, or melted butter
2 large eggs
1 teaspoon table salt or
  2 teaspoons kosher salt
About 4 cups unbleached
  all-purpose flour

1. Dissolve the yeast in ¼ cup of the water. Stir in 1 teaspoon of the sugar and let stand until foamy, 5 to 10 minutes.

2. Add the remaining water, remaining sugar, oil, margarine, or butter, eggs, and salt. Blend in 1½ cups of the flour. Add the remaining flour, ½ cup at a time, until the mixture holds together.

3. On a lightly floured surface, knead the dough until smooth and elastic, about 10 minutes.

4. Place in a greased bowl, turning to coat. Cover with a towel or plastic wrap and let rise at room temperature until double in bulk, about 1½ hours, or in the refrigerator overnight. (The dough is easier to handle when chilled, which is beneficial for cakes that require rolling.)

5. Punch down the dough.

VARIATIONS

Anise Sweet Yeast Dough: Add 1 to 2 teaspoons anise liqueur or 2 to 3 teaspoons anise seeds. (*Note:* Anise is a popular flavoring in Sephardic breads such as *roscas*.)

Citrus Sweet Yeast Dough: Add 1 to 3 teaspoons grated lemon zest or 1 tablespoon grated orange zest.

Sour Cream Yeast Dough: Substitute ½ cup melted butter for the oil, reduce the amount of water to ¼ cup, and add ¾ cup sour cream. (*Note:* Sour cream produces a richer, moister, heavier cake, desired in some smaller pastries and coffee cakes.)

Extra-Rich Yeast Dough: Increase the number of eggs to 3 and the amount of fat to ¾ cup (1½ sticks), and reduce the amount of water to ¾ cup.

Puter Kuchen

ASHKENAZIC BUTTER COFFEE CAKE
10 TO 12 SERVINGS

Austrians and Hungarians are masters of baking rich and elaborate creations. Even the more simple fare from this area deserves praise. Kuchen, literally "baked good" in Yiddish, refers to an assortment of yeast and baking powder cakes, commonly called coffee cakes, that originated in the central European kitchen.

1 recipe sweet yeast dough
(see page 294) or extra-rich
yeast dough (see page 295)
¼ cup (½ stick) butter or
margarine, melted

CINNAMON TOPPING
½ cup brown sugar or
granulated sugar
1½ teaspoons ground cinnamon
½ cup chopped walnuts
(optional)

Opposite: Marriage ceremony of Baron Alphonse de Rothschild (1827–1905) and Leonora Rothschild (1837–1911): the groom is breaking the wineglass.
The custom of breaking glass at the conclusion of the wedding ceremony derives from Talmud Berakhot (31a), which relates how Rav Ashi broke a piece of glassware at his sons' weddings in order to warn against unseemly celebrating.

1. Press the dough into a greased 13-by-9-inch baking pan or divide between two 8-inch-square pans. Brush with the butter or margarine. Cover and let stand at room temperature until nearly double in bulk, about 45 minutes.
2. Preheat the oven to 350 degrees.
3. Press narrow indentations into the dough. Combine all of the topping ingredients and sprinkle over the dough.
4. Bake until golden brown, about 30 minutes. Let the cake cool in the pan for 10 minutes, then remove to a wire rack to cool completely.

VARIATIONS

Frucht Kuchen (Ashkenazic Fruit Coffee Cake): Omit the butter, and before letting the dough rise in the pan, arrange 5 to 6 peeled, cored, and thinly sliced medium apples, 12 to 14 peeled, pitted, and quartered medium peaches, or 18 to 22 halved and pitted Italian or golden plums on the top.

Kirshen Kuchen (Ashkenazic Cherry Yeast Cake): Omit the butter. Combine ½ cup sugar, 3 tablespoons cornstarch, and a pinch of salt in a medium saucepan. Stir in 1 cup cherry juice or water. Cook, stirring, over medium heat until bubbly and thickened. Stir in 16 ounces drained tart cherries. Let cool. Spread on top of the dough and bake as for *puter kuchen*.

Streusel Topping

½ cup all-purpose flour
½ cup granulated sugar or
   brown sugar
1½ teaspoons ground cinnamon
¼ cup (½ stick) butter or
   margarine
½ cup chopped walnuts
   (optional)

Combine the flour, sugar, and cinnamon. For coarser crumbs, use less flour or more butter. Cut in the butter or margarine to resemble coarse crumbs. If desired, stir in the nuts. Or process all of the ingredients about 6 times in a food processor fitted with the steel blade. Substitute for the cinnamon topping.

Babka

EASTERN EUROPEAN YEAST CAKE

❧ 2 LARGE LOAVES ❧

Babka (literally "grandmother's loaf") is a rich egg-and-butter yeast bread from eastern Europe. There are actually two styles of *babka:* The Polish style is made from a soft yeast dough with a texture and shape that is similar to a *kugelhopf;* the Jewish style is a kuchen (coffee cake) dough that is rolled out, spread with a filling, rolled up jelly roll style, and baked in a loaf form. Chocolate and cinnamon are the most common fillings, but cheese, poppy seed, almond paste, raspberry, and apricot are also popular.

1 recipe sweet yeast dough (see page 294)

1 recipe babka filling (see pages 299–300)

1 egg yolk beaten with 1 tablespoon water or 3 tablespoons melted butter or margarine

1. Divide the dough in half and roll out each half into a ¼-inch-thick rectangle about 10 by 8 inches. Spread half of the filling over each rectangle, leaving a ½-inch border on all sides.

2. Starting from a narrow end, roll up jelly roll style, pinching the seams to seal. Place the rolls, seam side down, in 2 large loaf pans or large tube pans. (The *babka* can be prepared ahead to this point, sealed in a plastic bag, and left to rise in the refrigerator for up to 2 days, then placed directly into a preheated oven.) Cover loosely with a towel or plastic wrap and let rise at room temperature until double in bulk, about 1½ hours.

3. Position a rack in the lower third of the oven. Preheat the oven to 350 degrees.

4. Brush the loaves with the egg wash or, for a softer crust, brush with the butter or margarine. Bake until golden brown and hollow-sounding when tapped, 30 to 40 minutes. Remove from the pans and let cool on a wire rack.

Zimtfullung

CINNAMON BABKA FILLING

ABOUT ¾ CUP TO 1¾ CUPS

¾ cup brown sugar or
   granulated sugar
1 tablespoon ground cinnamon
½ cup raisins (optional)
½ cup finely chopped walnuts
   or pecans (optional)
¼ cup (½ stick) butter or
   margarine, melted

Combine the sugar and cinnamon. If desired, add the raisins and/or nuts. Brush the dough with the butter or margarine before sprinkling with the cinnamon-sugar.

Almond Paste Babka Filling

ABOUT 2 CUPS

½ cup (1 stick) butter or
   margarine, softened
1¼ cups almond paste
   (see page 362)
¼ to ½ cup granulated sugar,
   brown sugar, or confectioners'
   sugar
1 teaspoon almond extract or
   grated lemon zest

Beat the butter or margarine until smooth. Gradually beat in the almond paste. Add the remaining ingredients and beat until smooth.

VARIATION

Omit the butter and add 2 large egg whites. Or reduce the amount of butter to ¼ cup (½ stick) and add 1 to 2 large eggs.

Cheese Babka Filling

❧ ABOUT 1¾ CUPS ☙

12 ounces cream cheese or
   small-curd cottage cheese
   (or 8 ounces cream cheese
   and 4 ounces small-curd
   cottage cheese)
1 cup confectioners' sugar or
   ½ cup granulated sugar
¾ cup all-purpose flour
1 large egg
1 teaspoon vanilla extract or
   finely grated lemon zest

Beat together all of the ingredients until smooth.

Kahkahawfullung

CHOCOLATE BABKA FILLING

❧ ABOUT 1 CUP ☙

½ cup sugar
⅓ cup bread crumbs or ground
   walnuts
¼ cup unsweetened cocoa
   powder
2 tablespoons butter or
   margarine, melted
2 tablespoons water or milk
1 teaspoon vanilla extract

Combine all of the ingredients. If the mixture is too thin, stir in a little more bread crumbs or walnuts. If too thick stir in a little more water.

Schnecken

ASHKENAZIC NUT SPIRALS
ABOUT 5 DOZEN SMALL ROLLS

Schnecken, German for "snails," is a rich yeast dough spread with a cinnamon filling, rolled up, and cut into slices that resemble snails. They are a popular Shavuot (see page 315) treat.

1 recipe extra-rich yeast dough or sour cream yeast dough (see page 295)

GLAZE
1 cup brown sugar
½ cup (1 stick) butter or margarine, melted
2 tablespoons light corn syrup
About 5 dozen pecan halves (optional)

FILLING
2 cups chopped walnuts or pecans
1 cup dried currants or chopped raisins
1 cup granulated sugar or brown sugar
2½ teaspoons ground cinnamon
½ cup (1 stick) butter or margarine, melted

1. Grease 5 (12 cup) muffin tins or 2 large baking pans.

2. To make the glaze: Combine the sugar, butter or margarine, and corn syrup. Spoon a teaspoon of the glaze into each muffin tin or divide the glaze between the baking pans. If desired, place a pecan half in each muffin tin or scatter the pecans in the baking pans.

3. Divide the dough into 6 equal pieces. On a lightly floured surface, roll out each piece of dough into a ¼-inch-thick rectangle.

4. To make the filling: Combine the nuts, currants or raisins, sugar, and cinnamon. Brush the dough rectangles with the melted butter and sprinkle with the nut mixture. Starting from a long side, roll up jelly roll style. Place seam side down on a flat surface and cut into ¾- to 1-inch-thick slices.

5. Place the slices, cut side down, in the prepared muffin tins or baking pans. Cover and let rise at room temperature until nearly double in bulk, about 1 hour, or in the refrigerator for 12 hours.

6. Position a rack in the lower third of the oven. Preheat the oven to 350 degrees.

7. Bake the rolls until golden brown, about 20 minutes. Immediately invert the pans onto sheets of aluminum foil, a large baking sheet, or a heatproof platter. Let stand for 10 seconds, then slowly lift the pans to allow the *schnecken* to fall out and the glaze to drip over them. Serve warm or cooled. (After cooling, the *schnecken* may be placed in plastic bags and frozen for up to 4 months. Thaw at room temperature before serving.)

Kakosh

HUNGARIAN CHOCOLATE ROLL
2 LARGE OR 3 MEDIUM CAKES

Kakosh, one of the favorite desserts of Hungarian Jews, is made by spreading yeast dough with a chocolate filling and rolling up jelly roll style. The cake is then usually rushed straight into the oven without being allowed to rise, resulting in thin alternating layers of pastry and filling. The original cake rolls were filled with *mohn* (poppy seed filling; see page 320), which gave rise to the name *makosh*. Later, enterprising cooks experimented with a variety of flavors to produce new varieties, including walnut (called *dios*), cinnamon (use *babka* filling; see pages 299–300), almond paste (use *babka* filling), apricot preserves, raspberry jam, and, the most popular of all the fillings, chocolate. The combination of the words *makosh* and *kahkahaw* (Yiddish for "cocoa") produced the name *kakosh*. The recipe can be doubled.

*2 packages (about 5 teaspoons)
   active dry yeast or
   1 (1-ounce) cake fresh yeast*
*1 cup warm water (105 to 110
   degrees for dry yeast, 80 to
   85 degrees for fresh yeast)*
½ cup sugar
2 large eggs
*1 cup (2 sticks) butter or
   margarine, melted*
1 teaspoon vanilla extract
*½ teaspoon table salt or
   1 teaspoon kosher salt*
*About 4 cups unbleached
   all-purpose flour*

*1 recipe babka chocolate filling
   (see page 300)*

*1 egg yolk beaten with 1 tea-
   spoon water or ¼ teaspoon
   instant coffee powder*

1. Dissolve the yeast in ½ cup of the water. Stir in 1 teaspoon of the sugar and let stand until foamy, 5 to 10 minutes.

2. Stir in the remaining water, remaining sugar, eggs, butter or margarine, vanilla, salt, and enough flour to make a soft dough. Cover and refrigerate for at least 1 hour and up to 2 days.

3. Preheat the oven to 350 degrees. Grease a large baking sheet.

4. Divide the dough in half or thirds. Lightly flour a piece of waxed paper or a flat surface and roll out each piece into a rectangle about ⅛ inch thick. Halves will be about 15 by 8 inches.

5. Spread the filling over the dough, leaving a ½-inch border. Starting from a long end, roll up jelly roll style. Place seam side down on the prepared baking sheet.

6. Brush with the egg wash. Bake until lightly browned, about 35 minutes. Place the baking sheet on a wire rack to cool.

Roscas

SEPHARDIC SWEET YEAST BREAD

❧ 3 MEDIUM LOAVES ❧

Sephardim customarily shape this dough into 2 or 3 large doughnut-shaped breads or twisted rounds or 12 to 15 smaller doughnut-shaped rolls. In many Sephardic homes, *roscas* (Ladino for "screws") are served for *desayuno* (breakfast after synagogue; see page 29) on the Sabbath and festivals and *noche de Alhad* (after the Sabbath).

*1 recipe sweet yeast dough
(see page 294) or anise sweet
yeast dough (see page 295)
1 egg beaten with 1 tablespoon
water
About ¼ cup sesame seeds*

1. Divide the dough into 3 equal pieces and form each third into a ball. Poke a hole in the center of each ball and form into a doughnut shape about 6 inches in diameter and 2 inches thick.
2. Place the loaves on lightly greased baking sheets, cover with a towel or plastic wrap, and let rise at room temperature until double in bulk, about 1¼ hours.
3. Meanwhile, position a rack in the center of the oven. Preheat the oven to 350 degrees.
4. Brush the loaves with the egg wash, then sprinkle with the sesame seeds. Bake until golden brown and hollow-sounding when tapped, about 30 minutes. Transfer to a wire rack and let cool.

VARIATION

Panisicos Dulces/Pultabulkas (Sweet Yeast Buns): Panisicos are a traditional part of the meal to break the fast of Yom Kippur in many Sephardic homes. Divide the dough into 8 to 12 equal pieces. Shape into balls. Place on greased baking sheets, leaving 2 inches between. Cover and let rise until double in bulk, about 45 minutes. Brush the buns with the egg wash and sprinkle lightly with sugar or sesame seeds. Bake until golden brown, about 20 minutes. Makes 8 to 12 buns.

CAKES,
COOKIES, AND PASTRIES

Cakes

And he [David] gave to every one of Israel, both man and woman, to every one a loaf of bread, and a cake made in a pan, and a sweet cake.

—2 SAMUEL 6:19

In its simplest meaning a cake is a sweetened baked good. However, this food, laden with social significance and nostalgic connotations, possesses a much more exalted position in our lives and memories. Cakes are used to mark holidays, weddings, birthdays, and other important occasions.

It should be no surprise that the first wheat cakes, leavened by yeast, were sweetened with the world's first sweetener, honey. In the parts of Europe where wheat flour was scarce and expensive, however, bakers were forced to use rye or rye-wheat flour. Since yeast could not sufficiently raise these low-gluten batters, beaten eggs and chemical leavenings such as wood ash were used to lighten the cakes. Because of the disagreeable flavor of the primitive leavenings, larger amounts of honey and spices were added, resulting in heavy, strongly flavored cakes. Two of these early treats, *lebkuchen* (gingerbread) and

Opposite: **Moroccan Jewish woman preparing tea.** *Tea, the dried leaves of an evergreen shrub native to China, was introduced to the West at the beginning of the seventeenth century by Portuguese traders. It became particularly popular in England. Moroccans learned of tea from the British and embraced it to such an extent that mint-flavored tea (naa–naa) became the national drink.*

lekach (honey cake), were ubiquitous sights at medieval Franco-German celebrations. The rabbinic literature of Franco-Germany mentions a number of other cakes, including a spiced almond cake, a sponge cake fried in oil, a cake made from the skins of fermented grapes, *obleit* (a kind of waffle cookie), and various *gateaus* (a French word for cakes). Throughout the medieval period, European cakes remained crude and heavy.

The situation in the Arab world, where sugar had generally replaced honey by the tenth century, was very different. Innovative bakers, probably in Spain, discovered that beating sugar with eggs trapped air in the protein, resulting in one of the world's most enduring cakes, *pan esponjado* (sponge cake), also called *pan d'Espagna* (literally "bread of Spain"). The Italians adapted these new baking techniques to create light, airy cakes called tortes (from the Latin for "a round cake of bread"). Today, the term *torte* is used for rich cakes, generally containing little or no flour.

The evolution of French, German, and Austrian baking began with the arrival from Italy of *torten,* which first appeared in Franco-German rabbinic sources in the fourteenth century. In the seventeenth century, the popularization of sugar in Europe—with cheap supplies coming from new colonies in the Caribbean and the development of the sugar beet—resulted in a marked decline in the use of honey in European baking and a new era of cake making. Flavors became more refined and baking techniques more sophisticated. The English invented a cake lightened by beating butter with sugar, which evolved into the still popular pound cake, the forerunner of the vast array of butter cakes. The discovery of baking soda and later baking powder led to lighter, milder-flavored cakes.

Tishpishti

SEPHARDIC SYRUP-SOAKED SEMOLINA CAKE
ABOUT 24 (2-INCH) PIECES

*T*ishpishti*, also called *revani* (after a sixteenth-century Turkish poet), refers to syrup-soaked cakes and pastries common to the domain of the former Ottoman Empire. Sephardim adapted this sweet, heavy cake by using oil instead of butter and adding a touch of orange. An all-nut version (see Variation) is popular on Passover. *Tishpishti* is a traditional Rosh Hashanah (see page 126) dessert as well as a frequent sight at most special occasions. Although any kind of nut may be used, blanched almonds are traditional on Rosh Hashanah to produce a light color so that the year should be *dulce y aclarada* (sweet and bright). *Tishpishti* is served on Shavuot (see page 315) topped with dollops of whipped cream or yogurt. It is commonly accompanied by, as are most Middle Eastern sweets, Turkish coffee.

2 cups fine semolina meal or
  farina (or 1 cup semolina
  meal and 2 cups all-purpose
  flour)
½ cup ground almonds,
  walnuts, or hazelnuts
1 tablespoon baking powder
½ to 1 teaspoon ground
  cinnamon
6 large eggs, whites and yolks
  separated
1 cup sugar
½ cup vegetable oil
2 tablespoons orange juice or
  orange blossom water
2 teaspoons grated orange zest
  (or 1 teaspoon orange zest
  and 1 teaspoon lemon zest)
Pinch of salt
2 cups sugar syrup (see page
  372), cooled

1. Preheat the oven to 350 degrees. Grease a 13-by-9-inch baking pan or 9-inch springform pan.

2. Combine the semolina or farina, nuts, baking powder, and cinnamon. Beat the egg yolks and sugar until thick and creamy, 5 to 10 minutes. Add the oil, juice or orange blossom water, and zest. Stir in the semolina mixture.

3. Beat the egg whites on low speed until foamy, about 30 seconds. Add the salt, increase the speed to medium-high, and beat until stiff but not dry. Fold one-quarter of the egg whites into the batter to lighten, then gently fold in the remaining whites.

4. Pour into the prepared pan. Bake until a tester inserted in the center comes out clean, about 45 minutes.

5. Remove from the oven and immediately pour the cooled syrup evenly over the warm cake. Let the cake cool and absorb the syrup. Cut into diamond shapes or squares.

VARIATION

Tishpishti de Muez (Middle Eastern Nut Cake): Omit the baking powder. Substitute 1 cup matza cake meal for the semolina and increase the amount of nuts to 2 cups. Or omit the semolina and oil, substitute 1½ teaspoons baking soda for the baking powder, reduce the amount of sugar to ¾ cup, and increase the amount of nuts to 2 cups.

BUNDT CAKES

For generations, central Europeans baked butter cakes in fluted cast-iron tube pans called *bunds*. Since nothing similar was available in the United States, in the early 1950s a Hadassah chapter in Minneapolis, Minnesota, forwarded a request to Northland Aluminum Products asking if they could create a similar pan made from lighter-weight aluminum. Thus was born the Bundt pan.

Lekach

ASHKENAZIC HONEY CAKE

≈ 16 TO 20 SERVINGS ≈

*Thy lips, O my bride, drip honey. Honey and milk
are under your tongue.*

—SONG OF SONGS 4:11

Honey serves as the basis for one of the most enduring Ashkenazic baked goods, *lekach*
("honey cake," from the German word *lecke,* "lick"). By medieval times, honey cakes shaped
like ladders were prepared for Shavuot (honey being compared to Torah), loaves for Purim
and Hanukkah, and versions using matza meal for Passover. The works of Franco-German
rabbis such as Simcha ben Shmuel (died ca. 1105) of Vitry-en-Perthois in northern France, a
student of Rashi, and Eleazar ben Yehudah (ca. 1165–1230), born in Mainz, Germany, refer
to *lekach* in conjunction with a popular medieval Ashkenazic ceremony, later called *Aleph-
Bazyn* (from the first two letters of the Hebrew alphabet). At the initiatory appearance of a
child at *cheder* (elementary school), usually on Shavuot (the day on which the Torah was
given) or the first day of the month of Nisan (the first day of the Jewish calender), he was
escorted to the schoolhouse covered by a *tallit* (prayer shawl). Honey was smeared on a slate
containing the letters of the alphabet and the child licked them off so that the "words of the
Torah may be sweet as honey." Afterward, the aspiring scholar was presented with honey
cakes, apples, and hard-boiled eggs. Ashkenazim found special significance in the Yiddish
name for honey cake from the verse, "For I give you good instruction [*lekach*], do not
forsake my teaching" (Proverbs 4:2). Although the practice of giving the new student *lekach*
mostly disappeared by the eighteenth century, the custom of smearing honey on the letters of
the alphabet endures among some groups to this day.

The use of honey in Europe markedly declined beginning in the seventeenth century,
but it maintained a prominent place in traditional Ashkenazic cooking, adding a touch of
sweetness to everything from stews to desserts. *Lekach,* called *medianyk* in the Ukraine,
remains a common sight at an Ashkenazic kiddush, a Brit Milah, a wedding, and the meal
following Yom Kippur, and most notably as a traditional Ashkenazic Rosh Hashanah dessert,
starting the New Year off on a sweet note.

3½ cups all-purpose flour
   (or 2½ cups all-purpose flour
   and 1 cup whole-wheat flour)
2 teaspoons double-acting
   baking powder
1 teaspoon baking soda
1 teaspoon ground cinnamon
½ teaspoon ground allspice,
   cardamom, or ginger
¼ teaspoon ground cloves
½ teaspoon salt
4 large eggs, lightly beaten
1¼ cups granulated sugar or
   brown sugar
1⅓ cups honey
1 cup strong hot brewed coffee
   or tea
¼ cup vegetable oil
2 tablespoons whiskey, brandy,
   or thawed orange juice
   concentrate or apple juice
   concentrate
1 tablespoon grated orange zest
   (optional)
1 to 1½ cups raisins or chopped
   pitted dates, or ¾ cup each
   (optional)
Blanched whole almonds for
   garnish (optional)

1. Preheat the oven to 325 degrees. Line two 9-by-5-inch loaf pans, two 9-inch-square baking pans, or one 16-by-11-inch baking pan with waxed paper or aluminum foil, grease, and dust with flour.

2. Sift together the flour, baking powder, baking soda, spices, and salt. Stir the honey into the coffee or tea (the honey incorporates into the batter more easily when it is dissolved in a warm liquid). Add the oil, whiskey, brandy, or juice concentrate, and, if desired, zest.

3. Beat the eggs and sugar until light and fluffy. Add the honey mixture alternately in 3 parts with the flour mixture, starting and ending with the flour mixture. If desired, stir in the raisins or dates.

4. Pour into the prepared pans. If desired, arrange the almonds in a pattern over the surface.

5. Bake until a tester inserted in the center comes out clean, about 1 hour for the loaf pans, 35 minutes for the 9-inch-square pans, or 1¼ hours for the large pan. (If the cake looks like it is starting to burn before it is done, cover loosely with foil.) Let cool in the pans on a wire rack. Invert and remove the paper or foil. Wrap and store at room temperature or in the freezer. (*Lekach* keeps well and is even better after standing for a day.)

VARIATIONS

For a more intense honey flavor, increase the amount of honey to 2 cups. Reduce the amount of brown sugar to 1 cup and the coffee to ½ cup.

Apfel Lekach (Apple-Honey Cake): Add 3 cups (about 1 pound) peeled, cored, and grated apples.

Mehren Lekach (Carrot-Honey Cake): Add 4 cups (about 1⅓ pounds) finely grated carrots.

HONEY

Honey, the world's first sweetener, has long been valued for its purported therapeutic attributes, as well as for its flavor. Ancient Israelites viewed honey with high regard. Indeed, the Hebrew word for bee, *devorah,* is derived from the root *dvr* (word), alluding to the bee's creating honey, which, like the Divine Word, is unique and eternal. However, most of the "honey" consumed in ancient Israel was fruit honey extracted from dates and grapes. Indeed, most biblical references to honey refer to fruit honey.

"Honey out of the rock" (Psalms 82:17), the honey made by the region's fierce Syrian bees, was rather difficult to obtain. Only with the introduction of the European species by the Greeks did bees' honey become common in the Near East. And by Talmudic times, the word *devash* (honey) had taken on the specific connotation of bees' honey (e.g., "He who takes a vow of abstinence from honey is permitted to eat date honey" [Nedarim 6:9]). Ever since, bees' honey has been an integral part of most forms of Jewish cooking.

Nusstorte

ASHKENAZIC FLOURLESS NUT CAKE

❧ 8 TO 10 SERVINGS ❧

Since tortes rely on beaten eggs for leavening and contain little or no flour, they are perfect for Passover as well as any time during the year. This nut sponge cake is a typical Ashkenazic Passover dessert, customarily served plain or with *weinschaum,* a wine sauce similar to the Italian zabaglione. Modern cooks find it very versatile, adding chopped dates or candied citron; substituting 1 cup of mashed bananas or applesauce or 1½ cups of grated apples or carrots for the wine; or adding 3 tablespoons of cocoa powder.

1 cup finely chopped walnuts,
pecans, or hazelnuts
½ cup sweet red wine or orange
juice
1 cup matza cake meal
(or ½ cup matza cake meal
and ½ cup potato starch)
1 teaspoon ground cinnamon
½ teaspoon ground ginger or
cloves
¼ teaspoon salt
8 large eggs, whites and yolks
separated
2 cups sugar
¼ cup warm water
2 tablespoons lemon juice

1. Preheat the oven to 350 degrees. Grease and line with waxed paper two 8-inch-square baking pans, one 10-inch springform pan, or one 10-inch tube pan.
2. Soak the nuts in the wine or orange juice while you prepare the batter. Sift together the cake meal, cinnamon, ginger or cloves, and salt.
3. Beat the egg yolks, sugar, and warm water until pale and creamy, 10 to 15 minutes. Stir in the nut mixture and lemon juice. Fold in the cake meal mixture.
4. Using clean beaters, beat the egg whites until stiff but not dry. Fold one-quarter of the egg whites into the yolk mixture to lighten, then gently fold in the remaining whites.
5. Pour into the prepared pans. Bake until a toothpick inserted in the center comes out clean, about 35 minutes for single layers, 45 minutes for the springform pan, and 50 minutes for the tube pan. Let cool completely. Wrap the cake and store at room temperature or in the freezer.

VARIATION
Increase the amount of nuts to 2 cups and omit the matza cake meal.

———

Opposite: **Seder.** *Offenbach Hagaddah. Germany, circa 1800. A ceremonial dinner called the Seder ("order" in Hebrew) is held on the first two nights (one in Israel) of the Passover festival.*

Pan Esponjado/Tawrt

SPONGE CAKE

〰 8 TO 10 SERVINGS 〰

The Sephardic sponge cake, also called *pan d'Espagna* (literally "bread of Spain"), predates the expulsion from Spain. The cake eventually made its way to Ashkenazic tables. A version with flour is popular during the year; a matza meal version is a standard Passover dessert. Classic sponge cake contains neither chemical leavening nor fat (except that in the eggs). The high amount of sugar and relatively small amount of flour keep this cake moist. The citrus juice prevents it from being cloying.

8 large eggs, whites and yolks
   separated
1¼ cups sugar
¼ cup orange or lemon juice
   (or 2 tablespoons each)
2 teaspoons grated orange or
   lemon zest
1½ cups all-purpose flour
   (or ¾ cup matza cake meal
   and 1 tablespoon potato
   starch, or 1 cup potato starch)

Opposite: **Preparation for Passover.** Engraving, circa eighteenth century. *The Bible not only commands the consumption of matza on the first night of Passover but strictly forbids eating or even possessing any type of* chametz *(leavened/fermented flour) through-out the holiday. Therefore, all* chametz *must be removed from one's possession.*

1. Position a rack in the lower third of the oven. Preheat the oven to 350 degrees.

2. Beat the egg whites on low speed until foamy, about 30 seconds. Increase the speed to medium-high and beat until soft peaks form that curl over when the beaters are lifted. Gradually add ¼ cup of the sugar, 1 tablespoon at a time, and beat until stiff and glossy.

3. Using the same beaters, beat the egg yolks slightly. Gradually add the remaining 1 cup sugar and continue beating until thick and creamy, 5 to 10 minutes. (The entire beating process will take 15 to 20 minutes, but it completely dissolves the sugar, ensuring a tender cake.)

4. Stir in the juice and zest, then the flour. Fold one-quarter of the egg whites into the yolk mixture to lighten, then fold in the remaining whites.

5. Pour into an ungreased 10-inch tube pan, leveling the surface. Tap the pan to release any air bubbles. Bake until the cake springs back when lightly touched and a tester inserted in the center comes out clean, about 1 hour.

6. Invert the pan over the neck of a bottle (this ensures the cake will remain stretched out until set) and cool completely before removing the pan. Store the sponge cake wrapped at room temperature.

VARIATION

Torta de Almendras o Muez (Sephardic Nut Cake): Substitute 1½ cups ground almonds or walnuts for the flour. (*Note:* This is also baked in a 13-by-9-inch baking pan for about 45 minutes. For a Middle Eastern touch, pour 1½ cups cooled sugar syrup (see page 372) over the hot cake.

Kaesekuchen

ASHKENAZIC CREAMY CHEESECAKE
10 TO 12 SERVINGS

Milk and honey are the preeminent food themes of Shavuot, since the Torah is compared to milk and honey (Song of Songs 4:11) and the Bible refers to Israel as a "land flowing with milk and honey" (Exodus 3:8). In addition to the biblical references, tradition recounts that after receiving the Torah and the laws of kashruth, the Jews could no longer eat the meat foods they had prepared beforehand or use any of the cooking utensils that were now unkosher. Therefore, it was necessary to eat dairy products on the first Shavuot. Another legend adds that when the Jews returned to camp after receiving the Torah, they found that their milk had soured and begun turning into cheese. Because of their white color, dairy foods, as well as rice, are symbols of purity.

The predominant Shavuot dessert of France and Germany was *lekach* (honey cake). However, as the Ashkenazim moved eastward, they found honey less available. Central and eastern Europe were, however, lands where milk was very plentiful at this time of the year, much of it used to make soft cheeses and sour cream. Among Germans living in the East, dairy dishes were traditional fare on the holiday of Whitsunday (the seventh Sunday after Easter corresponding to Pentecost), and Ashkenazim adopted this practice for Shavuot. Eventually cheesecake, combining soft cheese and sour cream, supplanted honey cake. This creamy cake is a delicious treat any time. Since classic cheesecake freezes well, it can be prepared well in advance. To thaw cheesecakes, place in the refrigerator overnight.

CRUST

1½ cups graham cracker or
   zwieback crumbs
2 to 3 tablespoons granulated
   sugar or brown sugar
½ teaspoon ground cinnamon
6 tablespoons (¾ stick) butter or
   margarine, melted

BATTER

1½ pounds cream cheese,
   softened
1½ cups sugar

1. Position a rack in the center of the oven. Preheat the oven to 350 degrees. Grease a 9-inch springform pan.

2. To make the crust: Combine the crumbs, sugar, and cinnamon, then stir in the melted butter or margarine. Press into the prepared pan and chill.

3. To make the batter: Beat the cream cheese until smooth, scraping down the sides frequently. Add the sugar and beat until light. Blend in the sour cream, lemon juice, vanilla, and salt. Beat in the eggs, one at a time (do not overbeat, or the air will cause cracks).

4. Pour into the prepared pan. Bake until the cake is firm around the edges and lightly browned, about 1¼ hours. Turn off the oven and let the cake cool in the oven for 30

2 cups sour cream

1 to 3 tablespoons lemon juice

2 teaspoons vanilla extract

¼ teaspoon salt

4 large eggs

Sour cream topping (see below)

SOUR CREAM TOPPING

1½ cups sour cream

¼ cup confectioners' sugar or
   3 tablespoons granulated
   sugar

¾ teaspoon vanilla extract

minutes. Remove and let cool completely before garnishing with the sour cream topping. Cover and refrigerate overnight or up to 1 week.

5. Combine the sour cream, sugar, and vanilla and spread over the cooled cheesecake.

Hint: Dental floss held taut cuts cheesecake more smoothly than a knife. If using a knife, dip it into hot water.

VARIATION

To more than halve the calorie count of cheesecake, substitute 1½ pounds of part-skim ricotta cheese for the cream cheese and 1 to 2 cups of low-fat yogurt for the sour cream. This cake will be firmer and drier than cream cheese cakes but still quite tasty.

SHAVUOT

The festival of Shavuot (Hebrew for "weeks") is a two-day pilgrim festival (one-day in Israel) commemorating the giving of the Torah at Mount Sinai seven weeks after the Israelites departed Egypt. Also known as Chag ha'Katzir (Festival of the Harvest), Shavuot marks the end of the barley harvest and the beginning of the spring wheat harvest. In the synagogue, the Book of Ruth, which describes events occurring at this time of year, is read.

During the time when the Temple stood, two loaves of wheat bread—symbolizing the bounty of the season—were "waved before the Lord" (Leviticus 23:17–20) on Shavuot, this being the only occasion during the year when leavened bread was used in the Temple. Since the bread offering is one of the few biblical rituals for this holiday, a special emphasis is placed on the holiday challah. Saffron, the most expensive of spices, is sometimes added to the dough for this occasion.

PURIM

In response to a plot by the Persian prime minister Haman to physically annihilate their ancestors, Jews commemorate the events through physical enjoyment and riotous celebration. There are four central Purim rituals: reading the Megillah (Scroll of Esther), sending *mishloach manot* ("gifts of food," more commonly called *shalachmanot*) to friends, giving gifts to the poor, and eating a Purim *seudah* (feast).

Many Purim dishes involve a filling, alluding to the many intrigues, secrets, and surprises unfolding in the Purim story. The most common Purim foods are sweets, a symbolic way of wishing for a "good lot" or, in other words, a sweet future. For good reason Muslims have long referred to Purim as Id-al-Sukkar (The Sugar Holiday). Alcohol is liberally enjoyed, a practice that is most strongly disapproved of during the rest of the year.

Cookies

Hamantaschen

ASHKENAZIC FILLED TRIANGULAR COOKIES

The first mention of hamantaschen appears in *Machzor Vitry,* an eleventh-century prayer book compiled by Simcha ben Samuel of Vitry, a small town in Marne, France. (*Machzor Vitry* is based upon the rulings and practices of Simcha's teacher, the great commentator Rashi.) This ancient quintessential Ashkenazic Purim food can now be found on the shelves of many twentieth-century American bakeries, filled with fruits, nuts (nut-filled triangular pastries are sometimes called *pireshkes*), and even chocolate. However, poppy seed, the original filling, remains the most popular.

In no other area are poppy seeds so beloved and used in such diversity as in central Europe, where they flavor a large variety of vegetables, stews, confections, pastries, and cakes as well as serve in their most conspicuous role, as a topping for breads and rolls. Among the many medieval Teutonic pastries was a triangular-shaped treat called *mohntasch* (poppy seed pocket). The similarity of the German word for poppy seed, *mohn,* to the name of the villain of the Purim story, Haman (pronounced *Hamohn* in Hebrew), led to the renaming of this cookie to *hamantasch* (Haman's pocket). Subsequently, various symbolic meanings were ascribed to the hamantaschen. The triangular shape came to represent either Haman's pockets, alluding to the bribes the prime minister took, or his tricornered hat or ears, connoting his execution. This is in line with the widespread custom of symbolically eating some part of Haman and thereby erasing his name. According to the mystics, the three corners symbolize the three patriarchs—Abraham, Isaac, and Jacob—whose merit saved their descendants from Haman's plot.

Plums and prunes, long popular in central Europe, are used in many dishes, including preserves. Their role as a traditional hamantaschen filling started in 1731, when a Bohemian merchant named David Brandeis was accused of selling poisoned *povidl.* After the charge was proven false, he was freed from prison four days before the holiday of Purim. The entire

---

Opposite: **Purim games, 1726.** *Games reflect the nature of Purim, the most expressly joyous day on the Jewish calendar. During the Megillah reading, listeners make noise—Ashkenazim use traditional noisemakers called* groggers—*at every mention of Haman, literally blotting out the villain's name.*

city of Jungbunzlau, Bohemia, celebrated his release and, from that day forward, his family celebrated that day as a special holiday, the Povidl Purim (Plum Preserves Purim). Prune is second in popularity only to poppy seeds as a hamantaschen filling.

When the Jews of the Rhineland moved en masse to eastern Europe, they brought the hamantaschen with them and it became the preeminent Ashkenazic Purim pastry. At the same time, these triangular pastries lost favor among German, Alsatian, and Dutch Jews, who favor gingerbread men for Purim.

Cookie Dough Hamantaschen

ABOUT 40 SMALL COOKIES

½ cup (1 stick) plus
   3 tablespoons butter or
   margarine, softened
½ cup sugar
1 large egg
3 tablespoons orange juice,
   sweet red wine, or water
   (or 2 tablespoons water and
   1 tablespoon lemon juice)
1 teaspoon vanilla extract or
   grated lemon zest
¼ teaspoon salt
About 2¾ cups all-purpose
   flour
About 1½ cups mohnfullung
   (poppy seed filling; see page
   320), lekvar (prune jam),
   or povidl (plum preserves)

1. Beat the butter or margarine until smooth. Gradually add the sugar and beat until light and fluffy, 5 to 10 minutes. Beat in the egg. Blend in the juice, wine, or water, vanilla or zest, and salt. Stir in enough of the flour to make a soft dough.

2. Wrap the dough in plastic wrap and chill until firm, at least 1 hour. The dough can be stored in the refrigerator for several days or in the freezer for several months. Let stand at room temperature for several minutes, until workable but not soft.

3. Preheat the oven to 375 degrees. Have several baking sheets ready. (Do not grease the baking sheets.)

4. For easy handling, divide the dough into 4 pieces. On a lightly floured surface or piece of waxed paper, roll out each piece ⅛ inch thick. Using a 2½- to 3-inch cookie cutter or glass, cut out rounds. Reroll the scraps.

5. Place 1 teaspoon of the filling in the center of each round. Pinch the bottom side of the dough round together over the filling. Fold down the top flap and pinch the other two sides together to form a triangle, leaving some filling exposed in the center. (Hamantaschen can be prepared ahead to this point and frozen for several months. Defrost before baking.)

6. Place the hamantaschen 1 inch apart on the baking sheets. Bake until golden brown, about 13 minutes. Transfer to a wire rack and let cool completely.

Yeast Dough Hamantaschen

🔖 ABOUT 30 (3-INCH) COOKIES 🔖

Although yeast kuchen dough was originally used for these pastries, sugar cookie dough, which is easier to make, has become more common in recent times. Many connoisseurs, however, still consider yeast hamantaschen to be the best.

1 recipe sweet yeast dough (see page 294)
About 2 cups mohnfullung *(poppy seed filling, see page 320)*, lekvar *(prune jam), or* povidl *(plum preserves)*
1 egg beaten with 1 tablespoon water

1. Divide the dough into thirds. On a lightly floured surface, roll out each dough piece ¼ inch thick. Cut out 3- to 4-inch rounds.

2. Place 1 tablespoon filling in the center of each dough round. Pinch the bottom side of the dough round together over the filling. Fold down the top flap and pinch the other two sides together to form a triangle, leaving some filling exposed in the center. (The hamantaschen can be prepared ahead to this point and frozen for several months. Defrost before baking.)

3. Place the cookies 2 inches apart on several greased baking sheets. Cover and let rise at room temperature until nearly double, about 1 hour.

4. Preheat the oven to 350 degrees.

5. Brush the tops of the hamantaschen with the egg wash. Bake until golden brown, about 25 minutes. Transfer to a wire rack and let cool completely.

Mohnfullung

ASHKENAZIC POPPY SEED FILLING
ABOUT 2 CUPS

*1 cup poppy seeds, crushed
  or ground*
½ cup water or milk
*½ cup sugar or honey or any
  combination*
Pinch of salt
*2 tablespoons lemon or orange
  juice or ½ teaspoon vanilla
  extract*
*2 teaspoons grated lemon or
  orange zest*
*½ cup golden raisins or chopped
  dried apricots*
*½ cup finely chopped walnuts
  or almonds (optional)*

1. Combine the poppy seeds, water or milk, sugar or honey, and salt in a small saucepan. Simmer over medium-low heat, stirring frequently, until the mixture thickens, about 10 minutes.

2. Remove from the heat and stir in the remaining ingredients. Let cool. Store in the refrigerator.

POPPY SEEDS

The Dutch poppy produces dark blue seeds of different qualities: Fancy-grade poppy seeds are a lighter blue and have a slightly sweeter flavor; A-1 grade are darker and are slightly bitter. When roasted or steamed, poppy seeds have a mild, nutty flavor. Grinding the seeds releases the flavor more fully. Use a mortar and pestle, spice grinder, or blender to grind. If you cannot grind the seeds, use them whole. As with most seeds, poppies contain a large amount of oil, which can go rancid when left at room temperature for a long period, so store raw poppy seeds in the refrigerator or freezer.

Eier Kichlach

ASHKENAZIC EGG COOKIES
ABOUT 30 COOKIES

The name of this tender, airy cookie (singular, *kichel,* related to kuchen) reveals its Teutonic origins. Its popularity has survived with eastern European Jews, who commonly serve them at the Sabbath morning kiddush.

3 large eggs
¼ cup plus 1 tablespoon sugar
¼ teaspoon salt
½ cup vegetable oil
1 cup all-purpose flour

1. Position a rack in the center of the oven. Preheat the oven to 350 degrees. Grease several baking sheets.
2. Beat the eggs until light and fluffy, 5 to 10 minutes. Add the 1 tablespoon sugar and the salt, then the oil, and beat until thick, about 10 minutes. Gradually beat in the flour.
3. Drop the batter by teaspoonfuls, 2 inches apart, onto the prepared baking sheets. Lightly sprinkle the tops with the ¼ cup sugar.
4. Bake until puffed and golden brown, about 25 minutes. Transfer to a wire rack and let cool completely. Store in an airtight container at room temperature or in the freezer.

VARIATION
Mohn Kichlach (Ashkenazic Poppy Cookies): **Add 3 tablespoons** poppy seeds.

Lebkuchen

Ashkenazic Spice Bars
❧ ABOUT 48 COOKIES ❧

*L*ebkuchen, originally made from rye flour, were among the earliest European cookies. They are especially popular among European communities on Sukkoth (see page 146) because of the presence of fruit and nuts.

2 cups all-purpose flour
1½ teaspoons baking powder
½ teaspoon salt
1½ teaspoons ground cinnamon
1 teaspoon ground cloves
⅛ teaspoon grated nutmeg
2¼ cups brown sugar
4 large eggs
1 cup finely chopped almonds, hazelnuts, or walnuts
1 cup finely chopped candied citron, candied pineapple, pitted dates, or any combination

Icing
1 cup confectioners' sugar
About 2 tablespoons warm water
½ teaspoon vanilla extract or lemon juice

1. Preheat the oven to 350 degrees. Grease a 15½-by-10½-inch jelly roll pan.
2. Sift together the flour, baking powder, salt, and spices. Beat the brown sugar and eggs until light and smooth. Stir in the flour mixture, then the nuts and fruit.
3. Spread the batter in the prepared pan. (It should be about ½ inch thick.) Bake until golden brown, about 30 minutes.
4. Combine the icing ingredients and spread over the warm pastry. Cut into 3-by-1-inch bars and let cool. Store in an airtight container at room temperature.

Mandelbrot

ASHKENAZIC ALMOND BREAD
❧ ABOUT 42 SLICES ❧

Mandelbrot (Yiddish for "almond bread"), called *kamishbrot* in the Ukraine, is a favorite Ashkenazic cookie derived from the Italian *biscotti* (Italian for "twice baked") *alla mandorala* and the Turkish *paximadia*. The pastry is baked in logs or in a loaf pan, hence its name. The loaves are sliced while still warm and the cookie slices usually baked a second time, a step that lengthens their shelf life, making it perfect for unexpected Sabbath company.

2 cups all-purpose flour
1½ teaspoons double-acting
  baking powder
½ teaspoon salt
⅔ cup sugar
½ cup vegetable oil or melted
  vegetable shortening
2 large eggs
½ teaspoon vanilla extract
½ teaspoon almond extract or
  1 teaspoon ground cinnamon
½ to 1 cup coarsely chopped
  lightly toasted almonds,
  hazelnuts, or walnuts
½ to 1 cup raisins (optional)

1. Preheat the oven to 350 degrees. Grease and flour a large baking sheet.

2. Sift together the flour, baking powder, and salt. Beat together the sugar and oil or shortening. Blend in the eggs, one at a time. Add the vanilla, the almond extract or cinnamon, and then the flour mixture. Stir in the nuts and, if desired, raisins.

3. Using floured hands, form the dough into two loaves about 10 inches long, ¾ inch high, and 3 inches wide, smoothing the tops. Place the loaves on the prepared sheet, leaving 3 inches between them.

4. Bake until lightly browned, about 30 minutes.

5. Reduce the oven temperature to 300 degrees.

6. Using a serrated knife, cut the warm loaves diagonally into ½-inch-thick slices. Place the slices, cut side down, on the baking sheet. Bake, turning once, until golden and crisp, about 5 minutes per side. (The slices harden as they cool.) Store in an airtight container.

Hint: Mandel crumbs are customarily saved and used to sprinkle in sweet strudels.

HUNGARIAN HAUTE

"The Poles use too much sugar. I know Lithuanians who add raisins and dates to their fish," declares Lilly Weiss Levinson, a native of Satoraljaujhely, a small town in the northeast part of Hungary. "Hungarians only add a very little sugar to dishes such as stuffed peppers, stuffed cabbage, and gefilte fish. Just enough to bring out the flavor of the food. To be sure, Hungarians have a sweet tooth, but it's for dessert."

Jews lived in the area around the Danube now mostly occupied by Hungary as early as Roman times, but their numbers were greatly augmented with the arrival of German refugees in the eleventh century. A critical turning point in Hungarian history came with the Mongol invasion in 1241, during which more than half of the population was exterminated. This cataclysm left the country in such a weakened state that it subsequently found itself under the domination of its more powerful neighbors. From 1530 to 1687, the Ottoman Turks controlled most of Hungary. During this time, the area attracted a large number of Sephardim and, in the seventeenth century, Ashkenazim fleeing from Poland.

The many countries that controlled Hungary impacted on its cuisine. The nomadic Magyars, who settled in the area in 892 C.E., carried cauldrons called *bogracs,* convenient for preparing dishes over open fires. Levinson notes, "*Leves* [soups] and stews remain important elements of Hungarian cuisine and *bogracs* are still used in Hungarian

kitchens for preparing the national dish, *gulyás* [goulash]. Beef and veal are the predominant meats, which are rarely roasted but [in the Magyar manner] usually cut into small pieces and slow-simmered in their own juice. Vinegar, sauerkraut, or sour cream is often stirred into soups and stews, adding either a touch of tartness or a sour flavor. Noodles—*tarhonya* [dried pasta pellets dating back to nomadic times], *csipetke* [fresh pasta pellets], and *galuska* [soft dumplings]—rice, or potatoes customarily accompany stews.

"Hungarian cooking utilizes few seasonings other than paprika and onions, relying instead on cooking techniques for flavor," expounds Levinson. "In many dishes chopped onions are slowly fried in fat—ranging from a translucency to a light gold to a deep brown—to produce a rich, flavorful gravy. Schmaltz [which produces an intense red in conjunction with paprika] is the primary cooking fat. Tomatoes and sour cream often accompany paprika in a dish to mellow its sharpness.

"Since non-Jewish Hungarians use a great deal of pork and often incorporate sour cream into their meat dishes, Hungarian Jewish fare in many cases developed a different flavor," Levinson explains. "We also use garlic in dishes like *pecsenye,* which is similar to chicken paprikash but has a different taste.

"Hungary is justly renowned for its fruit," she continues, "used to make a large assortment of preserves, fruit soups, and compotes. My grandfather had a vineyard and we'd

hang bunches of grapes from beams in the pantry and they lasted for months. During the fall and winter we were generally able to import fruits from southern countries. My father would buy imported oranges and bananas as a Hanukkah treat."

Hungarians have a penchant for creating rich desserts (generally much sweeter than their Austrian counterparts), ranging from *makos metelt* (sweetened noodles with poppy seeds) to elaborate concoctions. Levinson reminisces, "On Sukkoth, we had *retes* [strudel], filled with both sweet and savory mixtures, and *palacsinta* [sweet crepes]. I remember on Shavuot that my mother had huge bowls filled with *delkel* [cheese Danish], *kakosh* [chocolate rolls], *makosh* [poppy rolls], and other pastries. But Purim was the time when my mother made all types of baked goods, especially *fluden* topped with a chocolate glaze."

Above: **Kosher restaurant, Budapest, 1990.**
The uniqueness of Hungarian cuisine is due to an assortment of historical and cultural influences: its Magyar roots; an Austrian domination that lasted almost six centuries; and the fact that it is a landlocked country surrounded by Turkey, Russia, Poland, the Balkans, and Austria.

Rugelach

Ashkenazic Pastry Crescents

 32 large, 48 medium, or 64 small cookies

In 1793, Austrian bakers, in celebration of the lifting of a lengthy Turkish siege of Vienna, shaped various baked goods into crescents (*kipferin*), the emblem on the Ottoman flag. *Rugelach* ("little twists" in Yiddish) and yeast *rugelach*—also called *Pressburger kipplach* and *Pozsonyi kifli*—are all delicious examples of Austrian crescents. (This is also the origin of the croissant.) Americans seem to agree, for it has recently become very popular over here. The dairy version of this pastry is popular on Shavuot and Hanukkah, and recommended for a rich, flavorful treat. This dough is also used for tarts, pies, cheese strudel, and cookies such as *polster zipfel* (Viennese jam pockets).

DOUGH

1 cup (2 sticks) butter, softened

8 ounces cream cheese, softened (or ⅔ cup sour cream and 1 egg yolk)

2 tablespoons sugar

¼ teaspoon salt

2 cups all-purpose flour

FILLING

1 cup finely chopped walnuts or pecans

½ cup dried currants or raisins (optional)

½ cup granulated sugar or brown sugar

1 teaspoon ground cinnamon

About 1 cup apricot jam, raspberry jam, strawberry jam, orange marmalade, or ¼ cup (½ stick) butter or margarine, melted

1. To make the dough: Beat together the butter, cream cheese, and sugar until light and fluffy. Add the salt. Gradually beat in the flour.

2. Divide into 4 equal portions, form into balls, wrap, and refrigerate overnight. (For quicker use, place in the freezer for about 1 hour. The dough can be frozen for up to 4 months.) Let the dough stand at room temperature until workable.

3. Position a rack in the upper third of the oven. Preheat the oven to 375 degrees.

4. On a lightly floured surface or piece of waxed paper, roll out each piece of the dough into a ⅛-inch-thick round about 15 inches in diameter.

5. To make the filling: Combine the nuts, currants or raisins, if desired, sugar, and cinnamon. Brush the dough rounds lightly with the jam, marmalade, butter, or margarine, leaving a ½-inch border around the edges. Sprinkle evenly with the nut mixture.

6. For large *rugelach*, cut each round into 8 wedges; for medium, cut into 12 wedges; for small, cut into 16 wedges. Roll up the wedges from the wide end toward the point, pinching the point to seal. Gently bend to form crescents.

(The *rugelach* can be prepared ahead to this point and frozen for several months. Defrost before baking.)

7. Place the *rugelach* on ungreased baking sheets. Bake until golden brown, about 20 minutes. Let the cookies stand until firm, about 1 minute, then transfer to a wire rack and let cool completely. Store in an airtight container at room temperature or in the freezer.

VARIATIONS

Roll the dough on a surface sprinkled with a mixture of ½ cup sugar and 1½ teaspoons cinnamon.

Flaky Rugelach: Substitute 1 recipe pastry strudel dough from *gebleterter kugel* (see page 347) for the cream cheese dough.

Chocolate Rugelach: Substitute ½ cup unsweetened cocoa powder for the cinnamon and brush the dough rounds with the ¼ cup butter or margarine (not the jam).

Polster Zipfel (Viennese Jam Pockets): Cut the dough into 2- to 3-inch squares, spoon ½ teaspoon jam in the center of each square, and fold one side over to form a triangle, pressing the corners to seal. (Or bring two diagonal corners together over the jam, pressing to seal.)

 **SALT IN BAKING**

Salt, an essential part of life on earth, is a crystalline compound long valued as a seasoning as well as a preservative. Salt is an important addition to baked goods, where it enhances flavor and aids the elastic properties of gluten, allowing it to rise better. In Roman times soldiers were paid in salt; thus fixed compensation became a *salarium* (literally "salt money" in Latin), or salary. Salt is obtained from deposits of rock salt (the residue of ancient seas) or from seawater. Sea salt is generally more expensive—as it is extracted through evaporation—but since it is purer, it has a superior flavor.

Biscochos de Huevo

SEPHARDIC COOKIE RINGS
❧ ABOUT 48 COOKIES ❧

These sweet cookie rings—also called *roskitas de gueve* and, in Syria, Iraq, Turkey, and India, *kaak*—are served at *desayuno* (Sabbath and festival breakfast; see page 29) and other festive occasions, including Purim (see page 316), where the rings symbolize Esther's jewelry, and the meal following Yom Kippur. Housewives take great pride in their ability to make cookies of uniform size and prepare large enough batches to always have some on hand for unexpected company.

4 cups all-purpose flour
1 tablespoon double-acting baking powder
½ teaspoon salt
4 large eggs, lightly beaten
1 cup sugar
1 cup vegetable oil
1 teaspoon vanilla extract or 1½ teaspoons ground cinnamon

1. Position a rack in the center of the oven. Preheat the oven to 350 degrees. Line several baking sheets with parchment paper or aluminum foil.
2. Sift together the flour, baking powder, and salt. Beat together the eggs, sugar, oil, and vanilla or cinnamon. Gradually stir in the flour mixture to make a soft dough. Cover and refrigerate for at least 30 minutes.
3. Roll the dough into ½-inch-thick ropes. Cut the ropes into 6-inch lengths and bring the ends together to form rings. If desired, cut gashes on the outer edges every ¼ to ½ inch.
4. Place the rings, 1 inch apart, on the prepared baking sheets. Bake until firm but not browned, about 20 minutes. Transfer to a wire rack and let cool completely.
5. For extra-crisp cookies, turn off the oven, return all of the baked cookies, and let stand for 20 minutes. Transfer to a wire rack and let cool completely. Store in an airtight container at room temperature or in the freezer.

VARIATIONS
Biscochos de Muez (Sephardic Nut Cookies): Dip the tops of the dough rings into a lightly beaten egg, then into 1 cup of finely chopped walnuts or almonds. Place nut side up on the baking sheet.

Biscochos de Susam/Taraleekoos (Sephardic Sesame Cookies): Dip the tops of the dough rings into a lightly beaten egg, then into 1 cup of sesame seeds. Place sesame side up on the baking sheet.

Reshicas (Sephardic Pretzel-Shaped Cookies): Loop the ends of the dough ropes over the middle to form a pretzel shape. Dip the tops into a lightly beaten egg, then into 1 cup of sesame seeds. Place sesame side up on the baking sheet.

Biscochos de Raki

TURKISH ANISE COOKIES
ABOUT 36 COOKIES

Raki, called ouzo in Greece, is a Turkish anise-flavored liqueur. These cookies are also called *anasonlis* (from *anason,* the Turkish word for anise seeds).

3 cups all-purpose flour
1 tablespoon baking powder
Pinch of salt
1 cup raki or ouzo
¾ cup sugar
½ cup vegetable oil
*1 large egg, lightly beaten
  (optional)*
*About 1 cup sesame seeds
  (optional)*

1. Sift together the flour, baking powder, and salt. Combine the raki or ouzo, sugar, and oil and stir into the flour mixture, adding more flour if necessary to make a firm dough. Cover and refrigerate overnight.

2. Shape dough and bake as for Sephardic cookie rings (see opposite page).

Ma'amoul

MIDDLE EASTERN FILLED COOKIES
ABOUT 36 COOKIES

Ma'amoul ("filled" in Arabic) is made throughout the Middle East and goes by a variety of names, including *menenas* in North Africa and *klaitcha* in Iran. Syrian cookies called *ras-ib-adjway* are *ma'amouls* filled with a date and walnut mixture, and *krabeej* are *ma'amouls* dipped into marshmallow fluff instead of confectioners' sugar. North Africans usually simmer the cooled cookies in warm sugar syrup (see page 372) for several minutes. Serious cooks use a special wooden press called a *tabi* to form the cookie and impress ornate designs on the surface.

Ma'amoul is traditional on many festive occasions, most notably Purim and Hanukkah. Middle Eastern Jews often serve similar foods on these two holidays, both of which occurred relatively late in Jewish history, "to connect miracle with miracle."

1 recipe semolina pastry (see page 43) or short pastry (see page 40)
Ma'amoul filling (see below)
About ¼ cup confectioners' sugar

1. Preheat the oven to 350 degrees. Line several baking sheets with parchment paper or aluminum foil.
2. Form the dough into 1¼-inch balls. Hollow out the balls using your thumb. Fill with a heaping teaspoon of the filling. Press the sides of the opening together to cover the filling and gently form into balls or crescents. If desired, make designs in the dough with a fork or knife.
3. Place the cookies, 1 inch apart, on the prepared baking sheets. Bake until lightly colored but not browned, about 20 minutes. Transfer to a wire rack and let cool completely. (The cookies will firm as they cool.) Sprinkle with the confectioners' sugar. Store in an airtight container at room temperature.

VARIATION

If you have trouble forming the dough balls into cylinders, there are several alternative methods of preparing the cookies. Divide the dough into 3 or 4 pieces, roll out the dough into thin rectangles (do not flour the surface), cut out 3-inch rounds, place a heaping teaspoon of the filling in the center of each round, and bring the sides of the dough over the filling to form a ball. Or place a teaspoon of the filling at the bottom of each round, roll up from the filling end, and form into a crescent. Or spread the filling over each rectangle, leaving a ½-inch border on all sides. Roll up jelly roll style, flatten the pastry slightly by rolling and pressing, and slice diagonally into ¾- to 1-inch pieces.

Ma'amoul Joz, Loz, wa Fisto

MA'AMOUL NUT FILLING

2 cups finely chopped walnuts, almonds, or unsalted pistachios

¾ cup sugar

1 teaspoon rose water or orange blossom water or ½ teaspoon ground cinnamon

Combine all of the ingredients.

WALNUTS

I went down to the garden of nuts.
—SONG OF SONGS 6:11

The Persian walnut (or, as it is sometimes called, English walnut) is the world's most popular variety. This is appropriate, since, according to Pliny and other Romans, walnuts reached Rome by way of Persia. The Romans then spread the walnut throughout their empire and it became the primary nut in Europe. Rabbinic literature is replete with references to walnuts, describing their characteristics in great detail. Walnut wood was used for the altar fire in the Temple and, in Talmudic times, walnut shells were tossed in front of a bride and groom. Many Jewish communities use walnuts to make *charoseth* and a wide array of baked goods, including pastries, cookies, pies, and cakes. Arguably no group loves walnuts more than Georgians, who add them to almost any dish.

Note: Walnuts are sometimes blanched in water for several minutes to remove an acid that some people find irritating to the stomach.

Ma'amoul Tamir

MA'AMOUL DATE FILLING

*1 pound dates, pitted and finely
    chopped (about 3 cups)*
½ cup water
*2 tablespoons butter or
    margarine*

Stir the dates and water over low heat for 10 minutes. Add the butter or margarine and cook until the mixture forms an almost uniform mass, about 5 minutes. Let cool.

VARIATION

Tamir wa Joz (Ma'amoul Date and Walnut Filling): When thick, remove the dates from the heat and stir in ½ to 1 cup chopped walnuts, 1 teaspoon grated orange zest, and 1 teaspoon ground cinnamon.

DATES

The righteous shall flourish like the palm tree.
—PSALMS 92:13

Dates are one of the oldest cultivated fruits. The sweetness of this native of the Fertile Crescent area has made it a favorite everywhere. Dates play a prominent role in Jewish tradition: The sages explain that the honey in the phrase "the land flowing with milk and honey" refers to date honey; it was under a date palm that Deborah judged the nation; the branch of the palm is one of the four species used during the holiday of Sukkoth; the Maccabees used the palm as a symbol of their military success; and a number of ancient Jewish coins bear a picture of the date palm. In Roman times, Jericho dates were considered the best in the world.

The name of this fruit of the date palm tree is from the Greek *dactylon* ("finger" or "toe"), a reference to its shape. Dates vary in size, texture, and color. Soft dates have a higher moisture content, a smaller amount of sugar, and a softer texture. Semisoft dates have less moisture, more sugar, and a firmer texture. Deglet Noor (literally "date of light"), the primary date variety grown in the United States, has a semisoft texture that lends itself to shipping and storage.

Hint: To prevent dates from sticking when chopping, first lightly oil the knife blade or kitchen shears.

Ghribi

MOROCCAN SHORTBREAD COOKIES
ABOUT 48 COOKIES

These cookies, based on a Near Eastern butter cookie, appear at all Moroccan celebrations. Although the omission of eggs results in an incredibly tender, slightly crisp cookie, it also makes them very fragile.

4 cups all-purpose flour
½ teaspoon salt
1 cup sugar
1 cup vegetable oil
1 teaspoon vanilla extract
Ground cinnamon for garnish

1. Preheat the oven to 350 degrees.
2. Combine the flour and salt. Beat together the sugar, oil, and vanilla. Gradually stir in the flour mixture to make a soft dough.
3. Shape the dough into 1¼-inch balls. Place on ungreased baking sheets and flatten slightly. (The cookies should be mounded.) Sprinkle lightly with the cinnamon.
4. Bake until firm but not browned, about 20 minutes. Transfer to a wire rack and let cool completely. Store in an airtight container at room temperature.

VARIATIONS

Kourabie (Middle Eastern Nut Cookies): **Reduce the amount of flour to 2½ cups and add 1 cup ground almonds or walnuts and, if desired, ½ teaspoon baking soda. (*Note:* Made with butter, this dough is similar to the Austrian *kipferin* [nut crescents].)**

Biscochos de Har Sinai (Sephardic Mount Sinai Cookies): **Press 1 walnut or pecan half into the center of each cookie. (*Note:* These cookies are made for Shavuot. The cookie mounds symbolize Mount Sinai; the nuts, the two tablets of the Ten Commandments.)**

Marunchinos

Sephardic Almond Macaroons
About 30 cookies

Almonds are a prominent feature in Sephardic cooking and the basis for many pastries. There are many variations of this popular Passover treat: Some versions call for as little as 2 cups ground almonds, others for as little as ¼ cup sugar. There is even a macaroon-style *marunchino* made by first beating the egg whites until soft peaks form and then gradually beating in sugar before folding in the almonds.

3 cups (about 1 pound) finely ground blanched almonds
1¼ cups sugar
3 large egg whites
1 teaspoon almond extract or 1 tablespoon rose water or orange blossom water
About ⅓ cup slivered almonds (optional)

1. Preheat the oven to 325 degrees. Grease 2 large baking sheets and dust with potato starch or flour.
2. Grind together the almonds and sugar. Stir in the egg whites and almond extract or flavored water to form a paste.
3. Drop by heaping teaspoonfuls onto the prepared baking sheets, leaving 1½ inches between the cookies. If desired, place a slivered almond on top.
4. Bake until lightly browned, 10 to 15 minutes. Let cool. Store in an airtight container at room temperature or in the freezer.

Variation

Hadgi Badah (Iraqi Cardamom Macaroons): Omit the almond extract and add ½ to ¾ teaspoon ground cardamom. (*Note:* Iraqis serve these cookies on Purim and at the meal following Yom Kippur.)

Mustachudos

SEPHARDIC NUT CRESCENTS

 ABOUT 48 COOKIES

These chewy Passover cookies get their name, "mustaches," because they are curved into a crescent shape.

3 large eggs, lightly beaten
1 cup sugar
3 tablespoons matza meal
1 teaspoon ground cinnamon
½ teaspoon ground cloves
2 teaspoons grated orange zest
   (optional)
4 cups (about 1 pound) ground
   walnuts (or 2½ cups ground
   almonds and 1½ cups
   ground walnuts)
Confectioners' sugar for dusting
   (optional)

1. Preheat the oven to 350 degrees. Grease 2 large baking sheets.
2. Combine the eggs, sugar, matza meal, cinnamon, cloves and, if desired, zest. Stir in the nuts.
3. Form the dough into 1-inch balls, then shape each ball into a 2-inch-long and ½-inch-thick crescent.
4. Place on the prepared baking sheets and flatten slightly. Bake until golden, 10 to 12 minutes. Let cool on the sheets for 10 minutes and sprinkle with confectioners' sugar. Move to wire racks and let cool completely. Store in an airtight container in the freezer or refrigerator.

ROSE WATER/ORANGE BLOSSOM WATER

Although Americans value roses almost exclusively for their aesthetic quality, Middle Easterners know that they have a beauty in the kitchen, adding flavor to baked goods, confections, and fruit dishes. Rose water, made by distilling fresh pink damask rose petals in water, is a popular flavoring on Shavuot among Sephardim, who call the holiday "the Feast of Roses."

To make rose water, cover rose petals with water and simmer over low heat for about 1 hour, then strain, discarding the petals. Cover additional rose petals with the rose water and simmer 1 hour. Repeat, at least once more, until the water has a pronounced rose aroma. Use rose water sparingly.

Orange blossom water, as the name indicates, is distilled from orange blossoms. It is used throughout the Middle East and North Africa in pastries and other desserts.

Bimuelos/Ponchiks

DOUGHNUTS

ABOUT 24 MEDIUM OR 48 SMALL DOUGHNUTS

Yeast doughnuts—called *lokmas* in Turkey, *loukoumades* in Greece, and *ponchiks* in Poland—are an ancient form of pastry, prepared in much the same way today as they were two thousand years ago. The Ladino word *bimuelos*—also spelled *bilmuelos, bulemas,* and *burmuelos*—(from the Spanish word for "fritter," *bunuelo*) can be a bit confusing, as Sephardim also use it in reference to a variety of small fried foods, including pancakes and fritters. However, pancakes usually have an adjunctive phrase attached, e.g., *bimuelos de patata* (potato pancakes). When used alone, *bimuelos* generally refers to these small dough fritters. A similar pastry made from *pâte à choux* (cream puff pastry) is called *zvingous.* These fried pastries are served on Hanukkah (see page 220), symbolizing the miracle of the oil, and on other festive occasions.

1 package (2½ teaspoons) active dry yeast or 1 (.6-ounce) cake fresh yeast

2 cups warm water (105 to 110 degrees for dry yeast, 80 to 85 degrees for fresh yeast)

1 teaspoon sugar or honey

2½ cups all-purpose flour

⅛ teaspoon salt

Vegetable oil for deep-frying

1 recipe sugar syrup (see page 372), cooled, or confectioners' sugar for dusting

1. Dissolve the yeast in ¼ cup of the water. Stir in the sugar or honey and let stand until foamy, 5 to 10 minutes.

2. Combine the flour and salt in a large bowl and make a well in the center. Pour the yeast mixture and remaining water into the well and stir until smooth. The dough will not be very thick. Cover and let rise at room temperature until double in bulk, about 1½ hours. Stir.

3. Heat 2 inches oil over medium heat to 375 degrees.

4. Dip a teaspoon or tablespoon into cold water and use the spoon to drop the dough into the hot oil. In batches, deep-fry the dough-nuts until golden brown on all sides, about 3 minutes. Drain on paper towels.

5. Dip the warm doughnuts into the cooled syrup or sprinkle with confectioners' sugar. Serve immediately. (To serve *bimuelos* later, let them cool without the syrup or sugar and store in an airtight container. Just before serving, dip into warm syrup.)

Below: **Beignet peddler, Marrakesh, 1950.** *Fried doughs have been common fare in the Mediterranean region since at least 2500 years ago. The trick to making nongreasy fritters is the temperature of the oil: If the oil is not hot enough, the dough will absorb it; if the oil is too hot, the outsides of the dough will brown before the insides have cooked.*

VARIATION

Zelebi (Middle Eastern Funnel Cakes): Drop the dough from a large spoon or squeeze it from a plastic squeeze bottle or pastry bag into the hot oil in a spiral fashion, forming a 6-inch-long coil. Makes about 26 cakes. (*Note:* This pastry, popular from the Maghreb to India, is called *chebbakiah/zangulas* in Morocco, *zinghol* in Syria, *zalabia* in Iraq, and *jalebi* in India.)

Oznei Haman

HAMAN'S EARS
ABOUT 36 PASTRIES

The underlying theme of most Purim pastries is shape, whereby a person symbolically erases Haman's name by eating a pastry formed to represent a part of the villainous prime minister's clothing or anatomy—most notably his pocket, hat, foot, or ear. The most widespread of these Purim pastries are "Haman's ears"—deep-fried strips of dough—known under an assortment of local names, including *oznei Haman* in Hebrew, *orejas de Haman* in Ladino, *gushfil* in Persian, *roscas di alhashu* in the Balkans, *aftia tou Amman* in Greece, *haman-muetzen* in Germany, *hamansooren* in Holland, and *orecchi de Aman* in Italy. Ear-shaped pastries are derived from the medieval custom of cutting off a criminal's ear before execution as well as a legend that Haman's ears were twisted or triangular in shape like a donkey's. On Hanukkah (see page 220), Sephardim also shape these dough strips into rosettes and pinwheels called *shamlias* (frills).

3 large eggs, lightly beaten

2 tablespoons vegetable oil

2 tablespoons water, rum, brandy, or orange juice

¼ teaspoon salt

About 2 cups all-purpose flour, preferably unbleached

Vegetable oil for deep frying

About 1 cup confectioners' sugar

1. Blend together the eggs, oil, water, rum, brandy, or orange juice, and salt. Gradually stir in enough of the flour to make a soft dough.

2. On a lightly floured surface, knead until smooth, about 3 minutes. Cover and let stand for 15 minutes.

3. On a lightly floured surface or piece of waxed paper, roll out the dough about ⅛ inch thick. With a pastry cutter or sharp knife, cut the dough into 1-inch-wide and 6-inch-long strips. Pinch each strip in the center and twist the ends.

4. Heat about 2 inches of oil to 375 degrees.

5. In batches, deep-fry the strips, turning to fry evenly, until golden brown on both sides, about 1 minute. Remove with a slotted spoon and drain on paper towels. Sprinkle generously with confectioners' sugar. Store in an airtight container at room temperature.

VARIATIONS

Orejas de Haman (Moroccan Haman's Ears): Cut the dough into 3- to 4-inch rounds, cut each round in half, and pinch the center of the straight edge to suggest an ear. *Orejas de*

Haman are sometimes drizzled with a sugar syrup (see page 372) instead of confectioners' sugar.

Heizenblauzen (Central European "Blow-Hots"): Cut the dough into 2-inch squares, cut a slit in the center of each square, and pull one corner through the slit. If desired, add 2 tablespoons ground cinnamon to the confectioners' sugar. (*Note:* These pastries are also called *schunzuchen* in Alsace and Switzerland.)

Fluden

ASHKENAZIC LAYERED PASTRY
10 TO 12 SERVINGS

Fluden—from the German *fladen* (flat cake), a word related to the French *flan* (an open-faced tart)—was for many centuries the favorite dessert of Franco-German Jews. The earliest recorded mention of *fluden* occurred in the writings of Rabbi Gershom ben Yehuda of Mainz (a city on the Rhine River) around the year 1000 C.E., in which he discussed an argument between his teacher Rabbi Yehuda Hacohain ben Meir Leontin (from León, France) and Rabbi Eleazar ben Gilo over whether it was permitted "to eat bread with meat even if it was baked in an oven with a cheese dish called *fluden*." This disagreement persisted, thus similar references appear in rabbinic writings on a frequent basis throughout this period.

Fluden is related to the Ashkenazic double-crusted meat-filled Sabbath pie called *pashtida*. The thick upper and lower layers of dough in this dish served several purposes: They kept the filling moist during baking and storage, they served as a base for eating the filling, and they were symbolic of both the double portion of manna collected for the Sabbath and the lower and upper layers of dew that protected the manna. Sometimes the dish was made with several thick layers so that each one could be separately removed and served at different times, while the remaining layers of filling stayed fresh. As the dish evolved, the hard, thick pastry was replaced with thin layers of soft-wheat pastry or rich yeast dough and was served by being cut into sections. Franco-German Jews developed several fillings for their favorite dessert: cheese for Shavuot and Rosh Hashanah (Franco-German Jews waited only one hour between eating meat and dairy, so a cheese *fluden* could be served as dessert after a meat meal), apples or raisins for Sukkoth and Simchas Torah, and jam and nut fillings for the Sabbath.

With the destruction of the Franco-German Jewish communities, the popularity of *fluden* declined. Yet descendants of this pastry are still served by Ashkenazim: In its native region, Alsatian Jews prepare a similar dish called *apfelschalet* (*Larousse Gastronomique* described *schalet à la Juive* as a sort of deep-dish apple pie made with layers of flaky pastry)—called *apfelbuwele* (German for "apple boy") in western Germany—which consists of an apple filling rolled up in a yeast dough; Hungarian Jews often use a different filling for each layer in this pastry, which they call *flodni* or *zserbo/jerbeau;* and in eastern Europe, *fluden,* sometimes called *gebleterter kugel,* became a version of fruit strudel made from flaky pastry. The term *fluden* is also used in eastern Europe for a beef stew containing fruit.

1 recipe extra-rich yeast dough (see page 295) or pastry dough (see opposite)
1 recipe fluden *filling (see pages 341–42)*
Sugar for sprinkling

1. Preheat the oven to 350 degrees. Grease a 13-by-9-inch baking dish.

2. Divide the yeast dough or pastry dough into 4 pieces, one slightly larger than the others.

3. On a lightly floured surface or piece of waxed paper, roll out the larger piece of dough into a 15-by-11-inch rectangle. Fit into the prepared baking dish so that it reaches up the sides. Spread evenly with one-third of the filling.

4. Roll out the remaining dough pieces into 13-by-9-inch rectangles and repeat layering the dough and filling, ending with a dough rectangle. Sprinkle with the sugar.

5. Bake until golden brown, about 45 minutes for yeast dough, about 1 hour for pastry dough. Let cool. Store at room temperature or in the freezer.

VARIATION

Apfelschalet (Western European Apple Roll)/Apfelbuwele (German "Apple Boy"): Roll the yeast dough into a 24-by-18-inch rectangle about ⅛ inch thick. Spread with half of the fruit filling, leaving a 1-inch border on all sides. Roll up jelly roll style, pinching the edges to seal, and place seam side down on a greased baking sheet, or bend into a circle and place in a greased 10-inch round pan. (*Note:* This adaptation of *fluden* is a very popular Sabbath dessert in Alsace and the adjoining parts of southwest Germany.)

Muerber Teig

FLUDEN PASTRY DOUGH

4 cups all-purpose flour
1 teaspoon double-acting baking
    powder
1 teaspoon salt
½ cup sugar
1½ cups vegetable shortening
    (or 1 cup vegetable shortening
    and ½ cup butter or
    margarine)
1 cup sweet wine, orange juice,
    or water
4 large egg yolks or 2 large eggs,
    lightly beaten

1. Sift together the flour, baking powder, and salt. Mix in the sugar. Using the tips of your fingers, a pastry blender, or knives in scissor fashion, cut in the shortening until the mixture resembles coarse crumbs. (The crumbs may be refrigerated for up to a week and mixed with the liquid when needed.)

2. Blend together the wine, orange juice, or water and egg yolks or eggs. Stir into the flour mixture until the mixture holds together. Using your fingertips, lightly press and knead the dough into a ball. Do not overhandle. Wrap in plastic wrap and refrigerate for at least 2 hours or overnight.

VARIATION
Oil Pastry: Reduce the amount of liquid to ½ cup and substitute 1 cup vegetable oil for the shortening.

Fruchtfulle

APPLE OR PEAR FLUDEN FILLING

10 to 12 medium apples or
    pears, peeled, cored, and
    coarsely chopped
1½ to 2 cups chopped almonds,
    walnuts, or hazelnuts or
    1 cup fine dried bread crumbs
About 1¼ cups sugar
1 teaspoon ground cinnamon
¾ to 1 cup raisins, chopped
    dried apricots, or chopped
    pitted dates

Combine all of the ingredients.

Kaesefulle

CHEESE FLUDEN FILLING

2 pounds pot, farmer, or drained   Combine all of the ingredients.
   small-curd cottage cheese
4 large eggs
About 1 cup sugar
¼ cup all-purpose flour
2 teaspoons grated lemon zest or
   vanilla extract
Dash of salt
½ to 1 cup golden raisins
   (optional)

Strudel

CENTRAL EUROPEAN ROLLED PASTRY

8 TO 10 SERVINGS

Strudel is the German word for "whirlpool," a fitting appellation for this roll of fruits or vegetables and delicate pastry. Strudel has its origins in a medieval German dish consisting of vegetables, and later fruit, rolled in a dough. This pastry eventually spread throughout central Europe. When the Turks, after their invasion of Hungary in 1526, introduced phyllo dough (which the Hungarians call *retes*) to Europe, the astute Hungarians promptly substituted these thin pastry layers for the original thick pastry. Austrians, Germans, Romanians, and Yugoslavians, all fanatic strudel makers, soon followed suit. The result is one of the most delicious of all pastries.

Strudel makers take their pastry very seriously, working the dough with gentle precision until stretched thin enough to read a newspaper through. Since classic strudel making was such a demanding process, housewives generally limited it to special occasions. Some cooks made strudel only once or twice a year—for Rosh Hashanah and/or Sukkoth. Strudel encompasses many of the High Holidays' traditional culinary symbols—sweet, "filled," and fruity. A cabbage filling was customary for Simchas Torah, dried fruit for Tu b'Shevat, poppy seeds for Purim (use a double recipe hamantaschen poppy seed filling; see page 320), and cheese for Shavuot (use the same filling as for *fluden;* see above, this page).

In this version, sheets of store-bought phyllo or strudel dough are arranged with overlapping sides to imitate the long sheets of dough traditionally used to make strudel.

About ½ cup (1 stick) butter or
   margarine, melted
8 sheets (about 18 by 16 inches
   each) phyllo dough
½ cup fine dried bread crumbs
   (optional)
1 recipe strudel filling (see page
   344)
Confectioners' sugar for dusting
   (optional)

1. Position a rack in the center of the oven. Preheat the oven to 375 degrees. Lightly brush a large baking sheet with the butter or margarine.

2. Place the long side of one sheet of the phyllo near the top edge of a tablecloth at least 4 by 3 feet and lightly brush with the butter or margarine.

3. Align a second sheet of phyllo along the bottom long edge of the first sheet, overlapping by 2 inches. Lightly brush with the butter or margarine. Align a third sheet of phyllo along the bottom long edge of the second sheet, overlapping by 2 inches, and brush with the butter or margarine. Align a fourth sheet of phyllo along the bottom long edge of the third sheet, overlapping by 2 inches, and brush with the butter or margarine. (You should have about a 42-by-18-inch phyllo rectangle.) For fruit strudel, sprinkle with ¼ cup of the bread crumbs.

4. Arrange the remaining 4 sheets on top of the bottom 4 sheets and brush with the butter or margarine. For fruit strudel, sprinkle with the remaining ¼ cup bread crumbs.

5. Mound the filling in a 4-inch-wide strip along the short side of the phyllo rectangle closest to you, leaving a 2-inch border along all three sides.

6. Fold the 2-inch uncovered sides of the phyllo over the filling. Fold the 2-inch short end of the pastry over the filling. Lifting the cloth from the filling end, roll the strudel jelly roll style. (The strudel can be prepared ahead to this point and frozen. Do not defrost before baking; increase the baking time by 10 minutes.)

7. Place the strudel, seam side down, on the prepared baking sheet and brush with the butter or margarine. Bake, turning the sheet halfway through, until the phyllo is golden brown and the filling tender, about 40 minutes.

8. Place the baking sheet on a wire rack and let the strudel cool slightly, about 30 minutes. Serve warm or at room temperature. (The strudel may be prepared 1 day in advance, covered loosely, stored at room temperature, and reheated at 400 degrees.) Sprinkle sweet strudel with confectioners' sugar. Cut into serving portions.

Apfel Strudelfulle

APPLE STRUDEL FILLING

2 pounds cooking apples,
   (such as Golden Delicious,
   Jonathan, Cortland, or
   Granny Smith), peeled,
   cored, and thinly sliced
¾ cup finely chopped walnuts or
   almonds
½ cup raisins or dried currants
About ½ cup sugar
1 teaspoon ground cinnamon
1 teaspoon grated lemon zest or
   ¼ teaspoon grated nutmeg
⅛ teaspoon salt

Combine all of the ingredients. (When the sugar is mixed with the apples, it melts as well as extracts juice from the fruit. Therefore, to avoid soggy pastry, store the apple mixture in a strainer or mix just before filling.)

Kirschen Strudelfulle

CHERRY STRUDEL FILLING

4 cups (about 2 pounds) pitted
   tart cherries (see Note)
¾ to 1¼ cups chopped blanched
   almonds or walnuts
About 1 cup sugar
1 teaspoon grated lemon zest or
   ¼ teaspoon ground cinnamon
3 tablespoons cake, cookie, or
   cracker crumbs (or ¼ cup
   dried bread crumbs sautéed in
   2 teaspoons butter or
   margarine) (optional)

Combine all of the ingredients.
Note: If using sweet cherries, decrease the amount of sugar to taste.

PHYLLO/STRUDELBLATTER

Phyllo, the Greek word for "leaf," is a simple dough of flour and water that is stretched paper-thin. It probably originated in Persia, spread throughout the Middle East, and was introduced to Europe by the Turks. Phyllo, the Middle Eastern version, is allowed to dry for a few minutes, then cut into pieces to facilitate stacking, while *strudelblatter* is left as one large piece of dough for easy rolling. When these delicate sheets are baked, they produce crisp, flaky, multilayered pastry used in a wide variety of savory and sweet dishes. Small phyllo pastries serve as an attractive appetizer or dessert, while larger pastries make a tempting main course.

Rolling out phyllo dough is a time-consuming and complicated procedure. Fortunately, frozen phyllo can be found in most grocery stores. One pound of frozen phyllo contains about twenty to twenty-four 13-by-9-inch to 18-by-16-inch leaves. Defrost the phyllo in the refrigerator for at least eight hours; defrost completely before using, or it will crumble. Do not defrost at room temperature, or the sheets will stick together. Remove the phyllo from the refrigerator about two hours before using.

Since phyllo dries out very quickly, keep it moist but not wet—if dried, phyllo becomes brittle; if too moist, the dough turns gummy. Before opening the phyllo package, prepare all of the ingredients called for in the recipe,

have all tools at hand, and preheat the oven. Remove from the package only the sheets needed, reseal the remaining phyllo, and store in the refrigerator. Do not refreeze. Unroll the phyllo onto a flat surface. When not in use, cover it completely with plastic wrap and then a damp towel. Work with only one sheet at a time. If the phyllo tears, use it between whole sheets or patch it with a little melted butter or margarine. Do not patch with water, or it will be gummy. Assembled phyllo pastry can be refrigerated for up to a day or frozen. If frozen, do not thaw before baking, or the pastry will be soggy.

Phyllo is always brushed lightly with fat. Do not soak the leaves with fat, or the result will be a clumpy mass. On the other hand, do not skimp on the fat, or it will be thick and heavy. One pound of phyllo will require ½ to ¾ pound (2 to 3 sticks) melted butter or margarine. Use a soft pastry brush or large feather for brushing. For a lower-calorie pastry, spray the layers with cooking spray.

Phyllo sheets are stacked on top of each other or rolled up for a multilayered effect. Moist fillings are suitable for large pastries but require six or more layers. Use drier fillings for small pastries. Scoring the top layers of a large phyllo dish makes it easier to cut into serving pieces. Use a serrated knife to cut phyllo pastries.

Gebleterter Kugel

ASHKENAZIC PASTRY STRUDEL

❧ ABOUT 36 PIECES ❧

Before phyllo pastry reached central Europe by way of the Ottoman Turks, strudel was made by rolling fruit fillings in a pastry dough. Although not as flaky as *strudelblatter,* pastry strudels, sometimes called *gebleterter kugel* and *fluden,* are much easier to make—since they are rolled out instead of stretched by hand—and less fragile. The sour cream or wine contains acid, which impairs gluten formation, thereby making a tender pastry, as well as adding an intriguing flavor.

1 recipe pastry strudel dough
*   (see below)*
1 recipe jam filling (see opposite
*   page) or 3 cups poppy seed*
*   filling (see page 320)*
Confectioners' sugar for dusting

1. Position a rack in the center of the oven. Preheat the oven to 350 degrees.

2. Working with one dough ball at a time, place on a lightly floured piece of waxed paper and roll out to a thin rectangle about 16 by 12 inches.

3. Spread one-third of the filling over each rectangle, leaving a ½-inch border. From a long edge, roll up jelly roll style. Place seam side down on an ungreased baking sheet.

4. Bake until golden brown, about 40 minutes. Let stand until firm, about 2 minutes, then, while still warm, cut into 1-inch-thick slices. Let cool completely. (The strudel may be frozen at this point for up to 3 months.) Dust with confectioners' sugar.

Pastry Strudel Dough

1 cup (2 sticks) butter or
    margarine, softened
    (or ¾ cup butter and
    ¼ cup vegetable shortening)
1 cup sour cream or softened
    vanilla ice cream
2 tablespoons sugar
½ teaspoon vanilla or almond
    extract
¼ teaspoon salt
2 cups all-purpose flour

Beat the butter or margarine until light. Beat in the sour cream or ice cream, sugar, vanilla or almond extract, and salt. Stir in the flour to make a soft dough. Divide the dough into 3 equal parts, form each part into a ball, flatten, wrap in plastic wrap, and refrigerate overnight. (The dough can be refrigerated for up to 1 week or frozen for up to 3 months.)

VARIATION
Wine Dough: Substitute ½ cup sweet wine and ½ cup vegetable oil for the butter and sour cream.

Jam Filling

2 cups finely chopped walnuts
1 cup shredded coconut
    (optional)
½ cup sugar
1 teaspoon ground cinnamon
2 cups apricot preserves, lekvar
    (prune preserves), or povidl
    (plum preserves)

Combine the nuts, coconut, if desired, sugar, and cinnamon. Spread the preserves over the dough and sprinkle with the nut mixture.

Teiglach

ASHKENAZIC HONEY DOUGH BALLS

36 TO 48 SMALL PASTRIES

Ancient man discovered that drizzling honey over fried and baked pieces of dough transformed them into a tasty treat. This ancient culinary practice, in the days before refrigeration and vacuum packaging, served another purpose, preserving foods. Thus soaking pastries and cakes in a syrup is a time-honored way of keeping them from drying out as well as refreshing them once stale. Baklava and *baba au rhum* are among the many delicious examples of this technique.

A popular dish among the ancient Romans was strips of fried dough in honey called *vermiculos* (see *chremslach*, page 215, for a history of this dish). Italian Jews adopted *vermiculos* and among its variations is a dish of deep-fried dough balls called *ceciarchiata* (referring to its resemblance to chickpeas, *ceci* in Italian). Sephardim prepare a version of this pastry called *pinonate*. It was among eastern European Jews, however, that these little pieces of dough in a honey syrup, called *teiglach* (dough pieces), gained the widest appeal. Ashkenazim traditionally enjoy this treat on such happy occasions as a Brit Milah, a wedding, and Purim (see page 316), but it is most prominently featured on Rosh Hashanah (see page 126), to symbolize the wish that the New Year will be a sweet one.

There are several variations of *teiglach:* The small dough pieces can be round, cylindrical, or tied into knots; the dough can be cooked in the syrup or baked first and then added to the syrup; a Passover version uses matza meal; and nuts or candied fruit can be added. Nuts were traditionally omitted from Rosh Hashanah *teiglach,* as eastern European Jews abstained from nuts on this holiday. Any leftover honey syrup was customarily saved and used to make other holiday dishes such as *lekach* (honey cakes), honey cookies, and tzimmes. The recipe can be doubled.

DOUGH

3 large eggs, lightly beaten (or 2 large eggs and 2 tablespoons vegetable oil)

½ teaspoon baking powder

¼ teaspoon salt

About 1¾ cups all-purpose flour, preferably unbleached

1. Preheat the oven to 350 degrees. Grease a large baking sheet. Oil a large plate or second baking sheet.

2. To make the dough: Combine the eggs, baking powder, and salt. Gradually stir in enough flour to make a soft, workable dough. Place on a lightly floured surface and, using floured hands, knead until smooth, 2 to 3 minutes.

3. Roll the dough into ⅓-inch-thick ropes. Cut into ⅓-inch pieces and roll each piece into a ball. (It is okay that the

SYRUP

1 cup honey

½ cup sugar

½ to 1 teaspoon ground ginger

1 cup coarsely chopped walnuts, blanched almonds, or hazelnuts (optional)

⅓ to ½ cup minced candied fruit (optional)

dough pieces are not smooth, as this will allow the honey to seep inside.)

4. Arrange the dough pieces in a single layer on the prepared baking sheet. Bake, shaking the pan occasionally, until very lightly browned, 10 to 15 minutes. Let cool.

5. To make the syrup: Stir the honey, sugar, and ginger in a large saucepan over low heat until the sugar dissolves. Stop stirring, increase the heat to medium-high, and bring to a boil. Reduce the heat to low and simmer for 10 minutes.

6. Add the dough pieces and cook, stirring frequently with a wooden spoon, for 10 minutes. Add the nuts and fruit, if desired, and cook until the syrup is a deep brown and the dough pieces sound hollow when tapped, about 10 additional minutes.

7. Pour the *teiglach* onto the oiled plate or baking sheet and let stand until cool enough to handle.

8. Using wet hands, shape into 2- to 3-inch mounds or shape into 1 large mound and cut into pieces. Let cool completely. Store in an airtight container at room temperature.

HAZELNUTS

Hazelnuts, also called filberts, probably originated in central Asia. They are particularly popular in western and central Europe, northwest Africa, and Turkey. These sweet, small, round, amber nuts are primarily eaten fresh but are also used in cakes and other desserts.

To skin hazelnuts, place the hazelnuts in a single layer in a baking pan and toast in a preheated 350-degree oven until lightly colored, 10 to 15 minutes. Place the nuts in a towel, cover, and let stand about 1 minute. Rub in the towel to loosen the skins. Method II: For each cup of hazelnuts, bring 3 cups of water to a boil. Add the nuts and ¼ cup baking soda and boil for 4 minutes. Drain, rinse under cold water, then rub off the skins. Toast in a preheated 350-degree oven until dry, 10 to 15 minutes.

Baklava

MIDDLE EASTERN NUT-FILLED PASTRY
24 TO 40 PASTRIES

Baklava, a Turkish treat that means "sweet-of-a-thousand-layers," is a traditional Purim dish throughout the Middle East, but it is also enjoyed throughout the year. A walnut filling is more prevalent in the Levant, while pistachios and pistachio-almond fillings are preferred in Iran. Blanched almonds are traditional on Rosh Hashanah to produce a light color so that the year should be *dulce y aclarada* (sweet and bright).

About 1 cup (2 sticks) butter or margarine, melted

4 cups (about 1 pound) finely chopped almonds, walnuts, pistachios, or any combination

½ cup sugar

2 teaspoons ground cinnamon or 1 teaspoon rose water or orange blossom water

¼ teaspoon ground cloves (optional)

1 pound phyllo dough

2 cups sugar syrup (see page 372), cooled

1. Preheat the oven to 350 degrees. Brush a 13-by-9-inch baking pan with the butter or margarine. Combine the nuts, sugar, cinnamon or flavored water, and, if desired, cloves.

2. Place a phyllo sheet in the prepared pan and lightly brush with the butter or margarine. Repeat layering and brushing with 6 more sheets. Spread with 1 cup of the nut mixture.

3. Cut the remaining phyllo sheets into 13-by-9-inch rectangles. Arrange 4 sheets in the pan, brushing each with the butter or margarine.

4. Repeat layering the nut mixture and phyllo 3 more times. End with a top layer of 6 sheets, trimming any overhanging edges. Baklava can be made with 1 nut layer or, as in this case, many.

5. With a sharp knife, cut 6 equal lengthwise strips (about 1½ inches wide) through the top layer of the pastry. (For very large pastries, cut 3 lengthwise strips.) Make 1- to 2-inch-wide diagonal cuts across the strips to form diamond shapes.

6. Just before baking, lightly sprinkle the top of the pastry with cold water. Bake until golden brown, about 1 hour.

7. Drizzle the cooled syrup slowly over the hot pastry. Cut through the scored lines and let cool at least 4 hours. Cover and store at room temperature or freeze.

Hint: If the baklava dries out while storing, drizzle with a little additional hot syrup.

Kadayif

MIDDLE EASTERN SHREDDED WHEAT PASTRY

ABOUT 12 PASTRIES

Kadayif—also spelled *kadaif, kadaife, kanafe,* and *konafa*—is unprocessed shredded wheat. Although Americans are most familiar with baklava, *kadayif* is equally as popular as a treat in the Middle East. It is available fresh or frozen in Middle Eastern and Greek specialty stores. Twelve ounces crumbled shredded wheat can be substituted for the *kadayif,* but the texture will be coarser. Nut-filled *kadayif* is a beloved Purim treat.

1½ cups (3 sticks) butter or
   margarine, melted and cooled
1 pound kadayif, *shredded*
1 recipe kadayif *filling (see*
   pages 352–53)
About 1½ cups sugar syrup
   (see page 372), cooled

1. Preheat the oven to 350 degrees.
2. Pour the butter or margarine over the *kadayif,* tossing to coat. Spread half of the *kadayif* in an ungreased 13-by-9-inch baking pan or a 10-inch round pie plate and press gently to flatten. Spread with the filling, then top with the remaining *kadayif.* Sprinkle with a few drops of water.
3. Bake until golden brown, about 45 minutes. Pour the cooled syrup over the hot pastry. For a smooth surface, invert onto a tray. Serve warm or cooled cut into 1- to 2-inch squares. Cover with plastic wrap and store at room temperature.

VARIATION

Multilayered Kadayif: Spread one-third of the *kadayif* in the baking dish, top with half of the filling, one-third of the *kadayif,* the remaining filling, then the remaining *kadayif.*

Individual Kadayif

18 TO 20 PASTRIES

1 pound kadayif

1 recipe kadayif *filling (see
    below)*

*1½ cups (3 sticks) butter or
    margarine, melted and cooled*

*About 3 cups sugar syrup
    (see page 372), cooked*

1. Preheat the oven to 350 degrees.

2. Unroll the *kadayif* and separate into 18 to 20 rectangles. Place a heaping tablespoon of the filling on the narrow end of each rectangle and roll up jelly roll style to enclose the filling.

3. Place on a lightly greased baking sheet, leaving a little room between each pastry. Drizzle with the melted butter or margarine and sprinkle with a few drops of water.

4. Bake until golden, 35 to 40 minutes. Pour the cooled syrup over the hot pastry.

Nut Kadayif Filling

*2 cups finely chopped blanched
    almonds, walnuts, unsalted
    pistachio nuts, or any
    combination*

¼ to ½ cup sugar

*1 teaspoon ground cinnamon or
    rose water*

*¼ teaspoon ground cloves or
    ½ teaspoon grated lemon zest
    (optional)*

Combine all of the ingredients.

VARIATION
Orange-Nut Filling: Add ½ cup orange juice.

Cheese Kadayif Filling

2 pounds ricotta cheese

2 tablespoons sugar

1 teaspoon rose water or ground cinnamon

Combine all of the ingredients.

Cream Kadayif Filling

¼ cup cornstarch

2 tablespoons sugar

2 cups milk

1 cup heavy cream

1. Combine the cornstarch and sugar. Gradually stir in 1 cup of the milk. Bring the remaining 1 cup milk to a low boil in a medium saucepan. Gradually stir in the cornstarch mixture.

2. Reduce the heat to low and stir until thickened. Remove from the heat and beat in the cream. Let cool.

VARIATIONS

Cheese-Cream Filling: Reduce the amount of cornstarch to 2 tablespoons and the milk to ½ cup plus 2 tablespoons. Cook the heavy cream with the milk, and after the filling is cooled, stir in 2 pounds ricotta cheese. If desired, add ½ teaspoon rose water and ½ teaspoon orange water.

Sour Cream Filling: Reduce the amount of milk to 1 cup. Cook the heavy cream with the milk, and after the filling cools slightly, stir in 1½ cups sour cream.

Travados

SEPHARDIC PASTRY HORNS

❧ ABOUT 50 COOKIES ❧

These filled crescents, the Sephardic version of the Middle Eastern *sambusak,* are a favorite pastry served on most holidays, particularly Purim (see page 316). Balkan Jews call these cookies *roscas di alhasu* (Haman's ears), an allusion to the curved shape's similarity to an ear. Moroccans enjoy a version called *kabulzel,* short for *kaab el h'zel* (gazelles' horns), with an almond paste (see page 362) filling.

DOUGH
1 cup vegetable oil
½ cup sweet wine
¼ cup sugar
½ teaspoon baking soda
⅛ teaspoon salt
About 4 cups all-purpose flour

GOMO DE MUEZ U
   ALMENDRA (WALNUT OR
   ALMOND FILLING)
2 cups ground walnuts or
   blanched almonds (or 1 cup
   ground nuts and 1 cup
   cooked rice)
½ cup honey or ⅓ cup orange
   marmalade (or ½ cup sugar
   and 2 tablespoons rose water,
   orange blossom water, or
   plain water)
⅛ to ¼ teaspoon ground
   cinnamon

1 recipe sugar syrup (see page
   372), or confectioners' sugar
   for dusting

1. Preheat the oven to 350 degrees. Grease 2 large baking sheets.
2. Combine the oil, wine, and sugar. Add the baking soda, salt, and 1 cup of the flour. Gradually add enough of the remaining flour to make a soft, nonsticky dough.
3. Form into 1-inch balls. On a lightly floured surface, roll out the balls into ⅛-inch-thick rounds about 3 inches in diameter.
4. Combine all of the filling ingredients.
5. Place a teaspoon of the filling in the center of each round and fold the edges over to form a half-moon, pinching the edges to seal. If desired, run a serrated pastry cutter around the curved side. Bend slightly to form a crescent.
6. Place about 1 inch apart on the prepared baking sheets. Bake until lightly browned, about 25 minutes. Transfer to a wire rack and let cool completely. (The *travados* may be frozen after cooling. Thaw before dipping into the syrup.)
7. Dip the cooled *travados* into the warm syrup, letting the excess syrup drip off. Or roll in confectioners' sugar. Place on a platter and let cool for at least 1 hour. Store in an airtight container.

VARIATION
Substitute ½ cup water for the wine and increase the amount of sugar to ½ cup.

Samsa

BUKHARAN FRIED DUMPLINGS
 ABOUT 30 DUMPLINGS

The caravans that traveled the Silk Road carried not only silks and spices but also the foods of China, including pasta. *Samsa,* the Bukharan version of fried wontons, are served on most festive occasions. Commercially prepared wonton wrappers can be used instead of homemade.

1½ cups all-purpose flour
½ teaspoon salt
About ⅔ cup lukewarm water
About 2 cups vegetable oil

FILLING
1½ cups ground walnuts
3 tablespoons sugar
1½ tablespoons butter or
margarine, softened

1. Combine the flour and salt. Stir in enough water to make a soft dough. Knead until smooth and pliable. Cover and let rest for 30 minutes.

2. On a lightly floured surface, roll out the dough into a thin rectangle about 18 by 15 inches. Cut into 3-inch squares. (Or roll out the dough in a pasta machine.)

3. Combine all of the filling ingredients. Put a teaspoon of the filling in the center of each square. Moisten the edges, bring the corners together to meet in the center, and press to seal. (The *samsa* can be frozen. Do not thaw; add about 3 minutes to the cooking time.)

4. Heat a wok or saucepan. Add at least 2 inches of oil and heat to 325 degrees.

5. In batches, deep-fry the *samsa,* turning frequently, until golden brown on all sides, about 3 minutes. Remove the *samsa* with a slotted spoon and drain on paper towels.

VARIATION
Meat-Filled Samsa: Substitute 1 recipe Sephardic meat filling (page 45) for the walnut filling.

CONFECTIONS

Honey and sweet food enlighten the eyes of man.
—TALMUD, YOMA 83B

Dulce de Bimbriyo

SEPHARDIC QUINCE PRESERVES

ABOUT 6 CUPS

The quince, a native of western Asia, is a tart-flavored, apple-shaped fruit with an intense aroma when ripe. Quinces must be cooked to be edible, since they have a hard, granular texture and an astringency when raw. The pale yellow flesh becomes pink and sweet when cooked. Poached quinces are often added to Middle Eastern meat stews or chicken dishes. Quince dishes are traditional Rosh Hashanah fare among Sephardim. In Greek and Iraqi communities, quince preserves and candied quinces are served on Rosh Hashanah in place of apples and honey. Persian Jews commonly serve stuffed quinces (*dolma bay*) on the Sabbath and Sukkoth. Candied quince is a beloved Passover treat.

Quinces, whose peel and core contain a high pectin content, have long been among the most popular fruits used to make jams. Indeed, they were the original fruit used to

Opposite: **A Jewish wedding in Baghdad, 1935.** *One of the first and greatest Jewish communities outside of Israel originated in 586 B.C.E. when the forces of Nebuchadnezzar captured Jerusalem and exiled much of the population to Babylonia. Baghdad, on the eastern bank of the Euphrates River, lies about 55 miles north of the ancient city of Babylon.*

make marmalade (from *marmelo,* the Portuguese word for "quince"). After marmalade reached Britain during the fourteenth century, the British began experimenting with fruits to substitute for the exotic quince and soon replaced them with oranges. Quince preserves, however, remain very popular in the Middle East.

4 medium quinces
   (about 3 pounds)
5 cups water
About 5 cups sugar
2 tablespoons lemon juice

1. Rub off any fuzz from the quinces. Core and, if desired, peel. Wrap the cores and peels in cheesecloth. (The peel contains a large amount of pectin.) Coarsely grate the pulp. (You should have about 5 cups.)

2. Place the cheesecloth bag into the water and bring to a boil. Add the grated quince pulp and parboil for 10 minutes. Add 1 cup of the sugar for each cup of grated quince and stir until dissolved.

3. Cook uncovered over medium heat, stirring occasionally, until the quinces are tender and pinkish in color, about 40 minutes.

4. Discard the cheesecloth bag. Add the lemon juice and return to a boil.

5. Pour into hot, sterilized jars, leaving a ¼-inch space on top. Clean the tops and threads of the jars with a damp cloth. Top with the lids, place in a boiling water bath, return to a boil, and boil for 15 minutes. Remove and let cool. (Unprocessed preserves can be stored in the refrigerator for up to 2 weeks.)

VARIATIONS

Honey Bimbriyo: Reduce the amount of sugar to 2 cups and add 2 cups honey.

Apple Preserves: Substitute 3 pounds apples for the quinces and reduce the cooking time to about 15 minutes.

Dulce de Cayeci

SEPHARDIC APRICOT GELS
ABOUT 36 CANDIES

Sephardim enjoy these confections on special occasions, especially Rosh Hashanah and Passover. Some Ashkenazim adopted this treat, which they call *aprikosen pletzlach*. Almost any fruit, fresh or dried, can be used in this dish, but hard fruits such as apples and quinces require cooking in water until soft before pureeing. Dried fruits need only to be soaked in water and they are ready to puree. The general rule of thumb is to use 1 cup of sugar for every cup of fruit pulp.

1 pound dried apricots
About 4 cups sugar
2 tablespoons lemon juice
Walnut halves or blanched
    whole almonds for garnish
    (optional)
Granulated or confectioners'
    sugar for dusting (optional)

1. Soak the apricots in water to cover for at least 2 hours or overnight. Drain, reserving 1 cup of the soaking liquid. Puree the apricots in a food grinder or food processor. (You should have about 4 cups.)

2. Combine the apricot pulp, reserved soaking liquid, sugar, and lemon juice in a large, heavy nonreactive saucepan (do not use iron, copper, or brass) over medium heat. Bring to a boil, reduce the heat to very low, and simmer, stirring frequently, until very thick, about 1 hour.

3. Pour the mixture onto a wet board or platter ½ inch thick. Refrigerate until set. Cut into 1-inch squares or diamonds. For fruit balls: Form into 1-inch balls (about 4 dozen) and, if desired, press a walnut half or blanched whole almond into each ball. If desired, roll in granulated or confectioners' sugar. Store between sheets of waxed paper in an airtight container at room temperature.

VARIATIONS

Dulce de Bimbriyo (Sephardic Quince Gels): Substitute 4 cups cooked quince pulp (about 3 pounds raw) for the apricots. For quince-apple gels: Use 2 pounds raw quinces and 1 pound tart apples.

Dulce de Mansana (Sephardic Apple Gels): Substitute 4 cups applesauce or cooked fresh apples (about 3 pounds raw) for the apricots.

Mishmish Helou (Syrian Apricot Gels): After the mixture thickens, stir in 1 to 2 cups ground unsalted pistachios or blanched almonds and, if desired, ½ teaspoon rose water.

Amsath (Indian Mango Confections): Substitute 4 cups strained mango pulp for the apricots. (*Note:* This is an Indian adaptation of the Middle Eastern apricot confection called *kamrooden* in Calcutta.)

Datils Rellenos

SEPHARDIC STUFFED DATES
 36 DATES

Stuffed dried fruits—also called *tamir mehshi* in Arabic and *forees* in Morocco—are a popular Sephardic treat. Although dates are the most prominent, you can stuff almost any dried fruit, including prunes and apricots.

36 whole almonds or 1 cup almond paste (see page 362)
36 medium pitted dates (about 1 pound)
Sugar for garnish or sugar syrup (see page 372) (optional)

Insert an almond into the center of each date. Or slit the dates open lengthwise, form the almond paste into thin rolls, place in the center of the dates, and press closed. Serve the dates plain, rolled in sugar, or dipped into cooled sugar syrup.

VARIATIONS

Apricot-and-Nut-Stuffed Dates: Mince ½ cup dried apricots and stir into the almond paste.

Sesame Dates: Blend together 1 tablespoon tahini (sesame seed paste), 1 tablespoon honey, 1 tablespoon water, and ½ teaspoon cinnamon. Roll the dates in the tahini mixture, then in sesame seeds, and place on waxed or parchment paper and let dry.

Badam Loozena

CALCUTTA ALMOND DIAMONDS

ABOUT 24 CANDIES

Loozena means "diamond," referring to the shape of these candies, which originated in the Middle East. *Loozena* is a traditional Purim treat in Calcutta.

1 cup sugar

6 tablespoons water

2 tablespoons rose water

1½ cups coarsely ground
   blanched almonds

1 teaspoon ground cinnamon
   (optional)

¼ teaspoon ground cardamom
   (optional)

1. Combine the sugar and water in a medium saucepan over medium-high heat. Bring to a boil and cook until the syrup reaches the thread stage or 230 degrees on a candy thermometer, about 8 minutes.

2. Stir in the rose water and cook for 1 minute. Add the almonds and, if desired, the spices. Cook until the mixture cleans the sides of the pan.

3. Spread the nut mixture onto an oiled baking sheet. Place a piece of greased waxed paper on top and roll out the mixture to an even ½-inch thickness. Immediately remove the paper. Cool slightly and, using a knife dipped into hot water, cut into diamonds. Store in an airtight container at room temperature.

VARIATIONS

Pista Loozena (Calcutta Pistachio Diamonds): Substitute 1½ cups coarsely ground unsalted pistachios for the almonds and omit the spices.

Nariyal Loozena (Calcutta Coconut Diamonds): Reduce the amount of water to ¼ cup, omit the cinnamon and cardamom, and substitute 2⅔ cups fresh grated coconut (or dried coconut moistened in 2 tablespoons water) for the almonds.

Tangerine Loozena (Calcutta Tangerine-Almond Diamonds): Substitute the juice and grated zest of 2 tangerines for the water and rose water.

Almendrada

ALMOND PASTE
ABOUT 1½ CUPS

Pounded almonds, a common ingredient in medieval kitchens, remained popular in Iberian and Sephardic cooking long after they fell out of use in the rest of Europe. Among the few almond dishes to retain their popularity were marzipan and almond paste. Marzipan is similar to almond paste but contains a larger amount of sugar and is cooked. The two should not be used interchangeably in recipes: Marzipan, which because of the higher sugar content is more malleable, is used in confections; almond paste, which has a more intense almond flavor, is used primarily in baked goods or for *fourées* (stuffed dried fruits).

Almond paste is a mixture of finely ground blanched almonds, sugar, and a binding agent. Egg whites produce a bright white paste, which is prominent at Sephardic weddings. Moroccan Jews often use egg yolks or whole eggs, producing an off-white color. Persians traditionally used fragrant rose water rather than expensive eggs. Since almond paste contains no flour, it makes a perfect Passover (see page 367) treat. A popular Greek treat for Purim (see page 316) is foot-shaped marzipan called *folares*. This recipe can be doubled (you can use 3 large egg whites or 4 small whites) or tripled.

1½ cups blanched almonds
1¾ cups confectioners' sugar or
   1 cup granulated sugar
   (or ½ cup confectioners' sugar
   and ¾ cup granulated sugar)
Pinch of salt
½ teaspoon almond extract or
   1 to 2 teaspoons orange
   blossom water or rose water
   (optional)
2 small egg whites, beaten until
   foamy

1. In a food processor or nut grinder, finely grind the almonds, sugar, and salt. If desired, add the almond extract or flavored water.
2. Add enough egg white to make a cohesive paste and knead until smooth, about 3 minutes. For colored almond paste, knead in several drops of food coloring. Wrap and refrigerate at least overnight, but preferably for 24 hours. (Almond paste can be stored in the refrigerator in an airtight container for at least 6 weeks and in the freezer for up to a year.) Let the paste come to room temperature before molding.

VARIATION
Persian Almond Paste: Omit the egg whites and increase the amount of rose water to ¼ cup. Or use ¼ cup water and 1 teaspoon rose water.

Masaban

SYRIAN ALMOND CONFECTION

ABOUT 72 CANDIES

1 recipe Persian almond paste
  or regular almond paste
  (opposite page)
About ½ cup ground unsalted
  pistachios

1. Remove 1 teaspoon of the almond paste and shape into a ball. Press the ball with the bottom of a glass to flatten. Sprinkle lightly with the pistachios, pressing gently into the paste. Repeat with the remaining almond paste.

2. Transfer to ungreased baking sheets and let stand, uncovered, at room temperature for 1 day. Store in an airtight container at room temperature.

ALMONDS

The almond, the kernel of a peachlike fruit native to the Middle East, comes from one of the earliest cultivated trees. There are two kinds of almonds—sweet and bitter. The sweet almond is edible; the bitter almond contains poisonous prussic acid and is therefore rarely available in America. When the bitter almond's harmful acid is removed, the remaining pulp is fermented and distilled to produce almond extract.

Almonds play an important role in all forms of Jewish tradition and cooking: They are one of only two nuts (with pistachios) explicitly mentioned in the Bible—as one of the "fruits of the land" sent by Jacob to Pharaoh (Genesis 43:11), as the rod of Aaron (Numbers 17:8), and as a symbol of human life (Ecclesiastes 12:5).

Hint: To blanch almonds, place in boiling water until the skins begin to wrinkle, 3 to 5 minutes. Drain, and rub off the skins.

IN THE SYRIAN STYLE

"In many ways, Syrian food is representative of Middle Eastern cuisine," explains Rae Dayan. "But it has its own identity. Syrians are known for the spiciness of their foods, the delicateness of their meze [appetizers], and extremely sweet desserts often drenched in syrup."

A strong Jewish presence in the land to the north of Israel dates back to biblical days. In Roman times, the Jewish community of Syria was one of the largest and wealthiest in the world. Tamerlane's sacking of Syria in 1400 greatly reduced the size and vibrancy of its Jewish community, but the Ottoman conquest in 1516 and the subsequent arrival of a large number of Sephardim resulted in a revival. Aleppo emerged as the center of trade between the Ottoman Empire and Europe, while Damascus became a banking center, with Syrian Jews playing a major role in these activities.

The cuisine of Syria is a blending of Persian, Arabic, Turkish, and Iberian influences. Dayan notes, "Elaborate meals are associated with various occasions in the community. The Sabbath, holidays, and other special occasions give Syrians opportunities to display their culinary, decorative, and organizational skills, subsumed under the term *suffeh*. Syrian women take pride in their *suffeh,* which requires much planning and preparation.

"Shabbat to a Syrian family revolves around the *keneese* [synagogue] and the table. To mark special events such as birthdays and anniversaries, *sebits* [buffets] are held at home following Sabbath morning services.

Although today many Syrians serve egg challah on the Sabbath, in Syria they served pita," she explains. In Syrian homes, the host tears the challah and tosses the pieces to fellow diners—placing food directly into someone's hand is a sign of mourning.

"A traditional Syrian Rosh Hashanah dinner might include *silka* [boiled Swiss chard or spinach], *karte* [sweet-and-sour meatballs and leeks], *lubiya m'sallat* [black-eyed peas with veal], fried or stuffed summer squash, and *ras-ib-adjway* [date-filled cookies] and *hellou* [candied fruits or vegetables]," Dayan continues. "Kaak [cookie rings], *sambusak*, and *jiben* [vegetable and cheese casserole] are traditional at the meal following Yom Kippur. Syrians adapt many of their favorite dishes for Passover, including matza meal *lahamagine* [small pies], *sambusak*, and *edjeh* [pancakes]. A typical Syrian Seder meal is composed of veal breast stuffed with fava beans or mushrooms, braised lamb shanks, rice with sour *kibbe* or *kibbe* with cherries, roast chicken baked with potatoes, and sweetbreads with mushrooms."

The period of time before a wedding calls for several parties, and one of the most beloved customs at this time is the *swenne*. Dayan explains, "A week before the wedding, the mother of the groom presents the bride-to-be with a table of perfumes, robes, candlesticks, and a silver tray bearing *lebas* [Jordan almonds] and *kaak ib loz* [nut confections] surrounded by flowers. Of course, a luncheon featuring Syrian favorites follows the *swenne*."

Kaak ib Loz

SYRIAN ALMOND BRACELET

ABOUT 36 RINGS

1 recipe almond paste (see page 362)

About 36 unsalted pistachios (optional)

1. Form the almond paste into 1-inch balls. Roll each ball into a 4- to 6-inch-long rope. Bring the ends together to form a ring. If desired, press a pistachio into the point of connection.

2. Arrange the rings on foil-lined baking sheets. Place under the broiler until pink, about 2 minutes. Let cool.

3. Invert the rings and place under the broiler for a few seconds to dry. Store in an airtight container at room temperature.

VARIATION

Mogados (Sephardic Almond Sticks): Roll the almond paste into a ¾-inch-thick rope and cut the rope into 1½-inch-long sections. (*Note:* These are a common sight at Sephardic weddings.)

Muez con Almendrada

MOROCCAN ALMOND-WALNUT CONFECTION

ABOUT 36 CANDIES

About 3 cups walnut halves

A few drops of green food coloring

1 recipe Persian almond paste or regular almond paste (see page 362)

1. Preheat the oven to 350 degrees.

2. Spread the walnuts in a single layer on ungreased baking sheets and toast until lightly colored, about 10 minutes. Let cool.

3. Knead the food coloring into the almond paste. Form the paste into 1-inch balls. Press a walnut half onto 2 opposite sides of each almond ball.

Noent

ASHKENAZIC HONEY-NUT CANDY

 ABOUT 48 PIECES

Honey candies are popular Ashkenazic Passover, Purim, and Hanukkah treats. The basic recipe is varied by adding poppy seeds, sesame seeds, matza, carrots, or spices. When ground ginger is added, the candy is called *ingberlach* (*ingber* is the Yiddish word for "ginger"). When the ginger is omitted, the candy is sometimes called *pletzlach* (board), because it is spread into a thin layer to cool. Since honey syrups absorb moisture from the air, it is advisable not to make this candy on a humid day.

1 cup sugar

2 cups honey

4 to 6 cups finely chopped
*   walnuts, pecans, or almonds*

1. Cook the sugar and honey over medium-low heat, stirring frequently with a wooden spoon, until the sugar dissolves, about 10 minutes.

2. Gradually add the nuts and continue cooking, stirring frequently and being careful not to burn the syrup, until the mixture is very thick and reaches the soft-crack stage or 280 degrees on a candy thermometer. (The candy will remain chewy at this stage; if it reaches the hard-crack stage—300 degrees—it turns brittle.)

3. Spoon the mixture onto a wet board or oiled baking sheet and spread to a ¼- to ½-inch thickness. Let cool until firm but not hard, about 10 minutes. Using a sharp knife dipped into hot water, cut into squares or diamonds. (The mixture can also be dropped by spoonfuls onto oiled baking sheets.) If desired, wrap the individual candies in plastic wrap or waxed paper. Store in an airtight container at room temperature.

VARIATIONS

Farfel Ingberlach (Ashkenazic Matza-Ginger Candy): Reduce the amount of nuts to 1½ cups and add 1 teaspoon ground ginger with the honey. After the syrup reaches the soft-crack stage, stir in 2 to 3 cups matza farfel (coarsely crumbled) and the nuts, and spoon onto a wet or oiled surface.

Mohnlach (Ashkenazic Poppy Seed Candy): Substitute 3 cups poppy seeds for the nuts. (Some versions add 1 to 2 cups chopped nuts.)

Mehren Pletzlach (Ashkenazic Carrot Candy): Reduce the amount of nuts to 1 cup. Add 2 cups (1 pound) finely grated carrots with the honey and simmer over low heat until thickened, about 1 hour. Stir in the nuts and spoon onto a wet or oiled surface. For *Mehren Ingberlach (Carrot-Ginger Candy):* Add 1 teaspoon ground ginger with the carrots.

Tzikel Pletzlach (Ashkenazic Beet Candy): Reduce the nuts to 1 cup. Add 2 cups (1 pound) finely grated beets with the honey and simmer over low heat until thickened, about 1 hour. Stir in the nuts and spoon onto a wet or oiled surface.

PASSOVER

Passover is an eight-day holiday (seven in Israel) commemorating the Exodus from Egypt. A ceremonial dinner called the Seder ("order" in Hebrew) is held on the first two nights of the festival (on the first night in Israel). In the time the Temple stood, the Seder centered on the paschal sacrifice, making ample use of the abundance of spring lambs. However, for the past two thousand years the paramount Passover symbol has been matza, a flat, crackerlike, unleavened bread.

During the Seder, the Passover story is recounted and relived through a progression of symbols and ceremonies as recorded in the Haggadah (literally "retelling"). On the table are three whole matzot and six traditional symbols: *maror*—a bitter herb, symbolizing the bitterness of the slavery experience; *charoseth*—a fruit mixture symbolizing the mortar that was used to construct buildings while in slavery; *karpas*—a green vegetable, such as celery or parsley, representing spring and renewal; *chazeret*—lettuce used for the Hillel sandwich (in the Baltic states, cabbage had to be substituted for the lettuce); *betzah*—a roasted hard-cooked egg, representing the festival sacrifice; and *zeroah*—a roasted shank bone or poultry neck, representing the paschal sacrifice. The Ashkenazic Seder adopted European characteristics in place of the original Middle Eastern flavor: no longer serving lamb; substituting horseradish for the bitter herbs and, when necessary, radishes or potatoes for the green vegetable; using salt water instead of vinegar for dipping; and replacing the Oriental small, low tables or trays, which were carried in and out of the room, with a Seder plate.

SESAME SEEDS

Upon ripening, the pods of a herbaceous Middle Eastern plant split open to reveal a cache of small oval seeds that have long been an important part of Middle Eastern cooking. There are two basic varieties of sesame—tan and black. The tan seeds, which are also hulled and sold as white seeds, possess a nutty sweet flavor. Black seeds are more pungent than the lighter ones. Unless otherwise specified, always use the tan or white seeds. Toasting brings out the seeds' attributes—to toast, stir the seeds in a dry skillet until lightly browned.

Sesame seeds are greatly valued in Sephardic cooking. Whole seeds are used to add flavor and texture to chicken, fish, and vegetables. Sesame oil—the seeds contain about 50 percent oil—has long been used not only for cooking but also to fuel lamps. Middle Eastern sesame oil is made from raw sesame seeds, while Oriental sesame oil— which has a dark brown color and nutty flavor—is made from toasted sesame seeds.

Ground sesame seeds are used to make a paste called *tahini*. Among the many uses of this paste is in making a sauce called *tarator bi tahina*. To make about 1⅓ cups *tarator bi tahina*, mix 1 cup *tahini*, about ½ cup water, 3 tablespoons lemon juice, 1 to 2 minced cloves garlic, and about ¾ teaspoon salt.

Susamit

MIDDLE EASTERN SESAME SEED CANDY
❧ ABOUT 36 LARGE OR 72 SMALL PIECES ❧

Sesame-honey candies, an ancient confection, originated in the Middle East, then spread to North Africa, India, and even to many parts of eastern Europe. Sesame candies—called *pasteli* in the Balkans, *simsimee* in Calcutta, and, on Purim *psires tou Amman* ("fleas of Haman") in Greece—are a standard holiday treat.

2 cups sesame seeds
1½ cups honey (or 1 cup honey
  and 1 cup sugar)

1. Stir the sesame seeds in a large dry skillet over medium heat until lightly colored, about 5 minutes. Transfer to a bowl and let cool.

2. Boil the honey in a 3-quart saucepan over medium heat until it thickens and reaches the soft-ball stage, or 235 degrees on a candy thermometer, about 5 minutes.

3. Add the sesame seeds and cook, stirring constantly, until the syrup reaches the hard-ball stage or 265 degrees, about 5 minutes.

4. Pour onto an oiled baking sheet or marble slab. Place a piece of greased waxed paper on top, roll out to an even ¼- to ½-inch thickness, and immediately remove the paper.

5. Let stand until firm but not completely cooled, about 10 minutes. Dip a sharp knife into hot water and cut the candy into rectangles, squares, or diamonds. Wrap the individual candies in plastic wrap or waxed paper and store in an airtight container at room temperature.

VARIATION

Gozinakhi (Georgian Walnut and Honey Candy): Substitute 3 cups finely chopped walnuts for the sesame seeds.

Opposite: **Banquet to celebrate a circumcision, Algeria.** Lithograph from *Voyage Pittoresque dans la Régence d'Alger*, Paris 1835. *Personal milestones, ranging from birth to death, are commemorated throughout the year as circumstances dictate. These life-cycle events take place in the presence of family and friends, thereby reinforcing the bonds of community. And food is an integral part of Jewish celebrations.*

SAUCES, CONDIMENTS, AND MISCELLANEOUS

Arrope

SEPHARDIC RAISIN SYRUP

 ABOUT 3 CUPS

Raisins have long been used in the Middle East to make honey, liquor, and syrup. This is a popular Sephardic Passover treat, customarily served with *bimuelos de massa* (matza pancakes; see page 216), and *revanadas de parida* (fried matzot, literally "toast of the new mother").

1 pound (about 3 cups) dark raisins

6 cups water

1 tablespoon lemon juice

1. Soak the raisins in the water until plump, about 15 minutes.

2. Bring to a boil, cover, reduce the heat to low, and simmer until very soft, about 2 hours. Strain through a sieve or food mill, discarding the skins.

3. Add the lemon juice. Simmer, uncovered, over low heat, stirring occasionally, until the syrup thickens, about 30 minutes.

***Opposite:* Passover Seder in Frankfurt, Germany. Painting by Moritz Daniel Oppenheim (1799–1882).** *During the Seder, the Passover story is recounted and relived through a progression of symbols and ceremonies as recorded in the Haggadah. On the table are three whole matzot and six traditional symbols:* maror *(bitter herb),* charoseth *(a fruit mixture),* karpas *(a vegetable),* chazeret *(lettuce),* betzah *(roasted egg), and* zeroah *(roasted bone).*

Sugar Syrup

   ABOUT 1½ CUPS

This basic syrup, composed of two parts sugar to one part water, is called *atar* in the Middle East and is used there to soak pastries, a way of preserving and moistening them. A thinner syrup, using equal amounts of sugar and water and cooked to 205 degrees, is sometimes used for lighter baked goods such as sponge cake. When pouring syrup over pastry, the rule is to use cold syrup and hot pastry or vice versa. The contrast in temperatures allows the baked goods to absorb the syrup, producing a moist rather than soggy result.

2 cups sugar (or 1 cup sugar
*   and 1 cup honey)*
1 cup water
2 teaspoons lemon juice

Combine all of the ingredients in a heavy 1-quart saucepan. Bring to a boil, stirring frequently. Reduce the heat to medium-low and simmer, without stirring, until the mixture is syrupy or registers 212 degrees on a candy thermometer, about 10 minutes. Let cool. Store in the refrigerator.

VARIATIONS

Cinnamon Syrup: Add 1 cinnamon stick or ½ teaspoon ground cinnamon.

Orange Syrup: Just before removing the syrup from the heat, stir in 1 tablespoon orange blossom water. Or add 1 tablespoon grated orange zest with the sugar.

Rose Syrup: Just before removing the syrup from the heat, stir in 1 tablespoon rose water.

SUGAR

Sugar cane is a tropical grass that grows to twenty or more feet and one to two inches in diameter. The word *sugar* is derived from the Sanskrit word *sarkara* ("grit" or "sand"), referring to sugarcane crystals. Long before its appearance in the West, Indians were adding crude sugar crystals to their foods.

Sugar was not a common commodity in the ancient world. It is mentioned only twice in the Bible, and then in references that reflect its rarity and foreignness: "You have brought me no sweet cane" (Isaiah 43:24) and "To what purpose is to Me the frankincense that comes from Sheba and the sweet cane from a far country?" (Jeremiah 6:20). The first mention of sugar by a Westerner can be found in the accounts of Nearchus, a Greek general who was introduced to the "honey reed" during Alexander the Great's campaign in India. Still, it was centuries before sugar became well known in the West.

The Arabs were the first to learn how to refine sugar cane, and the Nile River Valley became the home of the world's finest *sukkar,* primarily controlled by Egyptian Jews. By the tenth century, sugar had generally replaced honey in the Arab world. The Crusaders returned from the Middle East with a taste for the then exotic sweetener, which was soon mentioned by the Franco-German commentator Rashi (1040–1105). The Venetians developed a method of refining the cane into uniform crystals and gained a monopoly over Europe's sugar trade. Yet because of its high price, sugar remained the province of the upper class until the price dropped in the seventeenth century.

Sugar's first use in Europe was as a mask for the bitter taste of medicine, a role not unknown today. Apothecaries possessed exclusive rights to dispense it. For the next two centuries, because of its high price, sugar was the sole province of the upper class. The masses continued to rely on honey for sweetening.

In 1747, a German chemist named Andreas Marggraf discovered the process of producing sucrose from sugar beets. Sugar beets, unlike sugarcane, which grows only in tropical and subtropical climates, flourish in temperate climates. The first sugar beet refining factory was established in Silesia, Germany (now Poland), in 1786. About 1800, Jacob Herz Beer, father of opera composer Giacomo von Meyerbeer, established a sugar beet refinery in Goritz, near Venice. Soon the price of sugar plummeted and its availability rose. Ashkenazim who lived in regions where sugar beets grew, such as southwestern Poland, developed a preference for sweeter dishes and added plenty of sugar to their gefilte fish, kugels, and challah, while those from areas such as Galicia, where sugar remained an expensive item, generally used much less or no sugar in their cooking.

Agristada

SEPHARDIC EGG-LEMON SAUCE

 ABOUT 1⅓ CUPS; 3 TO 4 SERVINGS

*A*gristada is an ancient Mediterranean egg-thickened sauce called *avgolemono* in Greece, *brodo brusco* in Italy, and *beda b'lemune* in the Levant. Originally, this sauce was made with *agresto* (verjuice), an acidic and fruity juice made from unripe grapes. After lemons became prevalent in the West, they generally replaced the harder-to-find *agresto* as the souring agent in this sauce. (Vinegar is too sharp.) In the Balkans and the Levant, *agristada* serves a role similar to that of mayonnaise in the West, accompanying mild-flavored foods such as fried or poached fish, veal, poached chicken, brains, stuffed cabbage, rice, and fried cauliflower. For a brighter color and flavor, add a pinch of turmeric.

2 large eggs, lightly beaten
Juice of 1 large lemon
Salt to taste
1 cup water, chicken broth, or
  fish broth
1 tablespoon all-purpose flour or
  matza cake meal (optional)

1. Blend together the eggs, lemon juice, and salt. Gradually stir the water or broth into the flour to dissolve. (A little flour or matza meal is added to this sauce to help prevent it from separating, but it can be omitted.) Whisk into the egg mixture. (The ingredients can also be mixed in a blender.)
2. Cook in a 1-quart saucepan over medium-low heat, stirring constantly with a wooden spoon or whisk, until smooth and thickened, about 3 minutes. Do not boil. Serve warm or pour into a bowl, press a piece of plastic wrap against the surface, and let cool. Store *agristada* in the refrigerator.

FISH IN LEMON SAUCE

A distinctive dish among Iberian Jews was fish smothered in a tart egg sauce flavored with *agresto* (verjuice), pomegranate juice, or lemons. The latter combination remains popular today and, in many Sephardic households, poached fish fillets in *agristada*, called *pescado con huevo y limón* (fish in egg-lemon sauce), is served either warm or chilled as *la prima noche de Pesach* (the first course of the Passover Seder dinner) and on the Sabbath. (Use 2 to 3 pounds of skinless firm-fleshed fish fillets, such as striped bass, cod, flounder, haddock, halibut, grouper, or pike, for 6 to 8 servings.) This dish eventually spread to eastern Europe, where it was called *scharfe fische*.

Bazha

GEORGIAN WALNUT SAUCE

ABOUT 1 CUP

The Georgian love of walnuts manifests itself in dozens of walnut sauces, adapted from Persian cuisine, which are served with almost everything, including poultry, fish, meat, and vegetables. The most versatile of these sauces is *bazha*. Typical of Georgian cuisine, this uncooked sauce is slightly tart, as sweeteners are not used in cooking. The thickness of *bazha* varies according to the nature of the dish: a thicker sauce for *pkhali;* a thinner sauce for poultry and fish. *Satsivi,* a favorite Georgian party dish, is a richer, more elaborate walnut sauce served with poached poultry.

1 cup walnut pieces
3 to 4 cloves garlic
About ½ teaspoon salt
2 to 3 tablespoons chopped fresh coriander
½ teaspoon ground coriander
¼ teaspoon ground fenugreek
¼ teaspoon cayenne
¼ teaspoon ground turmeric or ½ teaspoon ground dried marigold petals
2 tablespoons red wine vinegar
About ⅓ cup water

1. With a mortar and pestle or in a food processor, grind the walnuts, garlic, and salt into a paste. Add the fresh coriander, ground coriander, fenugreek, cayenne, and turmeric or marigold.
2. Stir in the vinegar and enough water to make a sauce the consistency of heavy cream. Store in the refrigerator. The sauce thickens as it stands and may require thinning with a little water.

VARIATION

Substitute 1 to 2 seeded and minced jalapeño chilies for the fenugreek.

Ashkenazic Charoseth

❧ ABOUT 2½ CUPS ☙

This recipe is virtually identical in Ashkenazic communities from Alsace to the Ukraine. Ashkenazic *charoseth* tends to be a little chunkier in texture than Sephardic versions. In eastern Europe, many people could not afford to make *charoseth* at home, but obtained a little from the wealthier members of the community or purchased it from wine merchants. Today, the ingredients are inexpensive and easy to find in any grocery store.

3 large apples (about 1 pound), unpeeled but cored
½ to 1 cup chopped almonds or walnuts
1 to 2 tablespoons honey
About 1 teaspoon ground cinnamon
About ¼ cup sweet red wine

Combine the apples, nuts, honey, and cinnamon. Stir in enough wine to make a paste that holds together. Store in the refrigerator. Serve at room temperature.

Sephardic Charoseth

❧ ABOUT 2¼ CUPS ☙

There are many variations of Sephardic *charoseth*. Sometimes fruits such as apricots, raisins, oranges, pears, and prunes are added. Some contain a combination of almonds, walnuts, and pine nuts, while some are nutless. Some add a little wine vinegar or lemon juice for tartness, others a little honey or sugar. Some mix in chopped hard-boiled eggs. Some are cooked, while others are uncooked. Usually the *charoseth* is served as a paste, but sometimes it is formed into 1-inch balls. The common denominator among these many variations is that they all contain a large proportion of dates and the mixture is always made as a thick paste.

1⅓ cups chopped pitted dates
¾ to 1 cup chopped walnuts or almonds
About ¼ cup sweet red wine

Finely chop together the dates and nuts. Add enough wine to make a thick paste. Store in the refrigerator. Serve at room temperature.

VARIATION

Turkish Charoseth: Add 1 cup finely chopped dried figs, 1 cup finely chopped raisins or dried apricots, and 1 peeled, cored, and chopped apple.

Yemenite Charoseth

ABOUT 2 CUPS

15 dried figs, chopped

15 medium pitted dates, chopped

2 to 3 tablespoons sesame seeds, lightly toasted

1 teaspoon ground cinnamon

1 teaspoon ground ginger

Dash of ground coriander or cardamom

1 small chili or pinch of cayenne

Dry red wine

Finely chop the figs, dates, sesame seeds, cinnamon, ginger, coriander or cardamom, and chili or cayenne. Stir in enough wine to make a paste. Store in the refrigerator. Serve at room temperature.

CHAROSETH

Charoseth is a mixture of chopped fruit devised more than two thousand years ago to blunt the taste of the bitter herbs at the Passover Seder. *Charoseth*—a name derived from *cheres*, the Hebrew word for "clay"—symbolizes the mortar that the Israelites used to build with while in slavery in Egypt. The ingredients in this dish vary among communities, depending on symbolic meaning and availability. Sephardim and Yemenites use dried fruits that grew in Israel during biblical times—most notably dates, figs, and raisins. Since few of these fruits were available to Ashkenazim, they turned to a biblical fruit that thrives in the climate of much of Europe, apples. Italians and some Sephardim use both dried fruits and fresh apples, while Persians use a mixture of dates, apples, and pomegranates. Some Israelis add bananas, oranges, and lemons to zest up the basic Ashkenazic mixture.

Ground nuts are usually added to thicken the mixture, and red wine, in remembrance of the plague of blood, to loosen it. A little honey is often mixed in for extra sweetness. The final touch to *charoseth* is the addition of long-shaped spices, primarily cinnamon and ginger, symbolizing the straw with which the Israelites made bricks in Egypt.

Halek

CALCUTTA DATE SYRUP

ABOUT 2 CUPS SYRUP; 3 CUPS *CHAROSETH*

One of man's earliest sweeteners was in the form of honeylike pastes made from fruits such as dates and grapes. Indeed, Jewish tradition holds that the biblical description of Israel as the "land flowing with milk and honey" refers to date honey. In many locations in the Middle East and North Africa, *hullake* (date honey) serves as the basis for a version of *charoseth*.

Many Iraqi Jews prepare a syrupy variation of date honey, and Middle Eastern immigrants in Calcutta make a similar syrup called *halek*. Since this version requires a great deal of effort to prepare, it is usually made in a large quantity only once a year just before Passover. The leftover *halek* is then used throughout the rest of the year to add a distinctive touch to desserts.

1½ pounds pitted dates
1 cup finely chopped walnuts or
    almonds

1. Place the dates in a large bowl and add enough water to cover. Soak until soft, at least 24 hours. In a food processor or blender, puree the dates and soaking liquid. Let stand overnight.

2. In batches, place a little of the date mixture in a linen towel and squeeze out the liquid. Discard the solids left in the towel. (Some people use a small manual wine press in place of the more tedious towel method.)

3. In a saucepan, bring the date liquid to a boil over medium-high heat. Reduce the heat to medium-low and simmer, skimming the surface and stirring occasionally, until thickened and reduced to about 2 cups, about 1 hour.

4. Let cool, then pour into a jar. Store in the refrigerator. If sugar crystallizes, place the bottle in a bowl of hot water until the syrup is smooth.

5. To make the *charoseth,* stir the nuts into the 2 cups of *halek*.

Z'chug

YEMENITE GREEN CHILI PASTE

❧ ABOUT 2 CUPS ❧

There are many versions of this Yemenite green chili paste. Traditionally, the chilies are pounded with garlic in a mortar or on a flat stone, then spices are added. A blender makes the process much easier. *Z'chug* is fiery and therefore often served with crushed tomatoes or diluted with a little *chilbeh* (Yemenite fenugreek relish; see page 14) or tahini (sesame seed paste) to soften its potency. Add a little *z'chug* to stews and salads, and to meat, poultry, and fish sauces, or serve with such traditional dishes as *miloach* (Yemenite flaky bread; see page 271).

1 cup pureed small green chilies

1½ cups chopped fresh coriander (or ¾ cup chopped fresh coriander and ¾ cup chopped fresh parsley)

4 to 5 cloves garlic, crushed

1 teaspoon ground cumin or caraway seeds

1 to 2 teaspoons ground black pepper

1 teaspoon salt

3 to 5 cardamom pods or ¼ to ¾ teaspoon ground cardamom

2 tablespoons olive oil or 3 tablespoons lemon juice

Puree all of the ingredients to produce a paste. Store, covered, in the refrigerator for up to several months.

VARIATION

Shatta (Yemenite Red Chili Paste): Substitute 1 cup pureed red chilies for the green chilies. (Note: Red chilies tend to be milder than green ones.)

HINTS:

Most of the fire in chilies comes from the white membrane and seeds, so remove them if the chilies are too hot for your taste. When working with chilies, never touch your eyes or an open cut.

If the strength of the chilies in a dish begins to burn your mouth, do not reach for a beer or a glass of water—alcohol and water actually intensify the heat of capsaicin and spread it to the stomach. On the other hand, dairy products (such as milk and yogurt) mute the capsaicin, and bread absorbs it.

Choose smooth, shiny, firm pods that feel heavy for their size. Avoid those with soft spots and wrinkles.

Chrain mit Tzikel

EASTERN EUROPEAN HORSERADISH WITH BEETS

❧ ABOUT 1½ CUPS ☙

*Horseradish that does not bring a pious tear to the
eye is not God's horseradish.*

—SHALOM ALEICHEM, *TEVYE THE DAIRYMAN*

Horseradish is a fiery, white perennial root native to southeastern Europe. The root, which
can reach depths of two feet, grows best in cool climates and marshy land. After grating, it
loses its volatile oils and the bite fades quickly if not preserved. Vinegar is the most often
used preservative. Beets and sometimes sugar are frequently added to horseradish to
mellow the taste.

The sinus-clearing pungency of *chrain* (Yiddish for "horseradish," from the Slavic
khrin) has earned its place in Jewish cuisine as a topping for gefilte fish and sometimes as
the bitter herb at the Passover Seder. But horseradish proves much more versatile, as it
goes well with cold meats, vegetables, and fish. Add a generous amount for a tangy flavor
or just a bit for a subtle taste to salads, soups, or casseroles.

1 (4-inch-long) horseradish root,
    peeled and finely grated
2 medium beets, cooked, peeled,
    and finely grated
2 to 4 tablespoons distilled white
    or cider vinegar
About 2 teaspoons kosher salt
1 teaspoon sugar

Combine all of the ingredients, seasoning to taste. Let stand
at room temperature for 2 hours. Cover and store in the
refrigerator for up to 3 weeks.

Opposite: **Man selling greens in Jerusalem's Machane Yehudah
market, 1988.** *Some Halakhic authorities considered lettuce the preferable green to use for* maror *(the bitter herb) at the Passover Seder, since
"just as lettuce is first sweet and then (when left in the field too long)
bitter, so was the behavior of the Egyptians to our ancestors" (Talmud
Jerusalem, Pesach 2: 5, 29c).*

Huevos Haminados

SEPHARDIC BROWN EGGS

12 SERVINGS

In ancient Israel, eggs were collected from wild birds, making them an infrequent food and one scarcely mentioned in the Bible (Deuteronomy 22:6). With the widespread dissemination of the chicken during the Second Commonwealth period, eggs became an important part of the Jewish diet, as reflected by their prominent role in the Talmud and rabbinic literature. Eggs are cited as the only food that becomes harder as it is cooked, symbolic of Jewish history, and are regarded as a symbol of both fertility and death.

Originally, these eggs—called *huevos haminados* in Ladino or beid hamin in Arabic— were buried alongside the Sabbath stew in the embers of a wood-burning oven and left to bake overnight. With the advent of the modern stove, Sephardim developed the following technique to prepare one of their favorite dishes. The combination of a long cooking time, oil, and onion skins (usually saved from the previous week's cooking) gives these eggs a deep brown color, a creamy texture, and a rich flavor. *Haminados* are ubiquitous to nearly all Sephardic celebrations and life-cycle events, including the Sabbath desayuno (breakfast; see page 29), festival meals, Passover Seder, and *Seudat Havra'ah* (meal of consolation following a burial). Because of the similarity of the word *hamin* to Haman, the villain of Purim, *haminados* became a traditional Purim food and many Sephardim prepare pastries encasing hard-boiled eggs, representing Haman in jail. Cooks usually make a large batch of *haminados*, ensuring that there will be leftovers to add to salads during the following week.

Skins from 12 large onions
12 large eggs, at room temperature
About 4 quarts water
About 3 tablespoons oil

1. Arrange the onion skins in the bottom of a large pot. Place the unbroken eggs on top and pour in the water to cover.
2. Bring to a boil. Drizzle with the oil to cover the surface, cover the pot, and simmer over very low heat or bake in a 225-degree oven for 8 to 12 hours. Serve warm or at room temperature.

VARIATION
Omit the onion skins and oil and add ½ cup strong coffee and 1 teaspoon salt.

Index

(Page numbers in *italic* refer to illustrations.)

Photo Credits

Courtesy of the Library of the Jewish Theological
    Seminary of America: 8, 21, 24, 38, 60, 64, 86,
    96, 107, 133, 138, 146, 153, 178, 186, 211, 228,
    241, 278, 297, 316
Bill Aron: 6, 35, 81
Bettmann Archives: 52, 74, 142, 200, 217, 250, 287,
    313
Jewish Museum/Art Resource: 68, 122 *Page 68:*
    S0058298, JM4-63, black-and-white print.
    Kaufmann, Isidor. *Friday Evening.* Ca. 1920. Oil on
    canvas, 28½ x 35½ inches. Gift of Mr. and Mrs. M.
    R. Schweitzer. Jewish Museum, New York,
    U.S.A. *Page 122:* S0045995, black-and-white

print. Cholent pot. (Jewish Sabbath Stew Pot)
    Jewish Museum, New York, U.S.A.
YIVO Collection: 110, 157, 255, 259
Richard T. Nowitz: 150, 196, 381
Courtesy of Tabby and John Corré: 172
From the collection of Diana Newman and Isaac
    Corré: 167
Joint Distribution Committee: 262, 266, 271, 273
Israel Museum Jerusalem: 304, 337, 356
Ed Serotta/Joint Distribution Committee: 325
Foto Marburg/Art Resource: 370: S0059245, 1106522,
    black-and-white print. Oppenheim, Moritz
    Daniel. Passover Seder. Location not indicated.

Metric Equivalencies

Liquid and Dry Measures

CUSTOMARY	METRIC
¼ teaspoon	1.25 milliliters
½ teaspoon	2.5 milliliters
1 teaspoon	5 milliliters
1 tablespoon	15 milliliters
1 fluid ounce	30 milliliters
¼ cup	60 milliliters
⅓ cup	80 milliliters
½ cup	120 milliliters
1 cup	240 milliliters
1 pint (2 cups)	480 milliliters
1 quart (4 cups, 32 ounces)	960 milliliters (.96 liters)
1 gallon (4 quarts)	3.84 liters
1 ounce (by weight)	28 grams
¼ pound (4 ounces)	114 grams
1 pound (16 ounces)	454 grams
2.2 pounds	1 kilogram (1000 grams)

Oven Temperatures

DESCRIPTION	° FAHRENHEIT	° CELSIUS
Cool	200	90
Very slow	250	120
Slow	300–325	150–160
Moderately slow	325–350	160–180
Moderate	350–375	180–190
Moderately hot	375–400	190–200
Hot	400–450	200–230
Very hot	450–500	230–260